TWO HUNDRED YEARS OF AMERICAN BLOWN GLASS

The Schley pokal or large goblet, with cover, was made at the New Bremen Glassmanufactory of John Frederick Amelung in the glasshouse community he named New Bremen, near Fredericktown, Maryland. It was probably a presentation piece to George Jacob Schley, who was born at Pfalz, Germany, and came to America with his parents in 1746. The family settled in Fredericktown, and George Jacob lived there throughout his life. It was inherited by his great-great-great-great-grandson, from whom it was acquired several years ago. The metal comes closer to being colorless than any of the four known Amelung pieces dated 1788, each of which differs from the other in the thicker portions. In June 1790 Amelung wrote, "the quality of my glass is coming to perfection from degree to degree, almost every month owing to the experience I have acquired since the 6 years past." Therefore it is a reasonable conclusion that the date of the Schley pokal may be about 1790. This pokal is definitely of German inspiration, in form characteristic of the second and third quarters of the eighteenth century. Its domed foot is a type which had been discontinued in continental stemmed ware about 1775. Pokals were made with and without covers.

Free-blown from clear non-lead glass; deep semi-oviform bowl resting on an inverted baluster stem with large tear and supported by a high domed foot with plain rim; set-in domed cover with the characteristic Amelung feature of an applied band tooled into a half round to rest on the rim of the bowl, instead of a wide flange from the same gather as usually encountered in eighteenth-century covers; applied baluster finial with large tear; engraved by copper wheel in Amelung style and technique; decoration, on one side, composed of a foliated and floral wreath enclosing the name *"G. J. Schley."* in script above a small medallion showing a fish swimming in the sea below sunrays breaking through a small bank of clouds.

Over-all height, $11\frac{7}{8}$"; without cover, $8\frac{1}{2}$"; top diameter $4\frac{5}{8}$"; diameter of foot, $4\frac{7}{8}$".

Two Hundred Years of
AMERICAN
BLOWN GLASS

Helen AND George S. McKearin

BONANZA BOOKS · NEW YORK

All photographs, including color plates, were made especially for this book by Taylor and Dull of New York City, except the following:

PLATE 11, Bowl No. 2; PLATE 51, Vase No. 1; PLATE 53, Vases Nos. 1, 2, 3, and 4; PLATE 64, Bremen pokal; PLATE 81, Amelung tumbler, No. 2; PLATE 85, Decanters Nos. 4 and 5; PLATE 93, Pair candlesticks, No. 1; PLATE 95, Banks Nos. 1 and 2; PLATE 96, Banks Nos. 1 and 2.

CONTENTS

[ix]

LIST OF ILLUSTRATIONS

(Photography by Taylor and Dull of New York City except as noted)

NOTE

Unless otherwise stated, all pieces illustrated
in this book are from the McKearin Collection.

FRONTISPIECE. The Amelung Schley pokal

COLOR PLATES

PLATES NOT COLORED

[xi]

[xiii]

TWO HUNDRED YEARS OF
AMERICAN BLOWN GLASS

THE ANCESTRY
OF AMERICAN GLASS

GLASS is a familiar in so many divers forms that it is almost impossible for us to recapture the appreciation of its wondrous nature so eloquently expressed, often with poetic fervor, by early writers. Before modern times the only period in which it was so common an everyday article that it may have been accepted as a matter of course was when the Roman civilization was in full flower. That our own civilization would not have emerged without the aid of certain forms of glass is a truism undreamed of by the many, accepted as an unthrilling fact by the few who have given it thought. Yet glass, a transmutation of base matter by benefit of fire into a brilliant transparent or opaque, colored or colorless, briefly ductile and plastic substance which can be fashioned as man wills, has been one of civilization's essential tools in shaping his destiny.

Knowledge of all the marvelous properties inherent in man-made glass and of means to use them for man's benefit did not spring forth into the world like Minerva. Rather, it evolved at an erratic pace over centuries—now slowly, now swiftly, now marking time. And the ability to exploit those properties kept pace with knowledge. While the facts as to the genesis of glass still lie buried in the tomb of unrecorded history, legend and archaeology have sired more than one theory to account for it. Although after considering the theories one may feel that the weight of presented evidence tips the scales in favor of one rather than another, there is an inclination to suspect that some fortuitous circumstances, perhaps the hardening of glaze on pottery, familiar to the Egyptians by 3500 B.C., or the accidental fusing of sand and natron, as related by Pliny, awakened the inventive faculty of an exceptionally alert man and led to deliberate experiments. One tends to agree as well with Dr. Eisen's suggestion that glass "might also have been, and probably was, independently discovered at different places and at various times, where the imperfections of technic prevented the general use for practical purposes."[1] Be that as it may, while scholars may differ as to the exact time of its origin and the place where man first fused sand and soda to produce glass, they appear to agree that the locale was at the eastern end of the Mediterranean. It was another gift from the Middle East, the understanding and use of which expanded slowly from the first making of primitive beads about 2000 B.C. to a catalogue of objects rivaling the present day's in fabrication and ornamentation. There is agreement too that during those hundreds of years Alexandria, Tyre, and Sidon became the great centers of glassmaking and export, retaining their pre-eminence even when, under the aegis of the Roman eagle, the art of glass spread throughout the empire.

During those centuries the glassmaker gradually mastered his demanding yet responsive medium. His technique matured, progressing step by step from the primitive process of winding softened opaque rods of glass around a sand core, patting pads of glass into small molds (thereby forming small objects which had to be fused together to form the whole), and blowing by forming a tube from flat pads of glass, to the final achievement—"bubble" blowing.

That basic tool, the blowpipe, which around the first century B.C. made possible the full exploitation of the property of elasticity, has been attributed to the Sidonians. Then, as today, gathering a glob of molten viscous metal on the end of this hollow tube, the blower would inflate it, extending the resulting bubble to the size desired. With a simple tonglike spring tool he would fashion the bubble into the shape he envisioned. We call the process free-blowing. Always the artist among the blowers strove for beauty of form as well as utility. By the second century A.D. he had discovered and practiced the main techniques of glass decoration known today—the decoration of glass by and through itself, that is, glass applied and tooled; by the impression from a mold; by glyptic processes; by enameling and gilding. Materials for tools, new tools and molds, compositions of glass and chemistry of colors, all have been improved and expanded in scope, and mechanical aids to production and precision have been introduced, but in essence the fundamental processes of fashioning and decorating objects of glass have remained unchanged for nearly two thousand years.

While glassmaking, especially of free-blown pieces which embody the quintessence of artistry and craftsmanship, remains basically the same, most of the methods of fabrication and ornamentation have not been in continuous use over the ages. Toward the end of the fourth century A.D. the Roman Empire divided against itself with the proverbial result. In the west it carried the arts and crafts with it as it slowly fell into the pit of the Dark Ages. Glass was no exception. Before the close of the next century not only were vessels of glass no longer the rule: they were the wonderful exception. It was only in the hinterlands that the germ of the art of glassblowing was kept alive. Blowers in small, isolated, forest glasshouses evolved their own idiom from the "Roman" practices, an idiom of free-blown green or bottle glass fashioned into simple forms sometimes adorned with applied decoration such as threads, prunts, and crimped ribbons of glass. (Centuries later this bit of glass history was to be re-enacted—with some revisions, of course—in many of our American bottle and window glasshouses.) In the east survival took another path. Until the mid-eighth century glassmaking was among the arts fostered in Byzantium, but then Christian Iconoclasts, breaking artist and artisan of classical habits, drove them into the narrow lane of formalism. Finally the tattered mantle of the artist in glass passed completely to the Arabian glassmakers, especially at Damascus. While many of the Roman techniques had been preserved through exercise in Byzantium and the Middle East, enameling and gilding became the favorite methods of ornamentation. Their popularity, particularly after the rediscovery of uncolored glass, probably was attributable to their excellence as a medium for masking an imperfect metal.

As in the case of its beginnings, there is uncertainty as to the exact time when glassmaking as an art was reborn in the European world. But it is certain that when western man was overthrowing the totalitarian authority of ignorance by resurrecting the arts and learning, a renaissance in glass was taking place in Venice. While there seems no doubt that its revival was stimulated and nourished by eastern glass and artisans, Venetian glass at its best surpassed the products of the east in artistry. It not only reintroduced many long-forgotten techniques of antiquity but carried them to a greater peak of perfection, notably engraving, which in Venice was executed by diamond point. In the sixteenth century Venetian glassmaking attained unrivaled technical skill and its own distinctive styles. Its recipes for glass and methods of fashioning and decorating glass vessels were secrets as jealously guarded as the atomic researches of today. Death was the penalty paid by a traitorous glass blower who was caught betraying his house by teaching formulae or processes to princes of other countries. Nevertheless many were seduced and persuaded into France and the Low Countries, later into England, and a few into Germany. Everywhere, since glass was an art and a luxury beyond the reach and knowledge of the vulgar, nobility was no less noble for owning and operating a glasshouse or even participating in the processes involved. Of course some of Venice's monopolistic attitude regarding glassmaking arose from a desire to retain full enjoyment of any export trade and a reluctance to lose a profitable market . . . the day of cartels was as far away as that of glass for the commonalty.

In the main as, by hook or crook, other centers of glassmaking were developed, the style of Venice was unquestioningly and faithfully copied. The Germanic states, particularly in the north, were one exception. Perhaps because the more plodding German culture was always less in step with Italy's than was that of other western countries, the Germans were less susceptible to Venetian fashion in glass. Whatever the reason, it seems to be a fact that Venetian influence, although felt rather strongly at first, never dominated. On the other hand the influence emanating from the native forest glasshouse caused a continual undercurrent. Not only did Germanic artists fail to accept Venetian styles without reservation, but in traveling their path of rugged individualism they created their own, which subsequently eclipsed almost completely the popularity of the Venetian types. The trend of tenacious fashion they started was determined largely by copper-wheel engraving which they developed to its zenith, treating their glass as they did rock crystal. The process of wheel engraving, practiced in Roman days, had been rediscovered in the late sixteenth century by Caspar Lehmann, of Prague, who adapted to glass the lapidary's tools and equipment. For the first time, too, the ornamentation of glass passed outside the glasshouse where the objects were given form. Henceforth there were to be artisans— or artists—independent of the glasshouse who, while they used glass as a medium for displaying their art and skill, did so for commercial purposes, not in pursuit of a hobby as had the noble lords and ladies who engraved fine goblets with the diamond point.

In England the fashions from Venice, France, the Low Countries, and Germany all met and merged. But she, too, evolved her own glass idiom after making a tremendous contribution to the art, namely, her colorless glass of lead. This metal, called "flint," was considered far more brilliant than the continental "white" glass and, being softer, lent itself more readily to wheel cutting. It was in May 1674 that Charles II granted "George Ravenscroft, gentleman," a seven-year patent for his "Art and Manufacture of a particular sort of Christaline Glasses resembling Rock Christal, not formerly exercised or used in this Kingdom, and by his great disbursement having soe improved the same as thereby to be able to supply both inland and outland markets, whereby the public may be greatly advantaged."[2] The public was to be greatly advantaged, not only in all Britain

PLATE 1

1. Flask blown from pale amethyst non-lead glass: flattened chestnut shape; patterned in a part-size piece mold and expanded; checkered-diamond design, consisting of a diaper of large diamonds, eight in lateral chain and each containing four small concave diamond-shape ornaments.

These flasks, which usually occur in clear non-lead glass, are quite rare and are believed to have been made at the Amelung Glass Works. A fragment of one has been excavated at the site of the glasshouse. Two specimens patterned in the same or an identical mold, similar in shape and in typical Midwestern non-lead green glass with yellowish tone, have been found in Ohio. It is possible the mold was taken to the New Geneva Glass Works in western Pennsylvania by Amelung workmen who were later employed there.

2. Stiegel "perfume" bottle blown from clear amethyst non-lead glass; pattern-molded and expanded in daisy-in-hexagon design.

3. Stiegel "perfume" bottle blown from clear amethyst non-lead glass; pattern-molded and expanded in variant of diamond-daisy design.

4. Stiegel "perfume" bottle blown from sapphire-blue non-lead glass; pattern-molded and expanded in usual diamond-daisy design; only specimen known in blue, found in Ohio about twenty years ago.

5. "Perfume" bottle blown from clear amethyst non-lead glass; pattern-molded and expanded in checkered-diamond design; apparently patterned in same or identical mold, but not so greatly expanded as No. 1.

In the McKearin Collection there is a similar non-lead brilliant deep amethyst bottle blown by the so-called half-post method—a double gather. Another amethyst and a blue specimen, blown from one gather, are known, but we have not had an opportunity to check them to determine whether they are lead or non-lead, and whether patterned in the same or an identical mold. We know also of a clear glass specimen patterned in the same mold as the salt, No. 6, Plate 2, having seven checkered diamonds instead of eight in lateral row.

6. Stiegel "perfume" bottle blown from deep amethyst non-lead glass; pattern-molded and expanded in a design of ten lateral rows of twenty-eight small diamonds or ogivals above twenty-eight vertical flutes; smaller than most of these bottles.

7. Stiegel "perfume" bottle blown from brilliant amethyst non-lead glass; pattern-molded and expanded in a diaper of large ogivals or diamonds, twelve in lateral row.

While these bottles have been called "perfume bottles" it is doubtful if they were ever used or intended for that purpose. In Hunter's book, *Stiegel Glass,* they are called "toilet bottles." They might have been the bottles Stiegel listed in his inventories as "pocket" bottles. We have seen specimens which for many years had been used as camphor bottles. They are usually about half-pint size, somewhat bulbous in shape, with short cylindrical neck and plain lip and are typically eighteenth-century in form. Nos. 2, 3, 4, 6, and 7 have patterns which have been generally attributed to Stiegel and are different from any we know to be of English or continental origin. We think the checkered-diamond pattern was used by Amelung, but it is possible that it was first used at Stiegel's Manheim glasshouse. That this pattern did not originate with either Stiegel or Amelung is evidenced by a small amber bottle of characteristic early South German type and same pattern which was illustrated in Part I of an article on "A German View of Early American Glass" in *Antiques,* April 1932.

The usual diamond-daisy design consists of thirty graduated flutes below two lateral rows of five completed diamonds, each containing a 12-petaled flower. A third row usually shows at the base of the neck, only slightly expanded as the pattern opened into full bloom as blowing expanded the body of the bottle. In the variant of this pattern the number of flutes, diamonds, and petals are the same but the diamonds are larger, the petals of the daisylike flower longer and different in outline, and the center ovoid instead of round. The usual diamond-daisy is the pattern most frequently encountered in these Stiegel bottles. Three or four specimens in clear glass are known.

The daisy-in-hexagon is very rare, only about eight to ten specimens having been recorded so far as we know at present. One of these is clear non-lead glass.

In the ogival or diamond diaper patterns the diamonds appear as grooves on the narrow neck and gradually expand to full diamonds on the body of the bottle.

This group of bottles is from the Henry Francis du Pont Winterthur Museum.

but in America as well a century and more later as her glasshouses, founded for the manufacture of fine table and ornamental wares, turned to the making of lead glass.

Under the influence of national taste and customs each country eventually developed a characteristic style or idiom of its own. But always the kinship to contemporaries from other lands and even to the glass of the past was, and is, evident. The threads of continuity in techniques of fabrication and ornamentation converged in American glasshouses, for the men who founded our houses and blew our glass came from nearly every European country where glass was made. Two styles or idioms predominated, German and English, in many instances paralleling each other in a glasshouse at the same time. Eventually out of the babel distinctly American voices were to be heard.

Such, telescopically presented, is the family tree of our American glass.[3]

GLASSMAKING IN THE COLONIES

During the one hundred and sixty-eight years from the first settlement of Jamestown to the Declaration of Independence, Elizabethan crudities of manner and custom were gradually refined to the polished and sometimes delicate elegance of polite society. Slowly, nicety in living necessitated more compatible furniture and trappings. In the expanding catalogue of adjuncts to gracious and comfortable living glass was increasingly popular among the wellborn and, eventually, the people of substance, as a fabric from which more and more articles were made. In England, where the pace of progress was perhaps slightly behind that of the Continent, the real impetus to glass manufacturing, the aforementioned lead glass of Ravenscroft, came late in the seventeenth century. During the colonies' first hundred years the grim, unceasing struggle for existence must have drained all thoughts of such luxuries as fine glassware from the minds of most settlers. For that matter, while some of them may have been familiar with small windowpanes and, after the mid-seventeenth century, with black glass bottles, it is unlikely many had used or even seen a drinking vessel of glass. Nevertheless such was the fascination of this substance and the slowly growing need for it that there were five or six attempts at its manufacture—sporadic, miscarrying, or expiring in infancy,[1] except perhaps in New Amsterdam. There, by the 1650s, when Everett Dycking and Johannes Smedes supposedly established their glasshouses on Glass Maker's Street,[2] the Netherlanders had settled snugly on Manhattan, living well-ordered lives. Some among them may have desired fine drinking vessels such as one sees in the still lifes of Willem Kalf and interiors of Jan Vermeer of Delft, but doubtless all they demanded were bottles and windowpanes.

In the light of what is known of the seventeenth century it is little short of astounding to realize that the *first* American glass was blown long before George Ravenscroft solved the problem of using lead as a flux in the making of clear (crystal) glass, in fact before he was born. But Captain John Smith is one of the witnesses to the fact that glass was blown in the Virginia colony of James Towne. Moreover, the plan was to make glass for England, where in 1608 and for years to come so little was made that nobles indulging in the luxury of fine glass goblets and wines had to purchase imports. There, besides technical flaws and a paucity of skilled blowers and decorators, the drain on the nation's forests was a handicap to expansion. Much of the glass was made with potash instead of soda, and until about 1623 all furnaces were fired with wood.* Unfortunately for England, conservation of her forests had become a necessity. The consumption of wood and timber was so great that, whereas once she had had plenty for fuel, building, and, above all, her navy, and even a surplus for export, she now had to supplement her supply with

*Use of wood as fuel in glass furnaces was prohibited by law in 1617 (Dr. Robert Charleston, Keeper of the Department of Ceramics, Victoria and Albert Museum, London, England).

timber from the Continent. Since the use of wood in glassworks was "one of the greatest and chiefest means to consume and destroy tymber and wood"[3] it is understandable that the London Company in its utter innocence of New World perils took the reports of proper sand near unlimited forests as an invitation from Providence to establish a glasshouse. It is not beyond belief that a company of men who could so lightheartedly expect city dwellers to easily plant their modern society in a virgin wilderness as yet unraped by civilization also could envision supplying all the nobles of England with artistic drinking vessels as well as windowpanes.

Captain Smith and his fellow historians failed to record what forms or quantity of glass were made at Jamestown.[4] However, it would be an imposition upon the most febrile imagination to suppose any forms more sophisticated than small panes of window glass or bubblelike bottles ever were fashioned, even though the blowing was by the supposedly skilled Dutch or German glass blowers brought to the Plantation by Captain Newport in the spring of 1608. As soon as the men landed and Smith, then president of the Council, received the orders, the erection of the glasshouse was started in "a place in the woods mere a myle from Iames Towne." Subsequent events leave little doubt that only a small amount of glass of any kind could have been produced there. For, while Captain Newport searched dutifully for gold, a passage to the South Seas, and Raleigh's lost men, there was time only to clear the site, complete the glasshouse, and make trials of glass. These, with some small quantities of other special commodities, the captain took back to the London Company in the fall of 1608. With them went Smith's warning not to expect much from colonists scarcely able to sustain and defend themselves. Do not, he said, "send into Germany and Poleland for glassmen and the rest till we be able to sustain ourselues, and relieue them when they come."

Before the year ended the glasshouse was to be the rendezvous for all the "unsuspected villany" of the Dutchmen—Francis, Samuel, and Adam. They, seeing the Indians' plenty and the colony's want, abandoned their art for Powhatan's corn and, allegedly conspiring with him, were after Smith's scalp. Francis, soon caught near the glasshouse, was accused by some of being Conspiracy's errand boy, but believed by others to be searching, as he protested, for walnuts after escaping from Powhatan. Adam accepted a pardon early in the spring of 1609 and returned to the fold. Samuel did not. About that time another, apparently the last, trial of glass was produced. Before the next cruel winter overtook them Francis and Adam fled again to Powhatan but he, supposedly considering them proven unreliable, "caused his men to beat out their brains." As for the remaining workers at the glasshouse, perhaps, having cleared the land for the works and its fuel, they turned finally to agriculture, as did so many artisans and mechanics in later periods. In any event when Captain Argall arrived at the Plantation in 1617 there were no signs of manufacturing, and the energies of the remaining colonists were expended on the raising of tobacco. Oklahoma City's oil wells in the Capitol's grounds find precedent in Jamestown's cultivation of tobacco in "the market place, and the streets, and all spare places."

In spite of its initial failure the Virginia Company was so convinced that a busy glass furnace would prove to be the gold mine they had failed to find in America that, when Captain William Norton approached them on the matter of glassmaking in June

1621, they eagerly agreed to his propositions, including a fifty-fifty profit basis. In its enthusiasm the company overlooked the fact that the "common stock" was exhausted, so it could not fulfill its financial promises to pay even £150 for the equipment and transportation to Virginia of six foreigners skilled in making glass and beads, their servants, wives, and children, eleven persons in all. Consequently it was decided to approach private Adventurers who in July formed a joint-stock company with a capital of £500, of which each Adventurer invested £10. It was agreed that Captain Norton was to have complete charge of men and operations, the glasshouse was to be completed in three months, and the six Italians—two of them servants of his own—were to make "round Glasse, drinck-inge Glasses [and] Beads." The Virginia Company was to have a quarter share; the Adventurers a seven-year monopoly of the manufacture of glass and also of the soda used in making it. In addition the glass company was to have fifty acres for each person it transported in connection with the glassworks. Since the beads were to be the coin of trade with the Indians, the Virginia Company was to control that branch of the glass-making through its governor in the colony, recompensing the glass company through other commodities. On August 12, 1621, the company wrote to the governor and the Council, warning them that the beads should not be cheapened by abundance nor the Virginians permitted either to see or understand the manufacture of them. Furthermore, it recommended Norton's party, now sixteen in number, to their special care, stating frankly that it was the only group in the ship in which the company had any interest. Being so concerned for this veritable embodiment of its investment and hopes, the company instructed the governor to assist them in selecting as the site of the glasshouse and its community a "healthfull place . . . Charles Citty or Henerico, but by no means lower than James Cittie, nor remote from people."[5] The site chosen was on the mainland near Jamestown Island.[6]

This second attempt to plant glassmaking in America was as ill starred as the first. The erection of the glasshouse was well under way early in 1622 when its roof was blown down in a tempest. No sooner was it repaired than the Indians attacked the colony (the horrid massacre of 1622). Since this only interrupted the work it would seem that most if not all of the band escaped the tomahawk. The furnace was completed and two weeks later "when the fire was put in it flew in peeces." Whether this disaster was due to unintentional faulty construction or sabotage is uncertain. A vengeful wife (her husband had severely wounded her several times, and to avoid murder she was being returned to England) proclaimed that "Vincentio crackt it with crow of iron." Then sickness took its toll in time and men. Captain Norton and his servants died, but the Italians recovered. George Sandys, treasurer of the colony, vowing that "a more damned crew hell never vomited" and suspecting them of trying to be returned to England, nevertheless picked up the reins of direction, hired some more men, and rebuilt the furnace. Then the Italians adopted delaying tactics, complaining of the sand they had selected themselves. A year later the patient Sandys was still searching for satisfactory sand. The hopes of the company in London were starved on reports of continued troubles and little or no production. On June 15, 1625, the Virginia Council announced the end, reporting to London that because of the death of one of the principal workmen, the falling sickness of another, and other causes rendering "the work vnseruable" the glassmen were being allowed to return to England, duly cautioned, however, that they were still bound to the company by their covenants.

Under conditions so harsh and hostile it seems impossible that any quantity of glass of any sort could have been blown at this second Jamestown glassworks. Certainly the Virginia Company could have had no cause for worry about the debasement of the bead currency. Perhaps some beads were made between crises.* Perhaps, too, some of the specimens attributed to Jamestown and now in a few museums and collections were actually fashioned by the Italians sometime between 1622 and 1625. But as a matter of fact as little is known about the glass blown by the Italians as by their predecessors, the Dutchmen. These first attempts at glass manufacture ended in inevitable failure. Over a century was to pass before colonists ventured their money in glassmaking with any marked degree of success so far as we now know.

Life in the eighteenth century colonial towns, especially on the seaboard, was increasingly easier and more gently lived, that is, by the people of consequence. Its fashionable appurtenances, including glass, were enjoyed by the grace of England and a heavy purse or good credit. In the minds of the mercantile interests, the controlling group in the mother country, and of most Englishmen for that matter, the Colonies were a vast reservoir of essential raw materials to be siphoned off for their benefit and refilled, at a handsome profit, by goods made or supplied by them. On the eve of the Revolution, as at the beginning of the century, most Englishmen of substance heartily endorsed the long-held opinion that "all these Colloneys, which are but twigs belonging to the Main Tree (England) ought to be Kept entirely dependent upon & subservient to England, and that can never be if they are suffered to goe on in the notions they have, that as they are Englishmen, soe they may set up the same manufactures here as people may do in England."[7]

A home industrialist weaving a few yards of homespun or linsey-woolsey, an obscure undistinguished cabinetmaker-joiner turning out Windsor chairs, or even an ironmaster supplying pots and trivets could escape the exterminating wrath of the Lords of Trade because they were insignificant, but not so a manufacturer who was deemed hurtful to English interests. English manufacturers might tolerate an isolated glasshouse producing mediocre window glass and hollow ware, but fine wares were important, so as the English branch developed, they would have demanded ruthless pruning of even a tiny colonial twig. And an indication that glass products were an increasingly lucrative English export was the inclusion of glass among the five articles designated for colonial import duty in the Townshend Acts of 1767 from which Parliament hoped at least £40,000 revenue would be forthcoming.[8]

Actually as far as colonial glass manufacture was concerned English makers had little or nothing to fear from the ten or eleven houses projected in the eighteenth century before the Revolution. Most of them never passed beyond the stage of plans or else operated too short a time to have made more than a dent in local history.[9] Only one lasted very long, that of Caspar Wistar, in which there seems to have been no attempt to produce fine wares. Stiegel's two houses and those of the Glass House Company of New York were downed not by English blows but by those of colonial and personal economic conditions. In spite of the plethora of raw materials in almost any would-be glass manu-

*Archaeological excavations by the National Park Service unearthed neither beads nor evidence of bead making (J. C. Harrington, *Glassmaking at Jamestown*, 1952).

facturer's back yard, proper conditions for raising a husky young industry were virtually non-existent in most cases. By and large, while the need for glass utensils and window-panes was great, the demand was comparatively slight. As the use of glass tablewares spread, those who could appreciate and afford them were well supplied from England. Then, too, the ever present problems of financing, distribution, and labor were even more difficult to solve than at later periods. As in all arts and crafts skilled glassmen had to be induced to leave familiar surroundings and a modicum of security for the uncertainties of the New World. Moreover, to do so they had to brave the penalties of law and the wrath of princes, for the art of glass was guarded jealously. While a blower might be honored, his liberty of movement was limited by legal chains. Courage and venture-someness were necessary qualities no matter how alluringly the future in America was painted. In most cases they required the starch of hard cash to stiffen their resistance to timidity.

The colonial glasshouses which actually reached the stage of production were manned by imported glassmen, the majority of them from the Low Countries and western Germany. Their employers learned all too soon that even after the expense and worry of getting an experienced blower safely out of his country and into the colonies there was no surety he would not decamp or strike out for himself after his term was served. Both Stiegel and Richard Wistar had to advertise for absconding workers.* One of Wistar's was Jacob Stenger (Stanger), who later joined with his brothers to build the first Glassboro works not many miles from "Wistarberg" in South Jersey.[10] The problem persisted into the nineteenth century, though usually with apprentices. Perhaps the apprentice-blower who absconded from Bakewell, Page and Bakewell in the spring of 1815 heard the loud call of the land.[11] Land coupled with its attendants, dignity and independence, apparently caused more than one glass blower to desert his art. In 1767 Governor Moore, comment-ing on this and other hazards to employers, remarked:

> . . . The Price of Labor is so great in this part of the World, that it will always prove the greatest obstacle to any Manufactures attempted to be set here, and the genius of the People in a Country where every one can have Land to work upon leads them so naturally into Agriculture, that it prevails over every other occupation. There can be no stronger Instances of this, than in the Servants imported from Europe of different Trades; as soon as the time stipulated in their Indentures is Expired, they immediately quit their masters, and get a tract of Land. . . . The Master of a Glasshouse; which was set up here a few years ago now a Bankrupt, assured me that his ruin was owing to no other cause than being deserted in this manner by the Servants, which he Imported at great expense; and that many others had suffered and been reduced as he was, by the same kind of misfortune.[12]

Since the New York Glass House Company drew the fires in its Newfoundland and its New Windsor (Ulster County, New York) glasshouses about 1767 it seems quite likely that the royal governor had been discussing this colonial problem with a member of the expiring firm.

Like those of other early houses, the nature and character of the output of the Glass House Company at Newfoundland on Manhattan Island are matters of conjecture, not of knowledge. Unfortunately any enlightening fragments on its glasshouse sites were lost to students long ago as city and town crept over them. The diligent searches of Rhea

*Also, Lodewick Bamper advertised in July 1755 for "Christian Modther, German servant-man, run-a-way from the owners of the Glass-House at New Windsor" (Ulster County, N. Y.) (*New York Gazette and Weekly Post Boy*, July 4, 1755).

Mansfield Knittle and Messrs. Hunter and Kerfoot[13] failed to enlarge the picture beyond that drawn from a few bottles, belonging to the Van Cortland Mansion in New York City, which tradition credits to Newfoundland and inferences from a few newspaper advertisements. The tradition well may be fact, for the bottles are of the correct period. One has an applied seal bearing the name "Sidney Breese 1765"; another, one with the initials "F V C" (possibly Frederick Van Cortland). Also as early as 1754 the company advertised that all gentlemen could be promptly supplied with bottles of any size with their name on them. Bottles of all sorts and chemical wares were advertised and the annoyingly vague "any other sort of glassware."[14] Had fine drinking glasses or other vessels been fashioned, surely the fact would have been announced in bold type—in spite of the English. However, the possibility exists, slight as it may be. If any such wares were made they must have been unassimilated Dutch or German in form and ornamentation, probably similar to some of the engraved and enameled types attributed to Stiegel.

Caspar Wistar's glasshouse in southwestern New Jersey and William Henry Stiegel's in Pennsylvania were the two outstanding enterprises of the period. In 1914 Frederick William Hunter's *Stiegel Glass* brought out the importance of these two patriarchs of the industry and revealed the glass attributed to one as quite different from the other's in metal and decorative techniques. Consequently their glasshouses soon were regarded as the fountainheads of two distinct traditions in American glass fabrication and ornamentation, the South Jersey and the Stiegel, which flowed out into and through the houses that followed them. However, later researches showed that the two streams had many tributaries as other glasshouses were established and more blowers trained in the same techniques came to man them. Still these pioneer industrialists and their efforts to root glassmaking in America always will attract more than a passing glance.

Caspar Wistar, as we see him through the pages of Hunter's *Stiegel Glass*,[15] is not a romantic figure. He seems to have lived too normally and prospered too quietly for that. Yet his was the first successful glasshouse in the Colonies. In 1717, when he was twenty-one, he left his continental homeland for Philadelphia. Being well established within nine years, he married Catherine Johnson (or Jansen), a Quakeress of Germantown. Not until he had attained a position of honored prominence and had the security of a profitable button manufactory behind him did he turn to the glass industry. (Apparently "Brass buttons warranted for 7 years" were beneath the notice of the Lords of Trade.) In 1738 no glass was being made anywhere in the Colonies—so far as we know at present—and the needs of the people, if met at all, were met by imports. Perhaps this situation in itself explains his decision to cultivate a new field. At any rate, the decision once taken, he methodically made his plans for success in that field also. Late in the year, since he had no practical knowledge of glassmaking, he made arrangements with four expert glassmen to leave the Low Countries for America. He was to furnish the capital and equipment; they, the know-how. He was to receive two thirds of the proceeds; they one third. The agreement provided also that they should teach the art to him and his son Richard (then only twelve) and to no one else. Later, after the works were in production, more blowers were imported, this time from Germany.

In the meantime Wistar had acquired over two thousand acres of wooded land in Salem County, southern New Jersey. Sand of excellent quality and wood were abundant.

Equally important, there was a natural avenue of water transportation to any colonial port, for shallops could navigate two creeks running through the property,[16] Deep Run and Alloways Creek—Aloes or Allawas, in the Wistars' day.[17] This fact doubtless dictated the choice of the glasshouse site. The chosen spot on which construction of the glass furnace began in the summer of 1739 was about eight miles slightly southwest of the town of Salem, one and a half from the creeks,[18] and not far from the main road between Greenfield and Salem which crossed Alloways Creek about twelve miles from its mouth.[19] Although history and maps appear to have called the works and its brood of buildings only "Glafs House" and "Wistar's Glassworks" during its comparatively brief existence, it is supposed to have been called "Wistarberg"* in honor of its founder,[20] a name we have adopted because it is convenient and seems appropriate.

When Caspar died in 1752, thirteen years after the first glass was blown at his furnace, he left full control of his two enterprises, brass buttons and glass, to Richard, who apparently was as successful as his father before him. While it is possible that Stiegel's window glass and bottles may have cut into Wistar's market in the mid-sixties, it is doubtful if they sliced deep into his profits. That both glassmakers sought the same market is evidenced by their advertising in the same English- and German-language papers and both appealed to pocketbook and patriotism. One of Richard's 1765 advertisements, directed at merchants, reminded them that "because of the present great lack of money to send over in payment for such wares which we obtain from England, it is hoped everyone will try to support the manufactures of this country."[21]

After the news of the hateful Townshend Acts of 1767 reached these shores, such appeals must have had real effect. Probably there was a small boom at Wistarberg, especially following the Colonies' adoption of the 1768 Non-Importation Agreement in retaliation upon the English. But by the next summer Richard found it expedient to remind the paper's followers of their pact. With Quaker mildness of language quite in contrast with that of the times, he pointed to the Americanness of his glass, which exempted it from the justly complained-of duties and gently rubbed the burning sore, taxation, by adding, "it seems peculiarly the interest of America to encourage her own manufactures, more especially those upon which duties have been imposed for the sole purpose of raising revenue."[22] In the following year patriotism suffered a relapse; domestic manufactures did too. Business must have been progressively dull after 1770 and almost non-existent after the British forces occupied New York and Philadelphia. History and tradition seem silent as to whether, when the locality became a foraging area and skirmishing ground for segments of the British and patriot forces in 1778, there were any glasshouse people who rushed down to aid in the defense of Quinton's Bridge[23] or had the Nerolike aplomb to continue blowing during the months the war licked over the neighborhood. In 1780 the glasshouse and all its property were offered for sale.[24] The Wistar glasshouse apparently was one of many establishments for which the Revolution spelled stagnation or annihilation.

Information about the Wistars' regular output during almost forty years of presumably continuous operation has come mainly from Richard's surviving advertisements; about the probable blowing of household articles, from the conclusions of Messrs. Hunter and Kerfoot based on fragments from the factory site and on local inquiries. The adver-

*Also "Wistarburgh" in contemporary ad (*Pennsylvania Chronicle*, December 14, 1767).

tisements provide convincing evidence that window glass and bottles were the commercial foundation of the house. The window glass was carried in all "common sizes"—the largest 10 by 12, the smallest 6 by 8. The lights for lamps and lanterns—"lamp glasses"—and also all uncommon sizes under 16 by 18 were cut to order. "Most sorts of bottles" of full-gallon, half-gallon, and quart measures were steady products, as were also philosophical and chemical glass. Since case, snuff, and mustards were mentioned specifically they must have had distinctive forms.[25]

As for the fragments, while it is logical to assume that they revealed typical colors, perhaps some decorative devices and hints of form, inasmuch as Hunter did not differentiate between fragment evidence, local tradition, and personal opinion in presenting his material, one cannot be sure how much or how little the fragments enlarged the output picture. Apparently not even one complete vessel could be reconstructed from the fragments. It is regrettable that they were not catalogued and fully described for the benefit of other students and also that Hunter did not realize that South Jersey broke out with a rash of glasshouses, spreading the techniques from one to another. Today the chaff of inference and wishful attribution cannot be sifted from the wheat of fact; for one cannot be sure which of Hunter's assertions as to characteristic forms and types take their point of reference from the fragments and which from objects attributed to Wistar by tradition and opinion. Nevertheless an entire temple of American glass tradition was erected upon the fragile foundation of fragments, mortared with opinion and located at Wistarberg. For seasoned collectors it tumbled from its weak support long ago; for newcomers it seems to be raised again and again.

It was not until nearly ten years after the publication of Hunter's conclusions in *Stiegel Glass* that students and collectors discovered that not only were the "Wistarberg" decorative techniques practiced in nineteenth-century New Jersey, New York, and New England glasshouses but also that certain shapes, proportions, and treatments of details first appeared at different periods after 1800. For example the covered bowl, No. 3, Plate 27, which came from a private home near Glassboro, could have been blown at Wistar's glasshouse and may have been, but not that on Plate 6, which is typically nineteenth century. Consequently the term "South Jersey" eventually replaced the misleading "Wistarberg" in the informed collectors' vocabulary as a label for individual pieces and South Jersey tradition entered it to designate the techniques of fabrication.

Almost without exception, and no matter when they were made, the pieces with which the South Jersey tradition is associated were blown in our bottle and window glasshouses for friends and family or to supply local needs—many of the finest in the 1820–50 period, or even later. They were individual pieces fashioned to express the blower's ideas of combining functional form and beauty, or perhaps just to demonstrate his ability to master the difficult medium of his art. He drew on remembered forms and his skill. He was unguided by any blueprint from a design atelier and unhampered by the dictates of fashion. In the main his pieces were blown from ordinary window glass and green or bottle glass, a kind generally made from coarser and less pure materials than those necessary to the production of fine tablewares. Their principal colors were those which resulted naturally from the impurities in the ingredients—greens from pale aquamarine to deep olive-greens and ambers of varied hue and tone. Occasionally artificial colors were used, principally blues of which the pitcher on Plate 5 is an example, *rarely* deep wines or maroons, but neither of these, we suspect, in the Wistars' day. And toward the mid-nineteenth century opaque white and ruby joined the South Jersey spectrum.

With the rare exceptions of pattern-molding, glass was the medium of ornamentation as well as the substance from which a piece was formed. The various devices were achieved through tooling and manipulating glass applied to the piece in its formative stage, while still receptively soft and responsive, and taken usually from the same batch of metal as the piece itself. The simplest device was threading, that is, rather slender threads of glass were wound around the piece, mainly to embellish neck and rim as on the vase and pitcher, Plate 6, and the mug, No. 3, Plate 72. Threads were used also in obtaining the bi- and tricolored effects of loopings and draggings of one or more colors in the body color. In this instance parallel threads were applied around the parison (inflated, usually pear-shaped, gather of metal), dragged into loops with a tool, and then imbedded in the body by rolling on the marver, a long narrow slab of marble or polished metal on a low frame. The pitchers, Plates 39 and 40, are excellent examples of this type. Another decoration formed from threads was the chain or guilloche, to obtain which two applied parallel substantial threads were pinched together to form links. However, its use on the individual bottle-glass pieces was very occasional. The mug, No. 1, Plate 72, is one of the rare instances of its use. The most favored devices were applied prunts fashioned from globs tooled or molded into forms such as a "leaf" or "strawberry"; rigaree, from finely cross-ribbed ribbons of glass; quilling or pinched trailing, from ribbons pinched into spiny or wavelike formations; heavy swirled ribs and flutes, and lily-pad, formed from a "pearl" attached to the bottom of the parison, pulled over it, and tooled into the desired design. These are illustrated by the following: mug, No. 4, Plate 74; creamer, No. 1, Plate 41; jar, Plate 57; sugar bowl, Plate 7; (lily-pad Type I), creamer, No. 3, Plate 41; (Types II and III) pitcher, Plate 38.

A tooled device popular as a foot decoration was crimping, that is, a series of depressions which could be made with the narrow surface of a tool, for instance the edge of the shears' blade. Finials of covers were sometimes fashioned into fancy forms, for instance the flowerlike one on the Suncook bowl, Plate 32, the "chicken" on the New York State lily-pad bowl, Plate 8, and the swan on the South Jersey sugar bowl, Plate 30. All these varied forms, the principal decorative devices in the South Jersey tradition, are to be found on glass of nearly all ages, traveling from the Middle East through Europe to the Western Hemisphere. The jar, Plate 57, is a first cousin to contemporaries from Spanish and Persian houses. Only the so-called lily-pads found on nineteenth-century pieces such as those on the bowls and compote on Plates 15, 16, and 22, and the pieces on Plate 6 and others appear, at present, to be peculiar to our glass. At least in so far as we know now these have not been found on foreign glass.

While these devices—except, we believe, the lily-pad forms—were applied on crystal or clear commercial wares, for instance the chain or guilloche on the plate, No. 1, Plate 24, and the bird finial on the sugar bowl, No. 2, Plate 34, their use was not extensive. One reason was perhaps that as labor costs rose in the nineteenth century other manufacturing costs were reduced in most houses by eliminating as much handwork as possible on all but the most expensive wares, that is, the cut and engraved. However, it would seem that whenever a glass blower made a piece as a gift or for himself he chose to follow the method and create the decorative forms which called for the greatest skill in manipulating glass, for example, the Amelung covered bowls on Plates 28 and 29 and the banks on Plates 95 and 96. They are South Jersey type, in all but metal. They were fashioned from a sophisticated clear metal and in a glasshouse specializing in tablewares rather than from green glass in a bottle- or window-glass factory.[26]

It was the assignment to Wistarberg of all glass falling into the category of South Jersey type which caused the disagreement with Hunter's findings. Without doubt he was quite justified in his conviction that bowls, pitchers, and other household utensils were blown and occasionally adorned with some of the devices just described. There are several reasons for assuming the correctness of these two propositions. The custom of blowing utilitarian and ornamental pieces for friends and family was centuries old; it certainly persisted in later American bottle and window glasshouses. There is no conceivable reason why that of the Wistars should have been an exception. Moreover, it was the natural course of events to supply the communal needs. Often a bit of country produce must have been most welcome in exchange for a cream pot, especially when specie was scarce, as it usually was. The tiny community (ten workmen's houses and one mansion house in 1780)[27] and small nearby towns would not have been a large market for glasswares and its demands undoubtedly would not have been a tax on the blowers' capabilities. Not that the housewives would not have appreciated the fine imported wares but the sturdy individual pieces undoubtedly would have been more familiar and welcome. It is unlikely that their mode of living called forth even all of the household articles in the rather limited range then being made from glass. Jars with clean eye-satisfying lines, similar to that on Plate 55, may have been provided for storage and preserves. Bowls, milk pans, sugar basins, and pitchers, perhaps a salt stand or cellar, a few simple drinking vessels may have been sold in the retail shop which for over thirty years had been "as good a stand for the sale of goods as any in the country."[28]

Shapes and ornamentation would have been those characteristic of the eighteenth century. Then most of the purely utilitarian bowls would have been deep, narrow in proportion to their height, cylindrical with straight or slightly ogee sides having a plain or a folded rim, rarely with an applied circular foot; pans like the bowls but shallower. A fancier bowl would have been hemispherical with circular foot probably in the form of a straight-sided table rest—a bowl similar to the green one, Plate 4, and the Amelung bowl, Plate 11. The bodies of most covered bowls of the type today called sugar bowls also would have been higher in proportion to their diameter than those of the nineteenth century. Most of the covers would have had a low broad flattened dome with applied finial and a flange, formed by manipulation, above a short neck which set *inside* the top of the bowl—a "set-in" cover. Rarely the cover would have been given a truer dome and a cylindrical neck which fitted *over* the top of the bowl and rested on an applied ring like that of the Amelung bowls, Plates 28 and 29. In general the applied finials would have been tooled into either a simple form similar to that of the bowl, No. 3, Plate 27, or perhaps an elaborate one similar to that of No. 2, Plate 29. Most pitchers would have had very short necks and long bodies, proportioned like the bowls, and it is unlikely they would have been much if any larger than No. 4, Plate 27, which, having a slender barrel shape with pinched lip and strap handle, is typically eighteenth century. Some may have had ovoid bodies and applied circular feet; others, cylindrical bodies with short shoulder and neck with slight flare at the rim. Salts, which are rarely encountered in glass of the South Jersey tradition, probably would have had lines and proportions similar to those of the other articles. As for drinking vessels, they probably would have been either tumblers—from quarter-gill to gallon capacity—or mugs for such beverages as beer, ale, and flip. Tumblers and flip glasses would have been cylindrical, straight-sided or with slightly spreading sides, or slender barrel; mugs, either straight-sided or barrel; and both slender as compared with most examples from later periods. Wines blown from bottle glass are rarely seen today, perhaps because wine was not likely to be the beverage most popular among the folks who would use glass of this type, rather than because they were used so often they were broken.

That the decorative devices would have been of the applied and tooled variety would be natural, in fact inevitable. Since most blowers were Continental it would have been phenomenal had they not been familiar with the so-called forest techniques, those slender tough threads of continuity stretching from the time of ancient and classical glass blowers to their own. Also, being trained on the Continent, they must have been familiar with the so-called German half-post method of bottle blowing, in which procedure, after a gather of metal had been slightly inflated, it was reinserted into the pot of metal so that a second gather, a sort of outer coat, was formed upon it. The bottle or flask was then formed. However, confident as we are that such techniques were practiced and such articles blown at Wistars', *we do not know of a single piece that can be attributed with certainty to this glasshouse.*

Nevertheless the Wistars and their glassmaking will always be a part of the American glass saga; for it undoubtedly was their blowers who started these sturdy, wholesome individual pieces, American folk art in glass, on their march through the years. As late as the 1930s similar pieces were being blown in a small Jersey glasshouse operated by the WPA. But they, like most of their fellows from the mid-century on, were more crude than charming. The simplicity of form remained but the fine line flowing into pleasing proportions was usually missed. The heaviness of metal became a cloddish quality rather than one of strength. Unfortunately as the industry became more mechanized and centralized most of the small bottle and window glasshouses gradually disappeared. And in general the glass blower in such works, having lost the opportunity to practice blowing as an art, or even to learn the tricks of his trade, lost also his eye for line and beauty of simple form as well as manual dexterity to embody his vision in the material of his art.

In point of time the second towering figure in the American glass scene is Henry William Stiegel, so highlighted by Hunter[29] and later writers that all others have been cast into Rembrandtish shadows. Stiegel, like Caspar Wistar, was a native of the Palatinate. Unlike Wistar, the ambitious and energetic Stiegel had a dazzling, meteorlike career —rising from obscurity to prominence, then sinking into the debtors' prison. Besides the apocryphal tales of which he is the hero only a few facts are known. In 1750, twenty-one years after he was born in the Rhine City of Cologne, he emigrated with his widowed mother and a young brother to the province of Pennsylvania, already a haven for many of his Protestant countrymen. His activities during the two years after he landed at Philadelphia in August and as "Heinrich Wil Stiegel" signed the immigrant's declaration of loyalty to England's kings are uncertain, but his subsequent career suggests that he was fitting himself snugly into his new environment. Presumably he had been somewhere in the vicinity of Jacob Huber's prosperous iron furnace near Schaefferstown in Lancaster County, at least long enough to have won the affections of the ironmaster's daughter Elizabeth, whom he married in 1752. Apparently no unusual event ruffled the current of his life during the next six years. One assumes that he was mastering the business of an ironmonger. If he desired to be an industrialist he could have chosen no freer and more profitable branch, for England, as yet, had made no serious attempts to eliminate the colonial ironmasters. Chippendale furniture, fine porcelain and cut glass, frills and furbelows were doubtless more profitable exports than pedestrian objects of mere iron. Even the 1750 law forbidding the founding of new slitting mills and requiring the manufacturing to be done by England's own growing iron industry had not yet affected existing colonial enterprises.

The year 1758 was a difficult one of change for Stiegel. His wife died in February, leaving him with two small daughters; in October he married Elizabeth Holz; and sometime during the year, with some Philadelphia partners, he assumed complete ownership and control of the Huber furnace, henceforth called Elizabeth Furnace. Later, in partnership with a Lancastrian merchant, Stiegel acquired another furnace to be known as Charming Forge. Both furnaces prospered so that, again like Wistar, he had a ready source of capital when he turned to glassmaking. But unlike Wistar he drained the well dry. However, in 1763, when he built his first glasshouse, he was well on the way to the affluence which enabled him to live briefly in the baronial style to which he wished to become accustomed and which earned him the sobriquet of "Baron."

From our historical perspective Stiegel's sinking money in one such venture in such unsettled times, to say nothing of three, seems an open invitation to disaster. Yet not even his legal adviser and friend, John Dickinson, the lawyer-patriot who helped stiffen the colonists' resistance to England's colonial policy and was continually in touch with events, dreamed that a shooting war of independence would eventuate. In fact it is not impossible that Dickinson encouraged him in his projects. In 1763 the bubble of a war-bred prosperity had not yet burst even though pricked by the Treaty of Paris ending the French and Indian War. Colonial markets had expanded. Living had become more luxurious among the well-to-do; more comfortable for the common people. Near by there was Lancaster, a trading center buzzing with prosperous activities; about eighty miles away, Philadelphia, the most important commercial and financial center in the colonies, whence ships carried on a coastwise trade with the principal seaports and with the West Indies, where some of Stiegel's ironwork already had been sold. Also the only colonial competitor was Wistar, who had prospered. So perhaps Stiegel was not completely foolhardy when he determined to start a glasshouse. It was a modest establishment chiefly for the manufacture of window glass and bottles, employing only a few men, most of whom were German. During its few years of operation some household utilities undoubtedly were blown, probably individual pieces similar to those which had been made at Wistars'.

[17]

Although during the next two years the streams of commerce were continually roiled by postwar depression and acts of Parliament, colonial entrepreneurs, Stiegel among them, were far from worried. In 1764 England, empty of purse and head over heels in debt, decided it was high time her pampered and wealthy Colonies contributed to her support. Consequently Parliament not only raised duties on exports to the Colonies, which meant inflated prices, but also passed the Sugar Act, which, in the opinion of many, would smother the vital West Indian trade. The reaction of the manufacturers was to anticipate an increase in their business; for most colonists deeply resented having their pockets picked before being seated below the salt at the feast of commerce. There followed a widespread boycott. of English goods, which became even tighter after the Stamp Act was passed in 1765.

It was during these years that Stiegel expanded his own little empire. He and the Stedmans, his staunch tory partners, planned and laid out the town of Manheim. There Stiegel's own mansion and his second glasshouse were erected. Started in October 1764, the glasshouse was completed in 1765 and the first glass blown on October 29. Here, as the evidence of two cream jugs and a sugar purchased by a minister at York prove, tablewares as well as bottles were to be made. Like his Elizabeth Furnace glasshouse this first one at Manheim appears to have been at least moderately successful financially. A January 1767 report to the Lords of Trade perhaps deliberately belittled this enterprise, saying it was "still carried on, tho' to a very inconsiderable Extent, there being no other Vent for their Wares, which is of a very ordinary Quality, but to supply the small demands of the Villages and Farmers in the adjacent inland Country." [30]

Had Stiegel been content to halt the expansion of his enterprises he might have been able to ride the rising waves of economic distress, even the tidal wave caused by the Revolution. But he was not. Neither he nor John Dickinson had our hindsight. Glass and its making seem to have completely bewitched the man, as some of the Stiegel types of glass have bewitched collectors of today. He determined to build a large factory for the manufacture of "flint" glass, presumably lead glass. Here the popularly fashionable English flint glasswares were to be faithfully, accurately copied. Whether he conceived his plan before his trip to England, shortly after blowing started at Elizabeth Furnace, is not known. In any event his new passion must have been a beacon leading him inevitably to the English glass centers. Also he must have made the contacts which later enabled him to smuggle out of England the workmen necessary to the fulfillment of his desires.

In 1768, the year after the Townshend Acts levied duties on both of Stiegel's products, iron and glass, and the year industrialists were encouraged by the patriots' adoption of the Non-Importation Agreement, construction of the flint glasshouse was started. Completed in 1769, it was extended by an addition in each of the succeeding three years. In so far as we know today this second Manheim glasshouse to which Stiegel referred in his advertisements as the "American Flint Glass Works" [31] was the first in America to specialize in fine tablewares. Moreover, excepting the later New Bremen Glassmanufactory, it was by far the most ambitious project of its kind until well into the nineteenth century. At its peak of production about 130 men were employed, among them master blowers, "Flowerers" (engravers), cutters, and enamelers, from England and the Continent. The glass was widely advertised and, Hunter states, marketed as far away as Boston. At the time of his failure Stiegel listed unsold glass at dealers' or agents' at York, Hanover, Hagerstown, Carlyle, Frederickstown, Manheim, New York City, and Baltimore. Probably some traveled with his iron stoves to the West Indies. The advertisements made quite a point of equality in beauty and quality to Europe's wares and regularly appealed to purse and patriotism. In July 1770, about the time merchants in port cities were burying the Non-Importation Agreement, Stiegel, appealing to the herd instinct, eloquently pleaded the struggling manufacturers' cause in the following:

> As the proprietors have been at an immense expense in erecting said works, and engaging some of the most ingenious artists in said manufacture, which is now arrived at great perfection, and above all, as at this crisis it is the indispensable duty, as well as interest of every real well wisher of America, to promote and encourage manufactures amongst ourselves, they hope from the glorious spirit of patriotism at present voluntarily and virtuously existing here, to receive the approbation and encouragement of the public, which they expect to merit a continuance of, by selling their goods on much lower terms, than such imported from Europe are usually sold.[32]

Two months later he petitioned the Provincial Council of Pennsylvania for assistance. *A year later* he was "allowed and given" £150 "as a Public encouragement to his late manufacture of White Flint glass in this province."[33] That was a teasing sum when all costs, wages especially, were crippling industry.[34]

Unfortunately as the months passed patriots' purses were getting flatter, not fatter. Colonial prosperity was running out and war was close on its heels when in 1773 Stiegel resorted to a lottery, the "American Flint Glass Manufactory Lottery,"[35] in an attempt to raise the funds necessary to continue operation. It was not enough. The glasshouse was a Moloch which consumed all Stiegel's resources, leaving him only the ashes of bankruptcy. In the fall of 1774, several months after the glasshouse was closed, Stiegel was thrown into debtors' prison, from which, though his creditors were unsatisfied, he was released before Christmas. He soon slipped back into the obscurity from which he had erupted. After his death he was to emerge as the central figure of many a legend, and over a hundred years after his burial in an unmarked grave the annual Feast of Roses assured him a permanent niche in Manheim tradition. Each year since 1891, as required in his long-forgotten deed of the Lutheran church to its congregation, a single red rose has been paid as rent for the church he built.

Concerning Stiegel, his industries, and their products, there is more documentary evidence known to exist than in connection with any other American glasshouse established before that of the New England Glass Company in 1818. Most of these sources discovering the facts of Stiegel's life and enterprises were unearthed by Mr. Hunter. Again, as in the case of Wistar, attributions of specific pieces to Stiegel were made on the evidence of excavated fragments, local inquiries and traditions, and on personal opinions. The parallel extends further; for in the light of expanded information one feels that few pieces, even among those once confidently called Stiegel, can be categorically assigned to this glasshouse. Unfortunately for those who demand a label, Stiegel, through his imported *servants,* succeeded all too well in his avowed intention to copy popular imports of glass. Also, sad to say, many an English creamer did not emigrate to the United States to lose its identity among its American cousins until the twentieth

PLATE 2

1. Footed bowl blown from brilliant amethyst glass; circular form with folded rim, applied short-stemmed foot; patterned in 15-diamond mold and expanded in large ogival design. Collection of Dr. and Mrs. E. J. Carey.
Height, 4¾₁₆″; top diameter, 4¼″; diameter of foot, about 2⅝″.

2. Footed sugar bowl and cover blown from brilliant sapphire-blue lead glass; deep straight-sided bowl rounding to applied short-stemmed small circular foot; set-in flanged cover with the applied swirl-ribbed finial which is considered a Stiegel characteristic; bowl and cover patterned in a 16-diamond mold and expanded in ogival design; finial, twenty ribs.
Over-all height, 6⅛″; without cover, 3¹⁵⁄₁₆″; top diameter, 4⅛″; diameter of foot, 2¼″.

3. Footed bowl blown from brilliant emerald-green lead glass, of bluish tone; hemispherical bowl with plain rolled-over and turned-down rim; applied short-stemmed circular foot; patterned in a 15-diamond mold and expanded in ogival design.
Height, 2¾″; top diameter, 5″; diameter of foot, 2⅜″.

4. Salt blown from emerald-green lead glass, yellowish tone with pale amber discolorations; double-ogee bowl with short stem drawn from same gather, applied circular foot; patterned in a 14-diamond mold and expanded in ogival design.
Height, 2¾″; top diameter, 2⅜″; diameter of foot, 2″.

5. Creamer blown from light purple lead glass; ovoid body tapering to wide cylindrical neck with slightly flaring plain rim and small pinched lip; applied short-stemmed circular foot; applied solid semi-ear-shaped handle; patterned in a 15-diamond mold and expanded in ogival design.
Height, 3⅝″; top diameter, 2″; greatest diameter of body, 2¹¹⁄₁₆″; diameter of foot, 1¹⁵⁄₁₆″.

6. Salt blown from light purple non-lead glass; double-ogee bowl with short stem from same gather, applied circular foot; pattern-molded and expanded in checkered-diamond design, a diaper of seven large diamonds in lateral chain, each containing four small concave diamonds.
Height, 2¹¹⁄₁₆″; top diameter, 2¼″; greatest diameter of body, 2⅜″; diameter of foot, 2″.

On salts patterned in this mold there are usually three or four complete diamonds counting on the diagonal, the number depending on how much of the pattern was sheared off in finishing the rim. Another diamond, which was at the bottom in the mold, was distorted or eliminated in drawing the small knoplike stem from the bowl. These salts are found also in deep sapphire-blue, clear glass, and clear with pale blue tint. All that we have tested are non-lead glass. There is a strong probability that they, and flasks in a similar pattern but from another mold, were made at the Amelung Glass Works.

The forms of all pieces on this plate are typical of the eighteenth century. The relatively small foot of the two bowls and creamer was characteristic of the Stiegel period, 1764–74, and type was carried over into later years of the eighteenth and even into the first quarter of the nineteenth century. The green bowl and purple creamer were each blown from a relatively heavy gather.

century. Consequently—with a few exceptions—in spite of the fact that literally hundreds of examples of Stiegel's glass must be in collectors' cabinets and in ancestral corner cupboards, few of us have the courage to assign a given piece to Stiegel—unless, of course, its requisite physical characteristics are accompanied by reliable family history. More than one student of glass has placed authenticated English creamers and salts beside their counterparts, which there was good reason to believe to be Stiegel, or at least American, and has been unable to discover any differentiating features or qualities.

We believe that the typically eighteenth-century type pattern-molded pieces shown in color on Plate 2 are American and, excepting probably the checkered-diamond salt, quite possibly blown at Manheim. The blue bowl is characteristic of the period in its expanded diamond pattern and its shape, combining greater height in proportion to its width than in the nineteenth-century bowls, the applied short-stemmed foot, and plain rim fitted with a flanged set-in cover.[36] It is also typically English except for one detail, namely, the twisted ribbing on the pointed globular finial. Such ribbing, we understand, usually is not found on the finials of covers for similar bowls made in contemporaneous English glasshouses. The amethyst bowl has a folded rim, whereas most of the English coverless bowls have a plain rim. The other pieces have small imperfections of metal and irregularities of form that undoubtedly would have made them unfit for exportation from Britain or rather for importation into the Colonies. The diamond or ogival creamer and checkered-diamond salt, the latter of non-lead glass, are an odd shade of light purple, probably accidental and, we believe, not a commercial color. Such are the reasons for our opinion. Still, since we have no supporting proof, the pieces must be called Stiegel type.

The fact is that one is faced with an anomaly; for, while few pieces can be attributed to Stiegel, the articles of his output, the techniques employed in their fabrication, and their physical characteristics can be outlined with almost serene confidence. Because of his revealing advertisements and ledgers, coupled with authenticated foreign glass which he vowed to equal, it would be possible to deduce the nature of his glass even if there were no physical evidence in support of the conclusions. From the many articles advertised or listed[37] it is apparent that the majority, determined by the habits and tastes of the period, were containers for wines, spirits, fermented beverages, and condiments. There were decanters, plain and molded, from half-pint to gallon capacity; wineglasses and "Free Masons" (possibly firing glasses similar to those on Plate 60); glasses for wine, water, beer, and syllabub; mugs from half-pint to quart measure and lemonade cans; tumblers from quarter-gill to half-gallon and jelly glasses; and servers for cider, wine, and water. For condiments there were vinegar cruets, mustard pots and bottles, and quite an assortment of salts—with and without feet, tall, plain, common chain, and jacony. Other table articles included quart bowls (for punch?), cream pots or jugs, and, it would seem, four types of sugar containers, namely, boxes with covers, dishes, loaf, and round. Were the sugar boxes with covers similar to the covered bowl, Plate 2, which today we call a sugar bowl? Were the sugar rounds and dishes similar to the amethyst lidless bowl on the same plate? Ornamented candlesticks and blue flower jars were in his regular line. Extrinsic and molded decorations embellished these articles. Newspaper evidence and Stiegel's records are proof that wheel engraving, cutting, and enameling were regular methods of ornamentation. Also the small dip (pattern-mold) and the part-size piece mold had to be part of the equipment at Manheim if Stiegel was to produce the popular English types of glassware molded in the Venetian tradition.

Thus in the table and ornamental wares attributed to Stiegel two decorative idioms were expressed side by side, the English and the continental, generally called German today. The Stiegel type engraved and enameled wares identified by tradition with Manheim were mainly of clear glass, sometimes of deep blue, and undoubtedly non-lead metal. Quite apart from any other consideration, this would result naturally from a shop of artisans and a market which were part German and part British by birth or recent descent. Tumblers, plain and paneled, of various sizes were ornamented with shallow silhouettelike engraving of conventionalized motifs such as tulips and prim baskets of flowers, all decidedly continental in conception and execution. In fact they were closely related to contemporary folk art and their rendering was characteristic of the so-called peasant glass of the continent—the Low Countries and Germany in particular. Moreover, the pieces known to have been tested for lead content have proved to be non-lead as was the continental glass at that time, the sort made at Manheim before lead was introduced there, and probably afterward also. The same was true of the enameled pieces. Tumblers, drug or cordial bottles, and mugs were the principal articles which have been assigned to Stiegel, but enameled wineglasses, "Free Masons," salt cellars, three-footed cream jugs, servers, smelling bottles, and cruets were advertised, so presumably made. The engraved and enameled pieces attributed to Stiegel would have made the latest German immigrant to Pennsylvania feel perfectly at home in his new surroundings. It is likely such pieces were made with an eye on the patronage of the prosperous Pennsylvania Germans, and, moreover, when one considers the persistence of their folk art, were the only types which would have been acceptable to them.

However, Stiegel's own heart was given to the English types. These were the wares, principally tablewares, which it is believed were blown from the brilliant lead glass, the first of its kind to be made in America—so far as we know at present. Blues, amethysts, and, rarely, emerald-green were made in addition to clear or crystal glass. Of these artificial colors, blue predominated and was the only color we have seen mentioned in either advertisements or the account-book lists. The pieces blown from the fine flint metal were plain or pattern-molded.[38] In this method of decoration the blower making a creamer with expanded vertical ribs, for example, would insert the gather of glass into a small, deeply fluted dip mold; then, by blowing, inflate the gather so that it was pushed against the fluted sides of the mold, thereby impressing the pattern in the gather. Withdrawing the gather which now bore the pattern, he would proceed to fashion his creamer by blowing and manipulation. The processes of molding and blowing caused a physical characteristic by which pattern-molded glass may be distinguished from other types, namely, the exactly corresponding contours of the inner and outer surfaces. If the blower wished to produce swirled ribbing or fluting, he accomplished it by rotating the vertically ribbed gather as he inflated it. It is because the gathers were expanded *after* molding and *before* the shaping by manipulation was completed that the adjective "expanded" is used to modify the name of a design,—*expanded vertical ribbing* or *expanded diamond*. In the case of the diamond patterns, or for that matter any pattern which involved crossed lines, part-size piece molds were used, that is, a mold much smaller in size than the usual finished piece, used only to impress a pattern, and having usually two pieces or leaves hinged together.

The principal pattern-molded designs attributed to Manheim are the ribbed, fluted, various diamond, the daisy-hexagon, the diamond-daisy and its variant, which are illustrated by flasks on Plate 1. With the exception of the diamond-daisy blue bowl shown on Plate 11 and a few green and blue salts we have seen no pieces other than the bottles patterned in any of the *daisy* designs. Some students, we among them, believe that the diamond-above-flute, the daisy-hexagon, the diamond-daisy, and its variant were originated by Stiegel. The belief is held in spite of the fact that there is no proof of the proposition and the evidence, if it can be called that, is perhaps tenuous. The bottles, sometimes called "perfume" and sometimes "pocket" (perhaps for a coat pocket, but certainly not pants pocket in the 1770s), have the bulbous shape characteristic of the period and not of the nineteenth century. So far as we have been able to learn no student of foreign glass has ever seen or heard of an exact counterpart of these particular designs in any foreign glass, continental or British. Lastly Stiegel had the means at hand in his ironworks to manufacture molds and, equally important, improvements in the types and construction of his iron stoves furnish proof that he had the ingenuity or inventiveness as well as interest to conceive new designs. The ribbed and simpler diamond patterns characteristic of the Stiegel type glass were used almost universally wherever molded glass was produced. Diamond and ribbed pattern-molds were part of the equipment of most early nineteenth-century bottle houses in the Midwest as well as nearly every American glasshouse producing tablewares. Diamond salts similar in pattern and shape to No. 4, Plate 2, were made in all Midwestern early nineteenth-century bottle glasshouses and commercially in Eastern houses if one can judge from the presence of one among the objects decorating the billhead of the Boston Glass Manufactory,[39] in whose South Boston Works a general line of tableware was not produced until 1813.

Another design which, as far as we know at present, has no foreign prototype is the paneled vase, Plate 47.[40] These attractively shaped vases were attributed to Stiegel by Hunter on two bits of evidence—Stiegel listed blue flower jars and a small fragment of blue glass[41] appeared to Mr. Hunter to bear a portion of a panel and to be from a paneled vase. Actually the fragment is so small that it is impossible to determine either the specific type of panel or the object which bore it. Many students feel that the form of the paneled vase has a distinctly nineteenth-, rather than eighteenth-century cast and that the vases emanated from a New England factory—Boston, Cambridge, or Sandwich. One of the main reasons for this conclusion is the geographical distribution of those which we have been able to trace. Taking Albany, New York, as a focus, and describing a circle about one hundred miles in radius, we have found that the majority known to us have been located within its circumference, or within the environs of Boston. It is true, of course, that some of Stiegel's glass was sold in New York City and perhaps in Boston after the American Philosophical Society, exhibiting examples of it in 1771, judged it "equal in beauty and quality to the generality of Flint Glass imported from England." [42] Therefore the vases could have found their way to smaller and less sophisticated communities, though at that period customers outside the main "cities" in this area would have been few and very far between. But it is likewise true that in the early nineteenth century, when there were many more potential customers, Boston glass traveled by sloop around Cape Cod, down the sound, and up the Hudson to Troy, where many upstate country merchants replenished their stocks.[43] Of course, too, the arguments of means and inventiveness can be marshaled by those who believe Stiegel did make the vases. To many these seem outweighted by the shape and the fact that similar paneling was used extensively in the nineteenth century on bowls, pitchers, and celery glasses. On the basis of the present evidence, we personally incline to the New England theory. Wherever they were made, the design is one which redounds to the creator's credit.

Two or three years before the fall of Stiegel's little empire a rival glasshouse appeared on his horizon. Established by Leacock and Towars sometime in the period from 1771[*] to November 1772,[†] when it was taken over by John Elliott and Company,[44] the Philadelphia Glass Works was erected on a rented lot between Bank Street and the Delaware River[‡] next to Kensington.[45] The new firm not only competed with Stiegel for the glass market but denied his claim to being the first manufacturer of flint glass in the Colonies. And, probably more disastrously for Stiegel, shortly after he started his lottery it resorted to one of its own.[46] Apparently that of the Philadelphia Glass Works was the more successful; for on December 7, 1774,[47] while Stiegel was still in the debtors' prison, the proprietors announced that, "having procured a sett of good workmen, and the works being in blast," the public could be supplied with most kinds of white and green-glass ware. It seems extremely likely that those workmen were alumni of Manheim. The roll of articles headed by decanters and drinking vessels which they produced in 1775 was similar to Stiegel's and included some not mentioned by him. The character of the wares is largely a matter of conjecture from such phrases as "white" (clear) and "green glass" and "plain and cut" [48] and from the probability that the style was distinctly English in most aspects of its design. The colonial respect for English wares, undiminished by hostilities, was so glaringly evident even during the British occupation of Philadelphia that a German captain concluded that the colonial merchant or shopkeeper was a laughable creature who, if certain wares were fashionable and having a great sale in England, would push them in Philadelphia although he might know nothing about them.[49]

If one can credit the reports of the bibulous habits of the representatives to the 1774 Continental Congress and of the gay brotherly love during Howe's regime in the home of that commodity, the demand for flips and wines, decanters and punch bowls should have kept the furnace of the Philadelphia Glass Works in full blast through 1778, even allowing for the preference for imports. But early in 1777 the works and the stock on hand were offered for sale.[50] The works may have been taken over by Felix Farrell, once a "servant" of Stiegel, and George Bakeoven. However, inasmuch as it was reported early in 1778 that no white glass was made in America,[51] the glasshouse, if it was in operation at all, must have been producing green or bottle glass only. Be that as it may, in 1780,[§] the year the Wistar works was offered for sale, Thomas Leiper, a Philadelphia tobacconist, acquired the glasshouse.[52] By then the city had been vacated by the British, and American ports had been opened to the ships of all nations except Britain for over a year. Nevertheless England's blockade of shipping lanes was a definite handicap to the importation of goods, especially fragile ones, so perhaps Leiper was prompted by

*October 3, 1771, Robert Towars, skinner; Joseph Leacock, watch-maker (Philadelphia Land Records, Book D6, pp. 226 ff.).

†November 5, 1772, John Elliott, Sr. (merchant); John Elliott, Jr. (brushmaker); Isaac Gray (merchant); Samuel Elliott (tanner), ibid.

‡Town of Richmond, Northern Liberties (ibid.). Wares referred

to as made in Kensington (ad, *Pennsylvania Packet*, February 27, 1775).

§Indenture dated May 6, 1780; recorded, February 22, 1783 (Philadelphia Land Records, Book D6, pp. 268 ff.).

his own need for bottles and containers as well as by visions of a wider market. Contrary to former accounts, contemporary reports of events and manufactures indicate that he abandoned the project between 1783 and 1787.[53]* Even in 1796 glass was not mentioned among the listed manufactures of the state.[54] So probably the plant was idle until it was taken over by a new firm about 1800.† From then on until after 1900 glass—principally bottles and other strictly commercial utilitarian vessels—was to be made fairly continuously on that site in Kensington. Among the many owners was the fabulous Thomas W. Dyott,‡ entrepreneur of dynamic initiative, to whom collectors are indebted for some of the most interesting and well-designed historical flasks in the galaxy of American glass, one of which is shown on Plate 112. However, between the days of Leiper's snuff bottles and Dyott's historical flasks the face and heart of the United States were to undergo many changes. And many glasshouses were to be planned and built, some rising only to fall and some expanding into thriving concerns.[55]

*Inasmuch as the Philadelphia Glass Works (called also the Kensington Glass Works) is the only one known at present to have existed in the Philadelphia area in 1789, it seems probable that Leiper rented the works in that year to one Philip Stimel who advertised in September for two or three bottle blowers (*Pennsylvania Packet,* September 9, 1789). Since this is the only ad found as yet, it would appear that Stimel was unsuccessful.

†From April 13, 1798 (if not earlier), until after January 23, 1799, Leiper apparently rented the works to Christopher Trippel & Co. The firm produced mainly bottles. (Ads during this period appeared in *Claypoole's American Daily Advertiser.*) On March 6, 1800, Leiper sold the works to James Butland & Co. (Joseph Roberts, Jr., James Butland & James Rowland, merchants) (Philadelphia Land Records, Book EF1, pp. 320 ff.). On February 24, 1804, Roberts's share was acquired by Butland & Rowland (ibid., Book EF 18, pp. 346 ff.). On September 1, 1815, Rowland bought out Butland (ibid., Book AM 27, pp. 543 ff.).

‡Dyott purchased the property from James Rowland, Jr., on July 10, 1833 (ibid., Book AM 37, pp. 747 ff.). It seems significant that no glassworks was mentioned in the indenture or in the earlier indentures; however, three steel furnaces were. Dyott already owned abutting land purchased on November 3, 1830 (ibid. AM 10, p. 7), on which it appeared the new Kensington Glass Works had been built by Hewson, Connell & Co. in 1816. The firm's announcement of the works stated it was on the lot *next* to that of the "old glass works" (*Philadelphia Gazette and Daily Advertiser,* August 2, 1816). As indicated by ads (Philadelphia's *The Union for the Country,* February 9, July 24, and September 9, 1821), Dyott, sole agent by 1817, had acquired sole or controlling interest in the new Kensington Glass Works by 1821. These facts, plus Rowland's listing in city directories as "iron merchant," suggest that possibly no glass was blown at the old works after about 1815, after Rowland bought out Butland.

GLASSMAKING FROM 1780 TO 1800

WAR or no war, bottles and window glass were essential articles in continual and expanding demand. For that matter, if merchants could obtain them, fashionable tablewares did not sit long on their shelves. Life was spartan for many of the people, but for some it was luxurious. As always, war raised a fine crop of profiteers. Also, as the tide of fighting and foraging receded from a locality, commerce, trade, and even some manufacturing were coaxed into renewed activities. The interruptions and the blocking of the channels of commerce had created a demand far exceeding the supplies of most commodities. This glaring situation blinded more than one would-be manufacturer to conditions unfavorable to the success of his project. In this category were at least two glasshouses erected before the end of the Revolution for the manufacture of window glass and bottles.[1]

In 1780, the year Richard Wistar advertised his works for sale and Thomas Leiper purchased the Philadelphia Glass Works, the construction of a glasshouse was started by Robert Hewes in the forest near Temple, New Hampshire,[2] not far from Boston, a section which had been free from active warfare for some years. Trade, however, was not free. Hewes, a Bostonian and a theoretical rather than practical glassman, hoped to produce both crown and cylinder window glass and bottles for the local market at least. He "carried his works to his fuel" and to a spot so remote from civilization that during the building of the glasshouse the tracks of bears were frequently seen around his works in the morning.[3] Again a glasshouse was manned by Germans, this time mercenaries said to have been deserters from the British Army,[4] perhaps some of the many prisoners of war released from "Winter Hill" to earn their living[5] and pretending to a skill in glassmaking. In any case it is unlikely they were expert glassmen. Had they been master blowers they would have been too valuable at home to have been conscripted or even allowed to volunteer for military service in the cause of any king, certainly not a British king, Hanoverian or not. In fact they would have been exempted from military duty by law. In any event they proved to be an intemperate lot, contributing not a little to the disastrous end of the venture. But Hewes, in spite of being badly burnt, continued to preach the gospel of domestic manufacture of glassware. His vision and persistence were important factors in rooting the industry in Boston before the turn of the century.

The second glasshouse to be built during the Revolution was located in New Jersey, which also had been rid of the British for some time. Impersonal legal records contradict local history and traditions[6] as to the year the Stanger brothers started their furnace and disappointingly dispel the romantic mists of tales of debts and prison. There is confusion as to the names of the brothers, but general agreement that the glasshouse was an offshoot of the Wistar glassworks. Presumably some if not all of the Stangers were employed at Wistarberg, and apparently when blowing dwindled or ceased there they decided to stick to their blowpipes rather than turn to an unfamiliar trade or means of livelihood. It seems to have been about 1780 (one wonders why they did not take over the Wistar plant) that the brothers—Solomon, Daniel, Francis, Peter, and Philip—moved into Gloucester County and by the fall of 1781 completed their glass-house and small community, later called respectively the Olive Glass Works and Glass-boro. (Francis may have been the one for whom the Amelung flask, Plate 104, was made.) Two other brothers, Adam and Christian, were associated with them as glass blowers. They were the first practical glassmen in the new nation (so far as we know now) to attempt combining ownership, management, and production—a proud situation of brief duration. By 1784 financial stringencies had thrust them back into their familiar estate of glass blowers, making glass in the house they built but for its new owners. In 1786 Colonel Thomas Heston and Thomas Carpenter became sole owners. The tradition that they added window and flint glass to the output is supported by an item in the June 1788 *American Museum:* "A white glass manufactory has lately been set on foot in New Jersey, and the glass pronounced equal to the English White Glass." [7] It seems unlikely that by "White Glass" lead metal was meant. But it may have meant true flint glass, that is, glass made with calcined flints. "White" generally signified clear or color-less metal. Eventually this house and two later, nineteenth-century, Glassboro works in which members of the Stanger family were interested were owned by the Whitney brothers, grandsons of Colonel Heston. [8]

Perhaps it was this first Glassboro works to which Lord Sheffield referred in 1783 when he reported that bad window glass was made in New Jersey. [9] His may have been a statement of fact at the moment and the inferior quality may have contributed to the delayed success of the works, but it certainly was not prophetic. *Good* window and other glass were to be made in New Jersey, especially in the southern section, which was to become an extremely important center of the American glass industry. Various Stangers, as partners in at least seven different South Jersey ventures and as employees of glass-houses, [10] were to contribute to that growth. Though as managers and executives they were not destined to become tycoons, they continued to practice and nourish the art of glass blowing. It is almost axiomatic that they not only followed the South Jersey tradi-tion of blowing and ornamentation but passed it on to their apprentices and successors. The sugar bowl, No. 1, Plate 30, fashioned from non-lead glass of pale green tint and with the swan finial and square foot may have been made at Glassboro prior to 1800. It has a South Jersey pedigree. The blue pitcher, No. 1, Plate 40, was made at Glassboro in 1835 by Joel Duffield, one of the blowers. The rare lamp, No. 1, Plate 94, is said to have been blown by Julius Stanger about 1848 at his Isabella Glass Works in New Brook-lyn. The mug, No. 1, Plate 73, likewise was made there. Some of the houses with which Stangers were associated operated for decades, as in Glassboro. And there the glass blower was not utterly defeated by the machine until the early twentieth century, when the Owens Bottle Company, having taken over the Whitney Glass Works, installed its automatic machines for the production of bottles.

If the first Stanger glasshouse actually was in production in the fall of 1781, it had the distinction of being the first *United States* glassworks, since the birth certificate of the United States should bear the date when the last of her thirteen sponsors adopted the Articles of Confederation. However, even with the end of the physical combat to give reality to our Declaration of Independence, the struggle to be a nation was not to be decided before 1789. The brave assertion, "Our union is perfect," was still as vain a boast as in 1775,[11] perhaps keeping our courage up but fooling few, even among. ourselves. Unfortunately the end of the war snapped the strong danger-spun cord binding the states together and the Union parted into thirteen "free republics,"[12] each slipping back into the colonial mire of conflicting social philosophies blended with commercial interests. And, still nursing a sovereign-state complex, each was jealous of its rights—even carrying them so far as to erect tariff barriers. Massachusetts levied imposts so that other states had to pay her tribute, as Oliver Ellsworth reminded his fellow delegates weighing the proposed Constitution in 1788. He pointed out also that the people of Connecticut alone enriched the treasury of New York by more than fifty thousand dollars each year. About the same time a New Yorker opposed to federal control of imposts saw no equity in the independent state of New York becoming a dupe of Congress.[13] Most citizens, as well as some publishers, thought of the United States in lower case, of their states in capitals. More than one society for the encouragement of manufactures and the useful arts was formed, as in Pennsylvania, for the benefit of *its* State, not the united states.[14] In short the prevailing attitude was every state for itself and . . . Apparently Pennsylvania saw no reason to give aid and comfort to manufacturers of glass or any commodity in New York or Connecticut, nor the Carolinas and Virginia, to purchase their glass in Philadelphia or Boston when by buying it in London or Hamburg they might sell more cotton, tobacco, or rice.

In the meantime, while Congress might have the right to legislate for the common good, it lacked the power and, worse, the co-operation of the states to put a lid on the caldron of boiling trouble. It scalded only itself in attempts to stabilize or regulate trade and money, even though specie was scarce and confused. Imports, especially of luxury goods, so completely dwarfed exports that "this vast influx of goods soon drained the United States of a great part of the specie they had at the close of the war,"[15] thereby lowering the reservoir of capital for business. Individual states issued their own paper money and the paper of one state was not always at par with that of another. Such stipulations as Talmadge Hall's that the fare on his "Stage-waggon" between New York and Boston was "4 pence a mile Connecticut or Massachusetts currency"[16] may seem quaint to us but was not out of the ordinary in the 1780s. Finance, politics, commerce, all were in a state of flux in which only an essential industry with a receptive local market and convenient to water carriage had a chance of survival. And only the most optimistic and farseeing could believe that the fabric of a more perfect union could be woven with so many threads of disunity in the warp. Among them were a few men who felt there was a golden opportunity, or ought to be, to plant domestic industries as well as staple crops. Essential and luxury glass were high on the list of desirable imports, and therefore seemed one of the logical choices for domestic production. In this transition period before the adoption of the Constitution in 1789 a few more scattered glasshouses (seven or nine) were erected.[17]

With the exception of the New Bremen Glassmanufactory near Frederick, Maryland, only a little—or literally nothing at all—is known of the products of the glasshouses during that brief but critical period. Still the name Pitkin associated with one of them will long be remembered in connection with American glass. In 1783, the year the last redcoat left our shores, a glasshouse was erected by William and Elisha Pitkin and Samuel Bishop near Hartford in a tract called East Hartford, and later East Manchester, within a few miles of the Connecticut River—the first known to have been operated in the state. For over a hundred years members of the Pitkin family had been leaders in the colony; William and Elisha were no exception. Like their kin they had their fingers in several industrial pies. During the Revolution they not only ran an indispensable powder mill but manufactured snuff under a fourteen-year tax-free privilege. It is said that the twenty-five-year monopoly on glassmaking granted to them by the Connecticut Assembly in 1783 was a reward for their war services. As supplies of English crown glass were still cut off, apparently the time seemed ripe to capture its market. To realize this ambition Robert Hughes [Hewes?],* of Boston, was secured as superintendent, but it is said he was a failure.[18] On the other hand Mark Leavenworth writing from New Haven in 1787, attributed the lack of success to the owners not understanding their own business rather than to want of workmen who understood theirs.[19] Perhaps both management and employees invested the currency of ignorance. In any event the partners soon asked the Assembly for permission to conduct a £400 lottery to compensate for the losses. The lottery, we are told, was successful but the works still were not.[20]

Leavenworth, who thought the grant likely to be forfeited before any glass was made, expressed the opinion that if white glass was irresistible to manufacturers it should be fashioned into decanters, wineglasses, and similar vessels, which were expensive to import, rather than window glass, which was cheaper to import than to make at home. Bottles were the logical product, for, he said, if they could be had "at a reasonable price, the sale would be vastly extensive, and our farmers would be much benefited . . . our cyder might be shipped to the West Indies and Southern States to great advantage." About this time Tench Coxe and others pointed out that the manufacture of malt liquors for exportation actually was curtailed by an insufficient supply of the black bottles used as containers.[21] The Pitkins and Bishop may have taken heed or have been thinking along the same lines; for by May 1788 a new capital of $14,000 was subscribed and the works were in operation, promising "much advantage to the proprietors." [22] For the next forty years, until the holdings of wood were exhausted sometime in the 1830s, bottles of all kinds including flasks, carboys, demijohns or junk bottles were blown at the "Pitkin" glassworks. In addition to free-blown flasks it is probable that flasks in two other categories were made, namely, the pattern-molded type which today bears the Pitkin name and the full-size molded historical and pictorial flasks. As yet only five flasks in the second category have been attributed to Pitkin with any confidence.† Four are of pint size, one of half-pint, and all are extremely rare. One has the inscriptions "Jared Spencer" and "Manchester. Con." [23]

The pattern-molded flasks, long attributed to Pitkin by local tradition, were made by the German half-post method and were finely ribbed, vertically, spirally, or in a combination of both.[24] It was years before collectors realized that the same types must

---

*Hewes is correct: "Several bottles and a piece of crown glass, manufactured at East Hartford, have been brought to this town [Boston]. . . . This manufactory is conducted by Mr. Robert Hewes, late of this town" (Boston *Independent Chronicle*, December 4, 1788).

†But one or all five may have been blown at John Mather's glass-works [not known in 1950] established at East Hartford by August 1805 (Hartford *Connecticut Courant*, August 2, 1805), where figured flasks were made by 1817 (Hartford *Connecticut Mirror*, February 10, 1817). The Jared Spencer, Manchester, Connecticut, flask could not have been made before May 1823, when the town name was changed to Manchester.

have been made at other works *before* and *after* "Pitkin," especially in the early nine-teenth-century houses in the East and the so-called Midwest, that is, western Pennsyl-vania, West Virginia, and Ohio. Even now there is no proof they were blown at Pitkin's, but it is a reasonable assumption even though no fragments have been found, for they were a common type of the period. In fact they were more common before 1813 than afterward, when, it has been established, they were made at the nearby Coventry Glass Works, Keene-Marlboro-Street, and some Midwest houses. Hence Pitkin has been stripped of its factory significance and invested with a generic one. The Pitkin flasks which were made in the Eastern bottle houses, undoubtedly including the Pitkin works, were in clear olive-amber and olive-greens. In general the color range was limited; the weight, light; the ribbing, fine and patterned in a 32- or 36-rib dip mold, and more frequently swirled than vertical or double-patterned. (Double pattern was vertical ribbing upon swirled ribbing.) Usually in the case of the double pattern the vertical ribbing extended about three quarters of an inch above the swirled. The most common shape was a tapering ovoid with a slight concavity on the wide sides, a bit above the bottom of the flask. The Midwestern Pitkins, on the other hand, were blown mainly from a brilliant metal in varied shades of greens, ambers from deep to golden in hue, and aqua-marine. As a rule they were heavier in every way than the Eastern; more metal was used in their making; and the ribbing was generally patterned in a 16-, 20-, 24-, 26-, or 32-rib dip mold, more widely spaced and more frequently in a combination of vertical and swirled ribbing with the vertical usually terminating slightly below the top of the swirled. And they are flatter. A few—very few—"Pitkins" of blue or of amethyst glass have come to light. It is safe to say that the majority of the survivors of all types are from the early nineteenth- rather than the eighteenth-century bottle houses. Typical examples are shown on Plate 105. Of special interest to the collector are the rare individual pieces like the jar and bottle shown on the same plate. Pitkin inkwells, likewise, were made in the Eastern bottle houses.

One of the two glasshouses started in New York State in the 1780s was built in the same year as the Pitkin works, 1783. It was erected in the wilderness at Peterborough, Madison County, not many miles from the Mohawk River, presumably in anticipation of supplying the window-glass and bottle needs of the immigrants streaming into the central part of the state. As a matter of fact David Goff and his associates, who started the short-lived enterprise, had emigrated from Hartford, Connecticut. Early in the nine-teenth century, when the situation with England, which today would be termed cool war, was freezing commerce, glassmaking was revived. Operated by several firms as new members invested new money, the house met with moderate success until about 1830. Window glass was the main product and household wares of South Jersey type were blown.[25] We have seen an aquamarine powder horn, an individual piece in the South Jersey tradition, which was well authenticated as Peterborough, probably from the nineteenth-century period.

In 1785 the second New York State glasshouse of this period was built in the "pine, barren, sandy country" of Guilderland Township eight miles from Albany, and near the western turnpike to Schenectady.[26] John de Neufville and his son Leonard, late of Amster-dam, Holland, had sunk most of a huge fortune in the American patriots' cause; now the remnants of that fortune were ventured in wooded land and glassmaking.[27] On May 12, 1785, Leonard de Neufville, who seems to have had complete charge of all De Neufville affairs at the time, signed an agreement with Jan Heefke and Ferdinand Walfahrt whereby Heefke was to be the business agent and Walfahrt the manager of the new glassworks. The glass blowers were to be brought from the Continent.[28] Early in 1787, if not before, white or clear glass[29] was being blown at Dowesborough,[30] as the house was called. In addition to the windowpanes and "electrical glasses" for which undoubtedly the clear metal was used, pocket bottles, jars, and demijohns (the last wearing Indian-woven wicker jackets) were blown from common bottle or green glass.[31] Some at least of the window glass was sold by a New York representative to dealers in Pennsylvania, and Mr. Leiper (Thomas, who attempted to run the Philadelphia works around 1780, without a doubt) was supplied with bottles.[32] But production was sporadic and uncertain. Jan or John Heefke, writing from New York City to Leonard in December 1788, expressed his anxiety concerning the works and asked for glass as soon as possible. "I believe," he said, "the boat makes but one trip more this season, it will be of great damage to us if we do not get glass this winter for we may sell a great quantity if we have it as glass is high in town at present which makes people run to us for glass as ours comes something cheaper."[33]

Conditions at the glasshouse, however, were not healthy. Even in August when Elkanah Watson visited the works he found his former business correspondent, John de Neufville, an object of commiseration, in a shockingly impoverished state.[34] The new year brought not good tidings but the necessity of appealing to the state for help. Leonard submitted a petition stating that although the works had been a total loss to date they seemed on the verge of becoming profitable if assistance was forthcoming. Exemption from taxation, exemption of the workmen from militia duty, and a loan were his suggestions. In March on the last day of the session the Assembly by one vote and the Senate by four resolved that the treasurer should advance a loan of £1500 and the legislature at a future session would make provision to indemnify him.[35] If the treasurer ever took the chance of being indemnified we have been unable to find a record of it. A year later a petition from Leonard praying for an aid in money to enable him to continue the glassworks was read and referred to committee, where it went the way of so many good causes.[36] Nothing more about a loan appears in the records, but a year later, in February 1791, Leonard sent a memorial to the Assembly relative to persons confined to prison for debt. It too was read and referred to committee:[37] in August 1789 Walfahrt had landed in the New York jail as a defaulting debtor.[38] Dogged by one misfortune after another, the glassworks failed. By the spring of 1792 John de Neufville, probably his son too, had moved to Cambridge, Massachusetts, and from there was petitioning the United States Congress for reimbursement for monies and supplies advanced for the American cause.[39]

It probably was about that time that the glasshouse was acquired by four local American businessmen forming McClallen, MacGregor and Company, put into working condition, and rechristened the Albany Glass-House. By September they had on hand an assortment of window glass and bottles from half pints to five gallons which they were compelled to sell for cash only because the expected legislative loan had not materialized.[40] But in March 1793 they were actually granted an eight-year loan of £3000, without interest for three years and at five per cent for five, secured by a mortgage on the unencumbered real estate.[41] Shortly thereafter new partners brought in new money. Elkanah Watson who, having invested heavily in the project, was very active in the affairs of the company, wrote that in 1794 there were three furnaces in blast and nearly two hundred men employed,[42] most of whom were soon exempted from militia and jury duty. At the same time the glasshouse and its property were exempted from taxation for five years.[43] The company promptly expanded into more difficulties and reorganized in 1795. In June of the next year that copartnership dissolved[44] and a new firm formed the Hamilton Glass Manufacturing Society which, by the following March, "the busy opposition of some liberal minded patriotic gentlemen to the contrary not-withstanding," [45] was incorporated for fourteen years, a term later extended to 1821.[46] The firms really were, as a 1798 advertisement said of the great variety of Albany glass articles, "too tedious to enumerate." [47] The glasshouse community, which the new society named Hamilton in honor of the Secretary of the Treasury, who was a great friend to capital and domestic manufactures, boasted about thirty homes in 1808, and fifty-six two years later.[48] About 1815 when the company's wood lots were exhausted—probably the supply of new investors too—operations ceased. It was perhaps the first of the many works to earn the epitaph: factory closed—want of fuel.[49]

Advertisements, documents, and contemporary reports indicate that the main commercial output of the Albany Glass-House was window glass, with bottles, as in most such early houses, an important side-line product. In 1795 a foreign visitor pronounced the glass "pretty smooth,"[50] but whether it achieved equality with importations as its advertisements claimed apparently was a matter of indifference to a large portion of the callous public in the large centers until the period of the embargoes and the War of 1812. The house was, however, the principal source of supply for western Vermont, western and northern New York, and even nearby parts of Canada.[51] During the War of 1812 Albany window glass was good enough for Bostonians,[52] doubtless for New Yorkers also. For several years production had been on a scale considered extensive at the time. In 1808 Thomas Fessenden reported that, besides bottles and flint glass, a monthly average of 20,000 feet of window glass was being made by thirteen blowers who manned the three furnaces.[53] It seems unlikely that the flint glass was a lead metal; rather it is probable that Mr. Fessenden used the word loosely for white or clear glass. Possibly he meant true flint. Still, in at least two years before 1800, the firm advertised for broken flint glass, presumably for cullet.[54] But, whatever the metal, his report indicates that hollow ware, probably including some tablewares, was actually being blown at Albany and from metal of a grade superior to the bottle if not the window glass. Even if no clear glass tableswares were produced commercially it is safe to conclude that, since once more the blowers were from the Continent, the South Jersey techniques were practiced, flowing a little farther into a new land and expressing themselves in household articles. As a matter of fact Elkanah Watson claimed that the Albany or the Hamilton Glass Works, to use its more official title, "became a nursery for workers in all our other glass works in this state." [55] Perhaps one of them made the rare Vernon sugar bowl on Plate 7 or trained the blower who did.

Near the falls of the Schuylkill in Philadelphia, sometime between 1781 and 1786, it is said, a glassworks was started by John Nicholson and Robert Morris,[56]* famous as financier for the Continental Congress and somewhat infamous in his time as a merchant suspected of profiteering. If true, the project seems not to have been very active. After his visit in 1795 the Duke de La Rochefoucauld-Liancourt wrote:

> There is in America a scarcity of persons capable of conducting a business of this kind. There are also but few good workmen, who are with difficulty obtained, and whose wages are exorbitant. The conductors of Mr. Nicholson's manufactories [glass, buttons, and iron] are said to be very able men. But then a whole year may elapse before the workmen fall into a proper train of business, so that Mr. Nicholson's situation does not afford the most flattering prospects of success, if his returns be not rapid, as well as large.[57]

Although the history of this house is still to be traced, it warrants brief mention not only because of the light it sheds upon the difficulties of establishing a glassworks in the period but even more because its superintendent, supposedly from 1793 through 1796, was William Peter Eichbaum, a versatile gentleman who arrived in Philadelphia with a band of émigrés from the French Revolution. Eichbaum, like so many of our pioneer glass-makers, was German by birth, born at Attenback, Saxony, which he left for France, where he became glass cutter to Louis XVI.[58] While apparently he was thought to be a practical glassman capable of superintending all phases of the industry, his specialty was glass cutting. It was he who just after the turn of the century introduced this art to Pittsburgh, where he became a leading citizen and businessman. His presence at the Schuylkill house may just possibly indicate that an attempt was made there to produce fine table and ornamental wares. Also it is even probable that he snapped up some of the skilled craftsmen from New Bremen as the fires of Amelung's furnace turned to ashes.

In his pamphlet "Remarks on Manufacture, Principally on the New Established Glass-House near Fredericktown in the State of Maryland," printed for him in 1787, and distributed with the hopes of awakening Americans to the indispensability of manu-factures, especially his own, John Frederick Amelung revealed much of himself and his times. More important to the glass collector, he left posterity a richly detailed account of the promotion and founding of the New Bremen Glassmanufactory.

Amelung and his associates from prominent business houses in the imperial city of Bremen[59] on the Weser, possibly having followed and sympathized with the struggle across the Atlantic, either figured or were assured that so purely agricultural a land would be an Eldorado for the venturesome who helped it to secure industrial as well as political independence. Naturally all citizens would be aware that no country could flourish and become powerful without its manufacturers. Moreover, they would realize that every manufacture increased the population. Also, as soon as it could export its com-modities, it would bring in money from other countries or at least keep at home the money usually spent on the imports[60]—arguments which were to become *very* familiar to American ears during the next few decades. All this was elementary to Amelung, to his associates, and, evidently, to Benjamin Crockett, of Baltimore, who was then in Bremen. Apparently Crockett, fearing perhaps that a rival state might pluck so promising a plum, sang the praises of his Maryland to good effect. It probably was he who furthered the scheme by enabling the group to make contact with influential Americans in Europe.

*Evidence found since 1950 contains no reference to Robert Morris, and suggests the glassworks was not built until some time after 1790. Besides the quote above from La Rochefoucauld-Liancourt, which suggests erection of the works late in 1794 or early 1795, ads of John Nicholson's works and products appeared in the *Philadelphia Gazette and Universal Advertiser,* February 10 and December 8, 1795, August 25 to July 1, 1796.

At any rate, Amelung obtained letters of recommendation from John Adams, then at the Hague, from Benjamin Franklin, who was still at Paris, and from Thomas Barclay, our consul general in that city. Armed with letters to men of weighty influence—Thomas Mifflin, president of Congress; Thomas Johnson, ex-governor of Maryland and then member of Congress; William Paca, governor of Maryland; Charles Carroll, wealthy Marylander—and to well-known mercantile firms, he could but have had great expectations of instant and complete success in any undertaking. Doubtless the mercantile houses included Benjamin Crockett's own firm of Crockett and Harris and probably that of Charles Ghequiere, whose commercial ties were tightest with Hamburg and Bremen though his ships and cargoes sailed likewise to New England and the West Indies, Portugal and Spain. Another may have been George Repold, a merchant and neighbor of Ghequiere, and like him to become a personal friend of Amelung.[61]

Since by 1786 some £15,000 of combined German and American monies had been sunk in the project, Amelung must have obtained capital investments from some of these men or through their introductions. However, even before embarking for the United States some of those pounds had defrayed heavy expenses, heavier than anticipated, due to an act of God and of our erstwhile enemy, England. The winter of 1784 was so hard and bitter that some of the glassmen lured at great expense from Bohemia, Thüringen, and other parts of Germany, were "on the road half starved for the common want." The rivers froze before Amelung could set out with those who did keep the rendezvous, so the vessel which was ready to carry them and the equipment for three different glass furnaces could not set sail. However, any worry caused by the financial drain from supporting the men throughout the entire winter was overshadowed by the machinations of England, that "jealous nation, who look on the glass trade as an important one." He discovered that the sudden throwing of obstacles in his way such as the detention of glassmen by their princes was instigated by England, which, informed of his project by merchants and sea captains, asked the government of Hanover and other princes of the Roman Empire to do everything in their power to frustrate this plan which might result in losses to her and great benefits to the United States. Moreover, he was convinced that once he and his small band managed to set sail only the swift winds carrying them through the Channel in record time had foiled England's dastardly plot to take the brig *Fame* by force.[62] Conceivably, in 1787, Amelung stressed this evidence of the lengths to which England was prepared to go in order to prevent rival glassmaking, in the hope that it would jolt Americans into a realization of his glassworks' importance to the country. Perhaps he hoped also by unmasking her as the villain of the piece to rearouse so much animosity that the scales of trade would be tipped in his favor rather than in hers.

On August 31, 1784, no thoughts of such competition would have troubled Amelung when he landed at Baltimore with "68 hands." With the help of Messrs. Crocketts and Harris of Baltimore, and Abraham Faw, of Frederick-town, he lost no time in acquiring a 2100-acre tract of land[63] on either side of Bennetts Creek near the Monacacy River and about eight miles from Frederick.[64] In just under five months he offered window glass, also green and white hollow ware, to the public. Then he was more anxious about blowers than customers. While in the previous November fourteen workmen, brought over a circuitous route to avoid detention, had arrived, in October 1785 an assistant went back to Germany for still more workmen. But Amelung did not record whether this third group ever arrived at New Bremen, as the glasshouse community was christened.[65] However, the number of glassmen was enlarged from some source. Without doubt blowers from the earlier Manheim and Philadelphia houses seized the opportunity to preserve their art at New Bremen—perhaps replying to Amelung's first advertisement in February 1785 that "able glassmakers willing to engage themselves . . . on reasonable conditions . . . could find employment," [66] or Amelung may have sought them out. At least one of Stiegel's blowers, Baltazar (Baltzer) Kramer, and, for all we know to the contrary, one of the "sett of good workmen" at the Philadelphia Glass Works, was employed at New Bremen.[67]

By the time Amelung's pamphlet was printed in 1787 he had "erected all the necessary buildings for the Manufactory, as glass ovens for bottles, window and flint glass, and dwelling houses for one hundred and thirty-five now living souls." For himself there was a handsome mansion, complete with ballroom, as befitted the head of such an enterprise. A large community house, in which divine services were held on Sunday, had been built. A German school had been established under a competent master whose salary, paid by Amelung, was augmented slightly by a trifle from the parents of each pupil. Feeling this offered too narrow an education, he planned to have an English school in which, as he prospered, the curriculum would be expanded to include French, writing, ciphering, and also music, in the form of instruction in harp, harpsichord, flute, and violin for which purpose he had already hired the masters.[68] Also he intended to extend his domain by another thousand acres of land and his glass production through another glasshouse.[69] It was no wonder that overhead expenses and expansion confronted him with mounting costs for which his funds were inadequate, in part at least because, instead of husbanding his resources and starting out on a modest scale, he expended his capital in a princely fashion. There were no glassmaking Joneses in the United States for him to keep up with, so he must have aspired to European models.

While some of Amelung's glass had proven satisfactory to gentlemen in Baltimore, Frederick, and Elizabeth-town it was not being purchased eagerly by enough Americans. In fact Amelung obviously felt keenly that *he* had been oversold on the country and that he had not received the anticipated warm welcome as a manufacturer, even benefactor. He was deeply disappointed in ". . . the Flattering expectations to meet here [Maryland] with encouragement" from the people and, even more, from the government; for, he implied, the company had been assured encouragement and assistance would be given by the Maryland government.[70] Amelung was judging by European attitudes toward manufacturers, glassmakers in particular, and had been misled, it would seem, by Crockett, who apparently had overestimated his compatriots' desire for industries at home and underestimated the slowness with which the mills of Congress grind for the common good.

In his "Remarks," presumably sent to all state and federal representatives as well as likely investors, he politely presented a strong brief on the proper attitudes and actions of any government with even a modicum of common sense and a citizenry worth its democratic salt toward domestic manufactures and manufacturers, native or not. He stressed his own establishment's worthiness of wholehearted support and assistance in concrete form—dollars and cents, not kind words. He cited warning examples of what

PLATE 3

1. Sugar bowl and cover blown from brilliant light golden-amber glass; apparently non-lead glass, though "spot test" shows a slight trace of lead probably due to lead-glass cullet; bowl with spreading sides, angling sharply at shoulder and contracting to galleried rim, a type of rim not found on any covered bowls prior to the nineteenth century; flattened hollow circular foot drawn out of same gather as bowl; double-dome cover with infolded rim and ribbed ball finial from same gather; bowl and cover patterned in a 24-rib mold and expanded in vertical ribbing, slightly swirled on cover. Attributed to the Zanesville Glass Works, sometimes referred to as White Glass Works, Ohio. Circa 1815–30.

Over-all height, $6\frac{1}{4}''$; without cover, $4''$; top diameter, $5\frac{1}{8}''$; diameter of foot, $3\frac{1}{2}''$; diameter of cover at rim, $4\frac{11}{16}''$.

2. Vase blown from clear light green non-lead glass; globular body tapering to wide cylindrical neck with plain flanged rim; applied short-stemmed petaled foot (ten petals or scallops); applied double handle on each side of body and on each handle applied pincered trailing or quilling; body patterned in 24-rib mold and expanded, decoration of swirled ribbing to right. Attributed to Zanesville. Circa 1815–30.

Height, $6\frac{3}{16}''$; top diameter, $2\frac{1}{4}''$; greatest diameter of body, $3\frac{5}{8}''$; diameter of foot, $3\frac{1}{8}''$.

The bowl and cover and vase were patterned in dip or small open-top molds used primarily in making bottles and flasks.

3. Mug of golden-yellow non-lead glass; plain free-blown, barrel shape; applied flat heavy ribbed or corrugated handle with large thumbpiece (four horizontal ribs). Late eighteenth century.

Height, $5\frac{1}{4}''$; top diameter, $3\frac{1}{4}''$; greatest diameter of body, $3\frac{5}{8}''$; diameter of base, $2\frac{7}{8}''$.

4. Salt blown from amethyst lead glass; double-ogee bowl with short knoplike stem drawn from same gather; applied circular foot; patterned by two insertions in a 24-rib mold and expanded in broken-swirl ribbing. Midwestern, Ohio area. Circa 1815–30.

Height, $2\frac{3}{4}''$; top diameter, $2\frac{3}{4}''$; diameter of foot, $2\frac{1}{16}''$.

5. Salt blown from clear light green non-lead glass; double-ogee bowl with short stem drawn from same gather; applied petaled foot (five petals varying in size); patterned in 12-diamond mold and expanded in ogival design. Midwestern. Early nineteenth century.

Height, $2\frac{9}{16}''$; top diameter, $2\frac{1}{8}''$; greatest diameter of body, $2\frac{3}{8}''$; diameter of foot, $1\frac{15}{16}''$.

6. Small compote blown from brilliant golden-amber non-lead glass; shallow circular bowl with flaring outfolded rim, applied double-knop (dumbbell) stem and circular foot; bowl patterned in 32-rib mold and expanded in delicate broken-swirl ribbing, giving a sort of feathery effect. Midwestern, possibly Mantua Glass Works, Portage County, Ohio. Circa 1822–29.

Height, $3''$; top diameter, $4\frac{7}{8}''$; diameter of foot, $3\frac{1}{16}''$.

A "spot test" is a test for lead content by the use of hydrofluoric acid followed by ammonium sulphide. This consists of putting a tiny drop of the acid on the glass, preferably the bottom of the piece, followed by a drop of the sulphide on the same spot. If the glass is lead glass there will be a black or dark yellowish coloration of lead sulphide; if non-lead, a whitish effervescence. Cullet is fragments of broken glass which were cleaned, ground, and added to the batch—the mixture of raw materials for melting in the pot. If cullet containing a considerable percentage of lead glass was used in a batch in a glasshouse which did not customarily make lead glass, then a piece made from that particular batch might on spot test show some degree of lead content.

not to do: France, fallen from prosperity because she persecuted manufacturers instead of following Colbert's policy of unstinted assistance to them; Spain, weak largely because of envy toward them. He held up models of rewarding conduct: the King of Prussia's small state, now formidable and well settled because of the generous reception and liberal assistance to manufacturers; Great Britain, whose tender care of hers was well known. As no manufactory in the world was established without meeting great difficulties, rulers or governments should advance funds, loans without interest. Knowing that posterity would benefit, the Duke of Brunswick had assisted manufacturers even though he was in debt and no immediate returns could be expected. All of which tacitly demonstrated that the United States and its components ought not to wait until their debts were paid before lending a helping sum. Moreover, even though this new republic was "unaccustomed to grant particular privileges to any citizens" she should look into the advisability of doing so for manufacturers—privileges inexpensive to government, such as exemptions from taxes and protection from imports. Russia was a witness for protection. There when the empress decreed an impost of one hundred per cent seven glass manufactories sprang up where before there had been none. In all this Amelung was one of the first witnesses in the interminable case of Industry vs. Agriculture, of Protective Tariff vs. Tariff for Revenue Only. More than one nineteenth-century advocate was to take his place on the stand, using many of the same basic arguments in the cause of manufacturers as Amelung did in 1787.

Some of Amelung's readers must have been sufficiently convinced by his arguments to untie their purse strings: he was able to raise an additional £7000 to £8000 before June 1790,[71] bringing the total investment in New Bremen to about £22,000 or £23,000. Repold and Ghequiere might possibly have come to his rescue; Crockett could not since he and his firm had gone bankrupt in the spring of 1788.[72] Part of the new money may have been the £1000 loan granted him in 1788 by the Maryland legislature. The members perhaps had their minds prepared by his "Remarks" and some of them may have had the eloquence of interested parties.

He did not fare so well with the federal government: the committee, after the fullest inquiry into the large fire loss and other facts set forth in his May 1790 petition, reported in favor of a secured loan not exceeding $8,000, but the House did not concur.[73] Although by then some of the states were acting upon such advice and arguments as Amelung's, the doctrine of financial aid to an individual or any branch of the national economy was no more palatable to some republicans than it is to many Republicans today. Amelung's cause was eloquently pleaded in the House of Representatives by Daniel Carroll from Maryland and Elias Boudinot from New Jersey, representatives from states where glass factories were in operation. Among the points weighing heavily against the loan was the fact that Amelung was a foreigner. The sentiment of Robert Sedgewick from Massachusetts that while he was "in favor of giving all due encouragement to industrious foreigners" he doubted "the propriety of doing this in a partial manner and in preference to the natives of this country" was echoed by other members.[74] However, Amelung was hard to discourage; in December 1791 he again petitioned the House for a loan. It was "Ordered to lie on the table."[75]

In the meantime the new federal government had failed to provide adequate protection for the country's embryonic glass industry through its first tariff acts, 1789 and 1790. Early in the debate on imposts Elias Boudinot called the attention of the House to omission of glass from the proposed list of enumerated articles. A few days later Daniel Carroll moved to insert window and other glass, pointing out that a glass factory had been started in Maryland with considerable success and optimistically added that "if the Legislature were to grant a small encouragement, it would be permanently established." After brief and rambling conversation the committee agreed on a duty on glass, excepting black glass bottles. But 10 per cent ad valorem, even the increase in 1790 to 12½ per cent with an extra duty if foreign ships were the carriers,[76] was as futile as Canute in turning back the oceans of imports. In February 1794 three petitions for additional duty or other encouragement were sent to Congress:[77] Messrs. Walley, Tudor, Payne and M'Lean of Boston, M'Clallen, MacGregor and Company of Albany, and John Frederick Amelung in association with James Labes and Thomas Johnson.[78] Congress had no plum for them in the 1795 tariff pie; all they pulled out was 20 per cent ad valorem on glassware except window glass, which bore 15 per cent ad valorem and 21¾ per cent if not borne in American vessels.[79] As a matter of fact the probability is that, labor, financial, and transportation conditions being what they were, nothing short of a complete ban on imports would have helped Amelung. In addition the unprofitably small patriotic public which, in 1789, he thanked for giving its encouraging preference to American manufactured glass[80] apparently had not grown. In 1795 the property was offered for sale.[81] Before the end of the year Amelung deeded his unmortgaged interest to his son, John Frederick Magnus.[82] On December 24 Amelung and Labes were among the insolvent debtors whose bankruptcy petitions were found reasonable by the Maryland legislature.[83] Just when the last glass was blown under Amelung ownership is not known. Whether or not a less ambitious plant would have had a chance of survival one cannot say, but certainly it would not have drained the resources of the company sooner than need be.

One of the furnaces was operated, it would seem, for some years after part of the property was acquired in 1799 by Adam Kohlenburg and John Christian Gabler.[84] Gabler moved West; at least it is likely that this John C. was the same as the one who eventually joined the New Geneva group. Kohlenburg continued to manufacture window glass and bottles in a small way. In 1810 two furnaces, probably Kohlenburg's, were producing a yearly output of 40,000 square feet of window glass and 7000 bottles.[85]

Twenty-two years ago the name of Amelung, if familiar at all to collectors of American glass, signified for most of them only another futile attempt by another German to make glass in America for Americans. Those who read Rhea Mansfield Knittle's interesting account in her *Early American Glass*[86] realized that his career, like Stiegel's, had many of the elements of a romance. A few may have remembered that, while a John Frederick Amelung and Company had announced the intention to make "all kinds of Glass-Wares, Viz: Window glass, from the finest to the lowest sorts, white and green bottles, Wine and other Drinking-Glasses, as also Optical Glasses and Looking Glasses finished compleat," as yet only two kinds of window glass and white and green bottles had been produced.[87] They may have remembered, too, that four years later Amelung advertised that in addition to "window glass equal to London Crown, inferior to Bristol crown" the public could be supplied with "all kinds of flint glass such as decanters with glasses; tumblers, all sizes; every other sort of table glass" and have its glass adorned by "cut devices, syphers; Coat of Arms or any other Fancy figures." [88] But the name was not one to conjure with since no authenticated specimens had been publicized and illustrated, thereby giving the advertisement reality and impressing the story of the man and his house on the collector's memory. Today because numerous inscribed and dated pieces have been discovered to an appreciative public which would have warmed Amelung's heart his name is synonymous with the highest achievement in eighteenth-century American glass with extrinsic decoration.

While locally some family heirlooms of glass were attributed to Amelung's works probably not a baker's dozen of the collectors before 1928 knew of the pieces, including two or three now well-known case bottles from the set made for Baker Johnson, resident of Frederick-town and brother of Thomas. And some of the few questioned the origin because each of these bottles, fashioned by the German half-post method, bore an engraved design which was quite different in style and execution from any types then thought to be American. The decoration was composed of two small, facing, dovelike birds atop a compact wreath of slender bladelike leaves within which a suspended circle enclosed the inscription "*B. Johnson*" above "*1788*." Not long after 1928 they were taken into the Amelung fold without question; for then the Metropolitan Museum of Art in New York City acquired the now famous Bremen pokal, Plate 64, dated 1788. That was the year the pokal or covered goblet, wearing an engraved coat of arms of the city of Bremen, was sent back to Germany carrying the brave inscription "*New Bremen Glass-manufactory—1788—North America, State of Maryland*" on one side and on the reverse, "*Old Bremen Success and the New Progress*". The pokal which had cost the German stockholders in the neighborhood of £10,000 was probably the only dividend they ever received from their investment.

In the next few years other copper-wheel-engraved presentation pieces came to light, revealing the character of Amelung's finest glassware. One was an impressive, tall, and handsome covered tumbler made as a gift for Charles Ghequiere. This was inscribed "*Floriat Commercium*" above a rather dainty crown and delicate foliated and floral wreath enclosing "*Charles Ghequiere*" on one side and on the reverse at the bottom, "*New Bremen Glassmanufactory the 20th of June 1788*". That hope for a flourishing commerce must have come straight from Amelung's heart. Equally impressive and even more interesting in ornamentation is the 1788 Tobias and the Angel covered flip shown on Plate 76. The following year a tumbler bore witness to Boston of the achievement in New Bremen. It was engraved with the legend "*Our best wishes for every Glassmanufactory in the United States. God Bless the City of Boston.*" on one side and on the other "*Made at the Glassmanufactory of New Bremen in Maryland the 23 Jan. 1789 by John Fr. Amelung & Company.*" The gift may have been inspired by Robert Hewes's premature announcement that the Boston Crown Glass Company would soon be producing glass in its Essex Street House,[89] Boston's first glassworks. On the occasion of Thomas Mifflin's election as Pennsylvania's first governor following his long service as president of the Supreme Executive Council he was given a goblet engraved on one side with the state's coat of arms and the motto "*Virtue, Liberty and Independence,*" and on the other "*New Bremen Glassmanufactory 1791*"— as yet the earliest of the recorded pieces of American-made glass which might be classified as historical. The goblet, Plate 66, obviously a present from Amelung's wife, Carolina, to her friend Metha Repold, bears the date 1792, the latest recorded at the present time. Quite apart from the traditions associated with them, the presentation pieces shown in the frontispiece and the Plates 11, 28, 60, 66, 76, 77, and 104 can be attributed with the utmost confidence to New Bremen by analogy with those inscribed with the name of the glassworks.

Since the Bremen pokal seems to have been the only example sent to Germany it is likely its metal was the first to approach the quality Amelung desired. Therefore it seems probable that the window glass and bottles were the principal output at New Bremen during the first two or three years and that the year 1788 marked the beginning of tableware production on a commercial scale. In March of that year Andrew Keener, son-in-law of Amelung, advertised for sale in his Baltimore shop in the house formerly occupied by Mr. Benedick Stoope, besides six sizes of window glass, "Quart, Pint, Half-Pint, Gill and Half-Gill Tumblers, Wine Glasses; Quart, Pint, Half-Pint Decanters, exact measures; Goblets; Glass Cans with handles of different sizes; Phials assorted and green Bottles, from Pint to Gallons; with sundry other useful glassware, suitable for the Assortment." The most remarkable feature of the advertisement was its ending:

> This glass is all AMERICAN MANUFACTURE, very little inferior in Quality to any imported, and doubt not of its meeting the Approbation of the candid Friends of this Country, who wish to encourage its Artists in such useful Articles.[90]

This advertisement is unique among the literally hundreds we have read in the newspapers of the late eighteenth and early nineteenth centuries: it reveals a conscience which to most manufacturers would have seemed beyond the call of duty. It does not claim equality or superiority to imported glass; it admits inferiority. Therefore since James Labes's shorter advertisement of Amelung's glass, running from March 1789 through July 20, 1790,[91] contained no such comparisons it is likely that Amelung felt that his metal no longer called for apologies.

Amelung had suffered embarrassments other than financial: the available ingredients of glass were so unlike those to which his glassmen were accustomed that experience and experiment were necessary to determine the combinations and melting conditions which would result in the fine colorless metal he sought. The lack of uniform coloring or the presence of color in the identified specimens is physical evidence of the fact that he had not mastered his materials. Not one of the four 1788 pieces is perfectly colorless and each differs from the other in the thick portions—the Bremen pokal has a slight greenish cast; the Johnson bottle, a purplish; the Tobias and the Angel covered flip, deep grayish; and the Ghequiere covered flip, a deep smoky hue. The Schley pokal is the freest from color of all examples known to us and for that reason we believe it to have been made about 1790. As late as June of that year Amelung wrote, "the quality of my glass is coming to perfection from degree to degree, almost every month owing to the experience I have acquired since the 6 years past. . . ."[92] The characteristic greenish, amethystine, gray, or smoky tones, a condition moving Amelung to lamentations, today are not only attractive to the collector's eye but welcomed as Amelung earmarks which in conjunction with other and more vital features of metal, form, and decoration have provided a key to several enigmas of probable glass identity—for instance the goblet, No. 3, Plate 68.

The group of presentation pieces may have been born in America, but they retained the nationality of their ancestors. Quite naturally these pieces, presumably representatives of New Bremen glass at its highest degree of excellence, were German in character. The metal of those which have been tested is non-lead, a type with which the blowers and engravers were familiar and with which they would have attained the highest degree of artistry. Therefore the glass presumably used for the best tablewares was predominantly, if not entirely, the continental type. Lead glass is a possibility which must be considered since flint, which at the time usually meant lead, was advertised. And while the blowers and engravers who accompanied Amelung to Maryland would have been ill at ease with this unfamiliar medium those who had reached New Bremen by way of Manheim and possibly the Philadelphia Glass Works presumably had learned, or had had the opportunity to learn, its peculiarities. Be that as it may, the fine glassware, whatever its composition, was mainly clear, usually with a cast of color as previously mentioned. However, the Geeting amethyst sugar bowl and the creamer, Plate 28, and fragments unearthed on the factory site testify that colored glass was made also, but few colored specimens have been identified beyond doubt.

The forms, in contours and proportions, were likewise Germanic. The goblet or pokal with or without a cover was typical and was fashioned as were similar German stemmed drinking vessels of the late seventeenth and eighteenth centuries. Perhaps some of the common New Bremen goblets and wines were given the folded foot so prevalent in Amelung's day but none of the identified examples of which we know or those attributed by analogy, such as the goblet, No. 3, Plate 68, had this feature. The plain edge of the domed foot is one of those minor details of treatment which frequently differentiate the works of one artisan or his house from another. Also, it appears, the echo of a stem's baluster knop in a cover's finial was characteristic. There were two details in the treatment of covers which were quite different from those in English glass and, we understand, from contemporary German glass as well. The covers of the pokals and flips were the set-in type but instead of the rather wide flange fashioned from the same gather as on the usual eighteenth-century flanged covers the New Bremen covers had an applied band, tooled into a half round, to rest on the rim of the vessel. A more unusual treatment was the applying of a molding on a vessel itself as a support for the cover, which fitted over the rim, as on the Geeting sugar bowl. In their weight of form and metal these pieces are kin to some of the best of the modern glass, or perhaps the proposition should be stated in reverse. In any event there is definitely a sympathetic relationship between the goblets of Amelung and the Steuben Glass red wine, No. 1, Plate 63.

Without doubt, during the decade the New Bremen Glassmanufactory operated, all of the currently popular or familiar methods of ornamentation were practiced at one time or another. But the most favored method was copper-wheel engraving which, since Caspar Lehmann adapted the lapidary's equipment to glass late in the sixteenth century, had been perfected by German artisans and in which they excelled. While it would be folly to suppose that the most skillful designers and engravers consented to leave their security or were allowed to emigrate, those who did join Amelung were more than merely competent. Gustav Pazaurek, an authority on German glass, says of the Bremen pokal: "From the German point of view, it is a commonplace achievement, and with its elements of baroque and rococo, even rather antiquated for the year 1788." Nevertheless the quality of craftsmanship in the decoration of these pieces is of no mean degree. In comparison with the Stiegel type and even most of the early nineteenth-century examples the rendering is expert, mature in technique and design. The clean-lined, precise engraving gives depth and body to the motifs even though the modeling in planes is slight. The shallow silhouettelike engraving on the Stiegel type wares is but a shadow of Amelung's. In most instances the decoration is a medallionlike design, frequently a wreath or slender garland enclosing the name or initials of the person for whom the piece was made. It may be very simple and restrained as on the Stenger flask, Plate 104, or elaborated as on the Schley pokal, the frontispiece. The motifs are mainly a variety of stylized little flowers, some with many petals around a brilliant clear center, sprays of compact slender leaf blades and of flowers with leaves; a variety of scrolls, foliated and shell-like; heraldic renderings of the bearded awns of grain; and tiny dovelike birds. While wreaths and medallions created with these motifs have a somewhat formal air they are saved from prim conventionality, especially by the grace of the many curving lines which harmonize with the contours of the vessels. All have a family resemblance but so far no identical twins have been found. The over-all effect is far less bold than that of the forms themselves. There is a nice and pleasing balance between free metal and decoration, except perhaps for the vignette on the Repold flip, Plate 77, which is in itself an exception. The little primitive picture on glass, showing the tall Maryland farmhouse, its sentinel tree, and the fowl in the yard, has all the charm of genre. The inscriptions and initials, always in script, usually in size, shape, and arrangement of letters, enhance the effectiveness of the whole. The vignette of Tobias and the Angel, Plate 76, with its slightly overpowering and elaborate border, would be less effective without its framing arch formed by the appropriate inscription: *"Happy is he who is blessed with Virtuous Children. Carolina Lucia Amelung. 1788."* Moreover, to perfect his composition the designer took pardonable liberties with the tale, keeping the fish intact and having the little dog going ahead instead of after Tobias and his guardian angel.[93]

Engraving was not, however, the only form of ornamentation on New Bremen glass. The Ghequiere flip or tumbler and the small *"F.C.S.A."* enameled tumbler, Plate 81, offer proof that gilding was used, if only sparingly. Since this method of decoration necessitated a muffle in which to fire the pieces, it is not surprising that enameling, also a popular method at the time, was practiced as well. Maybe some of Stiegel's enamelers had found their way to the glasshouse in Maryland. The finials and ornamentation of the covered bowls on Plates 28 and 29 are evidence that the "forest techniques" of applied and tooled decorations were familiar to some of the workmen. But in the light of the prevailing French and English taste in glassware it is unlikely that they were used to any extent for commercial products destined for the seaboard cities.

It is likely that at first Amelung's commercial wares were as German in character as his presentation pieces. But before long he must have sought to make most of his output as thoroughly British or French as possible; for he faced an unreceding tide of competition for the limited market of which England, while sharing it with France, especially at

Baltimore and Philadelphia, naturally had the lion's share. In addition to the more expensive wares it seems certain that pattern-molded glass, involving so much less costly labor, was blown. Ribbed and diamond patterns probably were used. Perhaps some of the flasks of the Pitkin type were among the "green Bottles"; the half-post method by which Pitkins were fashioned was used for the Baker Johnson case bottles. At the moment the checkered-diamond design, which was used for bottles made in early South German forest glasshouses[94] and once tentatively attributed to Stiegel as the originator, is thought to have been used by Amelung. It occurs, but rarely, on amethyst bottles, like No. 5, Plate 1, of typical eighteenth-century form similar to the Stiegel type on the same plate. It is found also on clear, amethyst-tinted, and light green flattened ovoid flasks like No. 1, Plate 1. The last, similar in color and metal to some of the typical so-called Midwest chestnut flasks, have turned up in Ohio. The design occurs most frequently on the salts, usually clear or sapphire-blue and rarely purple (No. 6, Plate 2), which were patterned in a different mold and have the double-ogee bowl and applied circular foot characteristic of the period. These salts have usually been found in localities nearer to Amelung's New Bremen glasshouse, closer to Frederick, Maryland, than to Stiegel's at Manheim, Pennsylvania—some with a clinging Amelung tradition. A fragment of a darkish clear glass flask in this pattern, unearthed by Martin and Elizabeth Stohlman on the New Bremen site,[95] lends some support to the theory that the design was used by Amelung. Of course if each or one mold was—or were, if you are on the con side of the Stiegel theory—used at Manheim, its presence at New Bremen is easily explained, since some of Stiegel's workmen were employed there. In any event it is a fair assumption that, as some of Amelung's blowers were associated later with Albert Gallatin in founding the New Geneva Glass Works in western Pennsylvania[96] and as Amelung's son supposedly took molds to the Pittsburgh Glass Works,[97] the mold traveled westward too, and eventually was taken to an Ohio glasshouse.

The human-interest elements in the rise and fall of Amelung's American glasshouse arouse the sympathy and hold the interest of most collectors. The exciting fact that the surviving examples of the engraved wares from his glasshouse are without peer in early American glass makes nearly every collector covet at least one. But quite apart from these aspects, and actually more important, are the facts that the inscribed and dated pieces are, as such pieces always are in any era of glassmaking, invaluable as focal points of orientation in period, place, and glass tradition of other glass without such inherent documentation. And more, the glassmen who pioneered with Amelung or who, having already dared to take the precarious step into the New World, joined him here were the leaven of many subsequent enterprises gradually raising the industry to success. When Deming Jarves was writing his newspaper articles on glass manufacture in 1852 he turned to Thomas Bakewell, of Pittsburgh, son of the founder of the first successful flint glasshouse in the States, for data on the Western houses. Thomas Bakewell informed him that when Amelung's workmen dispersed some of them went to Pittsburgh, others to New Geneva, and still others established themselves in Baltimore and in all of those places some of their descendants were continuing the business.[98]

The truth about the building of the first Baltimore glasshouse with which Frederick Magnus Amelung and others from New Bremen were associated lies somewhere behind the mists of tradition and contradictory information. The earliest date has been given as 1790, 1795, and 1799.[99] In the Ihmsen family records Charles Ihmsen,* native of Germany, born at Ihmsen Hof, Westphalia, and one of the practical glassmen prominent in the early Pittsburgh industry, is credited with building Baltimore's first glasshouse in 1795, the year he left Germany. Perhaps this glasshouse was on the acre of land at the foot of Federal Hill and above the northwest branch of the Patapsco River, which Frederick M. Amelung leased from George Presstman in November 1799.[100] There is no doubt that from 1800[101] through 1804[102] Frederick superintended a glasshouse, making window glass and bottles, and that his father-in-law, Alexander Furnival, leading merchant and the postmaster of Baltimore, was associated with him in the glassworks until August 1802.[103] The venture did not prosper. Frederick had not escaped financial troubles: he had merely transferred them from New Bremen to Baltimore and carried his father-in-law with him. Notice of Furnival's bankruptcy was published on May 15, 1803; that of Frederick's on June 7,[104] his second trip to the bankruptcy courts in less than a decade.[105]† However, the blame for these failures probably should not be placed entirely upon glass. The main commercial ties of many Baltimore merchants were with the old Hanseatic port cities and Holland and they were strained to the breaking point during the brief recession while England and France were at peace and Napoleon was starting his European conquests. Furnival and Amelung, both named as merchants in the notices, were only two of sixty-one or more who failed between 1800 and 1805.[106] Among them was Charles Ghequiere, but his commerce ceased to flourish for only a short time. Frederick solved his difficulties temporarily by accepting Colonel O'Hara's invitation to the Pittsburgh Glass Works.[107] In the meantime the glasshouse and property were acquired by another merchant, John F. Friese.[108] Again a merchant's profits and glassmakers' knowledge were to form partnership, for it appears that from the first some of the Repperts, a family of glass blowers from New Bremen, had an interest in the business.[109] The house was to continue under different ownerships down into the twentieth century. The firm of Baker Brothers became proprietors in 1853 and exhibited "Druggist glassware of all descriptions, preserve and pickle jars, flasks, window glass, ink bottles, wine bottles etc" at the New York Crystal Palace, our first World's Fair and a miniature copy of England's.[110]

However, the glassworks' greatest interest to the collector and student of American glass—aside from the historical flasks made there in the nineteenth century—lies in the possibility, even probability, that in those early years some wares similar to those of New Bremen were produced. O'Hara, writing to Frederick M. Amelung on July 30, 1805, told him that he "was right in procuring the molds, I wish you to have them complete." [111] That statement implies not only that pattern-molded wares were made or to be made at O'Hara's Pittsburgh Glass Works but probably that they had been made at the Baltimore Glass Works *and* perhaps from molds used at New Bremen. It also brings to one's attention a circumstance upon which anyone should ponder if he cherishes the belief that a certain number of ribs or diamonds *ipso facto* indicates positive origin in one factory and one factory only. If pattern-molded tablewares were blown at Baltimore, then undoubtedly plain free-blown ones were likewise, and maybe engraving was a method of decoration. Moreover, it is possible that some of Amelung's artisans who engraved such pieces

*Though Ihmsen may have been an employee at the Baltimore Glass Works, no documentary evidence to support the family history or date has been found as yet. On the other hand, such sources as land records and ads indicate the works was started by John Frederick Magnus Amelung and Alexander Furnival, his father-in-law, on land rented by Amelung in 1799 (Baltimore,

"Maryland Products," *Glass*, Part I, February 1948).
†In 1803 was J. F. M. Amelung's first, not second, bankruptcy. Though Mrs. Quynn stated his first was at New Bremen, more recent examination of the evidence indicates the New Bremen bankruptcy was that of his father, John Frederick Amelung, with James Labes in December 1795.

as the Schley pokal and Repold goblet set up shop for themselves, engraving and cutting blanks from the Baltimore Glass Works. Be that as it may, obviously the works did not provide enough or give promise of enough employment for all of the Amelung workmen; before the end of the century some of them turned toward the West, the new land of promise.

From the end of the Revolution into the early 1790s the West's siren call to opportunity and a new start had been drawing the adventurous and the economically discontented—or distressed—among the Easterners. The unsettled conditions at New Bremen, as well as the land companies' fascinating propaganda, may well have decided the more daring of the glassmen to pick up their tools and move into the Western territory. Certainly in a section where all commodities transported over the mountains paid a wagon freight of five to ten dollars a hundred pounds and road conditions confined shipments of fragile wares mainly to the summer months[112] there should be no question as to whether a glasshouse would prosper. In any event some of the New Bremen glassmen, supposedly headed for the infant state of Kentucky, set out from Baltimore early in 1797. According to the oft-told tale, the westward trek of the glass blowers and the eastward journey of Albert Gallatin from his New Geneva to Congress crossed and paused at Tomlinson's Tavern between Uniontown and Cumberland on the Great Western Road, then little more than a rugged trail; the eloquent Mr. Gallatin supposedly diverted the glassmen from their planned course so that the final result of that coincidental need for rest and refreshment was the New Geneva Glass Works.[113] Like so many of our charming and colorful legends, this one, too, seems destined for the American Glass Apochrypha in so far as the inception of the works is concerned. It is possible there may have been a meeting between Gallatin and a second group from New Bremen, that of which John C. Gabler, whose name appears in all traditional accounts, was a member, but the evidence at hand indicates that Gallatin's contact with the original group was after plans for the New Geneva Glass Works were under discussion.[114]

On the tenth of May 1797 John Badollet, a friend whom Gallatin had persuaded to leave Switzerland for America[115] and partner in Albert Gallatin and Company, which owned considerable property and several enterprises in New Geneva and Greensburgh[116] just across the river, wrote a long letter from Greensburgh to Gallatin at Philadelphia, adding the following postscript:

> Since signing my letter we three [Badollet, Bourdillon, and Cazenove] *unanimously* have begun an affair. . . . It is no less than an undertaking of glass works. Six Germans containing all the necessary workmen we are trying to deal with and have a well grounded hope of success. Such an undertaking considered either in a public or private point of view ought to supersede every other and we will attend to it with the utmost of our abilities and by report inform you of the success.[117]

The following fall, September 20 to be exact, and about two months after Gallatin's return to New Geneva after the adjournment of Congress, articles of agreement were signed by a copartnership of Albert Gallatin and Company—Albert Gallatin, James W. Nicholson (Gallatin's brother-in-law), Louis Bourdillon, John Badollet, and Charles A. Cazenove, on the one part, and, on the other part, five glassmakers—George Kramer, Adolphus Eberhart, Ludowitz Reitz, Christian Kramer, and George Reppert—to erect and operate a glasshouse as a copartnership for six years. The Gallatin group put up the capital and land; the Kramer group, their knowledge of glassmaking and skill as blowers. But the blowers were to receive regular pay and from their share of the profits to pay their full share of the invested capital.[118] The sixth German was not, as we had supposed, Baltzer Kramer, who had blown glass for Stiegel and Amelung and wh   was later to become a partner in New Geneva. The first glass was blown in January 1798[119] in the small four-pot furnace[120] on George Creek about a mile from the Monongahela and just outside the village of New Geneva. All did not progress smoothly. Besides troubles with the furnace and materials there were conflicts between the partners which led to a reorganization of the firm and a change in management.[121]

It has been assumed that Albert Gallatin and Company was dissolved in 1803 and that the half interest in the glasshouse offered for sale by Gallatin and Nicholson was sold to the glassmen.[122] Actually that copartnership of Albert Gallatin and Company was dissolved prematurely in 1799 and its affairs dropped in Gallatin's lap, or rather taken on by him to settle. He and Nicholson took over the copartnership's interest in the glassworks, which were placed under the management of Gallatin's friend, Mussard. In 1803, the year the glasshouse agreement expired, it was Nicholson who withdrew from the company operating the glasshouse.[123] Soon after coal was discovered in 1804* in the mountains across the river, a new glasshouse with a coal-burning furnace was erected near Greensburgh,[124] or Greensboro, as it was also called. The group which financed this expansion consisted of Albert Gallatin, Lewis (Ludowitz) Reitz, Adolph Eberhart, Sr., George Reppert, Baltzer Kramer, Christian Kramer, and John C. Gabler. Apparently Baltzer Kramer and John C. Gabler replaced George Kramer and Nicholson of the original firm.† For a few years both houses were in operation with a fair profit and at the new house the glassmen-partners rotated as superintendent.[125] It may be that Nicholson re-entered the firm when Baltzer Kramer died about 1813,[126] as the New Geneva Glass Works was operated about that time by Messrs. Nicholson and Company.[127]‡ In 1816 the seven partners netted a total annual profit of about $8000 on a capital which had reached the sum of $40,000.[128] Ten years later Gallatin was still interested in the works.[129] After 1830 it was operated by B. F. Black and Company and the production of window glass continued until the factory was destroyed by fire in 1847.[130] That it never was rebuilt is explained perhaps by the fact that as numerous other factories had sprung up in its neighborhood the price of its window glass had fallen steadily without an increased demand for it.[131]

As would be expected in an area of a few farms and widely spaced hamlets and towns surrounded by wilderness, the chief demand, which of course determined the principal output of the New Geneva Glass Works, was for window glass and bottles. Its glass was sold mainly in the westward-creeping market, in the towns along the rivers, and it won a reputation for good quality. In 1801 eight hundred 10 by 12 lights were ordered for the Chillicothe Court House because New Geneva glass was considered superior to the Pittsburgh product. The glass was sold both directly to merchants or keepers of the general stores in the various towns or through agents.[132] In February 1806 the proprietor of The Sign of the Negro, a shop in Pittsburgh for china, glass, and Queensware, advised merchants descending the Ohio that he had a large general assort-

*The February 1807 Agreement (photostat of original provided by Cloyde D. Reppert) and Gallatin papers (New-York Historical Society) indicate the glasshouse was built in 1807 and probably in operation by that fall. According to an item in Gallatin records owned by C. L. Horn, coal was not used successfully until 1816.
†1807 Agreement signed "Christian Gabeler." In Gallatin papers (New-York Historical Society) the name appears as "John Gabler" and "J. C. Gabeler."

‡In the light of further study of Gallatin letters and records, it appears that Nicholson continued to look after Gallatin's interest in the works but had no financial interest himself. "Messrs. Nicolson & Co." did maintain a store in Greensburgh.

ment of superior quality New Geneva window and hollow glass for sale at the Pittsburgh prices.[133] The following year another merchant was given the Pittsburgh agency.[134] The hollow glass doubtless included utilitarian articles other than jars and bottles. For the immediate locality, if not for the Pittsburgh and river areas, pitchers of various sizes, large and small bowls, covered bowls for sugar or jam, drinking vessels—especially for beer, ale, spirits, and concoctions thereof—and, of course, decanter bottles were fashioned from non-lead green or bottle glass usually light green in color. It is likely they were blown from clear glass also; for clear half-pint tumblers appear on the account book sheets.[135] While in each house the majority of pieces may have been plain free-blown, a great many were pattern-molded. The glasshouse equipment is known to have included two vertically ribbed, or fluted, dip molds and a part-size, 16-diamond two-piece mold. One of the dip molds had twenty ribs, the other, and smaller, sixteen ribs, and in each the ribs converged at the center bottom. Today the glass is sometimes called Gallatin-Kramer: Gallatin because he was a national figure who in his roll of promoter and financer was instrumental in founding the house; Kramer because members of that family presumably were foremost in the glassmaking.[136] The goblet, Plate 69, so reminiscent of Amelung goblets, is an undoubted example of New Geneva glass. The deep footed bowl patterned in a 20-rib mold, No. 2, Plate 13, is a well-authenticated example.

Through Pittsburgh, the triangular heart of the growing Western body of the young United States of North America, passed much of the emigration from the East and flowed most of the commerce up and down the Alleghany, the Ohio, and the Monongahela rivers, and to the Canadian and Great Lakes regions by way of the Alleghany, Conewango Creek, and overland to Lake Erie.[137] Most of the trade between the seaboard states and the land west of the mountains was either transacted in Pittsburgh or passed through that city on its way east or west. When the "roads" were passable, loads of commodities—spices, teas, and the manufactured necessities and complements of a civilized socity—were dragged laboriously by five- and six-team wagons up the sides of mountain ridges, and, mainly by the strength of desperation of all available hands, kept upright on the sharp descents.[138] The products of the territory—grain, furs, whisky—were drawn as slowly and hazardously back. The more fragile the material, the less space allotted to it. So it was with glassware—if one can judge from the infrequent advertising of small lots in Pittsburgh newspapers at the end of the eighteenth and beginning of the nineteenth centuries.

For the optimistic, expecting continuance of the mushroom growth of population and wealth, every prospect for an increased consumption of glasswares was pleasing. A Pittsburgh glasshouse was an inevitability, especially as bottles were absolute essentials, even more so than in the East. For hard and fermented liquors—whisky, peach and apple brandy, beers and porters—were the red corpuscles without which trade and even living would have been anemic indeed. Moreover, "what a bank bill was at Philadelphia or a shilling piece at Lancaster, that was whiskey in the towns and villages that lay along the banks of the Monongahela river." [139] "It was the circulating medium of the country." [140] This state of affairs persisted long after the Whisky Rebellion, and in the more western sections as well. When John Badollet moved to Vincennes he sold his Greensburgh property for 1600 gallons of whisky to be paid in four installments over a year's time and, as he wrote to Gallatin, his family's support and the building of a new house depended upon their prompt payment.[141] In 1797 James O'Hara was advertising for this currency commodity, offering for a two-month period fifty cents a gallon in cash for barreled approved whisky delivered to his home.[142] After 1800, if not before, he was a steady bottle customer, for he owned the Pittsburgh Point Brewery. There he made strong and table beer and also porter, which would keep in warm climates and was barreled and bottled ready for export.[143]

It was in 1796 that Colonel James O'Hara and Major Isaac Craig, both prominent Pittsburgh businessmen with the vision to see the shadow of future developments, decided to include a glassworks among their many enterprises and schemes of promotion. Since neither of the partners was a practical glassman the staff to man the works had to be lured away from Eastern houses or from abroad. William Peter Eichbaum, superintendent of the Schuylkill Glass Works in Philadelphia, was invited to take charge of the building of the glasshouse and its production. He accepted. Accordingly, in 1797 a site for the house was purchased on the south side of the Monongahela, nearly opposite the tip of triangular Pittsburgh, and also lots on Coal Hill to provide coal for the furnace.[144] Right then the doom of many as yet unplanned Eastern wood-burning glassworks was sealed and the future hub of the American glass industry was determined. Erection of the eight-pot furnace began in June of that year. Frederick Wendt is said to have accompanied Eichbaum to the project[145] and the next year they were joined by Charles Ihmsen from Baltimore.[146] All were to become leading citizens active in the civic affairs of their adopted city as well as in building up its industry.

For the first few years events at the Pittsburgh Glass Works followed the pattern of other early houses—just one difficulty after another. There was trouble with materials; for instance, native clay proved so unadaptable for melting pots that New Jersey clay was imported.[147] Even in 1802 the search for a supply nearer home was still futile; seven months after it was offered, a $100 reward to anyone finding a bed "appearing to contain fifty tons" of suitable pot-clay was unclaimed.[148] Also as elsewhere, the paucity of trained glassmen was well-nigh crippling. It was small wonder that when the first bottle was blown in 1797 James O'Hara estimated its cost at $30,000.[149] The use of coal as the fuel instead of wood may account in part for some of the problems to be solved. Inasmuch as Eichbaum, Wendt, and Ihmsen were continental-trained their knowledge of the construction and operation of a wood-burning furnace would have been practical; that of a coal-burning furnace, presumably theoretical. Perhaps, too, this fuel explains why the glasshouse was in production only about six months after it was leased in December 1798 by Eichbaum and Wendt, who formed a firm of blowers, and when its operation was resumed by the owners in 1800 their superintendent was an English glassman, William Price,* of London.[150] To Price a coal-burning furnace would have been as familiar as it was unfamiliar to the Germans. About the same time an agent, sent to England, had been successful in obtaining workmen from English glasshouses, among them probably Edward Ensell, John Trevor, and others who later built furnaces of their own. However, the hunt for skilled glassmen continued. As we have seen, Frederick Magnus Amelung was hired by O'Hara in some capacity which he seems to have filled inadequately. For several years it was uncertain whether the pendulum of operation

*Price went to Pittsburgh as a result of reading the O'Hara & Craig Pittsburgh Glass Works ad in a Philadelphia newspaper in the spring of 1800 (letter in Craig Papers, Carnegie Library, Pittsburgh, Pa.). Price was not superintendent until after O'Hara bought out Craig in the fall of 1804 (O'Hara's Letter Book, Historical Society of Western Pennsylvania).

would stop at eventual success or complete failure. By 1804 the alarms sounded by his wife and brother-in-law caused Major Craig's faith to waver, so he withdrew from the firm.[151] James O'Hara saw the house through to prosperity, remaining with it until his death in 1819. Then Frederick Lorenz, head of another family to become famous in the glass annals of Pittsburgh, became the proprietor.[152] Much later in the century the works became a unit of one of the emerging early combines.[153]

Newspaper advertisements, letters, almanacs, and histories show that the main commercial products were window glass and hollow ware, principally bottles. William Price's attempts to produce lead glass apparently were abortive. In April 1804 the Pittsburgh Glass Works claimed their pint, quart, gallon, and half-gallon bottles, window glass, porter and claret bottles were superior in quality to any hitherto manufactured in the country and announced their determination to reduce prices.[154] Another advertisement included pocket flasks and pickling jars and stated that the Pittsburgh wares were 25 per cent lower in price than glass of the same quality brought from any seaport in the United States.[155] During the lifetime of James O'Hara tablewares also were produced to some extent, especially before rival houses were established in town. Chief among them were, of course, pitchers, decanters—big-bellied bottles—and drinking vessels. Moreover, not all were the usual light green bottle glass or clear of window glass: some were blue.[156] There is evidence that in 1810 James O'Hara "itemized to Joseph Carson of Philadelphia" gallon and half-gallon pitchers and pint, quart, and gallon jars.[157] Even during those days of curtailed importation it would be amazing if these articles and others actually were sold in *great* quantity in the Eastern markets. Most of the glass sold outside the environs of Pittsburgh would have followed the arteries of trade natural to the region—the rivers west of the Alleghenies. Regarding the glass from the Pittsburgh Glass Works, one circumstance should be remembered always: when Frederick M. Amelung arrived there he undoubtedly brought with him the molds about which he had corresponded with James O'Hara, so pattern-molded wares must have been made. All that's pattern-molded is not Ohio, Kent, Mantua, Zanesville, or New Geneva no matter how many ribs in its body. It is far from impossible that flips and pitchers like No. 1, Plate 79, No. 2, Plate 80, and Nos. 3 and 4, Plate 40, were blown at the Pittsburgh Glass Works.

One more important glasshouse of the eighteenth century remains to be considered. In July 1787, the year Amelung published his "Remarks," the Boston Crown Glass Company was organized by Robert Hewes of the Temple venture, four merchants, and six other Bostonians of speculative spirit fired by capital to invest. The General Court of Massachusetts repealed the 1783 act allowing Hewes to conduct a lottery to raise £3000 for starting a glassworks, which he had failed to do, and gave the new copartnership christening gifts of five years' tax exemption on the capital stock, exemption of the artificers and workmen from military duty so long as they were in the company's employ, and a monopoly on glassmaking for fifteen years upon which any infringement carried a £500 penalty—all provided the company carried out its plans.[158] Their pyramidal glasshouse was built at the foot of Essex Street during 1788[159]* and in December Hewes announced its imminent production of crown glass and bottles.[160]† He was far too optimistic. There were nearly five years of problems, trials, and errors before there was

*Completed in 1789 (Fessenden). Blowing announced (apparently prematurely; possibly a "trial") in August 1789 (*Salem* [Mass.] *Mercury*, August 11, 1789).

†Referred to East Hartford, not Boston—Hewes's connection with "Pitkin" glassworks not proved in 1950. See also 1, p. 29.

regular production of crown glass and some hollow ware. The advertisement of three shares or one seventh of the stock, part of an estate and for that reason only being offered for sale, sheds an interesting light on the situation: "The manufactory so eminently useful as to have obtained from the Legislature, an exclusive patent for fifteen years, is instituted upon a broad and ample basis. The almost impracticability of procuring suitable workmen, which has hitherto impeded the design, is at last happily overcome, by the arrival of European workmen, well acquainted with the business. These remarks are not made to magnify or mislead, as the means of information are in everyone's power." [161]

The first step toward the solution of the technical problem was taken when Frederick E. A. Kupfer was put in charge in 1790; [162] the second when the skilled workmen were obtained from Germany, arriving before October 1792. [163] In November of that year glass was made but, as the workers found the existing furnace unsuited to crown-glass production, operations were "interrupted by the transformation of the building." [164] Not until November 1793 did blowing begin in earnest. [165] In June of that year the company, minus some original members but plus new ones, was granted an exclusive ten-year privilege of manufacturing "window and plate glass" on which, provided it made four thousand 36-inch sheets each year, a premium of sixpence for each sheet equal to British crown and up to ten thousand sheets would be paid for three years. The same ten-year privilege was granted on all sorts of hollow ware if within three years the yearly output of hollow ware including bottles of all sorts amounted to £1000. Land and building were to be tax-exempt and workers exempt from military duty, each for five years. The penalty of £500, applying only to infringement on the window-glass monopoly, would be enforced only if the proprietors spent annually not less than £2000. At the time they had spent £6000, probably the sum to which William Winterbottom, contemporary English observer of the American scene, referred as more than $16,000. [166] In February 1794, as already mentioned, an appeal was made to Congress for increased duty or some form of aid. It was repeated in January 1797. Then the majority opinion of the committee on commerce and manufactures was that the high prices of labor, an evil curable only by time, was a greater obstacle in the path of manufacturers than lack of government protection and assistance. The company's prayers were not granted. [167] Still the works struggled along and, as the manufacturing climate improved, not only prospered but expanded, building their Chelmsford cylinder glasshouse in 1802, and in 1811 another crown glasshouse in South Boston. The company failed and blowing supposedly ceased in June 1827. [168] Long before then the persistence of those who believed in this glassworks had firmly rooted the making of glass in Massachusetts.

Though posthumous fame among twentieth-century glass collectors came to some of the founders of the glasshouses operated, erected, or merely planned in the troublous decades from 1780 to 1800, glassmaking brought fortunes to none. The miscalculations and conditions most detrimental to their enterprises were common to nearly all. As one critic in 1789 stated: "If we built a glasshouse it was at the expense of thousands and calculated to cover all that part of the country with glass, which was not covered by the house." [169] There is no doubt that in most instances the founders overestimated the demand for American-made glass and underestimated the difficulties of transporting and distributing their commodities. There was a scattered and scattering population having its points of concentration in a few urban centers—Boston, New York, Philadelphia, Baltimore, and Charleston. The local market was too small for a production large enough to be profitable, especially as the majority of customers perversely preferred the crown glass and the tablewares imported from England and even from the Continent. The conditions of transportation made expansion of that market practically impossible. There were few avenues of communication with potential outlets inland where inhabitants might not be so choosy. Moreover, on the avenues which did exist, moving wares was not only slow and costly even by water but limited to the months when the few roads and the waterways, in the North at least, were open to travel.

Also as they were pioneers in the industry—even the glassmen's experience was limited mainly to the practice of their art—without guiding precedent and experience, they habitually underestimated the amount of capital necessary to launch and maintain a glass-works. Establishment of a glasshouse could not be accomplished simply by building a pot-house and its oven, a melting furnace and annealing oven, perhaps facilities for making potash, and providing room for all materials and the mixing of batch. Nor could it be put into operation merely by hiring teasers or furnace tenders, clay tramplers and potmakers, batch mixers, master blowers and their assistants, including young apprentices. The operations of all these depended upon and entailed providing for many other activities. Trees, on land owned or leased by the company, had to be felled, hauled, cut into exact lengths and dried for fuel, perhaps for making potash, and frequently processed into lumber for the various buildings of the glasshouse and its community, and for making shipping containers—boxes and barrels. Provision had to be made for making and mending tools and other equipment. All these required men—laborers, woodcutters, wag-oners, carpenters, blacksmiths—and required teams of horses or yokes of oxen, wagons and sleighs to haul wood and supplies to the works and its glass to market or to transport. So, in addition to the glasshouse and its immediate adjuncts, there had to be carpentry and blacksmith shops, barns and stables, a sawmill and often even a gristmill and a general store. The farther the glasshouse was from an established town or city the more self-sufficient its own community had to be, as at Wistarberg and at Albany. The more, too, it needed a fire engine among its essential equipment. Elkanah Watson's estimate of 200 men in the company's employ does not seem an exaggeration when one thinks of all the collateral operations and expenditures involved. While some houses did not have to finance every one of them, none could escape all in the eighteenth and early nineteenth centuries.[170]

Labor, too, presented financial problems as well as those of scarcity and skill. In general, wages were very high, largely because of the small number of trained craftsmen and the lure of vast expanses of unoccupied land.[171] The trained glassmen who were available had been imported usually at great expense, and natives as yet were not per-suaded easily into apprenticeships. Other pastures did prove greener. If the call did not come from the land, then it was likely to come from the sea or an occupation, such as cabinetmaking, in which independence was more easily achieved than in glassmaking. Wages, however, were not the only financial concern in connection with the workers. Reserves were needed to tide the blowers and the whole establishment over the slack

PLATE 4

1. Footed bowl blown from clear light blue non-lead glass, a shade of blue similar to that encountered in flasks marked "Lockport Glass Works"; circular shape with outfolded rim and applied circular foot with seven long crimps. Lockport Glass Works, New York State. Circa 1840–50.

Height, $3\frac{3}{16}''$; top diameter, $8''$; diameter of foot, $3\frac{5}{8}''$.

2. Footed bowl blown from clear amethyst lead glass; circular shape with outfolded rim and applied circular foot; patterned in a 12-rib mold and expanded in wide-spaced vertical ribbing. Attributed to Pittsburgh, quite possibly Bakewell, Page and Bakewell. Circa 1815–35.

Height, $2\frac{1}{2}''$; top diameter, $5\frac{9}{16}''$; diameter of foot, $3\frac{7}{8}''$.

This bowl was patterned in the same or an identical mold as other hollow ware attributed to Pittsburgh such as sugar bowls and covers and pitchers like those illustrated by Nos. 1 and 2, Plate 27.

3. Footed bowl blown from light olive-green lead glass; deep bowl, circular shape, with a narrow band of applied threading at top, plain rim. Probably last quarter of eighteenth century.

Height, $3\frac{1}{4}''$; top diameter, $6\frac{5}{8}''$; diameter of foot, $2\frac{5}{8}''$.

An early technique was employed in forming the foot of this bowl. A small gather of glass was drawn out into a narrow ribbon, attached to the bottom of the bowl, and formed into a small straight-sided circular foot or table ring about a half inch in height. A similar technique was employed on the Amelung bowl, Plate 11.

periods, for furnaces were not in continuous blast. Sometimes they operated only six months out of the year. Also merchants laid in their stocks in the spring and fall so that sales were largely concentrated into two brief periods. These conditions prevailed in general well into the nineteenth century.[172]

In the 1790s conditions were to improve slightly for manufacturers. A turning point in our national economy had been made when the Constitution went into effect. The government's prompt adoption and implementing of stabilizing measures were a sedative to jittery business nerves and at the same time a stimulant to a confidence in the nation's ability to cope with its problems. The good business blown our way by Europe's ill winds of war created an unprecedented reservoir of capital, enough to satisfy many an American's keen appetite for speculation. As a result a small beginning was made in internal improvements. The public, clamoring to invest its dollars, built some needed bridges and inched along some turnpikes so desperately needed to bind the parts of the country together. While each new bridge and mile of turnpike might eventually be of importance to our glasshouses a few of them benefited immediately and more directly from the current prosperity. As we have seen, in the 1790s, the works at Glassboro, Albany, Hartford, and Boston got their second financial wind to carry them along into the nineteenth century and *its* problems. And glassmaking put down its Western roots in New Geneva and Pittsburgh, Pennsylvania, where, while facing obstacles similar to those confronting Eastern houses, it was spared having to meet the same vigorous and overpowering competition from imported glasswares. The federal government had taken its first, though feeble, step toward protective tariffs. Some states had granted loans and further assistance in the form of exemptions from taxation and of employees from militia duty for a limited term, and in some instances from jury duty also. By 1827 New York State included persons employed by the year, month, or season at glasshouses among those exempt from militia duty except, of course, in the event of an invasion or insurrection.[173] At the end of the eighteenth century the signs pointed to the survival of the manufacture of window glass and bottles.

GLASSMAKING IN THE CRITICAL PERIOD FROM 1800 TO 1830

IT IS inconvenient that, unlike its finite components, a growing industry does not pause or remain static long enough for one to say, "Here ends a phase in development with no overlappings." Instead, wherever one decides to put a period he will find it should have been a chronological comma. There will always be a good reason to select a date before or after the one chosen. There will be a fact to upset a neat generalization. With all this in mind we set apart the first thirty years of the nineteenth century as constituting perhaps the most critical period in the development of the United States' glassmaking, one falling roughly into two fifteen-year phases. Also, because with the spread and diversification of the industry the canvas needed to portray it becomes so large, the country has been divided into three sections: New England, with glasshouses mainly in Massachusetts, New Hampshire, Vermont, and Connecticut; the Middle States, with houses in New York, New Jersey, the Philadelphia area of eastern Pennsylvania, Maryland, and the District of Columbia; the Midwest, with works in western Pennsylvania or the Pittsburgh-Monongahela area, (West) Virginia, Ohio, and Kentucky.

In 1800, as an industry, glassmaking was close to non-existence. Its few scattered houses, subject to all the industrial ills epidemic at the time, gripped life more by their owners' stubborn belief in a future and hopes of salvaging investments than by any inherent strength of their own. During the next thirty years the nine or more houses which had survived the 1790s or had been revived around 1800 were multiplied more than tenfold.[1] Most of them were started during the hectic years before 1815, or in the 1820s after the postwar depression. Their mortality was high. Whereas before 1815 three or four were planned for the production of flint or lead glasswares, several of those established in the 1820s specialized in them. The majority, however, made chiefly window glass, bottles, or both. Scarcely more than half of the glasshouses in which a tumbler, bottle, or windowpane had been blown in the entire period from 1800 operated at all after 1829, and some of those only a year or two. However, cold statistics of the glasshouses—planned, built, sold, or leased—reveal but a fragment of the broken hopes and the pertinacity of purpose behind them. Quite apart from the seeming logic of investing in this branch of manufacture, the art of glassmaking must have fascinated men of the nineteenth century as hypnotically as it did Stiegel in the eighteenth, or it could not have lured so much good capital after bad to start and restart so many glass furnaces. The ninety-odd glasshouses of this thirty-year period were operated by three times as many firms formed by an even larger number of glassmen, merchants, and other businessmen.[2] In fact the genealogy of most houses is as intricate as that of a tenth-generation American.

Like any infant industry, glassmaking was very sensitive to all sorts of outside forces impinging on it and quite uncontrollable by any manufacturer. Its responses of course varied in individual cases and in different localities. In general the mushroom growth of glasshouses during the first fifteen years of the 1800s was germinated in the events leading up to the War of 1812 and in war-bred conditions. At last interference with our commerce by decrees and physical violence accomplished what memorials to Congress from hundreds of artisans and manufacturers could not. Repeatedly they had pointed out that because of government failure to foster manufactures the nation's wealth, instead of circulating at home, passed to foreign powers, giving "them the sinews of war, only to menace our peace and disturb our tranquility." [3] The Barbary pirates, France, and England were doing both. Tariffs were raised for building up our own resources for war, first against the pirates and later, as Congress was egged on by Henry Clay and other fledgling War Hawks ogling Canada with an imperialistic gleam in their eyes, against England. The makers of glass and other commodities did not object to their added protection being incidental to the revenues for war. In 1812 the permanent duties were doubled, with careful provisions for revoking the increases a year after peace, provisions never completely carried into effect. [4]

Imposts were welcome, but the embargoes of 1806 and 1807, the later Non-Intercourse Acts, even the war itself, were manna to manufacturers. Though as a defense against violations of our "Free Trade and Sailor's Rights" they were ineffectual, domestic industry profited by a larger market—especially as citizens' indignation led to the formation of local societies for the promotion of manufactures, and history repeated itself in pledges to wear and buy only American-made goods and wares—and also by the ephemeral quality of those resolutions. The volume of imports of glass shrank immediately. While glasswares—bottles, window glass, tablewares, the last still mainly decanters and drinking vessels—had been supplied principally by France and, in even larger quantities, by England, they had been imported also from Scotland, Ireland, the Netherlands, and other North European states. [5] In fact, during discussions of the 1806 resolution to stop importing any articles grown or manufactured in Ireland, Great Britain, or any of her colonies or dependencies, it was pointed out that increased importations from the Continent could make up any shortage of window or all other sorts of glass. [6] But it did not. For one thing, Napoleon soon took the old Hanseatic cities of Bremen and Hamburg, cutting off our trade with them.

Of course the measures against British wares and England's against our trade were not one hundred per cent effective; neutral channels and such devices as smuggling prevented that. Sometimes a privateer, especially during the war, would find in the cargo of a captured ship a few casks and cases of glassware which would be sold at public auction. [7] In the six years following the first embargo, 1809 was the only year in which New York City did not secure a few drinking vessels from Ireland; in the others it received a total of 321,090, a quantity far below our normal consumption. [8] Foreign glasswares became increasingly scarce. The supply of quart black bottles and window glass also fell off to a degree encouraging to glassmakers and stimulating to new ventures. In fact the market dreamed of hopelessly by all manufacturers had become a reality at a time when the country's manufacturing capacity was unequal to the task of supply. It could not produce essential commodities in quantities sufficient to make us independent of European manufactures—to say nothing of the luxuries. So while the near stoppage of

[55]

most imports resulted in crippling hardships for importers and merchants, it diverted a large portion of accumulated capital to manufacturing. Many a merchant invested in a factory, doubtless with hopes of filling his empty shelves as well as cutting out a middleman and sharing in both production and retail profits. Glassworks seem to have been especially attractive to merchants who specialized in porcelain, glass, and earthenware. Benjamin Bakewell was one.

A growing number of anti-industrialists were perceiving that, as advocates of domestic manufactures stated, "so long as we remain a nation of Farmers and Merchants merely, we shall be tributary to the Europeans." [9] Even Thomas Jefferson's ingrained antipathy to manufactures was wearing a little thin.[10] States were granting relief from taxes and exemption of workmen, including superintendents, from militia and jury duty more frequently. In 1809 the general concern had resulted in Congress' request to Albert Gallatin, Secretary of the Treasury, to conduct a survey of manufactures and submit recommendations for their promotion. As Congress was impatient, his report was submitted early in 1810. Based on "partial and defective" information, it drew an unfinished picture of the general situation.[11] By the time all replies were in and Tench Coxe's digest was ready in January 1813 the information was out of date. In 1810 the data secured regarding glasshouses indicated progress, and the more complete returns at Coxe's disposal showed the progress to have been slow but considerable.[12] But apparently there was no new information to change Gallatin's statement that the greatest advance had been in window glass, of which half the country's need was produced, and that expansion of glassmaking was prevented by the lack of glassmen.[13]

How very small the number of skilled glassmen in the country was and how tremendously production could have been increased by very, very few additions to their ranks is apparent from the fact that ten glasshouses averaging fourteen glass blowers each could produce 2,700,000 square feet of window glass a year.[14] It is easy to understand why labor —quality, quantity, and price—was considered almost the paramount factor in determining the life or death of a project. Moreover, not until some time after the end of the Napoleonic Wars of which our War of 1812 was an offshoot would there be anything like free emigration for skilled men in this field; all countries were still jealous of their glassmen, particularly England.[15] The scarcity of well-qualified men was only one facet of the labor problem. Another, highlighted in Thomas Bakewell's account of his father's handicaps in establishing the Pittsburgh Flint Glass Works, started in 1808, was the attitude of the skilled toward apprentices and employers, one cutting wider and deeper throughout the century. Even today Jarves' remarks on Bakewell's problem have a familiar ring, one of sympathy from experience:

> . . . to that [lack of skilled workmen] was added the great evil (which has too usually prevailed among the imported workmen) of a determination to prevent the instruction of apprentices by the most arbitrary and unjust means; and, so far as it was in their power, endeavoring to prevent competition, by not only controlling the hours of work, but the quantity of manufacture. In fact doing the least amount of work possible, for the largest amount of pay that could be coerced from the proprietors . . .[16]

All this long before the days of the glass blowers' union. There was no one to present their side of the issue in the early nineteenth century.

Even if manufacturers had had the personnel and equipment to produce all the glass, cloth, shoes, and other commodities the country required, transportation and distribution facilities were such that full advantage could not be taken of the suddenly expanded market. General stores in nearly every hamlet wanted merchandise; the problem was to get it to them at a profit. Too few and too poor roads, plus continued high freightage, limited the inland markets, geographically and numerically, and hindered deliveries to the most accessible. The privately owned turnpikes, the best roads in the country, not only required payment of tolls (bridges and ferries did too) but were not numerous enough to take care of all the transport forced off the sea. New companies for turnpikes, bridges, and canals were formed. In 1808 New York State alone incorporated twenty-two new turnpike and six toll-bridge companies.[17] Construction, however, takes time, so benefits were not immediate. State and national governments responded affirmatively to the vehement demands that they assume some responsibility for improving the conditions of inland roads and waterways and, above all, extend them. States accomplished more than the national government. It did facilitate correspondence; letters ordering wares could be sent at least once a week from an increasing number of villages even if delivery of the wares took weeks or months, for the miles of post roads were more than doubled between 1800 and 1815.[18] Otherwise federal plans and promises exceeded performance though a few projects were started. One of the most ambitious was the National Road from Washington through Cumberland to Wheeling—and, eventually, to St. Louis—which, being public, would be toll-free. Loud protests issued from Pittsburgh when this highway was authorized and started: the cities' butchers, bakers, and glassmakers, everyone in business, feared that the hub of the Western universe would be transferred to Wheeling, a would-be rival for its position and trade. This road, which did not reach Wheeling until 1819,[19] was only one of many projects contributing to the growing sectional solidarities with counterprojects aimed at the diversion or rediversion of commerce. Many canals were planned or started as part of the rivalry, especially when federal aid seemed imminent; scarcely any were completed until after 1825.[20] However, the very talk of them seemingly encouraged manufacturers to pick factory sites on or near the proposed routes. The plan for the Erie Canal, consummated in 1825, and other mid-New York State canals doubtless influenced the choice of location for several glasshouses built during this period. Proximity to navigable water lanes was to be an essential ingredient of success for glassworks for many decades to come.

In 1807 a revolutionary means of communication, suddenly drawing the country closer together, proved practicable; the *Clermont* steamed up the Hudson, as breath-taking and wonderful an achievement as Lindbergh's transatlantic flight one hundred and twenty years later. For all commerce, this new method of propulsion was to mean greater speed of transporting its commodities at lowered costs. Important as it was to the commercial development of the East, it was perhaps even more vital to the West. Pittsburgh, already a shipbuilding city and port with ships sailing some if not all of the seven seas,[21] launched its first steamboat in 1811.[22] Still, if President Jefferson, against his constitutional judgment but in accordance with his nationalistic common sense, had not purchased the Louisiana Territory this commerce might not have developed. After that deal was consummated in 1803 the port of New Orleans could never again be closed to Western

[57]

commerce as it had been by Spain. And if any country had illusions on that point Andrew Jackson's victory at New Orleans in 1815 dispelled them. The indispensable, if undependable, Mississippi was ours, and beyond its western banks would grow a market of a size outstripping even Lewis' and Clark's and Zebulon Pike's imaginations. The Far West and the steamboat were an important element in determining the prosperity of Midwestern glass manufacturing, of which Pittsburgh was the heart. The steamboat was also to be the means of bringing greater competition from, and to, the Eastern houses.

These bright prospects were but prophecies in 1814 when the Treaty of Ghent was signed the day before Christmas, and when peace came to Europe the following summer. Rather, by the fall of 1815, the future looked unpleasant. Many Americans became uncomfortably aware that "since an eternal war in Europe was not to be expected" the extension of our commerce and demands for our agricultural products had indeed been unnatural.[23] Other countries began to plow their own fields and sow their own seeds, and to step up all processes of production. Ruthless Europe, by retaking her former trade status, forced the United States to resume hers, a painful contraction for her. To attain her ends, Europe, England first of all, reset her trade barriers, barring our way to the markets within her control, and reinforced them. Our lighthearted and swollen prosperity was checked abruptly and the reins were being pulled tight by deflation at a time when credits and business of all kinds were running wild and the country's banking and currencies were almost out of control. By the end of 1817 what had started as a recession became a depression. Commerce was prostrated.

However, without foreign imports the situation might not have become so desperate. In effect the treaty was escorted home by a British armada loaded with the ammunition of merchandise to wage battle for markets. To England's delight the dammed-up wares—textiles, glass, china, earthenware—bursting out of British warehouses into the American stream of trade were caught up avidly by business-hungry merchants. And an equally eager public rushed to pay thousands and thousands of dollars for them. Thus American buyers and sellers cheerfully contributed not only to the failure of compatriots' manufactures but also to the problems of paper currency and specie scarcity. Before long American merchants and importers were being shelved along with American goods in favor of England's own agents here and of our auctioneers who had risen to the merchants' level during the war. England, doggedly and pitilessly determined that our infant industries should not mature to become competitors, resorted to all the tricks of trade to circumvent duties and taxes or any law detrimental to *her* interests.[24] One of her expedients was a bounty to her manufacturers, on glass among other articles, enabling them to sell below cost in the American market. Merciless competition pushed many already weakened firms into abysmal failure. Over half of the United States companies operating glasshouses failed between 1815 and 1820.[25]

The postwar difficulties turned affected groups, as always when hard times strike, to Congress to *do* something to save the situation. Naturally the first line of defense against foreign competition was a protective tariff; so another round in the fight for high duties began late in 1815. Now Jefferson was definitely aligned with protectionists, in so far as necessities were concerned, for experience had convinced him that manufactures were as vital to our independence as to our comfort, since it had been demonstrated that we could be excluded from commerce with other nations.[26] Textiles and clothing may have been uppermost in his mind, but for Thomas Jefferson to concede so much to any one branch of industry was to help all. Moreover, he consented to the publication of his new views because he felt "there was perhaps a degree of duty to avow a change of opinion called for by a change of circumstance." His letter must have produced higher-powered ammunition for Henry Clay and Henry Baldwin in their protective tariff fight than an avalanche of artisans' and manufacturers' memorials. The ceaseless activities of Henry Baldwin, citizen of Pittsburgh and representative from western Pennsylvania, with, therefore, a special interest in iron and glass, must have been heartening to the anxious owners of Eastern glassworks, especially of those in Boston, Keene, Vernon, and perhaps some in the Philadelphia area then making flint glassware. For the first time considerable consideration was given to specific imposts on this category of glassware; previously, window glass and bottles received greater attention.[27] However, the tariff act, finally passed in April 1816, while protective in intent was not so in result, since the imposts on most imported goods were practically nullified by England's tactics and our own love of her wares. Actually the supposedly protective duties on glass were a little lower than they had been under the war measure the bill replaced.[28]

Consequently, within a year Congress was again under pressure to raise duties on glass and most manufactured wares. Imports continued to soar. Treasury reports before 1821 do not give figures for glasswares paying ad valorem duty but do give them for quart black bottles on which a specific duty was paid. They probably indicate the trend for all types, perhaps in understatement. From Great Britain and her dependencies alone imports of these bottles leaped from 11,529 gross in 1815 to 28,269 gross in 1816.[29] Needless to say, manufacturers of glass joined gladly in a new campaign of memorials and also of citizens' meetings to inquire into the state of industry and ways to assist it—as a matter of form, one assumes, for its condition was well known to be one of financial and sales malnutrition. In the East, where glasshouses were scattered and manufacturing still secondary to shipping and merchandising, the voices of their owners were heard only in the chorus; in the Pittsburgh area, where the manufacture of glass was one of the principal mainstays of the community, its owners frequently had solo parts. A December 1817 report revealed that Pittsburgh houses were producing less than a quarter of their normal flint-glass output alone.[30] And, if business was bad there where foreign competition was not so major a factor as in the East, it was worse elsewhere. In October 1818, largely due to the persistent Baldwin, cut glass, an important Pittsburgh product, was treated individually and a thirty per cent ad valorem duty placed upon it.[31] This increase cheered only the few glass manufacturers who made their own cut glass and the independent firms of glass cutters who bought domestic and imported blanks. Their elation was a mere puff, for English wares still slipped by the guards. The ball of protection had been carried a few yards nearer the goal but there were more downs to go.

In 1819 the depression plumbed the depths; its survivors were none too fit. Memorials to curb and tax auctioneers, not to curb and tax auctioneers, to raise tariffs, not to raise tariffs, all bombarded Congress and made the news columns. One from Pittsburgh, among many, stated that where 169 hands had been employed in manufacturing and

PLATE 5

1. Large pitcher blown from a very heavy gather of clear, fairly deep blue non-lead glass; globular body with long narrow cylindrical neck flaring slightly to tooled rim with pinched lip, applied circular sloping foot; applied heavy ribbed (three ribs) strap handle; body decorated with lily-pad decoration Type II, and neck with wide-spaced spiral threading. New York State. Circa 1831–50. *Height, 8¾″; top diameter, 4¹¹⁄₁₆″; greatest diameter of body, 5¾″; diameter of foot, 3¾″.*

2. Small pitcher blown from aquamarine non-lead glass with loopings of mulberry; globular body, wide cylindrical neck with flaring plain rim with down-turned pinched lip; applied circular crimped foot and solid semi-ear-shaped handle. South Jersey. First half of nineteenth century.

Height, 3⅝″; top diameter, 2³⁄₁₆″; greatest diameter of body, 2⅞″; diameter of foot, 2¹⁄₁₆″.

3. Miniature pitcher blown from aquamarine non-lead glass; globular body with superimposed gather tooled into lily-pad Type I; wide cylindrical neck flaring slightly to plain rim with wide pinched lip; applied semi-ear-shaped handle and circular crimped foot. South Jersey. Probably first half of nineteenth century.

Height, 2¼″; top diameter, 1⁵⁄₁₆″; diameter of foot, 1⅜″.

Miniature pitchers with superimposed lily-pad decoration are very rare, as are pieces in blue with such decoration.

cutting glass worth $235,000 a year in 1815, there were only 40 hands producing $35,000 worth in 1819.[32] Everywhere glassmaking was sinking or in the doldrums, as were other industries.[33] Although the agriculturists were now allied with the manufacturers a new bill was defeated in 1820. By the time Congress was actually argued into constructive action on protective duties in the 1824 tariff, other forces in the business cycle had turned the wheel of fortune toward good times. Yet that tariff act was momentous: Congress at last chose the course of adequate protection of domestic industry.[34] In 1828, in so far as glass was concerned, Congress, without urging, took another step along the path. Although the volume and dollar value of imports continued to mount, consumption did also. As the Harrisburg Convention Committee, considering the expediency of increased protection for glass, found in 1827, both volume and dollars were moderate in proportion to the country's consumption.[35] As the ratio of foreign to domestic glass changed, it was to be mainly in favor of our own manufacturers. Since 1824, though units of the industry may have wished for higher duties on their particular products, the industry as a whole has had no well-founded complaints.

In 1820, almost in spite of itself, the national economy began to climb out of the depression to rise to greater heights than those from which it had fallen. During the next few years there were accelerated developments in all its components, especially the vital one of inland transportation. Many projects started before or during the war were extended or completed, improving the routes over which products of farm and factory had to pass. Among them were many miles of the Cumberland or National Road over which glass from Wheeling and western Pennsylvania could travel east to Baltimore and Washington at lower cost than hitherto. The Erie Canal, an even more vital artery of east-west trade, near which several New York State glasshouses were to flourish for years, was completed. More canals to join waterways and more turnpikes to fan out from urban centers were started, many of them with the hope and intention of diverting trade from rival centers. With the completion of the Ohio Canal in 1832 merchandise could travel from New York City and Montreal or Quebec to New Orleans without encountering ocean dangers.[36] Among carriers, the steamboat more than lived up to expectations, plying the oceans along the coasts as well as the lakes and rivers of the continent. By barge or sailboat the trip from New Orleans to Louisville took three months; by 1817 Captain Shreve had cut that time by Mississippi steamboat to twenty-five days. Such improvements were made in boats that ten years later the trip could be made in a little over eight days.[37] In 1822 it was of interest to Nantucketers and inevitably to those on the "continent," engaged in overland shipment of goods, that a Louisville merchant saved about $1200 in transportation charges by sending his New York and Philadelphia purchases via New Orleans (instead of over the mountains), receiving them on an average of six weeks after shipping.[38] That was a saving in time as awesome as nine hours and forty-one minutes from Idlewild to London by air is today. It may have been that in the 1820s Western window glass going to Boston was traveling the watercourse and the wares of the New England Glass Company of Cambridge to New Orleans and Louisville were going by steamboat.[39] The railroad, later to prove the best solution of the problem of inland communication, made its debut with horse-drawn carts, and a steam locomotive was tried out in 1828.[40] By all these means more markets became accessible and costs of distribution were reduced by greater speed in reaching them. Thus some of the handicaps under which many glasshouses operated were reduced, though at the same time that of domestic competition was increased.

Competition between American glasshouses was intensified and the demand for their glass stimulated by three instruments of promotion and advertising, namely, agents, newspapers, and organizations for promoting manufactures, which broadened and extended their activities after the depression. While each glasshouse always had its agent who had charge of the sales and of the business and one or more connections in the nearest market, it now secured as many agents in as many markets as possible. Boston and Cambridge glasshouses had agents in Philadelphia, Baltimore, New York, Troy, and Hartford, and doubtless elsewhere, as well as at home, and the agents advertised in the local papers. In a country where even in the 1790s the degree of literacy and widespread newspaper habit surprised foreign observers,[41] the value of advertising seems to have been appreciated. Also, shortly before the 1820s, companies and their agents began exhibiting their wares at nearly every opportunity, including those afforded by agricultural fairs. There, after all, the swarming visitors might be even more impressed by domestic achievements in glass tablewares than by a neighbor's prize pumpkin or friendship quilt. Many a farmer's wife might leave with a determination to own a glass sugar bowl and creamer set or other vessels of glass. Among the limited exhibits of manufactured articles at the Brighton Cattle Fair in the fall of 1819 was a New England Glass Company urn, not quite complete, cut by John Fisher and John Gilliland, both men destined to become proprietors of prosperous glasshouses of their own in the near future. The urn was intended for President Monroe, perhaps as proof that the cut-glass table set from Bakewell's in Pittsburgh could be equaled in New England. Before it was sent to Washington it was again on view, this time at Messrs. Nightingale and Neff's in Boston, as the "celebrated" cut-glass urn, and in company of a pair of cut-glass decanters marked with an "A" for John Adams, Secretary of State.[42]

About 1824 fairs for exhibiting manufactured articles, at first ending with an auction of the exhibits, became an annual event as societies, institutes, and associations for the promotion of "Agriculture, Commerce, Manufactures, and the Arts" (or similar phrase calculated to lull the suspicions of anti-industrialists) were firmly established. Nearly every important Northern community had one of these aids to the American System, the most prominent of which were in Baltimore, Philadelphia, New York, and Boston. One of the first fairs, however, was held in Washington by the "Artisans and Manufacturers of the United States" in the spring of 1825. Colonel Amos Binney, one of the committee members staging the exhibition, had not neglected the interests of his own firm, the New England Glass Company: among the exhibits listed was "a superb Glass Vase, diamond cut on diamond, from the Boston Glass Manufactory—produced by Col. Binney."[43] Glass manufacturers and glass cutters were quick to take advantage of this avenue of parade for their wares. The publicity value cannot be measured accurately today, although anyone who has attended a Grand Central Palace Exposition in New York City, a fair in Schaghticoke, or even watched a gadget demonstration in a department store, cannot doubt that it led to gratifying results in dollars and cents. Attendance ran into the thousands of the curious and the interested, quite undeterred by the cold water thrown by opponents of such institutions and exhibitions, "enemies among our own citizens," we are told, who uttered the fiercest imprecations upon internal improvements and the wildest denunciations of American manufactures. In 1828 the first fair of the American Institute of the City of New York, a spur-of-the-moment affair, was gratifyingly well received by the public in spite of the "ridicule of the presses in [allegedly] foreign pay." [44]

While some newspapers were indeed unfriendly to the American System of which domestic manufactures were an inevitable corollary, as many or more were partisans of the system or becoming converts to it. With increasing frequency these gave flattering publicity in editorial and news columns. They stimulated, then reflected the public interest in American-made glass as well as other articles. Often they took up the cudgel of the equality and superiority of American glass to any imports, a cudgel so long wielded by the manufacturers themselves with less effect. Some news items about glass were of sufficient importance to be reprinted by other papers, or the editors sufficiently interested in furthering the cause to republish them, so that they reached many localities, large and small. A typical item appeared in the Boston *Columbian Centinel,* June 27, 1821:

> American Glass. The beautiful bowl, which adorned the table of the Ancient and Honorable Artillery Company, on their late anniversary, is now placed in the store of Messrs. Wing & Summer, No. 3 South-row, for the inspection of the friends of American Manufactures. It was made at the South Boston Glass Works and is supposed to be the largest article of glass ever manufactured in the United States—its height being 26 inches and its diameter 24 inches. The body is cut in beautiful strawberry diamonds, and the color and brilliancy of the glass are equal to any ever imported. At the same place may be seen other samples of flint glass from this manufactory, which furnish full evidence that we can rival the proudest production of Europe.
>
> The Boston Crown Glass is celebrated everywhere for its strength, color, and brilliance—The Hail storms to which we are subject, while they shatter every other kind of glass, make no impression on the firm fabrick of the Boston Crown Glass as tests at Salem, in the Capitol at Washington, and numerous other places amply verify.

Niles' Baltimore *Weekly Register,* a Providence, Rhode Island, paper, perhaps others, carried versions of this notice. About two weeks after John L. Gilliland's Brooklyn Flint Glass Works opened in 1823 the Troy *Sentinel* reported that event.[45] When Bakewell's made the glass for President Jackson in 1829 papers in many places reprinted the Pittsburgh *Mercury*'s account or extracts from it or other newspapers. Many more instances could be cited. By 1830 if Americans were not proud of their glass it was not the fault of their newspapers.

One of the 1820s' most exciting developments was in foreign trade. Whereas our merchant shippers always had *re*exported manufactured articles of nearly every variety including glass, mainly to the West Indies and the South American colonies, their exports of native products were limited largely to those of the soil and the sea, furs and lumber, and a few by-products such as spirits and fermented liquors. Of manufactured articles there were few, among them furniture in steadily augmented quantities.[46] On the other hand if American-made glass went to market outside this country it was not in quantity worthy of the government's remark or individual record. Now this began to change as the demand for many American wares gradually increased and commercial treaties were signed, particularly with European countries and states. Our largest markets were the Indies (mainly the colonies *not* British), countries along the Caribbean, and the South American states as they achieved their independence. Packages of glassware were prepared for exporters to these markets by some of our glass manufacturers. The New England Glass Company, for one, advertised packages suitable for the African, West Indian, and South American markets as early as 1823.[47] The first Treasury report including figures on our glass exports was for the year 1825–26. Then American glass worth $44,557 went to twenty-four countries and their dependencies in amounts varying from a shipment or shipments valued at $32 to the South Seas to $15,000 to Cuba.[48] In 1828 the enterprising Jarves was proposing that the Cambridge and Sandwich houses send an agent to survey the possibilities of the South American market.[49] Fairly sizable sales already were being made there. Henceforth European factories encountered our competition in glass, especially in cheap wares after pressed glass became popular.

Still a foreign market, while gratifying, was not a fundamental factor in the success or failure of our glasshouses; the home market was, and it had been, growing steadily, almost abnormally. The number of people living and working in the United States nearly doubled between 1800 and the taking of the 1820 census. Almost a quarter of the population now lived west of the Appalachian range, fringing out beyond the Mississippi and along the Great Lakes. The postwar depression, this time as deep a chasm in European economy as our own, had again stimulated a westward movement of peoples. Many Americans moved out of the Eastern states; many Europeans moved in. Settlers wrested more of the West from the wilderness and the Indians for "civilization." The natural increase of the nation was augmented by a stream of immigration, chiefly from the British Isles, an immigration reaching flood proportions in spite of attempts to dam it at home. Fortunately for the United States, also entering its machine age, there were some men of capital and a goodly proportion of skilled mechanics and craftsmen, not a few of them glassmakers, blowers, and cutters. Several of the glasshouses established in the 1820–30 decade were started by British glassmen who had emigrated during or soon after the War of 1812 as well as later.

Quite as important to the glassmakers as the infusion of skilled craftsmen was the fact that continually a larger number of potential customers were becoming actual buyers. For at last a state was developing in which the majority of the people would constitute a market not only for window glass and bottles but for tableware likewise. The standard of living was rising again in the 1820s so that a greater number of housewives, hundreds quite unawed by or indifferent to the label "imported," were able to acquire more of the niceties of living. Moreover, Buying American was one manifestation of the lusty national consciousness arising from the stronger union into which war and hard times had helped cement the states, at least in so far as their stand against the world was concerned. In general, society, the wealthy ladder climbers, and the well-to-do would continue to patronize the importer for their fine tablewares, but more Americans of all classes were satisfied with the domestic brands. And for those unable to afford the fine cut and engraved glasswares there was a plenty of cheaper wares including substitutes simulating cut glass.

THE MAKING OF TABLE AND OTHER FINE WARES IN THE CRITICAL PERIOD

FRUIT to please all tastes was borne by the various branches of the glass industry before the end of the critical thirty-year period, from 1800 through 1829. The arrival at this state was achieved through developments in glassmaking itself, which nourished the very roots of the industry and, when the protective tariff was added, caused them to spread more rapidly. Moreover, they were to have far-reaching effects upon the entire industry for decades to come. Two of the developments were in methods of production; one was the successful production of a kind of metal. The methods were in molding; the extension of the use of the full-size piece mold from shaping to include lettering and decoration of the objects blown in them, which we shall discuss in detail later, followed in a few years by mechanical pressing. The metal was lead glass, the quality metal of fine glassware. The molded wares were to widen and hold the market for the cheaper wares; the fine flint- or lead-glass tablewares were to gain a foothold for American manufacturers in the competition for the carriage trade.

As we have seen, several attempts, short in duration or unsuccessful, had been made to manufacture lead or flint glass. The first in the nineteenth century was about 1800 under the supervision of William Price at the Pittsburgh Glass Works,* built by O'Hara and Craig in 1797. At least five of the fourteen or so glasshouses started in the Midwest during the following fifteen years were planned for the production of flint glasswares; one in Charleston, later Wellsburg, (West) Virginia; four in Pittsburgh.[1] Anticipation of success was reasonable: difficulties and costs of transporting fragile merchandise from the East over the mountain barriers limited supply and the demand was growing as the Midwest blossomed under the sun of prosperity. From about 2400 inhabitants in 1800 Pittsburgh nearly doubled itself by 1810, and again within five years.[2] By 1815 Ohio's 41,000 of 1803 had multiplied six times over.[3] Towns along the rivers were attaining a commercial importance as the hustling citizens fabricated their cities and society out of the raw materials of civilization. Even though the guilding motto, "every man to his business," left little time for entertainment and "the cultivation of refined social pleasure"[4] those who could afford to surround themselves with the fashionable and fine appurtenances of comfortable or, better still, luxurious living sought such earmarks of success. One was fine flint glassware. And it was in Pittsburgh that the manufacture of flint or lead glass was finally established in the United States, and in the Midwestern glassworks most famous with collectors today and most written about in book and magazine: Bakewell's, which operated from 1808 until nearly 1882. Although officially

*O'Hara's and Craig's letters (ms., Carnegie Library and Historical Society of Western Pennsylvania) contain the term "white glass" in connection with Price, not, so far as we have found, "lead" or "flint," though possibly by "white" they meant "flint." O'Hara's letters show also that little "white glass" was made until after 1806, and its production ceased in 1816 by agreement with Benjamin Page of Bakewell, Page and Bakewell (Daniels, "The First Glass House West of the Alleghenies," *The Western Pennsylvania Historical Magazine,* September–December 1949, p. 112).

the glasshouse was the Pittsburgh Flint Glass Works and, over the years the inevitable changes in the firm and its name occurred, the informal "Bakewell's" always sufficed to identify it. The business was a family affair and, according to all present accounts and available evidence, Benjamin Bakewell was the heart and head of the concern until shortly before his death in 1844.[5]

Born in Derby, England, in 1767, he was forty-one when he settled in Pittsburgh, where he was to become one of the leading citizens in the highest sense of that phrase—not neglecting his own material interests but furthering those of his community and contributing to its cultural improvement. From report and record he emerges as a man of unflagging energy and perseverance in his own and his city's affairs, of highest integrity and rectitude, and endowed with good taste empirically educated by contact with French and English arts and crafts. Benjamin Bakewell was not a practical glassman when he went to Pittsburgh. In England he had been an importer of French wares until 1794, when his supply line was severed by the French War. Then, like many others, he turned to the United States, setting up shop in New York City in 1795,[6] only to flounder again in the net of war as French and English interference with our commerce increased. Jefferson's embargoes did nothing to relieve the financial embarrassment of the importers. Bakewell was among those who failed. In September 1808 Bakewell, his friend Benjamin Page, and Thomas Kinder, one of his assignees, set out in search of business opportunities west of the Allegheny—employment for Bakewell and, for the others, investments for idle capital.

In Pittsburgh they were persuaded that the road to future prosperity lay through the manufacture of glass in the works built in the summer of 1807[7] by George Robinson and Edward Ensell, the latter, and probably Robinson, too, seceding from James O'Hara's Pittsburgh Glass Works.[8] Handicapped by lack of capital (a common condition of glassmen), proper raw materials, and, it would appear, a well-rounded experience in all processes necessary to glassmaking,[9] and probably a lack of practice in management, Robinson and Ensell dissolved their partnership on the twenty-fourth of August. The investment of the newcomers—Thomas Kinder representing his firm, Robert Kinder and Company—extricated them from a tight financial spot. The new glasshouse company, called Bakewell and Ensell, as Bakewell was to be the managing partner and Ensell the technical, lost no time in getting into production. On the nineteenth of October quart and pint decanters and tumblers of quart, pint, half-pint, and gill sizes, cream jugs and sugar basins, pocket flasks and salts were advertised.[10]

Bakewell was well equipped by nature and experience for administration, management, and selling; Ensell, a glass blower,[11] thought himself equally capable of superintending the glassmaking. However, he overestimated and hence overstated his ability to fill all the capacities requisite to that many-sided process.[12] As a result, Bakewell almost immediately discovered he had to master the manufacturing also, if only to salvage the capital invested.[13] Performing herculean labors of perfecting a poorly constructed furnace, locating and obtaining the best raw materials, and above all securing a staff of competent workers from mixers of batch, furnace men, and potmakers to skilled blowers and apprentices, he still was able to advertise in the spring of 1809 that the Pittsburgh Flint Glass Manufactory had recently enlarged its assortment of glass-

[66]

ware, advertised not only in Pittsburgh newspapers[14] but in a St. Louis paper also,[15] and if there, surely in local papers of other river towns. Under his guidance Bakewell's was to become a house without rival for years and reputedly never excelled in fine wares, a show place for all the curious travelers who visited Pittsburgh during the first third of the century. Starting from utter ignorance of the technology of glass and its manufacture, he later demonstrated a knowledge of his field so impressive that Deming Jarves conferred upon him an A.M. in glassmaking, summa cum laude.

Success, however, was not assured in the spring of 1809; it was possible. On February 1 the partnership of Bakewell and Ensell was dissolved; Ensell "withdrew." [16] It was the firm of Benjamin Bakewell and Company, called also B. Bakewell and Company by the three remaining partners, which announced the expanded output in April.[17] In March 1811 Robert Kinder and Company abandoned the project, leaving Bakewell and Page the sole owners. Two years later Thomas Bakewell, the son who from the first had been an invaluable assistant and to whom Benjamin finally handed over the reins of management, entered the firm.[18] Except for about a year ending in December 1815, when Henry Bostwick, a blower in the glasshouse,[19] was a partner,[20] the firm was Bakewell, Page and Bakewell until July 31, 1827. The next day John Palmer Bakewell, a second son, was taken into the firm and an s added to the second Bakewell in the firm name. From then on, barring the brief period from the summer of 1832 to that of 1836, during which Alexander M. Anderson was associated with them, the business was in the family. There were changes in firm personnel as Benjamin Bakewell's son, grandsons, and nephews retired or entered the business. From 1844 until 1880 the title was Bakewell, Pears and Company.

Although the background of Bakewell's glass is being filled in gradually by newly found historical data, the central subject remains in outline. Of the glass made during the first twenty-five years of operation few pieces are known which can be indisputably identified as Bakewell's. Yet there are many of which it can be said "attributed to Bakewell's because . . . " or "probably Bakewell's." As always, advertisements and various contemporary accounts are informative and, though not definitive, furnish clues to the character of the wares. Among the 1809 items[21] revealing not only an extensive output but also the public demand in glasswares, decanters and drinking vessels predominated, as would be expected then. The tablewares included:

Decanters of quart and pint size, of common or best double flint glass, either plain or ringed
   (collared) of half-pint and gill sizes, of common glass, plain or ringed
Wineglasses, common and best
Wine coolers
Water decanters
Goblets of pint, half-pint, and gill sizes, of common and best double flint glass
Tumblers of quart, pint, half-pint, and gill sizes, of common and best double flint glass
Jelly and syllabub glasses
Cups of quart, pint, half-pint, and gill sizes
Egg cups
Butter and sugar basins with covers, and cream jugs, assorted colors
Cruets and mustard pots
Finger cups

PLATE 6

1. Vase blown from non-lead glass, clear light amber with olive tone; globular body, wide cylindrical neck flaring to plain rim; applied plain circular foot; small applied solid semi-ear-shaped handle on each side; body with superimposed lily-pad decoration Type II; neck with applied threading extending to rim. New York State. First half of nineteenth century.

Height, 6¼"; top diameter, 3¾"; greatest diameter of body, 4 1/16"; diameter of foot, 3⅛".

2. Miniature goblet blown from pale aquamarine non-lead glass; ogee bowl and double-knop stem from one gather; applied circular foot. South Jersey. Circa 1825–50.

Height, 2"; top diameter, ⅞"; diameter of foot, 1⅜".

3. Tall wine blown from olive-amber non-lead bottle glass; conical bowl, graduated triple-knop stem; applied heavy circular foot with heavy folded rim. Circa 1816–25.

Height, 7 5/16"; top diameter, 3 1/16"; diameter of foot, 4⅜".

An unusual feature of this wine is the large upper knop formed from the same gather as the bowl, with the two lower knops attached to it. It is an example of exceptionally skillful free-blowing, which, although without a definite history, is believed to have been made at the Keene-Marlboro-Street Glass Works, Keene, New Hampshire.

4. Sugar bowl and cover blown from brilliant light olive-amber non-lead glass; globular body contracted below galleried rim and resting on applied pedestal foot with heavy folded rim; plain domed cover with stemmed button finial; body with superimposed gather tooled into lily-pad decoration Type II. New York State. First half of nineteenth century.

Over-all height, 7"; top diameter, 4 1/16"; greatest diameter of body, 3 15/16"; diameter of foot, 3⅛"; diameter of cover, 3⅜".

5. Pitcher blown from brilliant light olive-amber non-lead glass, slightly deeper in tone than sugar bowl, No. 4; pear-shaped body, wide cylindrical neck, flaring rim with wide pinched lip; applied solid semi-ear-shaped handle; body with superimposed lily-pad decoration Type II; neck with applied threading extending to rim. New York State. First half of nineteenth century.

Height, 5¾"; top diameter, 4"; greatest diameter of body, 4 3/16"; diameter of base, 2⅞".

Pieces in this light olive-amber glass with superimposed lily-pad decoration are extremely rare. We think the covered sugar bowl, No. 4, and pitcher, No. 5, are New York State glass but we have no definite history as a basis for this attribution. However, these bottle-glass pieces were found in New York State, and this lily-pad is a style and form which in our experience is characteristic of western and northern New York glasshouses of the 1831–70 period. Also the color is similar to the wineglass, No. 1, Plate 59, which was acquired about twenty years ago from a Buffalo collector and, according to its history, was made at the Lancaster Glass Works, Lancaster, New York, by a blower named John Lambrix. Historical flasks, including "Success to the Railroad" with locomotive, "Cornucopia and Urn," and "Scroll" flasks, were made in a wide range of colors at this glasshouse. Pitchers in aquamarine and cornflower-blue with quite similar lily-pad decoration were among the individual pieces known to have been made there. For these reasons we think it quite possible the sugar bowl and pitcher were made at the Lancaster Glass Works. We know of one other covered sugar bowl similar in lily-pad decoration and color.

We believe it possible that the vase, No. 1, also may have been made at Lancaster.

Among the miscellaneous articles were jars and beakers for chimney ornaments; inkstands; smelling bottles; globe and street, table and vase lamps, the last with shades;
and corals (teething rings) for children. There were also utilitarian jars from half pint
to half gallon in size, and a variety of apothecaries' furniture. Certainly only the best
table and ornamental wares were actually blown from flint or lead glass; the tinctures,
confectionary jars, and similar utility articles were blown from non-lead metal, that
referred to as "common." From the many advertisements for pot and pearl ashes[22] one
infers that potash was used for the common glass as well as the "flint," even though it
resulted in less brilliant glass than that in which soda was used.[23]

As others before and after Bakewell were to learn, American-made flint glasswares
were not yet in sufficient demand to carry a works, or rather, perhaps not within the
means of enough of the people willing to buy domestic glass. In June 1811, after building
a second glasshouse, the company informed their friends and the public that besides
the usual flint glasswares "articles of GREEN GLASS" could now be offered at the
usual prices.[24] Even after their tablewares had attained fame, green-glass wares were
produced for many years. A complete supply of bottles, flasks, and vials was mentioned
in an 1837 advertisement.[25] The articles listed in 1811 were bottles and jars of gallon,
half-gallon, quart, and pint sizes; pint and half-pint flasks, patent-medicine bottles; half-
gallon and quart square liquor bottles *and* half-gallon, quart, and pint pitchers. Were
the bottles and flasks similar to those shown on Plates 105, 106, and 107? Possibly. Were
some flasks blown in full-sized piece molds, as the patent-medicine bottles surely were?
Possibly. At least one of the American System flasks similar to that shown on Plate 111
was made by Bakewell's early in the 1820s. Were the green-glass pitchers similar to the
typically Midwestern shaped and proportioned pattern-molded pitchers, Nos. 3 and 4,
Plate 40, which *could* have been blown in almost any one of the houses of the area or
nearby Ohio in the early nineteenth century? Very possibly.

In general students are agreed that in the natural course of early nineteenth-century
glassmaking pattern-molded wares would have been produced at Bakewell's as they
were elsewhere. In fact, notwithstanding the lack of proof, amethyst, blue, and clear
glass sugar bowls and pitchers like Nos. 1 and 2, Plate 27, the fine amethyst bowl,
Plate 4, and other articles of tableware are believed to be probable Bakewell products.
Each of the pieces illustrated was patterned in a 12-rib mold and expanded with fascinating results in vertical shading of clear pure-toned color in brilliant lead metal. The
sugar bowl is of a distinctive shape and proportion quite different from Eastern sugar
bowls, for instance, Nos. 4 and 5, Plate 34, and even from the typical Pittsburgh-area
examples Nos. 1 and 3, on the same plate, also from the Ohio type shown on Plate 3.
In addition the geographical distribution of those known today points to Pittsburgh as
the most likely source. It is not impossible that the first of such bowls and pitchers were
among the covered sugar basins and pitchers of assorted colors advertised in 1809, but
perhaps it is more likely that they made their appearance after the war. Another type
which may represent a Bakewell product is illustrated by the typical "Pittsburgh"
cruet, No. 1, Plate 46, dark purplish amethyst in color and patterned in expanded vertical ribbing. The same is true of the later light blue pitcher, No. 3, Plate 45, and
the opaque white glass vase, No. 1, Plate 51, with eight wide-spaced vertical ribs

produced by the method of so-called pillar molding. This type of ribbing, which became popular about 1830, found favor throughout the century, and inevitably was used in many glasshouses producing tablewares.[26] The opaque white metal of the vase probably was similar to that from which the New England Glass Company made their enameled glass resembling "the finest Porcelain and Pearl and, surpassing what has been done in Europe." The New England Glass Company's ware, introduced in 1829, was a type which likewise became very popular in the next decade. Judging from continental and British pieces classified as enameled glass, we conclude that the term covered opaque white, with and without decoration by gilding, enameling, and painting, and colored and clear transparent glass with such decoration.[27]

The glass for which Bakewell's was most famous, especially in this 1815–30 period, was its cut and engraved wares, a branch supposedly added in 1810.[28] In that year William Eichbaum is said to have cut the chandelier for which Bakewell's received $300[29] and which has been mentioned by all who have had occasion to write of the glassworks. It has been supposed that Eichbaum, glass cutter to the King of France before the Revolution, worked for Bakewell's, executing some of their most important orders. Unquestionably he did cut glass for them, but seemingly in his own shop rather than in a department of the glassworks. Following his abortive attempt to operate the O'Hara glass furnace with Frederick Wendt and "company," Eichbaum established a tavern, The Sign of the Indian Queen.[30] A few years later,[31] after he had the financial security of his tavern behind him, he opened a cutting shop and retail store[32] in which he could supplement his own stock with imported articles. There was sufficient demand for his wares, or enough work for Bakewell's, to necessitate his employing more hands than his own, for by 1810 his son Arnold was a partner and they were advertising for apprentices, preferably thirteen- to sixteen-year-old boys from the country.[33] It is not impossible that the inexpertly cut compote, No. 1, Plate 18, so eighteenth-century in style and cut design—except for the nineteenth-century "strawberry diamonds"[34]— was cut by one of them. So far as we know at present no specimen of his cut tableware has been identified. Perhaps during his contact with French styles his skillful fingers and appreciative eye caught some of the French delicacy of line to lighten the stolidity of his native Germanic design, which, it may be hoped, he passed on to Arnold and the apprentices.

Newspaper advertisements and directory listings indicate that as William expanded his interests, including ownership of a wire manufactory, he was less active in his glass-cutting business. Even before 1815 that venture appears to have been conducted by Arnold alone.[35] Also he devoted increasingly more of his time to civic affairs and offices. Sometime between 1815 and 1826 Arnold, too, abandoned glass cutting and concentrated on the wire factory.[36] Perhaps his change was coincident with Bakewell's establishment of their own glass-cutting department on their own premises. That event we suspect took place about 1815 and doubtless was marked by the arrival of English and French decorators.[37] Perhaps Alexis Jardel, or Jardelle, who engraved the United States coat of arms on the glass for President Monroe[38] was one of them. In 1815 Thomas Bakewell went to England in search of skilled workmen. In 1820 glass cutters arrived from Belgium, then still part of the Netherlands.[39]

The year 1817 marked the beginning of a national as well as a local reputation for superlative glasswares. Bakewell's, it appears, had the distinction of being the first manufacturer of glass in the United States to provide the White House with glassware. When President Monroe visited the city and the glassworks in 1817 he was presented with a set of decanters and he ordered a complete set of tumblers, wineglasses, and decanters for the White House, occurrences not reported so extensively as were subsequent recognitions of the merit of Bakewell's glass. In 1824 the firm, taking advantage of the Franklin Institute's first Philadelphia exhibition to bring American manufactures to the public's visual attention, exhibited specimens of its cut glassware and received honorable mention. For years thereafter Bakewell's glass was shown at this annual event.[40] Bakewell, Page and Bakewell had a red-letter year in 1825. In March at the Washington Fair of "Artisans and Manufacturers of the United States" they exhibited decanters which afterward were presented to Henry Clay.[41] While not so highly honored at Washington as Colonel Binney with his vase, in October at the Franklin Institute they received an award for the best cut-glass decanters. In the same year, when Lafayette visited the glasshouse, he was presented with commemorative vases cut and engraved by Jardel.[42] All these pieces were executed without the benefit of steam power, as was all glass cut before the fall of 1827, when a 10-horsepower engine was installed, which, it was reported, facilitated the work and materially lessened its expense.[43]

Two years later Bakewell's made an entire table service for President Jackson. On August 1, 1829, the Nantucket *Inquirer* carried the following account from the Pittsburgh *Mercury*:

> *Elegant Specimens of American Manufactures*—President Jackson has ordered from Messrs. Bakewell, Page & Bakewell, of the city of Pittsburgh, a set of Glass for his own use. That order is nearly completed. We had last week an opportunity of witnessing this very splendid exhibition of American skill and ingenuity. It consists of large and splendid bowls with and without stands—celery glasses, pitchers, quart and pint decanters, tumblers, wine and champaign glasses, salts, etc., etc., the whole tastefully executed in the very best style of workmanship. The glass is as pellucid as crystal; and the beautiful cuttings give a brilliancy of effect not easily described. We think this specimen of American workmanship will vie with the best production of the French and English artists. It is very gratifying to witness the great perfection to which our artists have arrived in the various objects to which their skill and enterprise have been directed. We understand that the order is valued at about $1500.—Pittsburgh Mercury.

In July the New York *Commercial Advertiser* and Niles' Baltimore *Weekly Register* had reprinted the piece; other papers probably did also. On August 11 the Troy *Northern Budget* published an item from the Baltimore *American*: "Present— . . . a box containing a complete set of CUT GLASS, manufactured in Pittsburgh, Pennsylvania, was taken on board the steamer Colombia, Capt. Mitchell, on Saturday for Washington, as a present for President Jackson." The date usually accepted for this order has been 1832, the year given in several histories of the city including the *Standard History of Pittsburg*, which cites the "*Mercury* 1832" as its source. Its quotation is shorter but verbatim as far as it goes. As yet we have been unable to examine either 1829 or 1832 files of the *Mercury,* so we have not determined whether the "32" is a perpetuated error of an early historian or the original account was repeated in part for some reason. The latter seems a likely explanation. Perhaps the breakage during Jackson's first term was so great that a complete new set was needed for his second.

Although Bakewell's glass graced the White House board, Easterners did not demand it in quantity. Benjamin Bakewell, testifying before the congressional committee considering the 1828 tariff bill, stated that the output went principally to the Southwest and West and some to northeast Ohio.[44] And in 1832 it still was sold principally in the Western states.[45] However, as early as 1826 it was said that "the glass of Pittsburgh and the parts adjacent" was "known and sold from Maine to New Orleans" and that "Even in Mexico they quaff their beverage from the beautiful white flint of Messrs. Bakewell, Page & Bakewell. . . ." It was Samuel Jones who first wrote those words in 1826, not Anne Royall writing in 1828.[46] Perhaps because she considered his little work "the most accurate," to use her words, she quoted liberally without quotes when she gave statistics on the glasshouses in Pittsburgh, their histories and reports on their state and achievements.[47] Such flattering plagiarism was a rather common practice in her day, but one distorting and dislocating facts for us in the twentieth century. Mrs. Royall did give a glowing account of her visit to the Bakewell glassworks and an accurate graphic description of the fabrication of tumblers. The blower who was making them assured her that he made 600 a day and that his brother made 240 decanters in the same time. Fifty dozen tumblers . . . twenty dozen decanters . . . two blowers . . . one day . . . one glasshouse. Still, if reports of the times are true, the satisfaction and results of American drinking habits—and on that point Mrs. Royall's own acid tongue gave caustic utterance —would have kept many a blower producing at that rate.

The three rare tumblers on Plate 82, each with a sulphide portrait bust in the base, are among the few pieces which we feel confident are of Bakewell origin. Unquestionably the Lafayette tumbler was made in 1824, when so many commemorative objects were manufactured from every available fabric, in anticipation of Lafayette's grand tour of the country which adopted him. It is probable that the Jackson and the Washington tumblers were made at the same time. For the majority in the democratic West, Jackson was then the man of the hour. And Washington, first in the hearts of his countrymen, was a natural companion to Lafayette, or to Jackson, for that matter, since politicians were already using him as a mirror reflecting the qualities of each political favorite. Tumblers cut like these were made also with a portrait bust of Benjamin Franklin.

The New York Historical Society has two similar tumblers with a portrait bust of De Witt Clinton, which, according to their family history, were in a set presented to Clinton when he was governor. They differ from our three in that the cut decoration above the band of splits at the bottom consists of alternate fine vertical ribs, narrow rectangles of fine cut diamonds, and plain square panels. On one of the panels the monogram "D W C" is engraved in a style similar to that on the Washington tumbler. These, we believe, were likewise a Bakewell product. In 1825 Clinton as well as Lafayette was the central figure of many Pennsylvania and Ohio celebrations. In the West he was as exciting and important a guest as Lafayette; Henry Clay too. Henry Clay might be the father of the Internal Improvement policy, but De Witt Clinton was the "Father of the Most Distinguished Internal Improvement." In fact, after the two exponents of that policy met in Ohio and each had attended a public dinner in honor of the other, it was said that "Clinton seemed to wear the longest plume." From Ohio, where he had been invited to assist at the start of her Grand Canal, Clinton went to Pittsburgh. There he was greeted by a 24-gun salute, given a public dinner, and in the evening a Masonic supper. The following day a ship named for him was launched. Surely Pittsburgh placed Clinton high enough among America's benefactors for such glasses to be made in his honor and for him.[48]

The Bakewell attribution for all these tumblers is supported, we believe, by an advertisement which was given to the Pittsburgh *Gazette* on March 11, 1825, and appeared occasionally until January 13, 1827, if not later. In it Bakewell, Page and Bakewell of the Pittsburgh Flint Glass Works announced that, in addition to their very complete assortment of plain, molded, and cut glass, they had for sale at reduced prices "LAFAYETTE & MEDALLION tumblers, ornaments, etc." The phrase "at reduced prices" would seem to indicate that their reception by the buying public had been less eager than anticipated.

Another field in which apparently Bakewell's had the distinction of being the first to attain success was that of pressing glass mechanically. Small hand-operated tools and molds for pressing stoppers and parts such as feet for salts and bowls had long been glasshouse equipment. Apparently, starting from there, John Palmer Bakewell had been experimenting with mechanizing the process, for in 1825 he took out the first patent ever granted in connection with this revolutionizing process of fabricating glass objects: one for pressing knobs.[49] As within a year the Eastern houses followed suit, it is probable that experiments were paralleling each other in several houses and the process was speedily extended to other articles. Mrs. Royall commented on the difference between the Bakewell glass, made by the new method, which she saw in 1828 and that of Boston which she had seen earlier.[50]

In the four years after Benjamin Bakewell staked his all on glassmaking, three more houses for the production of flint or lead glass were built in the Pittsburgh district. In 1809, the year after Ensell and Robinson sold their works to Bakewell, the undaunted George Robinson erected another for himself. While it is said Bakewell acquired this house also, Robinson apparently was able to operate with moderate success until about the end of the war.[51] The following year (1810), Edward Ensell joined with Frederick Wendt, Charles Ihmsen, and others from the Pittsburgh Glass Works to establish a factory in the new settlement of Birmingham on the south side of the Monongahela a little above Pittsburgh near Kizer's ferry.[52] (No wonder James O'Hara was writing to Eastern correspondents for assistance in securing competent glassmen.) The new enterprise's prompt and urgent need for capital was met early in 1812 by some local businessmen. Henceforth there were several changes in corporate title and personnel. Around 1850 the ownership of the glasshouse, known first as the Birmingham Glass Works and later as the Pennsylvania Flint Glass Works, was merged with that of other houses in which the Ihmsen family had a substantial interest, forming a business which continued in operation until about 1900.[53] The only piece of glass attributed to its early years, that is, piece of which we now know, is the extremely rare decanter, Plate 83, depicting the engagement between the *Hornet* and the *Peacock*, one of our famous naval victories of the War of 1812. It may have been blown and engraved, rather crudely, not long after that engagement in February 1813 or as late as 1815. That great victory of the *Hornet*, a matter of intense national pride, was an ingredient of a soothing balm for that pride so badly burned at Washington. Perhaps the model for the decanter's scene was an engraving of one of the paintings made from Captain James Lawrence's sketches, or even a painting itself if, for example, Michael Corney's *Naval Panorama* of celebrated victories was exhibited in Pittsburgh.[54]

The flint-glass manufactory erected by John B. Trevor and John Encell, the third on the south side of the Monongahela, was in operation before Christmas 1812.[55] One of their first moves to insure success attracts attention to them even though as far as their plain and cut flint glass is concerned one can conlude only that it was similar to that of their competitors. That move was to obtain a Philadelphia outlet through the firm of Dorsey and Peterson[56] at a time when little glass was transported over the poor roads but a good Eastern market existed since imports were few and far between. Perhaps theirs was the Pittsburgh manufactory sending to Philadelphia the seven boxes of pint and seven of half-pint tumblers which were sold at auction in May 1815.[57] After Trevor sold his interest to a commission merchant by the name of Bolton, in May 1816, the firm rounded out its line of glasswares by arranging for a regular supply of window glass and green bottles.[58] Apparently they were unable to survive the depression; in 1819 blowing ceased.[59]

In 1813 at Charleston, later Wellsburg, (West) Virginia, Isaac Duval in partnership with Nathaniel and John Carr built the first flint-glass furnace in that area. Duval is said to have been another of the émigrés from the New Bremen Glassmanufactory and an ex-superintendent of that ill-fated house. Until his death in 1828 the company produced some excellent cut wares reputedly of exceptional metal, but, apparently like other glass manufacturers, found it expedient to add green glass to the output.[60] The rare little bowl, No. 3, Plate 24, was attributed by family tradition to Duval and Company. In fact it was said to have been fashioned by Mr. Duval himself. It was not, however, blown from lead but from bottle glass of pure light green color and metallic brilliance characteristic of early nineteenth-century Midwest bottle or green glass. Its pattern-molded diamond-above-flute or ogival design was impressed in a part-size piece mold like the one believed to have been used at Zanesville for bottles and other hollow ware. The same mold could have been used at each furnace, carried from one house to the other by a migrant glass blower. On the other hand it is barely possible that there were identical molds or perhaps the attribution was legendary, though the circumstances of the story make this seem unlikely. Whatever the explanation, the bowl is a choice and distinctively American example of early glass.

For a few years war's rank aftermath of economic ills discouraged attempts to start new flint glasshouses in the Midwest. In 1820 the small, short-lived, and mysterious Zanesville White Flint Glass Manufactory was started by Edmond, Bingham and Company in Zanesville, Ohio. Nothing as yet is known about it beyond that fact and one advertisement, though it undoubtedly was the Muskingum County flint glasshouse which in 1820 was "declining for lack of funds and legislative aid." [61]

In 1823, when John Robinson erected his Stourbridge Glass Works, or Flint Glass Works, for the production of white or flint glass only, not a real competitor to Bakewell's was left in the city of Pittsburgh. At the end of 1825 the year's production of engraved and fancy cut glass in the new works was valued at $22,000, slightly under half that of Bakewell's output for the same period.[62] By then glassmaking was a firmly rooted industry of the United States. Pioneering in the future was to be mainly in the technology of glass and its production and, following closely upon the heels of John P. Bakewell, Henry Whitney and Enoch Robinson of the New England Glass Company, and Phineas C. Dummer of the Jersey Glass Company, John Robinson pioneered in pressing glass. In 1827 he obtained a patent for pressing knobs, the third granted in connection with those articles.[63] While fine lead metal was used even for some of Robinson's beautifully colored and clear glass historical flasks, like No. 1, Plate 112, apparently Robinson or his sons Thomas and John, Jr., found it expedient to add common metal, at least for their cheaper line of glassware. (The well-known pressed plate marked "T. & J. Robinson" is non-lead glass.) However, in general, the works continued to maintain a high standard during its comparatively brief existence. It was operated only ten years after John Robinson's death in 1835.[64] When Alexander M. Anderson withdrew from Bakewell's in 1836 after an association of four years, he joined the Robinsons.[65]

Of the three other Midwestern flint glasshouses in this period, two were started in 1829 and one in 1827. The Fort Pitt Glass Works, which was to have a long and successful career, operating rather steadily from 1827 until almost 1900, was established by Robert B. Curling, his two sons, Alfred B. and William, and William Price, men with practical experience in the manufacture of glass. William Price, it will be remembered, was brought from England by O'Hara and Craig in 1800* to superintend the Pittsburgh Glass Works. He was also the first glassman in the United States to take out a patent on a composition of glass, in 1815.[66] Robert Curling had begun his Pittsburgh career as a potmaker at Bakewell's and progressed to the position of clerk.[67] The name Curling was associated with the Fort Pitt Glass Works until 1863. In 1828 large quantities of plain and cut flint wares were being made.[68] By then, or soon afterward, mechanically pressed glass was added to the output—a type of ware becoming an increasingly important factor in determining the longevity of many glasshouses.

In 1829 the short-lived Union Flint Glass Works was launched by Captain John Hay and William McCully.[69] This house marked the beginning of McCully's career as an entrepreneur after serving an apprenticeship at Bakewell's and perfecting his craft at the Pittsburgh Glass Works when owned by Frederick Lorenz;[70] his success was in the manufacture of window glass and bottles. The same year, 1829, the Wheeling Flint Glass Works was built by John Ritchie and Jesse Wheat in Wheeling, (West) Virginia, and advertised cut, pressed, and plain glasswares. Its career of swinging from prosperity to failure and owner to owner ended about 1850.[71] Although neither of these 1829 houses was a success, each did produce cut and other flint wares, so that the present-day problem of factory identification is the more complicated.

While the manufacture of flint glass was progressing in the Midwest, it was developing in the East on a bigger though not better scale. The War of 1812 provided the occasion for its start; Thomas Cains, an English glassman, the foresight; and the Boston Crown Glass Company the place.[72] By the time the company's superintendent, Charles F. Kupfer, returned from his 1811 journey to England in search of competent crown-

*See 1, p. 48.

glass blowers the country was at war. Consequently, just when the supply of labor was augmented, that of Demerara sand from British Guiana was cut off, in a short time forcing the glasshouse into a state of nearly complete idleness. Thomas Cains, a new recruit arriving in April 1812, was not only a glassman skilled in mixing batch and blowing, but a man of sufficient imagination and enterprise to start the flint-glass business in the Atlantic states.[73] He persuaded the company to erect a small six-pot flint-glass furnace in their South Boston plant; leased it, with the company's responsibility for accounting and selling as one of the conditions; secured sand, first from Plymouth Beach, then from the Maurice River beds in New Jersey, and later from the nearer Berkshires,[74] for his flint and their window glass; and was in production late in 1812 or very early in 1813.

In a December 18, 1812, advertisement in the *Columbian Centinel,* the first which we have found in this period, tumblers were the only articles of tableware listed specifically. Since *flint* was not mentioned, presumably they were blown from window-glass metal along with the chimney and lamp tubes and apothecaries' furniture. Seven weeks later flint glass was mentioned, but so modestly as to seem almost an afterthought to the thousands of feet and boxes of "Boston Superior Crown Glass, ready packed for exportation by land or water" and thousands of feet of Chelmsford glass, all obtainable from C. F. Kupfer, superintendent, at the Glass-House, Essex-Street. The *Columbian Centinel's* February 6, 1813, advertisement, which appeared off and on for more than a year, contained the simple phrase "with a variety of Flint Glass ware" tagging after those devoted to Chelmsford glass. Not until a new advertisement appeared in the paper, September 10, 1814, was the flint glass given headline emphasis as South Boston Flint Glass Wares, and even then it was placed after the window glass. While the term covered many articles, decanters, wines, mugs, and pitchers were the only table glass named. Perhaps the order and phrasing arose from the local market conditions. Even though some window glass came through from England and more from Russia, importation of this commodity was almost at the vanishing point. But the Boston crown and Chelmsford cylinder glass was meeting an unprecedented domestic competition particularly from the Utica, Woodstock, and Albany glasshouses in New York and the young war baby, the Franklin Glass Works at Warwick, Massachusetts.[75] On the other hand, competition for any tableware custom was slight, if advertisements are any indication of the state of the trade. True, occasionally English and Irish glasswares were heralded, some probably smuggled (smuggling was less frowned upon in anti-war Boston than in some quarters), some from prize cargoes and some having traveled roundabout routes of trade. Most of the infrequently advertised shipments which had run the blockade were of Dutch and Russian glasswares, especially tumblers.[76] Consequently for about two years local demand for flint glass must have been met mainly by South Boston.

Still, the young flint-glass business was not immunized to the aftereffects of the war; instead, being in a seaboard city, it was the more susceptible to the resurgent foreign competition. This condition may have been one reason for publishing, in May 1815, an expanded list of tablewares from its "Peace Establishment." [77] Apparently for the next few years not only enumeration of more articles, a practice of auctioneers and importers, was found expedient, but also reiteration of claims that the flint glass, which by 1816 included cut and engraved wares, was equal to any imported and was sold both wholesale and retail as cheap as if not cheaper than any similar glass of equal quality from any part of Europe.[78] In the summer of 1817 extension of local outlets was another move in the game of competition. Though retail selling was continued at their warehouse in charge of Edward A. Pearson, all such sales at the factory were stopped and ten merchants in Boston were appointed agents.[79] It was probably about the same time that agents were secured in other centers. Cambreleng and Pearson of New York City were handling their products late in 1816.[80] In 1819 business was so slim that production almost ceased.[81] Perhaps for that reason, when the South Boston Flint Manufactory caught fire on Columbus Day, its owners were the more thankful to the "gentlemen Firewards" and their fellow citizens for saving the house so quickly that no time was lost "except the usual intermission allowed to the workmen at noon."[82]

From 1823 until 1827, when the intention to cease manufacturing was announced, business deteriorated, not because of the times but from poor management. Failure followed. Internal politics and intrigue had shaken up the firm and when the new one had been formed Charles Kupfer and Thomas Cains were out. The furnace at which Cains had made glass history was leased to one Andrew A. Jones, who, later with Daniel Jackson, incorporated the South Boston Flint Glass Works. They appear to have been no more successful than the furnace's owners.[83] In June 1829 the directors of the Boston and Sandwich Glass Company approved a purchase of their glass.[84] But closing out a glass factory was not accomplished by one such sale. In April 1831 the "South Boston Flint Glass Works" was still trying to dispose of an extensive assortment of cut, plain, and pressed glasswares, glassmakers' tools, molds, lathes, and other equipment.[85]

In the meantime Thomas Cains had built his own glasshouse, the Phoenix Glass Works, which was in operation in 1824. When he retired in 1852, with "an independent property, the honest fruit of his skill and industry,"[86] the management of the glass-works was left to his son William and his son-in-law William Johnston. His leisure was ended in 1855 when the death of Johnston necessitated his again picking up the reins. Perhaps, like many businessmen before and after him, he welcomed the opportunity to return to the driver's seat. Be that as it may, he guided the business through the depression of the late 1850s. After his father's death in 1865 William managed to keep the business alive another five years.[87]

Even less is known about the actual pieces blown in the first successful Eastern flint-glass works than about Bakewell's early glass. Among the articles of tableware which we have found advertised during the Cains regime were decanters, plain or ringed neck, and liquor bottles with stands; quart and pint cans and plain and cut lemonades; jelly glasses; and wines of different patterns, some of which were said to be very elegant, some best, and some tale. (The tale wines, or any article to which that term was applied, were those sold at wholesale by number instead of by weight as was the fine glass, and generally were inferior in quality of craftsmanship, for instance, not fire-polished to remove marks of the marver or glassmaker's tools.[88] Also it is said they were usually blown from the less pure metal in the pot, that at the top or bottom.[89]) There were tumblers of several sorts: quart, pint, half-pint, and gill and barrel of the same sizes, half-pint tavern, figured and plain double flint, ground and engraved ship, best and tale.

There were goblets and mugs; pitchers from gill to three-quart capacity and creams; plain and cut sugar bowls; castors, vinegar cruets, mustards, common and cut salts; dishes and plates; sweetmeat baskets and fingerbowls. Interesting items in the miscellaneous glassware were traveling bottles, bird fonts, fish globes, and inkstands.[90]

Some forms, presumably characteristic of the early period, are shown in the engraving which decorates a Boston Glass Manufactory's billhead,[91] obviously designed about the time Cains began producing tablewares. It shows a large pitcher similar to No. 4, Plate 27, but with a little fuller body and ordinary semi-ear-shaped handle. Five drinking vessels appear, a goblet with a bowl similar to but flaring a bit more than that of No. 3, Plate 67; a wine apparently with drawn bowl and stem like that of No. 1, Plate 60, and one similar to No. 3, Plate 61, except for the cylindrical bowl; two tumblers, one cylindrical and one with slightly spreading sides. The stemmed pieces all seem to have a flaring folded foot. Incidentally in 1815 half-pint barrel tumblers sold for ten cents each, the regular for eight cents.[92] There is a ringed-neck plain decanter akin in shape to the eagle decanter on Plate 84. The only startling item is an anachronistic Stiegel type diamond salt in pattern similar to those on Plate 2 but in shape more like the early nineteenth-century Midwest version, No. 6, Plate 58, except again for the foot, which in the engraving at least appears to be blown and folded instead of the usual applied solid foot. The salt can be taken as evidence that pattern-molded wares as well as the great variety of plain and, by 1816, "elegantly cut" were regular products.

The probability is that full-size piece molds were also part of the equipment, used perhaps for the bottles which could be ordered to any pattern. There can be no doubt they were used before 1820 and extensively afterward. Advertisements of glass which may have been produced either by the South Boston Flint Glass Company or at Cains's Phoenix Glass Works mentioned "plain" and "fluted" decanters; "plain" and "moulded" wineglasses; "moulded" plates and very "elegant diamond moulded" plates; "twisted cruits" (doubtless pattern-molded in vertical ribbing, then swirled); "knob" tumblers,[93] an unidentified form made widely here and abroad in the 1820s and perhaps molded.

Information gleaned from contemporary sources such as advertisements may form the basis for conjectural conclusions but rarely are specific enough to provide even clues for attributions today. Rather their revelation of the number and quantity of apparently similar wares made by so many, many manufacturers arouses one to extreme caution about categorical attributions, unless of course a given piece is accompanied by a reliable genealogical history and has the inherited characteristics which agree with the history. Nevertheless there is one type of simply decorated glass which we have believed was made in or near Boston because, in so far as we have been able to learn, it has been found principally in the environs of that city. It is clear glass, and decorated with either one or two bands of guilloche or, as the English call this chainlike ornament, trailled circuit. Besides plates of various sizes, bowls, sugar bowls and creamers, pitchers, and decanters were fashioned in this style. The plate, No. 1, Plate 24, is an example blown from lead glass, as probably were its relatives. It is the opinion of Lura Woodside Watkins, an opinion generally accepted without reservation, that pieces of this type were made under Cains at South Boston.[94]

Perhaps Cains's flint glassmaking was the magnet of success drawing other Bostonians into the field. A little more than a year after the South Boston furnace was in blast, February 14, 1814, to be exact, the Boston Porcelain and Glass Company was incorporated and soon built its factories at Lechmere Point, Cambridge.[95] The company began a brief career of crises; the glassworks, a long one of success. The glasshouse, which had been under the management of a Mr. Thompson, was leased in 1815 to three ambitious glassmen from Cains's project: William Emmett, George Flowers, and one Fisher, probably John Fisher since he was later in the employ of the New England Glass Company.[96] "Want of concert of action prevented a successful result" and they "dissolved without loss." [97] This event must have occurred before the end of February 1817 inasmuch as on the twenty-sixth, the Boston Porcelain and Glass Company announced that, as an accommodation, orders for glasswares and common earthenware sent to R. Sudgen at their works and destined for neighboring traders or going to Eastern and Southern states would be forwarded to any wharf or store within two miles.[98] Circumstances had forced the concern into operation of its plants, but it was neither prosperous nor happy in the situation. Hardly any manufacturer was in 1817. On September 3 a meeting of the corporation was held to decide whether or not part or all of the real estate should be sold. The glasshouse and its property were disposed of at public sale in November.

Apparently three members of the corporation, Edmund Munroe, Deming Jarves, its clerk in 1817,[99] and Daniel Hastings, believed in the future of glass in spite of the depression and foreign competition. They, with Amos Binney, one of Boston's leading citizens and businessmen, formed the New England Glass Company, which they incorporated in February 1818, purchased the works, promptly expanded them, and added a cutting department, operated not by foot but by steam power. Shortly afterward Jarves, "aided by a director" whom he leaves nameless in his account, installed the first lead furnace to be operated in connection with a glasshouse, thereby insuring a steady and less expensive supply of lead used as a flux in making flint glass.[100] Seemingly the company was not so distressed by the hard times as others, although it did resort to the services of the auction house, so generally excoriated at the time, to dispose of its large surplus stock in the fall of 1819 and again in the spring of 1820.[101]

The New England Glass Company had a keen appreciation of the value of advertising and was accorded favorable publicity. As we have seen, its bowl for President Monroe, and decanters for Secretary Adams, exhibited at fair and shop, were lauded by a friendly press. Like Bakewell's, it exhibited at the Franklin Institute's first Philadelphia Exhibition in 1824 and, like its Pittsburgh rival, received honorable mention. The vase, Colonel Binney, and the Washington fair already have been noted. In subsequent years its glass was publicized at exhibitions of the Franklin Institute and the American Institute of the City of New York, at the fairs of the Massachusetts Charitable Mechanics' Association in Boston and, of course, at the New York Crystal Palace in 1853 and at the 1876 Centennial.[102] Usually the displays were staged by the company's local agent. The New England Glass Company was well represented in the seaboard cities and in some of the smaller important centers such as Hartford, Connecticut.[103] And its glass was known not only from Maine to New Orleans and Mexico but also in the West Indies, South America, and Europe.

The first setback came about 1864 with the advent of the cheaper lime glass and the company's decision not to debase its metal. However, though steadily weakened by competition from the Midwest, where production costs, other than labor, were lower, the factory was run until 1888. Then a glass blowers' strike proved the impracticability of continuing production in Cambridge. The Libbeys, who had been operating the house since 1874, closed it and moved permanently to Toledo, Ohio.

Once more the situation exists in which conclusions as to the nature and appearance of the wares made prior to 1830 by one of our most important glasshouses are largely matters of supposition and deduction. While inevitably advertisements[104] throw some light upon the varieties of articles, the type of metal and methods of ornamentation, the illumination is rarely strong enough to identify specific types of glass known to us today. The glasswares, as revealed by advertisements, were fashioned from either flint (lead) glass or window glass, the common clear or white metal made usually with a combination of soda or potash and lime but always without lead.[105] The best and most expensive glass was free-blown from lead metal and ornamented by copper-wheel-engraved or wheel-cut decoration. Among the interesting items were "taper and French shape" wines and goblets; figured and printed dessert plates; and Prussian decanters with tall and pressed stoppers, possibly inspired by some currently popular German type. One of the richly detailed advertisements was that of Joseph Hastings, the Boston representative appointed in 1819. In October he offered, among other things, complete table and dessert services which included center dishes, salad dishes of all shapes, celery stands, plates, decanters, wines, tumblers, jellies, claret, "champaign," lemonades, custards, "liquers," salts, castors, and liquor stands. Also among the many types of lamps were richly cut Grecian lamps from twelve to twenty inches tall priced at $120 to $300 a pair. At that time and for many years to come, as whale oil and other lighting oils or fluids were rather costly, the use of lamps was an earmark of at least moderate prosperity.[106]

In 1819, if not sooner, molds were used to produce tumblers and decanters, fan-end salts and castor bottles, peppers and cruets, soy cruets and mustards, and jugs or pitchers. Japanned and plated four-, five- and six-hole castors for the bottles were carried. Inasmuch as the small dip mold and part-size piece mold had been used in American glasshouses for going on one hundred years and "moulded" is a term which, in our experience, is rarely encountered in advertisements of glass prior to 1818, it seems probable that the "moulded tumblers" and other articles were formed in full-size molds of the two-, three-, or four-piece type or shallow dish type. It is not unlikely that the sugar bowl, No. 2, Plate 32, was made at Cambridge. Moreover, there is good reason to believe that Blown Three Mold glass was one of the Cambridge lines and that one of its patterns was the Arch GIV-6, in which the large pitcher, No. 4, Plate 43, was patterned. It was blown in a quart decanter mold and the neck and rim formed by manipulation.[107]

The occurrence of "prest" and "pressed" in 1819 and 1820 advertisements gives one pause even though it seems inconceivable that *mechanical* pressing was meant at that early date. The pressed star stoppers undoubtedly were made in a sort of hand-operated pinch tool. While one may speculate as to the exact method denoted by "pressed" in 1820, it seems certain that after 1825 or 1826 mechanical pressing was meant. The New England Glass Company was the second glasshouse to institute and develop this revolutionary method of production—so far as we know at present. In November 1826 Henry Whitney, who succeeded Jarves as agent, and Enoch Robinson took out the second recorded patent for pressing, and like John Bakewell's, in 1825, theirs was for knobs.[108]

Also before 1830 gilding was used as a means of ornamentation with increasing frequency; likewise painting and possibly staining, which was an inexpensive simulation of flashing. In 1829 the company introduced a new line called enameled glass, which has been mentioned already in connection with the Bakewells' wares. The company continued to make all kinds of pressed glass; added fancy blown types made popular as "Bohemian" influence permeated the industry; adopted novelty types and even developed some of the late nineteenth-century art glass like the Amberina and Wild Rose shown on Plate 99. Among the novelties were gilding and silvering on glass, which it exhibited in 1850 at the Franklin Institute. Perhaps its now famous apple and pear paperweights, one of which is illustrated on Plate 98, were the types exhibited in 1856. With all its digression to conform with current tastes it never compromised on its high standard for fine lead cut and engraved glass. It undoubtedly was the leading house in New England in the production of the highest quality of glassware, as Bakewell's was in Pittsburgh, and Gilliland's and later Christian Dorflinger's were in Brooklyn.

Before 1830 five other important flint glasshouses were established.[109] Four of them were founded by men who had been connected with the New England Glass Company; three by practicing glassmen, one by Deming Jarves. On December 8, 1819, not long after their celebrated urn had been completed to be sent to President Monroe, John L. Gilliland, John Fisher, with Fisher's brother Richard, purchased a tract of land on the Hudson River in the Bloomingdale section on Manhattan Island[110] and erected their Bloomingdale Flint Glass Works, usually referred to locally as Fishers' Factory.[111] It was not long before plain and, as one would expect since at least two of the partners were skilled glass cutters, cut flint glasswares were ready for the market. In November 1822 the Fishers bought Gilliland's interest in the business. For a few years before the hard times of 1836 became a panic they maintained a downtown New York store as an outlet for their druggist and chemical wares and their fine cut glass.[112] But, when exhibited at the fairs of the American Institute of the City of New York, their cut glass appears to have won official recognition only twice, once in 1829, when it received a "Discretionary Premium," and again in 1835, when it was rated second best.[113] After Richard's death in 1840 the factory closed. So far as we have discovered, the Fishers never made any pressed glass, which may in part account for their difficulty in weathering the depression of the late 1830s. The large cut-glass pitcher, No. 1, Plate 42, is quite like three owned by a descendant of Richard Fisher and illustrated in an article in the New York Sun on April 1, 1933.

Unquestionably before he withdrew from the Bloomingdale project John L. Gilliland had determined to establish a flint-glass factory of his own and promptly formed John L. Gilliland and Company for that purpose.[114] Brooklyn was decided upon as the location and property purchased near Mr. Pierpont's place opposite New York. The project was hailed as a boon to the community. The May day in 1823 when the cornerstone of his glassworks was laid was one of celebration. The Brooklyn artillery paraded and fired a salute at the ceremony. "Every friend of this country," said the Mechanics Gazette of

New York City, "must wish him success in this important branch of manufacture." [115] When the house was completed in September and blowing began on the fifteenth many Brooklynites, curious about and proud of the new industry, were on hand to observe the various processes. Interest, however, was not merely local. Even the Troy *Sentinel* ran a congratulatory editorial pointing out the favorable situation of the works, "so near the great commercial emporium of the United States and at a point where so many channels of water transportation concentrate," and expressing the hope that Gilliland would find "his enterprise abundantly rewarded while . . . honorably contributing his part toward the substantial independence of the country. . . ." [116] The *Sentinel* was, of course, an "American System" supporter and a Whig paper. Its hopes were realized: John L. Gilliland conducted his works with great skill for about twenty years. In 1864 a controlling interest was acquired by the Houghtons, Amory, Sr., and Jr., who had established the Union Glass Company in Somerville, Massachusetts, in 1851. Four years later the old, old problem of bringing fuel and materials together most economically led them to seek a new location. They moved to Corning, New York, and established the well-known Corning Glass Works.

The Brooklyn Flint Glass Works was to become famous for its metal. In 1824 its blown and uncut glass exhibited at the fair of the New York Mechanical and Scientific Institute was considered equal in brilliancy and beauty to anything of its kind ever seen by the reporter, who, to be sure, was from a paper advocating domestic manufactures. But the judges must have agreed with him, since they awarded the First Premium to Gilliland and Company. [117] The following year the well-known Philadelphia firm of McCord and Shiner, glass cutters, using Brooklyn blanks, won acclaim at the exhibition of the Franklin Institute for its cut glass. By 1826 John L. Gilliland and Company was cutting its own glass, which, exhibited at Philadelphia, was awarded a silver medal— not for the cutting, but as the best flint glassware in the quality of the material and the form of the articles. The judges reported that not one bad piece was seen in the entire Brooklyn exhibit. Moreover, the American glass exhibits of Gilliland, McCord and Shiner, Jackson and Baggott of New York City, the New England Glass Company of Cambridge, Bakewell, Page and Bakewell, and the Jersey Glass Works were hailed as proof that "this country need not remain tributary to foreign manufacturers." Brooklyn glass was shown at most of the subsequent exhibitions of the Franklin Institute and at those of the American Institute of the City of New York, beginning with its first in 1828. Nearly always there were comments on the metal, such as "pure whiteness," "best metal for color exhibited," "contrasts strikingly with imported material of the same variety from Europe [which is] often yellow and dingy," "sparkles like the diamond." At the London Crystal Palace in 1851, the first World's Fair, and against all comers, Gilliland's exhibit received the prize for the best flint glass. Even the English remarked on its purity and absolute freedom from all color. [118] Deming Jarves was not alone in his opinion that John L. Gilliland was the "best metal mixer in the United States"; though in the 1865 edition of his *Reminiscences* he toned it down to "remarkably skillful in mixing metal." [119]

Once more it must be said that little or nothing is known about the wares of an outstanding glasshouse. During its first seven years it supplied New York City with glass cups for its lights and then with gas lamps; [120] it provided some of the firms of glass cutters with their blanks; produced plain and cut, molded and pressed glass on an expanding scale. In 1829 its pressed wares were of a quality to merit the award of a premium by the American Institute of the City of New York. As yet we have found no evidence revealing more about the period, but one can rest assured that in form and decoration the wares of the Brooklyn Flint Glass Works resembled those of its competitors. The same can be said safely of the later periods, when the trend in fancy glass was followed. However, students and collectors of paperweights have attributed some of the fine American weights, such as No. 6, Plate 97, to Gilliland's Brooklyn Flint Glass Works.

In 1824, the year after Gilliland started his well-rewarded career as head of a glassworks, George Dummer, William G. Bull, and Joseph K. Milnor founded the Jersey Glass Company[121] and erected a glasshouse on Paulus Hook near the village of Jersey City.[122] George Dummer probably initiated the plans for both the glassworks and the pottery which was started the next year. He was another of the merchants handling glass, earthenware, and porcelain who sought a steady and more profitable supply of stock for his shelves. He had been an importer in New York City for many years. His firm headed the signers of a petition to Congress in November 1811 asking permission to bring into the country the goods, wares, and merchandise which had been purchased by the petitioners before the passage of the Non-Importation Act in March.[123] About 1820, perhaps as a defense against the competition of auctioneers and English agents, he established his own glass-cutting department in conjunction with his store. This department doubtless was moved to Jersey City when the glasshouse was completed. First George Dummer and Company—which still continued for several years to import earthenware and porcelain, plain and cut glass, almost by the shipload—then succeeding Dummer firms were the principal New York agents for the glassworks. Another was the wholesale and retail firm of Shirley and Taylor, extensive advertisers of the Jersey products. Like other houses of the period it had representatives in Philadelphia and Baltimore also, and exhibited occasionally at the New York and Philadelphia exhibitions. Apparently it was one of the many glassworks succumbing to the depression which started in 1857; at least it disappeared from the directories after 1862.[124]

Very few pieces of glass have been identified with this glassworks, which operated for nearly forty years; yet the production was tremendous and its output varied. At the beginning the glasshouse had two departments, one for blowing glass, which was under a Mr. Glaze, and one for cutting the glass, which was under the supervision of a Mr. Young. By 1826, when Thomas Jones, the editor of the *Franklin Journal and American Mechanics Magazine*,[125] visited the factory, there were thirty-two steam-driven cutting wheels in operation and twelve more were soon to be installed in another room. Mr. Young showed him glass cut by boys having only a few months' training which nevertheless, to the superintendent's eyes, appeared of the best. The opinion probably was a fond overestimation, but such was the report. Engraving was also a method of ornamentation. In the meantime experiments in mechanical pressing must have been in progress, for in the fall of 1827 Phineas C. Dummer took out one patent and he with George Dummer and James Maxwell took out another.[126] It would seem that pressed glass became an important line of the Jersey Glass Company. Its wares—any article,

PLATE 7

1. Candlestick, one of pair, blown from brilliant bluish-aquamarine non-lead glass; long socket, with straight-sided bobêche, tapering slightly to shaft composed of hollow inverted baluster between graduated rings and resting on applied circular foot. Made at the Redford Glass Works, near Plattsburg, New York. Circa 1831–50.

Height, 9″; top diameter, 1¾″; greatest diameter of inverted baluster in stem, 1¹¹⁄₁₆″; diameter of foot, 3³⁄₁₆″.

The stem of the mate, larger, the greatest diameter being 2⅛″.

2. Candlestick blown from aquamarine non-lead glass; extremely long slender socket with flanged lip; at base of socket a gather of glass tooled into gadrooning; shaft composed of a hollow baluster between triple rings and heavy double ring at center of broad quatrefoil foot; a United States Indian cent dated 1862 in the hollow baluster. Attributed to New London Glass Works, Connecticut. Circa 1862–70.

Height, 9½″; diameter of foot, 4¼″.

3. Mug blown from brilliant bluish-aquamarine non-lead glass; cylindrical form tapering slightly to rim tooled to give effect of a band; applied heavy solid semi-ear-shaped handle; superimposed lily-pad decoration Type II. Redford Glass Works, New York State. Circa 1831–50.

Height, 4″; top diameter, 3½″; diameter of body, 2⅝″.

4. Sugar bowl with cover, blown from brilliant bluish-aquamarine non-lead glass; globular body contracted below shallow galleried rim, applied solid globular-knop stem and broad circular foot; high domed cover with applied flattened globular finial; body and dome of cover decorated with superimposed gather tooled into heavy swagging. Probably Mount Vernon Glass Works, Vernon, New York. Circa 1810–40.

Over-all height, 8⅝″; height without cover, 5⅛″; top diameter, 4⅛″; greatest diameter of body, 4″; diameter of foot, 3⁷⁄₁₆″.

5. Pair of small vases free-blown from deep bluish-aquamarine non-lead glass; short globular body, with wide cylindrical neck and flaring rim, applied plain circular foot; applied fine threading on upper part of neck and rim, a heavy double ring applied around base of neck; on each side, applied heavy solid semi-ear-shaped handle with lower part trailed over horizontal ring. Redwood Glass Works, located near Watertown, New York. Circa 1833–50.

Height, 5⅝″; top diameter, 3³⁄₁₆″; g. eatest diameter of body, 3¹⁄₁₆″; diameter of foot, 2⅜″.

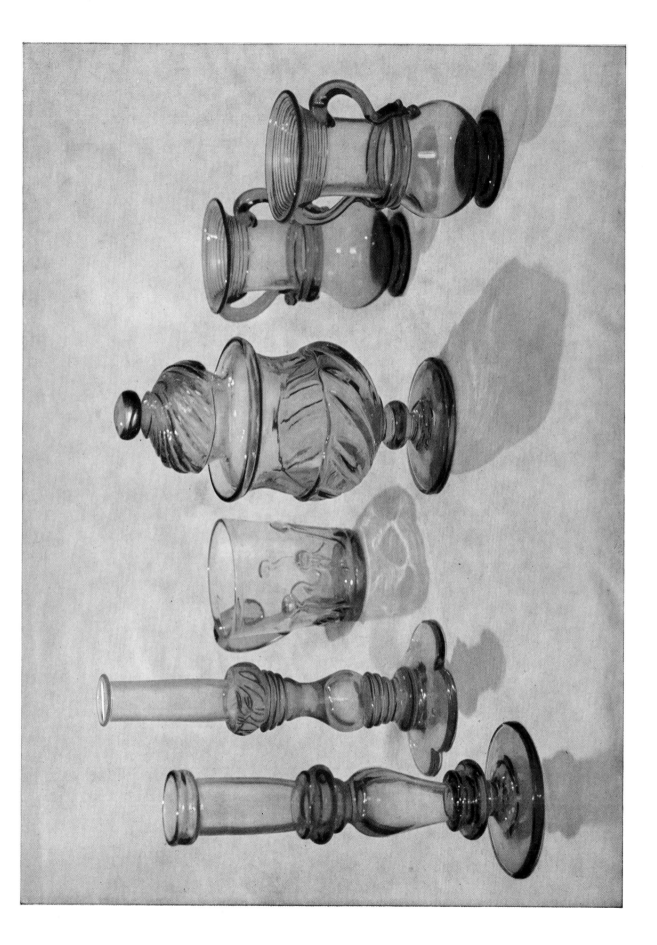

cut, plain, pressed, molded, or made to pattern—were offered by their agents and themselves at wholesale and retail to Southern and country merchants, families, hotels, shops, and steamboat owners, and for export. The articles enumerated in advertisements were just about the same as those of their competitors. One interesting group, offered to the trade only, consisted of knobs of assorted sizes, ribbed, twisted, plain, cut, opaque, and pearl. Although such knobs were a standard article of manufacture with most houses, as yet we have found only those of the Jersey Glass Company advertised extensively.[127] Notwithstanding the fact that this company was one of the first to press glass and produced wares in this category for years, the only design identified with it today is a marked salt. And only a few blown pieces have been attributed to it, among them the green wineglass, No. 4, Plate 59.

In 1825 another cutting from the New England Glass Company took root. Deming Jarves built his glasshouse at Sandwich.[128] As in the case of Baron Stiegel, so much more has been written about Jarves and his glassworks than about his contemporaries and their accomplishments that, as in many primitive paintings, the proportions of the subjects are distorted. Apparently Jarves was an enterprising and shrewd businessman, an imaginative and capable manufacturer inventive and unafraid of innovation, and a keen merchandiser, but he was not a giant among pygmies. Like Bakewell and Dummer, Jarves was a merchant at the start of his career, but in drygoods rather than glass and china. In 1812 he was selling French ribbons, satin and lustrings, netting for indispensables, plain and embossed galloons, and gentlemen's white silk hose. He was a frequent advertiser and varied his bait more often than most merchants of the period. For nearly four years, from April 1, 1814, he was the copartner of Joseph B. Henshaw, a Boston dealer in crockery and glassware.[129] Perhaps his contacts with the fine objects in these categories first gave him the urge, stimulated by the recent difficulties in securing importations, to associate himself with their manufacture, first through the Boston Porcelain and Glass Company, and then its successor, the New England Glass Company. His Sandwich glassworks, located on a tidal creek about a mile from the sea, was ready for production three months after the ground was broken for its erection, even the workmen's homes were completed, and on the fourth of July glass was blown at the eight-pot furnace. Early in the following year Jarves sold the works to a new company, consisting of himself, Henry Rice, Edmund Munroe, and Andrew T. Hall, which incorporated as the Boston and Sandwich Glass Company. But Jarves, like Benjamin Bakewell, whom he admired so unreservedly, was the activating spirit of the works. Under his guidance the factory mushroomed quickly, expanding its manufacturing and sales facilities—the last through agents in strategic cities—and sending its glass far and wide, at home and abroad.[130] Frequently Sandwich products, pressed and blown, were displayed at the exhibitions in Boston and also at a few of those in Philadelphia, where in 1833 the pressed glass received an award.[131]

Five years before, after securing the services of the Boston moldmaker, Hiram Dillaway, a mold department had been added and in the same year Jarves obtained his first patent connected with mechanical pressing.[132] However, unquestionably, experiments in pressing had been made at Sandwich for some time previous. Pressed glass apparently was the product insuring prosperity until the 1880s. The fires were drawn in 1888. Jarves did not run the full course with it, however. In 1857, when there was a change in ownership and management, Jarves left and started the Cape Cod Glass Works, the sixth glasshouse with which he had been connected in about forty-two years.

Just as more has been written and is known about its founder than about his contemporaries, so more has been written and is known about the products of the Boston and Sandwich Glass Works than about those of its competitors. In fact, "Sandwich" has become almost as common a household term for glass as for a picnic mainstay. For so many years it was the only well-known nineteenth-century Eastern manufactory of tablewares that any piece of table or ornamental glass which could not be fitted with the supposed Stiegel or Wistar mantle automatically wore that of Sandwich. Most of us have had the painful experience of unlearning Sandwich glass facts; for, as Homer Keyes once said, "All that glitters is not Sandwich." However, because the factory was located on the rim of a small village which never grew into a city, exhaustive excavations on its site have been possible, thereby determining the types and patterns of many of its products. Studies of the fragments confirmed the attribution of many early pressed-glass patterns to Sandwich and also revealed many Cassandras among the students and collectors of American glass who had believed, and so stated, that Sandwich must have been one source of Blown Three Mold glass. Aside from these, little evidence aiding identification of other wares produced during the first five years was uncovered. In these two categories, however, more designs are identified today with Sandwich than with any other one glassworks. The trouble is, one cannot be positive the works had a monopoly on them.

Sandwich's pedestal in the glass Hall of Fame is of pressed glass. Nevertheless fine blown glass with and without extrinsic decoration was produced there, though probably in comparatively limited quantities until after 1830. In the course of our research we have found no long itemized advertisements of Sandwich wares before the mid-1830s, but writers have recorded items listed in the factory's first account book. Among the blown and molded articles mentioned during the first year of production were decanters and toy decanters; star and ball stoppers and cruet stoppers, the last presumably for the cruets and twisted cruets; "flint champaigns, licquieres," tumblers, and ship tumblers; center dishes, sugar bowls, and common salts; pint pocket and cologne bottles. Molded articles were hats, half-pint jugs (pitchers), 5-inch patty pans, 9-inch oval dishes; mustards, salts for cutting; and, doubtless, the 6-inch round dishes and 7-inch, 8-inch, 9-inch, and 10-inch octagon dishes. Lamps, also made from the beginning, were entered as small and large rose foot, on foot, peg, and high blown stem and button stem short lamps. Perhaps the rare lamp, No. 2, Plate 94, was one of the short ones with button stem. Its font and base fall in the Blown Three Mold category, which will be discussed later.

The banks on Plate 96, and No. 1, Plate 95, bear witness to the expert craftsmanship of Sandwich glass blowers and also to the fact that when they made special gifts they used the most difficult glass technique, fashioning the pieces entirely by hand and ornamenting solely by glass itself. Molds might be time- and money-savers, but as crutches for craftsmanship they were unnecessary. The paperweights, Nos. 1, 2, and 4, Plate 97, and the floral bottle stopper on Plate 98, which have been attributed to Sandwich, are evidence of skill in another category.

The last important flint glasshouse of this thirty-year period, like Sandwich, was established after the American System had been implemented by the 1824 protective tariff, a more effective financial aid than any government loan. Jarves in his *Reminiscences* states that another secession of workmen from the New England Glass Company in 1820 resulted in the Union Flint Glass Company of Kensington, Philadelphia, and disposes of it quite summarily as an ill-fated venture passing into other hands as death thinned its ranks and mismanagement its funds.[133] Actually the company was not formed nor its glasshouse operating until 1826. So if any of its founders deserted the Cambridge house in 1820 they must have spent the interim either at one of the works in or near New York City or at the Philadelphia and Kensington Glass works "about a mile above Philadelphia at the further end of Kensington."[134] The company was formed by William Granville, William Swindell, William Bennett, and William Emmett (the last a familiar name in connection with South Boston and Cambridge), all of Kensington, and Joseph Capewell, of Cambridge, and James Venables, of Boston.* On the first of November 1825 William Granville, acting for the group, purchased for $3600 a tract of land in Kensington along the Delaware River. The cornerstone of the glasshouse was laid the same month and the works was in operation early in 1826.[135] Before the end of the year Granville and Swindell had withdrawn and Charles Baldren Austin had entered the firm,[136] which became Charles B. Austin and Company. Austin, an Englishman and apparently one of the skilled craftsmen who left Europe during the postwar depression, landed at New York in January 1819 with his family. He was probably the Charles Austin listed as a glass cutter in the New York City directories for 1821–24. So long as Austin was the agent and head of the Union Flint Glass Company the works prospered. But when the management passed to William Bennett after Austin's death in 1840, he was hampered by strife within the firm. He, his wife, Sarah Synar, and Joseph Capewell were soon at litigation with Austin's widow. The firm dissolved in 1844. The glasshouse was shut down. In 1847 it was taken over by the firm of Hartell and Lancaster and operated for many years.[137]

Here was a firm operating successfully for at least fifteen years, employing a hundred hands, and producing glass in such quantities that almost from its inception two warehouses were maintained in the city of Philadelphia,[138] yet all we know of its wares at present is that its specialty was cut glass and it made pressed glass including cup plates, a few of which have been tentatively identified. When Thomas Porter, author of the second volume of *Picture of Philadelphia from 1811 to 1831*, visited the works and inspected their blown and cut glass he reported that he felt "no hesitancy in pronouncing the workmanship to be of the most elegant kind." In 1827 specimens of their cut glass were shown at the exhibition of the Franklin Institute, and also in five subsequent years before 1849.[139] Colored as well as clear glass was made. Like other houses of the period it started pressing before 1830. Its infringement—in the jury's opinion—on the New England Glass Company's 1826 patent involved it in a suit which lasted over two years.[140]

We believe it quite likely that the cut-glass tumbler with pictorial engraving, No. 5, Plate 79, was a Union Glass Company product. But the belief rests on faith in the logic of a conclusion drawn from two facts rather than on direct evidence, namely, that the

*Also Richard Synar; see ref. 135.

[87]

glass company made cut and engraved glassware and the engraving depicts the Widows and Orphans Asylum in Philadelphia as shown in an 1830 publication.

Besides all the glasshouses operating their own glass-cutting departments by 1830—some long before that year—there were many firms of glass cutters and engravers dependent upon glassmakers only for their blanks to cut. Nor were they a new departure in Ameican business; there had been such shops in the seaboard cities in Stiegel's day. Moreover, it is probable that many a crest was engraved on a prized decanter by the local lapidary or jeweler. It is safe to say that in the early nineteenth century nearly every sizable city had a glass-cutting and engraving shop, even if it was no more than an adjunct to a jeweler's shop. In 1813 Richard James, of Pittsburgh, whose shop was on Third Street between Grand and Smithfield, styled himself "Lapidary and Glass Engraver." [141] Also in Pittsburgh, Jardel or Jardelle, who had engraved glass for Bakewell's, was in business for himself by 1826.[142] Before 1830 O'Leary, Baily, and Smith had launched their Franklin Cut Glass and Watch Chrystal Manufactory with the claim that long experience in Europe and America enabled them to compete in quality and price with any glass-cutting establishment in the United States.[143] McCord and Shiner were perhaps the largest producers in Philadelphia. In New York City, Jackson and Baggott were the principal manufacturers producing cut glass on an extensive scale even in the depression year 1819. But since they were "determined to sell on such terms as shall ensure them a share of the public patronage," it apparently was accorded to them by the private families, storekeepers, and exporters to the Southern states who were invited to call.[144] Although the owners of glass-cutting and -engraving shops vociferously opposed increased duties on imported blanks[145] many of them were able to expand after the 1824 duties became effective. Jackson and Baggott enlarged their manufactory and replaced foot power with steam. Moreover, in 1825 they were able to inform the public that they could now afford to sell at least twenty per cent below the price on imported wares.[146] We have their assurance also that they used the best London patterns.[147]

It must be remembered that at the same time that increasing hundreds of thousands of articles were being cut and engraved in the glasshouses and cutting shops of the United States almost unimaginable quantities were being imported from abroad. Also, as the country recovered from the depression, the center of gravity of our glass imports shifted steadily from England to the Continent—Bohemia and northern Germany via the port cities of the old Hanseatic League, and France.[148] Consequently there was a larger reflection of French and German fashions in our own wares. In most instances, as yet, few of us have the knowledge or, lacking it, the temerity to say with confidence that this piece is certainly foreign and that positively American, to say nothing of which American glasshouse or cutting shop produced it. True, there are certain types which are quite certainly English; others, surely French; still others, undoubtedly Bohemian or German. But—and here is the rub—our makers of cut and engraved glasswares, with growing impartiality, used them all as models. They had to; their commerce survived by remaining in the train of fad and fashion. And the closer to 1830 a piece was cut or engraved, the less likely it was to have national earmarks. By then even English glassmakers, their initiative sapped and creative impulses checked perhaps by heavy taxation and government excisemen, were frankly copying the French and German styles themselves.[149] Moreover, in so far as an exhaustive comparative study of early nineteenth-century reputedly American cut and engraved wares is concerned, these categories are still the neglected offspring of the industry. It is not impossible that, while conforming to the current taste, some of the glass still was not a slavish copy. And it is possible that an analysis, if ever made, may reveal a blend of the immigrant designs, or perhaps one should say pirated designs, into an American version of the popular types. Yet, if this should be so, such a development would probably have been before 1824 and the days of mass production. At present, however, one could identify the honeybee on the honey-suckle vine as a worker from Hive 11 as surely as to assign a piece of engraved or cut glass, *on the evidence of appearance and physical characteristics alone,* to a particular American glasshouse or shop.

On the other hand, a few studies, particularly English, Irish, and German, have provided standards by which the period and probable nationality of some late eighteenth- and early nineteenth-century cut and engraved glass can be determined with fair accuracy. For the most part *un*likeness to known foreign types has been the basis for the attributions to the United States of pieces unaccompanied by any evidence as to their source other than their own appearance. Recognition of the differences from foreign cut glass, we now realize, entails a knowledge of not only English and Irish patterns and styles but continental as well. In British glasshouses the emphasis started gravitating in the late eighteenth century from glass itself to its decoration, with accelerated speed as the influence from the Continent combined with other forces and finally overpowered English resistance to it.[150] Decoration encroached upon more and more of the surface, grew bolder in composition and, as restraint slackened the reins, became "exuberant," to use Mr. Thorpe's word.[151] The decoration of the compote, No. 1, Plate 18, illustrates a typical composition of the very early nineteenth century; perhaps because the shallow cutting is extremely amateurish, the lines are not quite so fluid as in some decoration of the period, and the strawberry diamonds are merely simulated by crosshatching. Whether or not this diamond motif, which may have been used sparingly before Pellatt adopted it around 1810, deserved its popularity, it became one of the most commonly used of the cut-glass motifs, and was even adapted to pressed glass.

It was not long after 1800, if one can judge from the attributions in books showing glass of the nineteenth century, that the evolution of a new and stereotyped style of lavish but not exuberant cutting began. It was characterized by rigidity and primness resulting from reiterated simple geometric forms, small in scale and composed mainly in tight ranks or in diapers, for example, bands of vertical ribbing and bands of diamond diaper-ing. The rectilinear motifs predominated—flutes or ribs, splits and prismatic cutting, as on the large pitcher, No. 1, Plate 42, and diamonds—little diamonds, medium-sized diamonds, big diamonds, strawberry diamonds, crosscut diamonds . . . Seldom were the regimented strait-laced motifs relieved by curvilinear forms more complex than the simple circle or oval, or their arcs. From these, occasionally, more complex motifs were evolved such as a sunburst formed from a circle or concentric rings with fine raylike ribs, or the conventionalized palm on the celery vase, No. 3, Plate 50. But the norm became a banded composition, one band above another. Sometimes the designer restrained himself to two or three bands, often he was prodigal in their use. Examples of typical designs of the 1815–30 period are illustrated by the sugar bowl, No. 3, Plate 34, the punch cup and mug, Nos. 2 and 4, Plate 75, the sulphide tumblers, Plate 82, and the celery vase mentioned above, which has a less crowded and bolder design than most. The large pitcher, also mentioned, is an example of a type which enjoyed years of popularity. Typical cut-glass patterns which were adapted to the full-size mold are illustrated by the Blown Three Mold decanters, Plate 86, and No. 4, Plate 87. The two bottom bands of the latter have an exact English cut-glass counterpart. Though all too few in number, there were exceptions to the general prevailing style, not only before 1830 but throughout the century.

The typical shallow engraving and design styles found on some commercial wares are shown by the compote, No. 2, Plate 18; the sugar bowl, No. 1, Plate 34; the pitcher, No. 3, Plate 42; and the celery glasses, Nos. 1 and 2, Plate 49, and No. 1, Plate 50. In shape and style of decoration, particularly the basket of flowers, the celery glasses on Plate 49 are quite French in feeling, Empirish. The high incidence of their type in Maryland and eastern Pennsylvania, particularly the Baltimore–Philadelphia area, led to their attribution at one time to Amelung and also to the glassworks in Washington, D.C. The form is too late for Amelung and the only product of the Washington works was cylinder window glass. Though almost nothing is known about the glass made in other early nineteenth-century glasshouses in the area, it is believed that some of these celery glasses may have emanated from one of them. As it is probable that many of them were made in the late 1820s and even shortly after 1830, Kensington's Union Glass Works may have been a source also. But today Pittsburgh is accepted generally as the principal source. The other pieces bear decoration which in our experience has been confined mainly to glass found in the Pittsburgh area; this is one reason why they are considered products of glasshouses in that section of the country. The pitcher, moreover, was fashioned in a distinctive Midwestern shape characteristic of individual pieces from the bottle and window glasshouses as well as of commercial wares. Since flowers and leaves, motifs of almost timeless popularity, were most common, more curving lines occur in the engraved than in the cut designs, but generally stiffly curbed. In the main, though not completely conventionalized, most motifs are basically conventional.

The tumbler, No. 5, Plate 79, probably made in 1830 or shortly afterward, combines cutting and engraving. The style and disposal of the cut design with its heavy pillar ribs, its very fine diamonds and medium diamonds, and the tumbler's proportions appear more continental than English. The view of the Widows and Orphans Asylum in Philadelphia, partly perhaps because it was a special subject and partly because of the trend in engraving, is more carefully modeled than the decoration on the other illustrated pieces of this period. While designs and their rendering, similar to those on the compote and pitcher on Plates 18 and 42, for example, continued in use, fashion was turning to more naturalistic renderings and subjects, some highly romanticized. And steadily through the ensuing years the craftsman was allowed greater freedom in the play of his wheels upon the surface of glass, often creating, when the thickness of the metal permitted, the illusion of three dimensions. Even in 1828 Mrs. Royall, on her visit to Bakewell's, was astonished by the engraving of a greyhound—"not an inch in length, it was perfect and entire, the ears, nose and eyes were life itself."[152]*

In evaluating the cut and engraved wares of the early nineteenth century, and later for that matter, like the glassmakers themselves, one is caught between two extremes of thought on the subject of the proper relation between glass and its decoration; for only rarely is the perfect balance of one to the other achieved. According to one point of view, the glass is a vehicle bearing the creation of the designer or decorator. And in any event, whether the design is that of an artist or an artisan, its execution on the glass is by the artisan—glass cutter or engraver—who has no aversion to unstinted demonstration of his skill. According to the other point of view the metal, the glass itself, is of prime importance; the decoration merely a handmaid to its inherent qualities. The former might be said to be the extreme German and the latter the extreme English school of thought. It was the German approach which won out. In character, however, designs everywhere succumbed to the French. Not only in glass, by the 1830s, but also in manners, dress, and all the outward manifestations of nice living, society took its cues from Paris.

Then and later Fashion's habit of grinding individuality under her heel must have been resented by more than one glassmaker, but acquiescence to her whim was the usual price paid for commercial success. By 1830 it was the ransom for continued existence. Strangely enough, while the wares which were the finest in metal and craftsmanship were forced to conform to current tastes, glassmakers, for a few years at least, were able to indulge in flights of fancy and originality in the designs of their cheaper molded tablewares and the whisky bottle.

*A gross exaggeration if the tumbler acquired by the Historical Society of Western Pennsylvania about 1953 is the one Anne Royall saw—as it is said to be.

HISTORICAL AND PICTORIAL FLASKS AND BLOWN THREE MOLD GLASS

THE American glass manufacturers' successful establishment of flint-glass tableware production by 1830 was equaled in importance to the industry as a whole by the extension of the full-size piece mold from the mere shaping of an object to its lettering and, more important, its ornamentation. As a matter of fact, if this method of fabricating bottles and tablewares had not been developed, thereby making those wares more abundant and cheaper, the roots of the industry would neither have been so strong by 1830 nor spread so rapidly afterward. By 1809, if not earlier, the full-size piece mold was being used for bottles and flasks; a few years later, for the tableware today called Blown Three Mold. These molds, made of metal, were composed of two or more pieces with or without an intaglio pattern or inscription. When closed they were the size and shape of the article to be made. It was a long stride toward mechanization and away from true craftsmanship. Whether the possibility of an almost infinite variety of molded designs was sufficient compensation for the loss of the artisan's touch is one of those matters of opinion the discussion of which can lead to broken friendships. But there is no arguing the point that from a production standpoint their use was labor-saving and timesaving, hence making for greater production at a lower cost, both important elements in meeting competition. Also, since such ware *could* be made cheaper than those completely "handmade," it could tap a wider market.

Full-size piece molds, a glassmaker's device as old as molded glass itself, were redis-covered sometime during the Western renaissance in glassmaking. Pazaurek says the "metal molds of several sections" were used in Venice and Germany in the sixteenth century and that, while never popular in Germany, in France they were used extensively in the eighteenth century for bottles and decanters.[1] Though we have no proof of their use in United States glasshouses before the nineteenth century it seems likely some were used to shape certain types of bottles, such as those for porter. The first *proof* we have found of their purpose being extended beyond mere form was in a February 16, 1810,* advertisement in the Pittsburgh *Gazette*. In it J. P. and J. W. Skelton, druggists, included among their various panaceas Dr. Robertson's Genuine Family Medicines, and at the end of the roster placed the following warning:

> Dr. Roberton's Family Medicines are put up in square flint glass bottles American manu-factured, with these words impressed on the glass—Dr. Robertson's Family Medicines, prepared only by T. W. Dyott.

Such a bottle for his medicines is just what would be imagined and wanted by so

*Since 1950 found in the *Federal Gazette and Baltimore Advertiser,* May 17, 1809.

ingenious a man as Thomas W. Dyott, who about 1807 started a patent-medicine business and soon tacked an M.D. after his name.² If, as is not unlikely, the medicines were shipped in demijohns to Pittsburgh* these advertised bottles may have been of local manufacture, probably Bakewell's or Robinson's. About two years later, after B. Bakewell and Co. had started their green-glass house, "Patent Medicine" bottles were mentioned among their bottle products.³ It seems to us that the word "patent" implied that names and inscriptions were molded in the bottles. From such bottles to the pictorial and historical flasks was a short step in moldmaking but a long one in design conception.

The category of historical and pictorial bottles and flasks is richer in variety of design, decorations, color, and interest than any other division of American blown-molded glass.⁴ And the historical flasks have a more opulent background of national traditions and historical significance than any other category of American glass except perhaps the pressed cup plates. Too, their numbers reflect the causes perhaps of such street names as Philadelphia's Drinkers Alley and Baltimore's Whiskey and Bottle alleys. Over four hundred flasks made prior to 1850 have been charted in groups according to their principal subjects or decorative motifs.⁵ Those bearing purely decorative motifs are classified under pictorial; under historical, those decorated with portrait busts of national heroes, Presidents, or other personages connected with notable events important in our national life and history; with emblems and symbols of our sovereignty, of societies and of political parties; with inscriptions related to the various subjects, or recording some famous sayings or popular slogans of the period. Many are embodiments of history in the making and all form, whether we like it or not, a part of our "cultural heritage." The designs are reflections of the democratic trend of the times. They reached the hands of the common man of slim resources and limited political privileges even more than those of his more fortunate fellow citizen. The makers of the flasks produced something entirely new in containers, but without a growing market acutely sensitive to national pride and politics there probably would have been few historical flasks. It could have been no mere coincidence that the designers of flasks turned to men and events at the same time ardent nationalism expanded or that the production of this type of flask grew with the growing vital masses of people whose political voice by the mid-1820s was gaining the right to be heard and would soon begin to speak with authority.⁶

Just when the first historical or pictorial flask was blown is still a matter of conjecture; it may have been as early as 1810 or during the War of 1812. As we have mentioned in connection with the Pitkin Glass Works, that house probably made a few of the varieties which, because of the treatment and type of decorative design and the shape, are considered representative of the first types originated. Below an American eagle on one of these flasks are the initials "J.P.F.", supposedly those of Jeremiah P. Foster, who, it is said, had been superintendent of the glassworks and took them over in 1810.⁷ Foster may well have signalized his new estate by a flask identified with himself—after all Thomas W. Dyott had his own name and portrait bust on some of his, for example No. 2, Plate 112. Beneath the cornucopia on the reverse of the "J.P.F." flask is "CONN," for Connecticut, bolstering the logic, if one may call it that, of the attribution. Again, since one variety of the Cornucopia-Urn flasks and two flasks of the 1824–35 period—a Horse-and-cart Railroad and a Lafayette-Masonic—were produced at the

*An illustration heading Dyott's March 4, 1820, ad in *The Union* depicts his drugstore, warehouse, and carboys or demijohns about to be loaded into a covered wagon drawn by two teams of horses. It is nearly identical with an engraving by Tiller from a drawing by the Philadelphia artist George Strickland (c. 1825 or possibly earlier) in which JACOB SLOUCH / PITTSBURGH appears on the cover of the wagon.

Mount Vernon Glass Works in central New York, it is possible that flasks of this species were made there soon after the house was started in 1810. Some of the other houses with which such flasks have been identified began operation during the war.

Whenever their birth, it was not many years before the pictorial and historical flasks, and their unadorned, full-size-molded brothers, completely replaced the lovely free-blown flasks, pattern-molded chestnuts, and the Pitkins, like those shown on Plates 105 and 106, which perhaps were less uniform in liquid capacity. Too, the color range of the pictorial and historical flasks was even more attractively wide than that of the free-blown and pattern-molded types. However, the colors natural to bottle glass predominated, that is, ambers, olive-ambers, olive-greens, and aquamarines with many nuances of tone. As nearly as one can judge by the surviving numbers in emerald and other greens, blues, amethysts, and related hues from deep reddish to the very rare purple, artificial colors were used lavishly. Also recent tests have proved a surprising number of the early flasks were fabricated from lead glass instead of the ordinary green or bottle glass, especially the heavy Sunburst and Masonics from Keene-Marlboro-Street, New Hampshire, and flasks from houses in the Pittsburgh area. Like the free-blown and the pattern-molded, the pictorial and historical flasks were predominantly of half-pint and pint sizes. The present records indicate that quart flasks, about one variety to ten in smaller sizes, were not made until after 1830 and then mainly in a few Eastern glasshouses, and that the quart calabash bottle came at the end of the first period, about 1850.

Whereas by the use of two or three dip molds and part-size piece molds a wide variation of design on flasks of nearly any desired size could be produced, each size and design of flask formed and decorated in a full-size mold necessitated an individual mold. In some instances, perhaps most, manufacturers purchased their glass molds, custom-made or perhaps stock designs, from makers of molds and dies. Others maintained their own moldmaking departments. Joshua Laird, who made the mold for the Washington-Eagle flask on Plate 112 for John Robinson of the Stourbridge Flint Glass Works, was a moldmaker in Pittsburgh prior to 1837.[8] Flasks showing close similarity in technique and lettering leave little doubt that Laird supplied many of the early bottle houses in the Pittsburgh-Monongahela area with their molds. He was sufficiently proud of or satisfied with Robinson's Washington-Eagle mold to sign it as sculptor. That the molds varied in quality of craftsmanship is evident from the flasks blown in them. By the flask, the mold is judged; few would have borne close scrutiny. In a select minority the designs were carefully modeled and detailed; in most, they were sketchy, sometimes little more than crude incised drawings. And one feels that deliberate advantage was taken of the refractive property of glass to create an illusion of modeling and realism. The molds for the Dyott-Franklin flask and Laird's Washington-Eagle, Plate 112, were far more skillfully sculptured than that for the later 1840 Harrison flask, Plate 114, which, as close examination of the flask reveals, was little more than a linear caricature of the man. In general it can be said that, with the usual one or two exceptions, the earlier the flask the more expertly sculptured and more elaborately detailed its mold. As the mid-century approached, the designs and their modeling became progressively simplified.

One of the most popular designs in the pictorial group was that of the "Scroll" flask molded in a decorative form suggesting the present name and fitted with "scrolled" ribs which usually enclosed or bordered a small neat motif such as a star, palmette, rosette, or anchor. Made over a period of many years, they probably were produced in more glasshouses and have survived in more sizes than any other design. In size they range from the extremely rare miniature to the rare gallon. The purely decorative motifs which predominated were the cornucopia and the eternal and universal sunburst, both of which graced some of the earliest of these flasks. A sunburst, so easily adapted to nearly any space or shape, was used on both sides of at least thirty varieties, on the reverse of one American Eagle and of two Scroll flasks. The cornucopia or horn of plenty, that symbol of prosperity so often an attendant to the personification of Peace, was chosen for at least thirty-six different flasks, mainly with the American eagle or an urn filled with produce on the other side, natural associations. But on the reverse of five Eagle flasks and three Geometric-medallion flasks there is an upside-down cornucopia spilling out its plenty. Perhaps in the inverted position the motif seemed to conform more harmoniously with the shape of the flasks. Whatever the designer's reason, the little half-pint inverted Cornucopia flasks are unusually attractive.

As might be expected in a period when Masonry was important and prominent, socially and politically, many flasks were designed to catch that market. Masonic emblems and symbols form the principal decoration on about forty pint and half-pint flasks of which examples are shown on Plates 110 and 113. On the reverse of the Masonic flasks there was usually an American eagle, quite distinctive in character and treatment. In most instances he was below a plain or an "E Pluribus Unum" pennant and often without one or more of the appurtenances of his office—his shield, thunderbolt, and olive branch. He was not so finely modeled as most of the eagles and, as a comparison of the one on Plate 110 with those on Plates 112 and 113 will illustrate, he was made stolid, quite lacking the verve and spirit of most others. By far the majority of Masonic flasks were produced in glasshouses in New England and New York, strongholds of Masonry. The largest number have been identified with the Keene-Marlboro-Street Glass Works, where the earliest were blown from flint glass, clear and of many colors—greens, blues, amethysts, and purples. On the other side of two, a Wheeling, (West) Virginia, and a Mantua, Ohio, flask, there was a portrait bust of Andrew Jackson. These probably were brought out during the 1824–28 presidential campaign, for west of the Alleghenies Jackson was not only a popular native war hero and a Mason but also the People's Choice. The other two Western Masonics had a bust of Lafayette on the obverse and were occasioned by his second visit to the United States in 1824, when he was feted by Masonic Lodges at nearly every stop. About 1830 the popularity of the Masonic flasks ceased; Masonry suffered an eclipse. Anti-Masonic sentiment aroused by reports of the notorious abduction in western New York and disappearance of Morgan, who had threatened to divulge the secrets of the order, provided the justification for an Anti-Masonic political party which was promoted and fostered by those who wished to alienate voters from the groups in power.

The emblems and symbols of the United States which were used as decorative subjects were the American flag, Columbia, and, of course, the American eagle. The flag flies on only a few and Columbia graces only six varieties, whereas the eagle appears on more flasks than does any other motif. Each of the molds having the flag and Columbia was well modeled, Columbia in particular, as befits a lady and as the example on Plate 113 shows. Aside from the Masonic flasks, the American eagle, inspired by the Great Seal of the United States, was rarely without his shield and seldom without his thunderbolt and olive branch. In most instances he was an exciting bird, seeming to embody the qualities attributed to him and in pose and treatment so akin to many of our coins that it seems logical to conclude that some of them were the moldmakers' model for him. Among the exceptions, the rare canteen-shaped Eagle bottle, Plate 111, is considered by collectors one of the most desirable of the Eagle flasks, even though the bird is poorly drawn. Rarity, it seems, more than compensates for lack of craftsmanship.

One woman and fifteen men were selected as subjects of portrait busts on flasks and calabash bottles. Many of the representations are unrecognizable and quite unidentifiable were it not for the inscriptions. Three having no names in their molds must be listed as unknown. Of the others all but one were of national and even international fame—five Presidents: George Washington, John Q. Adams, Andrew Jackson, William H. Harrison, and Zachary Taylor; Henry Clay, so long the perennial candidate for the position, Benjamin Franklin, Lafayette, De Witt Clinton, and two foreigners, Louis Kossuth and Jenny Lind. The one exception to contemporary fame was Thomas W. Dyott, M.D. But today he has his own Hall of Fame in nearly every collection of American bottles and flasks, deservedly, for more varieties of the known historically interesting flasks were created by him than by any other one producer. If the enterprising Dr. Dyott did not start making flasks after he acquired an interest in a New Jersey glasshouse, probably the Olive Glass Works at Glassboro, during the war period, he did early in the 1820s, when he was owner of the Kensington and Philadelphia Glass Works, later expanded into Dyottville. Moreover, the molds for his flasks of the 1820s, perhaps a little earlier and a little later too, were exceptional in quality of craftsmanship, as the surviving flasks blown in them testify, for instance the Dyott-Franklin, Plate 112. Dr. Dyott contributed so much color to the history of American glass and so many exciting flasks to the historical category that flattery of himself by placing his portrait with Benjamin Franklin's on at least four flasks calls only for an understanding smile. So far as we know he is the only owner of a glass factory immortalized in glass by more than initials.

Of course George Washington was a "natural" for a patriotic flask with appeal to all citizens of the United States. Nearly everyone had forgotten the accusations of monarchial aspirations so many had believed and continued to believe, although at his death he had been canonized by most of the press and the orators and in the hearts of most people as The Father of His Country. By the time of our second war probably few diehards remained who proposed such toasts as the one "Drank or *Drunk,* at Newton (Pennsylvania) in celebration of the *'Glorious triumph of Republicanism'*: 'GEN'L GEORGE WASHINGTON—MAY TRIBUTE DUE HIS MEMORY NOW BE FORGOTTEN!!!!' "[9] In the early period of the historical flasks, during which about half of the more than sixty varieties bearing his portrait bust appeared, Washington was depicted as the soldier in uniform, the commander in chief of the Revolutionary Armies, usually and appropriately with the American eagle on the reverse. Later, when time, while not dimming the glory of his military feats, had enhanced his achievements as our first President (and perhaps the cost of molds had increased) he was cast in a simple classical bust, the statesman. On some flasks, early and late, his bust was coupled with that of presidential aspirants. To adorn common whisky bottles with the likeness of our great has seemed close to sacrilege to some critics, or merely vulgar. Unsuitable and in bad taste as the practice may have been, it did not belittle the man or the country in the eyes of the citizens who bought the flasks, filled or unfilled. And if sometimes the buyers became even more vociferously proud of their heroes and their country, no great harm came to either. Washington himself probably would not have felt honored. Certainly the coupling of his portrait with that of Andrew Jackson as a potential president would not have pleased him by its implication of Jackson's equality to him as, of course, was the intent.

The major designs on the historical flasks, that is, the majority of them, were a new form of political propaganda in presidential campaigns or in the nature of souvenirs of memorable events or people, as well as novel packaging to catch the customers' attention. The bitter and ungentlemanly campaign which was waged between the adherents of John Quincy Adams and Andrew Jackson from 1824 through 1828 certainly was not the first in which liquor was used either as a goad or a persuader but it doubtless was the first in which liquor containers played a part. The democratic forces were mustering their numbers to form a new party, especially in the West, less tradition-bound and class-conscious than the East. Jackson was their man—a fellow Westerner fast becoming the Champion of the Common Man and advocate of moving the Indian tribes farther into the West. But in the East, too, especially among the immigrant laborers, the Jacksonian ranks were swelling. Adams was painted by the political brush as a king-lover, an aristocrat, and a man of intrenched privilege. John Q. Adams had little attraction for John Q. Public. Even as late as 1834 the old campaign songs were timely. One verse is typical:

> While Johnny was gorging the fat of the land,
> And bartering for cod, d'y see,
> Brave Jackson was feeding his patriot band
> On nuts from the Hickory tree,—
>> The ground was his bed
>> While the bold hero fed
>> On nuts of the hickory tree.[10]

But Adams had one partisan in the Pittsburgh area who made, or caused to be made, a mold for a pint flask having a portrait bust of Adams on one side and the American eagle on the other. Old Hickory had more Eastern supporters; Coventry and Keene-Marlboro-Street each put out two Washington-Jackson flasks. Of seven Western flasks, two with Masonic emblems, five having caricature-like portraits of Jackson combined once with an elaborate floral medallion and four times with the American eagle, five were from molds undoubtedly made by Joshua Laird. Jackson's hair was standing on end, probably in horror over the alleged Clay-Adams Secretary-of-State deal.

Henry Clay also was the subject of historical flasks, though strangely enough the only ones definitely known to have existed, those advertised in 1824 by Pugh and Teeter of Moscow, Ohio, are yet to be identified. Nor can it be said whether they were in celebration of the American System victory so inextricably woven into Clay's career or of his role as presidential favorite. However, the exceptionally realistic but unnamed portrait bust on three quart flasks from the Baltimore and one from the Bridgeton Glass

Works seem to portray Henry Clay. The flasks, characteristic of the 1840s, doubtless were put out during the 1844 campaign when Clay finally obtained a party's nomination at a time, unfortunately, when issues of slavery, anti-Masonry, and the annexation of Texas, to name a few, were so personal, sharp, and bitter that the man who had earned the title of The Great Compromiser was not acceptable to the people.

The 1840 and 1848 Whig battles with the Democrats brought forth portrait flasks of their successful presidential candidates, William Henry Harrison and Zachary Taylor. The Log Cabin and Hard Cider 1840 campaign was the most tumultuous our young country had yet seen, and it was thoroughly enjoyed. The actual issues submerged by trivia made the political spree the more emotional. As never before, and never afterward outdone, newspaper diatribes and stump speeches were supplemented by slogans and emblems in tangible form made from nearly every available material, including glass. Among the glass items were two or three flasks, presumably for hard cider, a favorite drink of the common people, and a taste, according to the Democrats, shared with Harrison. All three flasks, rare today, were made somewhere in the Pittsburgh-Monongahela district. One is illustrated on Plate 114. On one side the voter saw the portrait bust of Harrison in uniform, and on the other the fabled log cabin with the cider barrel near its hospitable door and the plow to remind him that Harrison was a poor farmer ever willing to leave his plow in its furrow to help save his country from the corruption of undemocratic forces and the Eastern aristocrats, as he had once saved it from the Indians and the British for the Western pioneers. If the voter had been subjected to the classical schooling of the day all this was symbolized by the current Whig headline, "The Cincinnatus of the West." Another flask, GX-22,[11] featured the American flag, the log cabin, the cider barrel and plow—all derisively attached to Harrison only to backfire on the Democrats—and bore the words "Hard Cider." The third flask, GII-9, pictorialized its message a little more subtly. On one side it had the American eagle drawn from our Seal and on the other the eagle in flight with the snake of corruption in his beak. It mattered little that Harrison was far from a practicing farmer, that he had never lived in a log cabin, that he was actually a gentleman of some means: the propaganda worked. Perhaps in part at least it was effective because so very many of the voters could put on the shoes so rashly fitted to Harrison by the Democrats.

In 1848 Zachary Taylor, another soldier untainted by expressed political views on the hot and splitting issues of the day, had been nominated seemingly as the result of the spontaneous combustion of the people's wishes. He stated emphatically that he would neither be brought before the people as the candidate of any party nor would he be the exponent of any party doctrines.[12] The build-up started soon after his impressive Buena Vista victory over the Mexicans in 1847 and it reached a mighty crescendo at the Washington Birthday celebrations in 1848. Ostensibly Taylor and the public which elected him were convinced that he was "drafted." With the exception of two Taylor-American Eagle flasks which undoubtedly are earlier, all the twenty-eight or more depicting him in uniform were of that political campaign. On about twenty, made chiefly at the Dyottville Glass Works, the classical bust of Washington was on the obverse, giving graphic reality to the current comparisons of Taylor to Washington

[98]

as a military hero, a statesman, and even as The Father of His Country. The majority have an appropriate inscription arching above the portrait bust such as "I have endeavored to do my duty," "General Taylor Never Surrenders," and "A Little More Grape Captain Bragg." This last became a much-quoted Taylorism shortly after the Battle of Buena Vista when a letter from an eyewitness was published in several newspapers.[13] Of this, one of the many incidents described, he said, "While Bragg was slaying them, right, left and center, Gen. Taylor quietly rode up behind him without being observed, and in an undertone of voice said *'A little more grape, Capt. Bragg!'* These few words so completely inspirited him and his men, that they fired with redoubled vigor, and the result shows the effect of, *'a little more grape.'* " For the reverse of the remaining flasks the American eagle was used on two; the Baltimore monument commemorating the lives lost in defending the city in 1812[14] on one; the bust of Major Samuel Ringgold, Maryland's Mexican War hero, on two; and on two more a cornstalk and the slogan "Corn for the World." On the obverse of the Ringgold and "Corn for the World" flasks the bust of Taylor is accompanied by his most famous sobriquet, "Rough and Ready." These are attributed to the Baltimore Glass Works. One of the last, an obvious attempt at portraiture, is shown on Plate 114. Perhaps the model was the portrait painted in Mexico in 1847.[15]

Visits of two foreigners and an adopted son were among the notable events publicized or celebrated in flasks and calabash bottles. One was that of Jenny Lind, the Swedish Nightingale, brought to this country by P. T. Barnum in 1850 and paid $1000 a concert, and all expenses;[16] another, that of Louis Kossuth, the Hungarian revolutionary patriot who found that, while our sympathies with democracy's struggles were ardent, our government was coldly cautious in foreign affairs. And in 1824 Lafayette, honorary citizen of the United States, arrived to pay his last visit. Of the portrait flasks, celebrating this event, some prepared before his arrival, fourteen have been recorded. However, without the identifying name molded in the glass, our most feted guest would never be recognized. The subjects on the reverse, in addition to Masonic emblems of which one is illustrated on Plate 110, were the American eagle, the French liberty cap and pole (he was a patriot of French as well as American democracy), and De Witt Clinton. Two of the Masonics were products of the Mount Vernon Glass Works; Masonics, Liberty Cap, and Clinton, of the Coventry Glass Works. In 1825 not only Lafayette was being lionized but also Clinton, whose Ditch at last mingled the waters of Lake Erie with those of the Hudson.[17]

On the invitation of sponsors of internal improvements Clinton made a grand tour West to attend the ceremonies at the beginning of the Ohio Canal. In the West he was considered almost as responsible for the advancement of internal improvements as Henry Clay. Moreover, he was as important a guest as Lafayette and citizens traveled as far to see him.[18]

The country-wide interest in the American System, or in less cryptic terms a governmental policy of extended improvements of internal transportation facilities and higher tariffs to protect our manufacturers and, incidentally, help finance the internal improvements, was expressed in two main varieties of flasks, the American System and the Railroads. The American System flasks were a manifestation of Pittsburgh's ap-

PLATE 8

1. Pitcher blown from bluish-aquamarine non-lead bottle or window glass; globular body, wide cylindrical neck flaring slightly to plain rim with wide pinched lip, applied large hollow knop stem and broad circular foot; applied small solid semi-ear-shaped handle; body decorated with superimposed gather tooled into lily-pad Type II; neck threaded to rim; in the hollow knop a United States silver half dime dated 1829. New York State. Circa 1835–50.

Height, $6\frac{7}{16}$"; top diameter, 3"; greatest diameter of body, $3\frac{1}{2}$"; diameter of foot, $3\frac{5}{16}$".

2. Sugar bowl and cover blown from bluish-aquamarine non-lead bottle or window glass; globular body contracted at top below high galleried rim and resting on applied large hollow knop stem and broad circular foot; high domed cover with applied large hollow ball supporting an applied chicken finial; bowl and cover, with superimposed gather tooled into lily-pad Type II; in the hollow knop of the bowl, a United States silver half dime dated 1829, and in the hollow ball of the cover, a similar coin dated 1835. New York State. Circa 1835–50.

Over-all height, 11"; height without cover, $6\frac{11}{16}$"; top diameter, $4\frac{1}{4}$"; greatest diameter of body, $5\frac{5}{16}$"; diameter of foot, $4\frac{1}{16}$"; diameter of cover at rim, $3\frac{7}{8}$".

This set, unique as far as we know, was inherited by a member of a New York State family but with no definite history as to the particular glasshouse in which it was made. The characteristics would indicate a strong probability of its having been made at either Redwood or Redford Glass Works. One other similar pitcher with a silver half dime in the hollow knop of the stem is known, and that also turned up in central New York State. Inherited with the sugar bowl and pitcher was a free-blown aquamarine footed pitcher with a pale amber applied rim.

proval of the twin policies—excepting the Cumberland Road, of course. That phrase was as common in the early 1820s as the New Deal is today, and as praise-evoking or ire-provoking. It was also as closely identified with one protagonist, who in the case of the American System was Henry Clay. Still, while to the country at large Henry Clay was considered the father of the American System, to Pittsburgh and its neighbors he was only its godfather; Henry Baldwin, "the darling of Pennsylvania and the pride of Pittsburgh," [19] was the father. In so far as they were concerned Henry Baldwin had secured singlehanded the substantial raise in the duties on iron and cut glass in 1818. The same year he was re-elected to Congress after a hard-won fight on an American System platform.[20] Though the 1820 tariff bill, dubbed a "Pittsburgh, a cut-glass bill," [21] was defeated, he came out fighting for that of 1824. At home he was given credit for its passage. Twice Baldwin was given enthusiastic ovations upon his return home from Congress, in 1822 and again in 1824 when the men of industry held a thanksgiving banquet in his honor.[22] Since Pittsburgh's spotlight of interest was focused most directly on the System and its champion in the years from 1818 through 1824 we believe the three varieties of American System flasks were made during those years. One is illustrated on Plate 111.

In the late 1820s the imagination of the country was caught by a momentous innovation in transportation which, if it proved practical, would solve the problems of vast distances, poor roads, spring thaws, and winter freezes. Railroads—lines of wooden rails over which horse-drawn carts could travel—were initiated. Early in the 1830s the steam locomotive began to replace natural horsepower. This new means of transportation at the time was more important to the East than to the West, though important to all sections since Jackson's veto of the Maysville Road in 1830 blasted hopes of a national road system. It was the subject of twelve known varieties of Railroad flasks, all made in Eastern glasshouses, and the first probably before 1830. A horse and cart on rails appears on both sides of seven, the reverse of three American Eagle, and one Symbolical figure. These were made in Coventry, Keene-Marlboro-Street, Mount Vernon, and the Baltimore Glass Works. Two flasks having a locomotive and the inscription "Success to the Railroad" have been attributed to the Lancaster Glass Works, established in 1849, at Lancaster, New York. Perhaps they were occasioned by the New York Central's reaching Lancaster and making the town one of its stops en route to Buffalo.[23] The continued excitement over Railroads as their networks spread across the country doubtless explains the fact that the popularity of even the Horse and Cart varieties was still strong in the forties. The mold for the Mount Vernon Glass Works' variety was used at Mount Pleasant near Saratoga after the works were moved there in 1844.

Among ships decorating bottles and flasks were two United States vessels of war: the steam frigate *Mississippi* because it brought Kossuth's family to this country and the brig *Franklin*, for reasons which are a matter of conjecture. The "*Franklin* 74" was built and launched with great fanfare in 1815 at Philadelphia,[24] which was also the home of the Kensington Glass Works, where some of the few ship *Franklin* flasks were made by Thomas W. Dyott. Two of these bear the inscription "Free Trade and Sailor Rights," the battle cry of the War of 1812, probably taken from one of Henry Clay's war-inciting speeches in which he used the phrase "Free Trade and Seamen's Rights." It was carried over into peacetime through adoption by the Free Traders. The *"Franklin 74,"* which became the flagship of the Pacific fleet in 1821, was looked upon as a protector of our trading rights both when she was launched and when she was in the Pacific.[25] Consequently either occasion could have inspired the flasks.

Less interesting pictorially and historically but doubtless more important in the competitive struggle between the European and United States glasshouses for the American market were the tablewares also molded in full-size piece molds but in patterns imitating cut glass, which was the glass of luxury and fashion. Actually two types of full-size molded ware were evolved to simulate cut glass, namely Blown Three Mold[26] and a heavy variety which, for lack of a known trade name, we shall call "imitation cut glass." Generally the creation of the latter is credited to Britain, probably Ireland, but whether the former, the Blown Three Mold, originated in Britain or the United States is not established as yet. Arguments can be marshaled for each thesis and the conclusion still remains a matter of opinion. However, there is no doubt that it was made on both sides of the Atlantic and that the production of this non-luxury glass, while very limited in output and in number of patterns and articles in Ireland and in England (if made there at all), was almost unlimited in all these aspects in the United States.[27]

It is thought that the forerunners of the tablewares in this type of glass were in the form of bottles—large castors and decanter bottles—which were introduced during or soon after the War of 1812. While several varieties and patterns have been recorded we know of only two which have exact cut-glass prototypes and also Irish or possibly English molded counterparts, both of which were often put in silver castors. These two varieties, which one would expect to be the earliest since they do have British mates, were hexagonal cruets and bottles, blown in three-piece molds in a pattern of a band of vertical ribbing below one of diamond diapering (GII-16),[28] and square cruets and castors or decanter bottles, blown in two-piece molds also with a band of vertical ribbing below one of diamond diapering but with fan fluting on the shoulder (GII-28) like the deep amethyst square example, No. 4, Plate 87. Both patterns were used for bottles molded from clear and artificially colored lead glass and from non-lead green glass in its natural colors. In fact Keene-Marlboro-Street is so likely a source that we attribute certain of these bottles to it rather confidently, the one illustrated for example. The basis for the attribution is the similarity between a large proportion of the colored decanter bottles and Keene Masonic and Sunburst flasks in colors, metal, and weight of lead and non-lead glass, a similarity so close that one feels sure a chemical analysis would reveal an identity of composition in many instances.

Whether the first of these bottles was made at Keene-Marlboro-Street is, however, another matter. It is, we believe, far from impossible that they were introduced in clear glass by Thomas Cains, who, by renting the flint-glass furnace which he persuaded the Boston Crown Glass Company to erect in its South Boston works during the War of 1812,[29] became "the father of the flint-glass business in the Atlantic States." [30] He may have brought the idea with him when he arrived from England in the spring of 1812 or he may have originated it. (Of course this is all speculation, justified, we trust, because speculation sometimes establishes a starting point for searching out facts.) Perhaps the

"Castors and Vinegar Cruets" advertised without descriptive adjective on November 29, 1815,[31] were of this type. Perhaps, too, the use of the full-size mold had already been extended and the "Best double flint half-pint tumblers figured" were in a molded cut-glass pattern. Since "cut" and "engraved" occur in the advertisement, "figured," it seems likely, had another significance, one which, logically, could have been "molded."

Whether it happened in England or Ireland, in South Boston or Keene, the extension of the use of the full-size mold from bottles to other articles was an inevitable progression in tableware production. The carriage trade demanded cut glass, therefore cut glass was the most desirable of all glassware and it was the most expensive for both its maker and its buyer. The success of a glassware resembling or imitating cut glass sufficiently to catch and hold the custom of the growing number of those for whom cut glass was beyond pocketbook reach was almost axiomatic. Any pattern that could be cut on glass by the wheels of the glass cutter could be duplicated in a full-size piece mold. These molds might be a heavy initial investment but that would soon be covered by the cut in production costs and increased unit output since handwork on many articles could be reduced to a minimum and the labor of one or more highly paid skilled glass cutters completely eliminated. Considerations such as these, among others, probably led to the imitation cut glass and Blown Three Mold. Moreover, in glassmaking, as in other fields, the spirit of innovation was abroad.

Blown Three Mold, Contact-three-section-mold-glass, Stiegel, Stoddard, Blown-molded, Insufflated, Three Mold, to give it all the names by which it has been or is known, is like a foundling left on a doorstep: no one knows its name, if it ever had one. Since the glass was *not* a product of either the Stiegel or the Stoddard glasshouses, and the other names, in our opinion, are even more misleading as to the glass so named, we continue to call it Blown Three Mold, the familiar name for the past quarter century or more. Whether this type of ware preceded, followed, or developed concurrently with the "imitation cut glass" is still a matter of conjecture. In any event it appears to have been more popular in the United States than in Britain and to have reached the peak of its production and popularity in the late 1820s.

It, like glass in other categories, had its inherent identifying characteristics arising from its designs and the method of its fabrication. In general the glass, especially that blown from clear lead metal, has a liveliness of appearance akin to that of cut glass, though its liquid brilliance is to the brilliance of cut glass as the glow of polished pewter to that of silver. Quality of metal, contours of pattern, and type of molding, all together determined the degree and quality of brilliance. But the method of molding determined the type of impression from the mold, wherein lies one of the distinctive characteristics of the glass, namely, a softness and rounding of edges without being so diffuse as on pattern-molded glass and in contrast to the usual definitiveness of planes and edges on cut glass or on the later mechanically pressed imitations of cut glass. The difference in the appearance of the three types of decoration—that is, pattern-molded, full-size molded, and wheel-cut—is apparent from a comparison of the Midwest pattern-molded and Blown Three Mold flip glasses on Plate 80 and the Blown Three Mold and wheel-cut celery glasses on Plate 50. Equally inherent identifying characteristics, and more easily recognized, are the nature of the mold marks and the concavo-convex relationship of the inner and outer surfaces of the individual pieces. Except in the rare instances in which an abnormally heavy gather of metal was used, wherever there is a protuberance on the outside there is a corresponding hollow on the inside of a piece. The mold marks, whether they be two, three, or four in number (in ninety-nine out of a hundred pieces we have found three), are faint vertical linear expressions from the mold, about the width of a heavily penciled line and no more defined and sharp than such a line appears on the reverse. Frequently when reheating and manipulation were required to fashion the object the marks were partially obliterated and are consequently difficult to locate.

About 150 characteristic patterns of Blown Three Mold glass have been recorded and classified in three main groups according to the predominant motif: namely, Geometric, Arch, and Baroque. Naturally, since the type of ware was inspired by cut glass, many of the patterns, in the Geometric group principally, faithfully reproduce those of cut glass and others are plainly derivative. Many seem more becoming to glass when it was molded rather than cut, perhaps because of the softened contours. Still the designers not only shuffled the same old motifs for a new deal in combinations but also, it seems, originated a few patterns of their own, especially in the Arch and Baroque groups.

The patterns in the small Arch group of about eight have either a Roman or a Gothic arch as the most conspicuous motif. Two of the most interesting of these patterns are illustrated by the pitcher, No. 4, Plate 43, probably made by the New England Glass Company, and the Sandwich decanter, No. 3, Plate 85, which has the molded word "NIƆ" upside down and reversed. As yet only one Arch pattern and four Geometric have been recorded which include the name of a liquor, though this method of labeling was a logical step from the engraved and enameled labels which succeeded the silver and other "ticket" necklaces for decanters. All the patterns have "WINE," "RUM," and "BRANDY"; all but one—GI-8—have "GIN." The Sandwich version of GI-29, the pattern of the Mount Vernon carafe, No. 1, Plate 87, has an "H. GIN" (Holland Gin), and quart decanters in Sandwich's GIII-2 Type II like the flip, No. 3, Plate 80, has a "CHERRY". Besides the liquors mentioned the Arch and Fern comes with "WHISKEY". This pattern and GII-27 are the only ones in which we have record at the moment of labeled pint decanters. The pint Arch and Fern has "GIN" and "WHISKEY"; GII-27, "BRANDY". So far as we know at present these labeled decanters occur only in the American Blown Three Mold glass, in which they are either scarce or rare.[32]

The Baroque patterns, about twenty-five in number, have simple arabesques and motifs such as hearts, palmettes, shells, and gadroonlike ribs. Four of these patterns are illustrated on Plate 43. These Baroque patterns, like the Arch, are in comparatively high relief and the motifs of more generous proportions than those of the Geometric. Also whereas the Geometric are tight and compact like the cut glass of the day, the Arch and Baroque are usually free and flowing in line. The sharp contrast between typical Geometric patterns and those in the two other groups is well demonstrated by the decanters on Plate 86 and the pitcher and creamers on Plate 43. They illustrate also typical shapes of the period. The number of articles molded in the Arch and Baroque patterns was limited largely to decanters and pitchers, a few cruet bottles and tumblers.

As the name indicates, geometric motifs, mainly rectilinear, form the patterns in the Geometric groups. In a few a single motif has been used; in most, two or more, as a rule in horizontal bands. Ribbing is the predominating motif. Hardly more than half a dozen patterns have been recorded without ribbing in some one of its many forms: vertical, horizontal, herringbone, swirled, or spiraled; rounded or flat; broad or narrow; long or short. Vertical, horizontal, and diagonal flutes, also convex or concave circles and ovals as beading, have been used sparingly. The most elaborate of the motifs are the sunbursts and the diamond motifs.³³ There are three of the latter, each having a plain field and a ringed center; and eleven of the former. The sunbursts progress, or from a design point of view perhaps retrogress, from the simple sunburst with its beams radiating from its focus as on the decanter, No. 5, Plate 87, through nine steps to the most complex, the sunburst-in-square, which forms the middle band on the flip on Plate 80. With the exception of three, the other sunbursts appear in the patterns of articles illustrated on Plates 10, 24, 34, 41, 42, 75, 80, and 86. Like their sunbursts, the Geometric patterns seem to have progressed from utter simplicity of design to one of extreme ornateness, falling naturally into three groups on their way. Group I contains the simplest of the patterns, those composed mainly of flutings and ribbings, of which the rare sugar bowl, No. 4, Plate 34, is an example; Group II, principally of ribbings or flutings and diamond diapering in bands or blocks; Group III, a diamond or a sunburst motif in addition to the others. The decanters on Plates 86 and 87 illustrate typical patterns in Groups II and III. The rare tumbler, Plate 81, with a band of ribbing which might be called angular-festoon, is in a class by itself: being inscribed "WELCOME LAFAYETTE", it is the only pattern of historical significance as yet recorded in Blown Three Mold.

From an analysis of the pieces and the surviving numbers there is no doubt that Blown Three Mold, particularly in its Geometric patterns, was a type of tableware made on a scale approaching mass production. There were decanters, from miniature to over a quart in capacity, bottles and carafes and their companion drinking vessels—cordials and punch cups, mugs and wines, goblets and tumblers ranging from whisky to flip glasses. There were dishes of many sizes; small plates; and bowls, large and small, with and without a foot or standard. There were preserve pots with cover and stand, celery glasses, pitchers from miniature to water size holding a quart or more, and sugar bowls, sometimes with their matching creamers. In fact there were most of the articles which the auctioneers and importers of fine cut glass after the war and during the lush 1820s felt should be listed in their notices. And besides the table glass there were hats and inkwells, lamp fonts and night lamps, and individual pieces like the little Keene inkwell on Plate 10. Most of these articles were fabricated from clear or colored flint (lead) glass, but an interesting minority were made from bottle glass. They consisted of the decanters, bottles, and inkwells in particular which were blown in houses where bottles constituted the main output or part of it. These last, as a rule, were drab olive-ambers and olive-greens, occasionally aquamarine and light greens. Naturally by far the greatest number of the flint-glass pieces were colorless but, fortunately for the collector, there was a goodly proportion in blues, sometimes a light hue, sometimes a true sapphire, principally a deep purple-blue appearing amethyst when held to an electric light. While, as in the eighteenth century, blue was the color most favored, amethysts, true even when in daylight, and emerald-greens were made sparingly. One or two pieces in canary-yellow are known. Also there were pieces, like the heliotrope tumbler on Plate 10, in odd tones defying verbal description and possibly puzzling their makers as well; whether they were achieved by intent or by accident is a question.

Even more than the great number of Blown Three Mold pieces surviving the hazards of usage and time, the anatomy of individual pieces has revealed that it must have been a popular ware produced in many glasshouses, especially in the 1820s. The present survey has been based on the examination of well over five thousand pieces of this glass. More than one thousand were analyzed to determine the molds in which they were patterned. That analysis established that more than *four hundred* basic individual molds were used in their making. From our present data it appears that the basic molds for the production of all articles of tableware were bottle molds from gill to quart or more in size and in the various shapes and patterns for castors, cruets, and decanters; for bottle stoppers; and for tumblers from gill to large flip size, in barrel or cylindrical shape. Of course there were molds for a few other articles, for instance inkwells and lamp fonts. In one pattern alone, GII-18, having a band of diamond diapering between bands of vertical ribbing and a variety of base designs, we have determined more than fifty molds made for bottles, decanters, tumblers, castors, or inkwells. And these molds were used also to pattern such articles as salt cellars, dishes, hats, pitchers, sugar bowls, celery glasses, and bowls with and without foot. The unusual example of the former shown on Plate 20 was patterned in a decanter mold and its flaring foot in another mold, one having a sunburst pattern. In other words, in the fabrication of most articles of Blown Three Mold (other than the bottle and tumbler forms) the full-size mold was used almost solely to set the pattern, that is, as a pattern-mold of either the dip or the part-size piece type was used. And the piece was fashioned mainly by offhand methods, its ultimate form shaped by manipulation, frequently having little resemblance to that of the mold in which it was patterned. Consequently the creation of a Blown Three Mold sugar bowl, for example, like those on Plate 34, took as much or nearly as much of the blower's time and skill as the pattern-molded bowls on Plate 2. Probably the example, No. 5, Plate 34, took more time than the Stiegel type, for its foot was pattern-molded. Nevertheless, since so many of the articles, bottles, and tumblers, for instance, necessitated little or no more handwork than the shearing of a rim or turning of a flange, Blown Three Mold represented a considerable saving in labor and time as well as a substitute for cut glass on the Empire and possibly early Victorian tables of the "middling classes."

From the geographical distribution of the Blown Three Mold glass which has been collected it would appear that this manifestation of blown-molded glass was a specialty of Eastern rather than of Midwestern glasshouses. It must have been included in the molded wares made and advertised by many of the glasshouses of its period which were devoted chiefly to the production of tablewares. Unfortunately, since most of them were located in cities and towns, any physical evidence which might have been found on their sites has long since been destroyed. Consequently it may not be surprising that fewer than one third of the recorded patterns and considerably fewer than a third of the individual molds which have been determined can be attributed to specific glasshouses. That even those attributions can be made is largely because of excavations on factory sites.

The excavations of the late Harry Hall White on the sites of the Mantua and Kent, Ohio, glasshouses and of the Keene-Marlboro-Street, the Coventry and the Mount Vernon glasshouses in New Hampshire, Connecticut, and New York respectively, unearthed fragments in sufficient quantity to establish the certainty of production in certain Geometric patterns.[34] Those of Francis L. Wynn on the site of the Boston and Sandwich Glass Company's factory, combined with other determining factors, indicated that Sandwich, as long believed, produced the ware on a large scale in patterns falling in all three main groups.[35] Actually the output of the other proven sources may have been minuscule by comparison. Several of the patterns were used by more than one of the houses. One mold in the pattern, GII-33, having a band of diamond diapering between bands of vertical flutes, has been identified with Mantua, but this pattern, in which the unique bowl and the decanter on Plates 19 and 86 were molded, was not used at Mantua only. This is likewise true of the two patterns used at Kent, one of which is illustrated by the bowl on Plate 14. Three patterns (used principally for inkwells) have been identified with Coventry; five patterns with Keene; four with Mount Vernon; and at least twenty-six with Sandwich. The commonest pattern in the entire category, GII-18, was common to all these Eastern houses. Mount Vernon and Sandwich both used the Geometric pattern of ribs and fan flutes, GI-29, in which the Mount Vernon carafe, No. 1, Plate 87, was molded. Also they combined the sunburst-in-square with broad vertical and swirled ribbings in a comparatively simple pattern. The Sandwich variation is illustrated by the flip glass, No. 3, Plate 80. Except for a slight difference in the treatment of the sunburst, their patterns were nearly identical. The flip glasses, Nos. 1 and 3, Plate 80; three creamers, Plate 43; punch cup, No. 1, Plate 75; small glass, No. 2, Plate 79; cordial, No. 1, Plate 61, and quart "NIƆ" decanter, No. 3, Plate 85, were molded in other Sandwich patterns and show the factory's tendency toward elaboration in design. Two Keene patterns are illustrated by the rare inkwell with little applied birds perched on its rim, Plate 10, and the aquamarine decanter with sunburst having a bull's-eye center, similar to that of some Keene Sunburst flasks, Plate 86, No. 2. These pieces demonstrate not only typical patterns from known sources but also shapes and detail treatments characteristic of the period.

At present only about a baker's dozen of all the remaining patterns can be attributed with any degree of certainty to either a glasshouse or a region. One Geometric, one Baroque, and three of the Arch patterns, one illustrated by the large pitcher, Plate 43, undoubtedly were among those which the New England Glass Company used for its common run of wares.[36] Inasmuch as the scarce pieces molded in the three Geometric patterns, GII-32, GIII-10 and 11, have been found almost exclusively in the Midwest, it is probable that these patterns were used by one or more of the Midwestern houses specializing in tablewares. Among these pieces are the amethyst sugar bowl and creamer, Plate 9, which, by their very shapes, lend credence to the theory. The creamer is typical of the early nineteenth-century Midwest pitchers and the sugar bowl, with its eighteenth-century proportions and the nineteenth-century galleried rim and typical double-domed pattern-molded cover, is likewise purely Midwest.

Seven other Geometric patterns in Groups I and II, including GII-28 and 16 which have been discussed in connection with the large cruets and square decanters, were as British as they were American. However, Blown Three Mold glass in England and Ireland was restrained in its number of patterns and motifs. Only ribs, or, as the British call them, pillar flutes, and diamonds were employed; such motifs as the sunbursts were not carried over from cut glass to the molded. Moreover, the number of articles and the quantity produced was limited; not, certainly, because Britain did not have her classes unable to indulge in the luxury of cut glass but because their wants were met by other types of ware.

Blown Three Mold glass was in that twilight zone between the brilliance of craftsmanship and the darkness of mechanization in production of the ordinary wares. In the "imitation cut glass" the glassmaker seems to have come even closer in some respects not only to simulating cut glass but also to a final transfer of craftsmanship from the glass blowers to the moldmakers. It was molded in patterns composed from simple motifs, principally shallow diamonds, usually in blocks or diaper bands as in Blown Three Mold glass, and ribbings—chiefly vertical, horizontal, curved, sometimes forming a fan. Each piece was made from a generous gather of metal so that it was quite heavy, varying from an eighth to a quarter of an inch in thickness. And it looked stolid, as a rule quite lacking the sparkle and life of the glass it imitated, perhaps because so much metal was used and its contours rounded. In contradistinction to that of Blown Three Mold glass its inner surface was almost always even and smooth as on cut glass or the finest of the pressed glass. While an overwhelming majority of the pieces were made from clear glass, artificial colors were made occasionally. A few colored salts have been recorded. It would appear from the articles found today that the output in the United States, at least, consisted mainly of salts, dishes, and sugar bowls. The salts were of many shapes, with and without foot or standard; the dishes, round, oval, and octagon; the sugar bowls, globular with circular foot or, rarely, rectangular, as No. 2, Plate 32, similar to Staffordshire sugar bowls of the early nineteenth century. The dishes were formed either in piece molds or shallow molds such as those used in blowing blanks for oval and octagonal dishes for cutting. Probably the molds for blanks gave some ingenious glassman the idea of having an incised pattern to simulate a cut design.

Among the many reasons for believing that production of this type of ware began before 1820 is the fact that by 1817 the oval, round, and octagonal cut-glass dishes were sufficiently popular to be mentioned specifically in auctioneers' and merchants' listings of imported glass. A sketch of one of the octagonal dishes was used by the New York City firm of glass cutters, Jackson and Baggott, at the head of their April 1819 advertisement announcing the opening of their store at 36 Maiden Lane.[37] Moreover, molded fan-end salts which undoubtedly belonged in this category of imitation cut glass were among the articles listed in the announcements, made in the Boston papers, of the New England Glass Company's wares to be sold at auction on October 16, 1819.[38] In Ireland, we understand from Mr. Westropp, the authority on Irish glass, this type of molded ware was being made in limited quantities around 1830, but how long it was made in the United States we do not know. It seems probable that little was made after mechanically pressed glass became popular.

By 1829 at least six Eastern and four Midwest glasshouses were pressing glass on a commercial scale. Henceforth in so far as most of the non-luxury tableware and ornamental glass were concerned craftsmanship was to be in the hands of the moldmaker. For many decades the luxury wares were to be almost totally under foreign domination and freedom of expression in glass was to be found mainly in the small bottle and window glasshouses of the United States where blowers continued to fashion individual pieces.

INDIVIDUAL PIECES FROM NINETEENTH-CENTURY BOTTLE AND WINDOW GLASSHOUSES

THE collector of American glass, especially one seeking examples purely and simply exemplifying the art of the glass blower, must be everlastingly thankful that part of our heritage from the Old World was the custom of blowing and fashioning individual pieces by the oldest traditional techniques. In the houses devoted to table and ornamental ware production this custom was followed to a limited extent for the purpose of making gifts or, perhaps, to show off skill. It prevailed mainly in the many bottle and window glasshouses. During the late eighteenth and early nineteenth centuries, mainly in those houses removed from the most populous and fashionable centers, besides the gifts and whimseys, articles of table and utility ware were produced on a small scale for the housewives of the community, probably of the nearby towns also, and for the neighboring tavernkeepers. Most early window glasshouses had a "corner pot" or two of metal for such wares, made from the same ingredients as the window glass but not rendered colorless. Since the materials were usually more nearly free from impurities than those used for ordinary bottles, the color of uncleared batch was generally on the light green side of the spectrum. Consequently most individual pieces blown in the window glasshouses are aquamarine or some tint of light green, whereas those from bottle houses occur in all colors natural to glass. Mr. Isaac Craig informed Joseph Weeks, who made the government's 1880 survey of manufactures, that he remembered seeing tumblers and decanters made from green glass (type of glass, not color), presumably at the Pittsburgh Glass Works started by James O'Hara and Isaac Craig. "In the old days," he said, "decanters were used in every house, most commonly by the poorer families, who could not afford cut glass."[1]

Generally speaking, the gulf between the tumblers, decanters, and other articles blown from the window and green glass and those from flint (lead) glass was as wide as that between the common people using the humble unpretentious pieces and the wealthy and well-to-do using fine and stylish glassware. The pieces blown from window and bottle glass, even while following a type, retained a distinct individuality, whereas the finer glass, no matter how perfectly made, was stereotyped in conformity with whatever fashion was ruling the day, a circumstance arising largely from the conditions under which they were made. The blower in a commercial tableware factory was an employee hired to execute the designs of his employer, who rarely deviated from the styles popular at the moment; by comparison the blower in the bottle or window glassworks was a free lance, restricted mainly by the limitations of his own skill, taste, and creative ability. One

[109]

reason the individual pieces sometimes are called American folk art in glass is that they do not conform to a sophisticated fashion but are traditional. There is no doubt they were made for the folk of the country. Certainly it is quite unlikely that sugar bowls and creamers, candlesticks and salt cellars like those shown on Plates 3, 5, 6, and 7 ever rested on the mahogany of Philadelphia's Savery, New York's Duncan Phyfe, or even Albany's Tunis Singerland.

While the unfettered blower was not completely immune to the tastes of his time, he did not carry imitation very far. When, in the Victorian era, most commercial table and ornamental wares waxed fancier and fancier in form and ornamentation, sometimes so grotesque as to do less for glass than a hoopskirt or a bustle for a woman, their influence invaded the concepts of most glass blowers. But, it would seem, that influence was confined chiefly to the proportions of one part of a vessel to another. In spite of the contemporary design currents eddying about them, the blowers of individual pieces continued for many years to make honest vessels of clean line and good functional form, very rarely overloaded with decoration. Their pieces emphasized the peculiar qualities of glass itself. The majority were free-blown and strictly utilitarian—pitchers, pans, or bowls for milk, and jars for preserves; the minority were ornamented. Needless to say the latter are the most prized by the collector today. Strangely enough, in the decorative techniques employed there was a sharp line of demarcation between those of the Midwest and those of New England and the Middle States. The Midwestern blowers followed the so-called Stiegel tradition of pattern molding; the Eastern, the South Jersey tradition which has been outlined in the discussion of Wistar and the South Jersey types and techniques.

These individual pieces came from more houses and more parts of the three glassmaking sections of the country than did the commercial tablewares. This is hardly surprising since more than two thirds of the two hundred and fifty or more glasshouses planned or started between 1800 and the United States' hundredth birthday were for the production of bottles for innumerable concoctions and of window glass.[2] The local demand for utility and table articles from these houses, and any profit in making them, diminished rapidly as the result of several interdependent conditions—distribution and transportation improvements, rising living standards, establishment of the tableware industry with steadily declining prices after 1830, and the eventual realization of mass production through the mechanical press. By the mid-nineteenth century individual pieces such as the sugar bowl and pitcher on Plate 8 were made for fun, friend, and family. The opportunity for the glass blower to exercise his skill was further reduced as glasshouses became big instead of little, factories instead of craft shops, and more specialized in their production. All these factors subtracted continually from the attitude and practice of craftsmanship to leave diminishing returns, quantitatively and qualitatively. There were exceptions, of course, because an old-school blower cherished his art. However, when he had to be replaced, his successor was unlikely to be either so skillful or interested in his craft. So many get-rich-quick schemes dazzled American boys and mechanical methods seemed so effortless that long years of apprenticeship in most crafts were too irksome. Glass blowing was one of the most exacting of the industrial arts. The proportion of late nineteenth-century individual pieces comparing favorably with those fashioned earlier in the less industrial-revolutionized glasshouses is relatively small.

A thumbnail sketch of each house in which we know or suspect individual pieces were blown and of the innumerable companies operating them, if it could be made, would be exceedingly boring to reader and writer as well. Actually little or nothing is known about most glassworks beyond the facts of their existence, location, sometimes span of operation, and the supposed, advertised, or known type of output. Still, even such stark facts contribute to the over-all picture of the trends of United States glassmaking and of its growth from a neglected infant industry to such a stature as to command the attention of the anti-trust forces. However, in this survey the majority of glasshouses will be anonymous in the background of glasshouse statistics of period or area[3] and those with which illustrated pieces have been identified, definitely or tentatively, will fill in a few typical details.

While in New England as elsewhere the number of glasshouses planned or established for the production of window glass and bottles exceeded that of those for table and similar hollow wares, the differential was smaller. Massachusetts was the home of the greatest number, whatever the product. There were three spurts of enthusiasm for the manufacture of these essential articles, the first during the war-caused shortage when between 1812 and 1815 about thirteen glasshouses were established, most of them unlucky. The end of the war and the depression was the end of them, though new firms revived a few. Four of the Massachusetts fatal postwar casualties were located near the Housatonic River in the northeast county of Berkshire. Presumably the discovery of the fine Berkshire sand about 1812 dictated the choice of sites. The second spurt was in the 1824–27 years. It included the New England Glass Bottle Company at Cambridge founded by Edmund Munroe and Deming Jarves. Its works was the scene of a seven-day wonder. In September 1829 William Cumming gathered the metal which was handled by James Proudlock to fashion "A great bottle" weighing forty-three pounds and holding thirty-one gallons.[4] The third spurt produced around fourteen houses in the thirty years from 1840 to 1870. In the meantime several had drawn their fires; for as their wood became scarcer fuel became an overbalancing item of expense. The westward trend nearer cheap fuel was irreversible.

Vermont had only four glasshouses, two of the war period and two of the 1820s. Three were located on or near Lake Dunmore[5] and near the Otter River, which empties into Lake Champlain. The fourth was at Burlington, a little farther north on Lake Champlain. Each was established for the production of window glass, and each was short-lived. On the other hand, with the exception of two window glasshouses in New Hampshire, all the glassworks in that state and in Connecticut were primarily bottle houses and at least moderately successful.

In the years between Robert Hewes's abortive enterprise in 1780 and 1815, when the first Keene glassworks, the New Hampshire Glass Factory, began producing window glass, no one attempted glassmaking in New Hampshire. Keene, deep in the southwest corner of the state, was considered a strategic spot for such a manufactory. It was on the main road from the North to Boston, eighty miles away, and on the Ashuelot River, which joins the broad Connecticut twelve miles to the west. Moreover, fuel and the ingredients for glass were abundant in its neighborhood. The advisability of such an undertaking had been discussed for several years. The war-bred scarcity brought several businessmen, including the merchant, John Elliott, and Nathaniel Sprague, his partner, to a decision.

The company was formed in the summer of 1814; its glasshouse and workmen's dwellings were ready for occupancy early in 1815. The glasshouse was operated by many firms in its forty years of existence. In 1817 one failed; in 1825 another changed the name to Keene Window Glass Factory. Never a very large house, the North Works, as it was called, was nevertheless fairly successful and content with a New England market. It burned to the ground in 1855.[6]

The large pitcher of light aquamarine glass, No. 2, Plate 39, was made in the North Works by Matthew Johnson, a blower from Stoddard, during one of his periodic visits with cronies in Keene. It was sometime in the five years before the fire that Johnson—Matt to his familiars—blew the pitcher, skillfully threaded its neck, and adorned its body with the lily-pad Type II. In general lily-pads of this type have a rather broad vertical stem and roughly round or oval pad; on this pitcher of Matt's they rear like a music-charmed cobra. According to gossip, the company Matt sought did not belong to the Temperance Society.

In the summer of 1815 plans were made by Timothy Twitchell of the North Works and Henry Rowe Schoolcraft to establish a Keene flint glasshouse. Schoolcraft, who had become familiar with glassmaking at the Hamilton Glass Works near Albany when his father was superintendent there, was attempting to follow in his father's footsteps. After graduating from Union College in 1811 he had gone first to the Ontario Glass Manu-factory at Geneva, New York, thence to the Vermont Glass Factory, where his contract called for the princely salary of $1000 a year. As the company had been behind in his salary and its finances, in general, were unstable the situation at Salisbury had not been a comfortable one. Consequently the decision to join Twitchell had not been too difficult to make. Their agreement was signed on July 25, 1815, and their glassworks was in opera-tion about four months later. Early the next year Nathaniel Sprague of the North Works replaced Twitchell. By the spring of 1817 they had failed. The partners abandoned glass-making. They were too young to be much discouraged by one failure: Sprague was twenty-seven, Schoolcraft, twenty-four. After a year or two Sprague became a school-teacher and later an Episcopal minister; Schoolcraft entered the government service and achieved fame as an authority on the American Indians. In the meantime, in fact in 1817, Justus Perry, a local merchant, acquired the works which, with various partners, he operated until 1835. The house closed in 1850; its fuel—wood—had become so expensive it could not compete with more fortunate works.[7]

Information as to the house and the glass first produced comes from Henry School-craft himself through a letter published in the *Literary and Philosophical Repertory* for February 1816.[8] The glasshouse, about half a mile from the village, was on the Boston road (a stretch later named Marlboro Street). The seven-pot furnace was in an "octagon wooden building, forty-two feet at the base," rising in a fifty-three-foot cone which ter-minated in a wide ventilator for the escape of smoke and gaseous matter formed by the burning fuel and cooking batch of glass. On each side was a wing "divided into convenient apartments for preparing the materials and crucibles and for various other processes necessary in the Manufacture." There was space, too, "for cutting and polishing all sorts of glass," so it could be "finished with a beauty . . . long called for in American glass." Also Schoolcraft stated explicitly that the manufactory of *flint* glass had been in operation about three months, employing sixteen men besides the woodcutters hired during the winter.

There can be no doubt that Schoolcraft and his partners intended to manufacture flint-glass tablewares and there is no doubt that they and their immediate successors did, though probably to a limited extent. The heavy Masonic flasks, one with Henry School-craft's initials, another with Justus Perry's, and the "J.K.B.," Plate 110, and Sunburst flasks are proof of flint-glass manufacture. The production of Blown Three Mold has been mentioned already in connection with that category of American glass. Actually bottle production was the backbone supporting the factory, and the probability is that all the Pitkin type flasks, later historical flasks, and common bottles were the ordinary non-lead bottle glass. Bottles brought a moderate success to the Keene-Marlboro-Street house, but like its fellow townsman, the North Works, it never became a colossus. When the 1832 information was sent to the Secretary of the Treasury for his report on manufactures, the annual output was figured at $16,000, of which a small proportion was exported to South America.[9]

The individual pieces blown in the Keene-Marlboro-Street Glass Works are more varied in color than those of other New England glasshouses largely because flint glass in artificial colors was made in the early years. Moreover, among them are pieces patterned in full-size piece molds, some of which might be classed as whimseys, for example, the little aquamarine inkwell with the tiny swans sailing on its rim, Plate 10. However, the majority identified with this house are the usual dark olive-ambers and olive-greens of non-lead glass. The tall dignified jar or vase of ageless form and fluid line, Plate 56, is one example. Another is the unique olive-amber wine, Plate 6, with its drawn bowl tapering into a large knop which seems to hold it securely upright and is in turn supported strongly by the knop stem and generous circular foot held in bounds by a heavy folded rim. One could wish that the blower had taken his metal from a pot of clear flint metal or perhaps one of the beautiful greens or amethysts of the Masonic flasks. The little amber wine, No. 3, Plate 59, is not so well realized as the tall one and was blown at a later day, either at Keene in the last days of the Marlboro Street house or at one of the nearby Stoddard houses.

Six years before the Keene-Marlboro-Street Glass Works closed the first of Stoddard's four bottle factories was erected.[10] In 1842 Joseph Foster left Keene and built a glass furnace in South Stoddard. Foster failed and his small works was taken over in 1850 by the Granite Glass Company which had built its glassworks in 1846 at Mill Village. Also in 1850 the South Stoddard Glass Company was started and in 1865 Joseph Foster's sons established the New Granite Glass Works. Because of the impurities in the local sand used by the houses, their products were dark ambers, olive-ambers, or olive-greens in color. No artificially colored glass and no clear glass was ever made there. The rapidly growing preference for clear glass bottles was one of the main causes of the factories closing one after the other in 1871, 1872, and 1873.

Four individual pieces attributed to Stoddard are illustrated: the candlestick, No. 3, Plate 89; the goblet, No. 2, Plate 70; the pitcher, Plate 38; the large jug, Plate 109. The small, rather crudely formed candlestick is deep reddish amber and has a long socket, a throwback to the eighteenth century, as do most candlesticks in the South Jersey tradition. Incidentally they are articles less frequently encountered than the more strictly utilitarian vessels. The tall chalicelike goblet with the curving lines of its bell bowl, collared stem, and domed foot was more lovingly than skillfully fashioned. We suspect that it may have been inspired by the communion chalice in its maker's church. The expertly formed and ornamented "blood amber" pitcher was probably the creation of Matt Johnson. It is one of the few examples known to us having the double lily-pad decoration formed by the Types II and III. The jug's symmetry, full-bellied capaciousness, and the use of Type III lily-pad with its stem sweeping along the curve of the body all point to Johnson as its maker.

New Hampshire's second window glasshouse started in 1839, when a works was moved from one place to another in the hope of reducing costs. The firm, which had taken over the Chelmsford cylinder-glass works after the South Boston Crown Glass Company's failure,[11] ran into bad luck from the start. Within about a year, early in 1829, the glasshouse on the bank of the Merrimac River, about two miles from Lowell, Massachusetts, was destroyed by fire and rebuilt.[12] Next production costs began to rise; fuel became scarce. Suncook in southern New Hampshire, not far from Lowell, was selected as the new site because the sand of nearby Massabesic Pond supposedly was suitable for window glass. It proved unusable. The company, instead of saving money on sand, spent more in buying the Maurice River sand from New Jersey. After a decade of slight success the fires were drawn in 1850,[13] the same year the Keene-Marlboro-Street Glass Works closed. Although, considering the period of Suncook's operation, one would expect many examples still to be found in its neighborhood, few individual pieces have been attributed to it. Of those known to us none have elaborate applied decoration, most are plain free-blown. The brilliant deep aquamarine sugar bowl, Plate 32, is an example which is rare and, in form, unique in our experience.

Connecticut was another state in which there were few glasshouses, and all, except possibly one in the late nineteenth century, made bottles. When the nineteenth century opened, the only one operating was the Pitkin Glass Works in East Hartford, later East Manchester, which, it will be recalled, produced bottles until around 1830. There is definite record of only three others during the first thirty years of the century. One is still a mystery; the other two, by-products of the War of 1812, were the Coventry and West Willington bottle houses established in 1813 and 1814 respectively. The Coventry Glass Works and the Willington Glass Works were built by stock companies, that of Coventry by the townspeople with Nathaniel Root as their agent. Both were located in Tolland County, not far from Hartford but nearer the Willimantic than the Connecticut River. Both served many masters; for a time in the 1830s the same one. In 1848 the Coventry Glass Works, like its Pitkin neighbor about two decades earlier, closed for "lack of wood." The Willington Glass Works ceased operating, too, but resumed again in 1849. After about eight dividend-paying years the works limped along until 1872. Then the company failed.[14]

The archaeological researches of Harry Hall White proved that Coventry made Pitkin, historical, and other flasks and bottles and some Blown Three Mold and that Willington also made historical flasks, jars, and other utility ware. The fragments established, too, that the colors of their glass were similar to those of the New Hampshire bottle houses. The olive-ambers and olive-greens were undistinguishable from those of Keene-Marlboro-Street. Some of the Willington ambers, probably made in the late years of operation, were like those of Stoddard, including the blood amber. At Coventry a limited quantity of aquamarine glass was made. The fine free-blown goblet, No. 2, Plate 71, which is attributed to the early period of the Willington Glass Works, is a deep rich olive-green, appearing black in reflected light. One of the most unusual individual pieces of Connecticut glass is the jar on Plate 57. The lavishly applied decoration is quite consistent with the name by which it was known in the family from whom it was acquired, a workman's fancy. It was made, we believe, at either Willington or Westford.

From the establishment of the Coventry and Willington glassworks over forty years elapsed, and Pitkin and Coventry had ceased blowing before another glasshouse was started in Connecticut. Then two bottle houses were started, also east of the Connecticut River; one in 1856 on Ford Neck, New London, at the mouth of the Thames, and one in 1857 at Westford, not far from West Willington. The facts of the life history of the one or possibly two New London factories still are to be unscrambled. The Westford Glass Works, joining the death march of the Stoddard and the Willington glassworks, closed in 1873.[15] The making of bottles was no longer profitable in Connecticut either. Two individual pieces from Westford and two from New London are illustrated which are typical of the late period. Definitely the unusual "black" glass candlesticks, No. 1, Plate 89, and probably the rather fascinating crude cruet, No. 2, Plate 46, are Westford glass. The brilliant aquamarine pitcher, No. 1, Plate 45, made at the New London works as a presentation piece, is the only Connecticut piece of which we know that is ornamented by the superimposed lily-pad decoration. The blower evidently had caught the contemporary aversion to the purely functional in form. But by perching his perfectly good pitcher on a knop stem rising from a broad circular foot he created a unique heirloom for posterity. The rare aquamarine candlestick, No. 2, Plate 7, is completely atavistic in design—in the shapes and decorative treatment of its elements, that is, socket, composite shaft or stem and foot, and in the proportion of each to the others. Yet it is highly improbable that its maker ever saw any of the eighteenth-century candlesticks of which it is reminiscent.

In the Middle States from 1800 to 1876 more than eighty glasshouses were established for the production of window glass and bottles.[16] Washington, D.C., had one making window glass from 1806 to 1835. The Baltimore and the Philadelphia areas each had about five. The rest were rather evenly divided between New York and New Jersey. In New York State, where the window glasshouses outnumbered those specializing in bottles, not a decade passed unmarked by at least three new houses until the 1860s. In New England war shortages brought forth a large crop of glasshouses but in New York it was the talk of canals and the embargoes prior to the war that turned considerable sums of idle capital into glasshouses, especially across the central part of the state. In 1811 when John Melish, returning from his Western journeys, traveled that route he found that citizens of Utica had taken advantage of what they and he considered the "new order of things" and even surplus Albany and New York capital had been invested in manufactures. The consensus was: "The foreign trade is gone never to be recalled to its former state." [17] A few of the houses did survive the war's aftermath.

The first nineteenth-century New York State glasshouse about which very many "facts"

PLATE 9

1. Pitcher blown from clear sapphire-blue lead glass; globular body, broad cylindrical neck with flaring rim and wide pinched lip, applied short-stemmed petaled foot (ten petals), applied solid semi-ear-shaped handle; patterned in a 10-diamond mold and expanded, the design consisting of a large diamond diaper, ten diamonds in lateral chain. Circa 1815–30.

Height, 5"; top diameter, $3\frac{1}{2}$"; greatest diameter of body, $3\frac{5}{8}$"; diameter of foot, $2\frac{3}{8}$".

2. Sugar bowl and cover blown from clear sapphire-blue lead glass; globular body contracted at top below slightly flanged galleried rim; applied short-stemmed petaled foot (eight petals); double-domed cover with infolded rim and ball finial drawn out of the same gather; bowl and cover patterned in 10-diamond mold and expanded, the design consisting of diamond diaper, ten diamonds in lateral chain; by drawing the ball finial out of the same gather the diamond pattern is changed to vertical ribbing. Circa 1815–30.

Over-all height, $6\frac{7}{8}$"; height without cover, $4\frac{7}{16}$"; top diameter, 5"; greatest diameter of body, $4\frac{11}{16}$"; diameter of foot, $2\frac{7}{8}$"; diameter of cover at rim, $4\frac{1}{2}$".

The mold in which these pieces were patterned was probably a part-size two-piece mold and similar to that used in making the 10-diamond chestnut flasks which are attributed to Zanesville. They were found in the Zanesville area and may have been made in the early Zanesville glasshouse.

3. Blown Three Mold salt, brilliant clear amethyst lead glass; ogee bowl in pattern GII-18, band of diamond diapering between bands of vertical ribbing; applied short stem and plain circular foot.

Height, $2\frac{1}{2}$"; top diameter, $2\frac{3}{8}$"; diameter of foot, 2".

4. Blown Three Mold pitcher, clear brilliant amethyst lead glass; pear-shaped body in pattern GII-32; wide cylindrical neck, flaring rim with pinched lip, applied solid semi-ear-shaped handle with fine ribbing.

Height, 4"; top diameter, $2\frac{7}{8}$"; greatest diameter of body, $3\frac{5}{16}$"; diameter of base, $2\frac{3}{8}$".

5. Blown Three Mold sugar bowl and pattern-molded cover, blown from clear brilliant amethyst lead glass; deep circular bowl with galleried rim and applied short-stemmed circular foot; domed cover with heavy infolded rim and globular finial drawn out from same gather; bowl molded in same pattern as pitcher, No. 4; cover patterned in a small 16-rib mold and expanded in a design of swirled ribbing which continues on the finial.

Over-all height, 6"; height without cover, $4\frac{1}{4}$"; top diameter, $4\frac{3}{16}$"; greatest diameter of body, $3\frac{5}{8}$"; diameter of foot, $2\frac{9}{16}$"; diameter of cover at rim, $3\frac{13}{16}$".

We believe the three Blown Three Mold pieces to be of Midwestern origin although we have no definite information as to the glasshouse in which they may have been made. Only a few of the salts, this one pitcher, and seven of the sugar bowls are known at present. The cover of one of these bowls has vertical instead of swirled ribbing. All have been found in the Midwest, the sugar bowls in one section of the Ohio-Indiana territory. They are all Midwestern in form.

The pattern numbers used in the text and captions refer to the Blown Three Mold pattern numbers in the book, *American Glass*.

have been gathered is the Rensselaer Glass Factory on Glass Lake and the southeastern turnpike to Bath and Williamstown, ten or twelve miles from Troy and Albany. Its history, though incomplete and sometimes blurred by contradictory accounts of events, is typical of its period. Traditions differ about the start of the house. And so far we have been unable to substantiate the exciting Pied Piper tale that one of the founders, a Scotsman named William Richmond, returned to his native land for Scotch glass blowers, naturally the best in the world, donned kilt, wore a patch over one eye, and played the bagpipes as he vagabonded through the Cambria glass district, seducing the blowers with glowing accounts of America, and eventually smuggled some over the sea.[18] But no matter how deviously craftsmen were secured or when the factory started, the following advertisement leaves no doubt that it was operating in the fall of 1805:

James Kane & Co.
Have opened a store at the *Rensselaer Glass*
Factory near the *Sand-Lake*, in Stephentown; where
they will keep a constant supply of
Dry Goods and Groceries
. . . .
Rensselaer Glass Factory, Nov. 4, 1805.[19]

James Kane, of Albany, was one of four merchandising Kanes who singly and in partnerships established general stores (in those days usually a Lilliputian Sears, Roebuck) in several communities.

February 28, 1806, the Rensselaer Glass Factory was incorporated for fourteen years by nine men, including Jeremiah Van Rensselaer, Elkanah Watson, George Pearson, and James Kane, members of the Hamilton Manufacturing Society operating the Hamilton or Albany Glass Works. Their agent (an office for which James Kane was selected), superintendent, all artificers and workmen were exempted from jury and militia duty so long as they were in the company's employ.[20] As the works, a crown and a cylinder glasshouse, had been erected in a veritable wilderness it was necessary to establish a nearly self-sufficient community, an expensive undertaking especially as business was not booming. In December 1806 the company joined with its alter ego, the Albany firm, in an appeal to Congress for higher duties, a subject on which, at the time, Congress was hard of hearing and of heart.[21] In the early fall of 1812 the crown house burned to the ground. Immediately the president and board of directors levied upon the stockholders for the purpose of rebuilding it. Each share was assessed $50—$20 to be paid in thirty days, $20 in sixty, and $10 in ninety. Failure to pay up meant forfeiture of the stock.[22] By January 1813 the house had been rebuilt; Rensselaer crown as well as cylinder glass "superior to any made in this state" was once more on the market.[23] If the company did not possess a fire engine before the fire, it did afterward—two of them.

Another calamity was in store for the works; by 1815 its prospects were submersed by the flood of postwar importations. In November the coming auction of the glassworks was advertised far and wide by its agent, John Reid, Albany merchant. On Tuesday, February 6, 1816, the cleared land and wood lots, glassworks, sawmill and ashery, two houses for the superintendents and twenty-four workmen's dwellings, the general store, and undoubtedly the barns itemized later, were to be put on the block. On the following Tuesday the personal property was to be sold at the factory—horses, wagons and sleighs, tools for blowers and a complete set for a crown house, bar iron and iron castings, fine stone and sand, clay and other materials for making glass, and two fire engines.[24] In 1816 the cylinder glasshouse, it is said, burned down; presumably henceforth the crown house was used for making both types.[25] From then until the spring of 1819 the record is obscure except for continued advertising of cylinder glass. In April, about the nadir of the depression, the New York Assembly passed an act for the relief of the president and directors who, having kept the house in operation in spite of continuous loss, wished to sell their estate and pay their debts. Permission was granted.[26] It is said that at this point Isaac Fox, who ran the general store at Rensselaer Village (the glasshouse community), Nathan Crandall, and Abraham Gregory first entered the picture.[27] In any event the works was in blast that fall.[28]

In the fall of 1824 Crandall, Fox and Company failed for $14,766.71 and Richard J. Knowlson, of Albany, purchased the property at the sheriff's sale March 11, 1825. Fifteen months later, since it had not been redeemed, Knowlson took title and promptly advertised it for sale.[29] Again the picture fades. But a few scattered advertisements show that window glass was being made at Rensselaer and, moreover, that at Troy it had to compete with New York Cylinder, Ontario, New England Crown, Champlain, and "Common Western" window glass.[30] Since in the spring of 1830 the Rensselaer Glass Manufacturing Company was incorporated for twenty-one years by Richard J. Knowlson, Daniel M. Gregory, and Isaac B. Fox,[31] it may have been they who had been operating the factory. Three years later the Assembly refused the request of "Knowlson and others" to reincorporate with an increased capital stock on the ground that the factory was doing very well on its current basis.[32] About this time, according to local tradition, blowers from South Jersey arrived at the glassworks, which some of them soon rented. There is no doubt that William and John Gabler were there then, for they purchased property.[33] And in 1835 Stadlers, Rush and Company—Anthony Rush (Antony Rosch), Francis and Joseph Stadler, and Joseph Welser—paid Richard Knowlson and his wife $3500 for the glassworks property. Perhaps a victim of the 1837 panic, the company failed in 1838. Knowlson and Isaac Fox were appointed trustees and immediately sold the works to Fox's sons,[34] Albert R. and Samuel H., who operated it until 1853, when it was consumed by fire.[35] In the meantime the Foxes had become interested in a factory started at Durhamville, Oneida County, in 1845.[36]

Quite a number of individual pieces have been located in homes in the vicinity of the Rensselaer Glass Factory, or Sand Lake Glass Works, as it is called locally. Almost without exception they have been accompanied by a Sand Lake history, a tradition associated with the South Jersey blowers and the 1830 period. The articles consist principally of bowls, pitchers, jars, and whimseys such as canes. All are free-blown from aquamarine glass and, in our experience, free of ornamentation. The goblet, No. 3, Plate 70, said to have been blown by John Gabler, is an exception in two respects—its color, a clear brilliant deep green, and its function, a drinking vessel.

The talk of a canal to join Lake Erie and the Hudson and later the completed project led to a concentration of the state's glasshouses along its route or within easy access to it. Of the eleven companies incorporated between February 1809 and March 1811, ten were scattered across central New York, four of them in Oneida County.[37] Apparently two never materialized, and four never completely recovered from the postwar depression. Of those in Oneida County the one at Utica and two at Vernon met with more success. The first of the trio apparently was built in 1808. It started perhaps under the supervision of Lawrence Schoolcraft, who, after disagreement with one of the owners, left the Hamilton Glass Works that fall and joined the group establishing the Oneida Glass Factory at Vernon.[38] The tenses of the verbs in the February 17, 1809, act of incorporation seem to indicate that the glasshouse was already in operation when the twenty-two named investors and "their associates" sent their request to the Assembly. The company was incorporated for fourteen years and allowed the same exemptions as the Rensselaer Glass Company. They were not given, however, to the Utica Crown Glass Works, which was incorporated the following spring by twenty-five stockholders, also for fourteen years. Its crown glass seems to have had a wider, if temporary, sale and reputation than the cylinder glass of the Oneida Glass Company. During the war it was sold as far east as Boston and as far south as Philadelphia.[39] It was no exception to the rule of postwar difficulties but, being a crown house, it suffered even more than a cylinder glassworks. In fact in 1822 it was leased by the Oneida Glass Company. In the same year the incorporation of the latter was extended to 1837; and in May 1836, for another thirty years. The owners must have had a bad case of overoptimism in the spring, for supposedly when the fires were drawn in August 1836 they were never relit. Perhaps by then the firm recognized the storm signals of the coming panic.

The second Vernon glasshouse was established by the Mount Vernon Glass Company, incorporated February 17, 1810, for fourteen years and with the exemptions from jury and militia for its agent, superintendent, and workers. Among the seven named incorporators was Oliver Lewis and probably among its unnamed was Nathan Granger, whose sons followed him in the concern. In April 1824 the act of incorporation was renewed and extended for four years from the previous February.[40]

Unlike its neighbors this glassworks was a bottle house making all the various types of such containers as were in demand throughout its existence. Though most early bottle houses must have made "black" glass wine bottles of tall cylindrical form and having a shoulder seal with the initials of the gentleman for whom they were made, the Mount Vernon Glass Company is the only one from which examples having the company's name have been recorded as yet. One bearing the seal with "Mᵀ VERNON GLASS Cᵒ" encircling the initials "M S M" is illustrated on Plate 223 in *American Glass*. In addition to the usual chestnut bottles, patent-medicine bottles, historical and pictorial flasks, and Blown Three Mold glass (the last two previously mentioned), Harry Hall White's excavations on the glasshouse site revealed the making of offhand, that is, free-blown, vessels and the production of aquamarine and of clear flint as well as the dark olive-amber and olive-green bottle glasses. Moreover, much to the amazement of collectors and students, there was evidence that light green and dark olive-green salts were pressed at Mount Vernon (also pressed later at the Saratoga Mountain Works), and in a pattern identified, by fragments, with Sandwich. Apparently the pressing was confined to these salts, which are not common today. It is unlikely that the company ever invested in a pressing machine for so limited a production. Therefore the probability is that the salts were pressed manually in the mold, one which may have been taken to Vernon by a workman from Sandwich. Just when the flint glass and tablewares were added to the output and how long they were made is not known at present. The earliest date was probably prior to 1833, the year Granger, Southworth and Company advertised in the Utica City Directory that it manufactured flint glassware, flasks, and bottles of all kinds.

The brilliant bluish-aquamarine sugar bowl shown in color on Plate 7 is believed to have been fashioned in the Mount Vernon Glass Works. Its superimposed decoration of swagging, a device seemingly chosen by blowers less frequently than the various lily-pads, makes it an outstanding piece. It is almost identical in form and decoration with one made for Gideon Granger, one of the proprietors of the glasshouse, and illustrated on Plate 67, *American Glass*. Another individual item which may have been made either at Mount Vernon or at the later Saratoga (Mountain) Glass Works is the crude but rare tall dark olive-amber wineglass, No. 2, Plate 59.

Sometime in the early 1840s the company realized that, as its wood lots were nearly exhausted, if it wished to continue in the glass business it would be expedient to move the works closer to an abundant supply of fuel. After a survey of possible locations Oscar Granger, apparently the leader in the company, decided upon Mount Pleasant, about eight miles from Saratoga Springs. Like Robert Hewes nearly seventy-five eventful years before him, he figured it was cheaper to haul the sand to the wood than the other way round. Consequently a cord road was laid up the mountainside to the site of the new community. Trees were felled, the land cleared, then the glasshouse, homes for the owners and married workmen, a "hotel" for the bachelors, a church and schoolhouse were erected. In 1844 when the little community was ready for living and working the Vernon works and workers were uprooted like Mrs. Oscar Granger's flower garden and transplanted to Mount Pleasant.[41] For twenty-one years the Mountain Works, as it was nicknamed, was operated for the production of bottles. Its best customers were the Saratoga spring-water companies. In 1865 the Congress and Empire Spring Company in which Oscar Granger was a stockholder bought the glassworks and moved it to a section of Saratoga Springs which Granger dubbed Congressville. There containers for the various spring-water companies were made until about 1890.

Inasmuch as the molds used at Vernon were taken to the Mountain Works along with other equipment, some of the historical flasks and even some Blown Three Mold pieces were produced there. These molds, however, apparently were not removed to Congressville. In color the village glass was consistently a bright deep emerald-green whereas the Mountain Works' metal was aquamarine and the olive-greens and olive-ambers, "black" glass similar to that made at Mount Vernon. For this reason family tradition is sometimes hazy as to the factory origin of many individual pieces fashioned by blowers who worked at both the Mount Vernon and the Mountain glassworks. A case in point is that of the tall wine, No. 2, Plate 59, to which reference has been made. Perhaps the decline in manipulating skill, as glass blowing in bottle houses passed from a craft to a factory operation, is nowhere more graphically demonstrated than by a comparison of the average individual pieces blown at the Mountain Works by the older blowers and those made later at Congressville by the younger members of the occupation. Most of the Congressville pieces are of immature workmanship, and if the line happens to be pleasing so much metal was used that the object is cloddish. Three examples of individual pieces blown at the

Mountain Works are illustrated by the "black" glass mug, No. 3, Plate 71, and the hand basin and ewer, Plate 25, which speak for themselves. The creamer, No. 5, Plate 41, attributed to the Mountain Works, is a workman's fancy. The use of a hollow cylinder for a stem is uncommon.

In northern New York, at opposite sides of the state, there were two window glass-works in which were created many of the finest individual pieces in the South Jersey tradition. In connection with each, John S. Foster, a veritable cork on a stream of personal failures, bobbed up again. After the failure of the South Boston Crown Works, of which he was superintendent and stockholder, Foster went to Burlington on Lake Champlain to superintend the Champlain Glass Works established in 1827 by a local stock company.[42] About three years later he turned up across the lake in New York State, where he erected a saw- and gristmill and the large crown glasshouse in which Gershom Cook and either Charles or Gurdon Corning, merchants of Troy, New York, were interested. The present record is not clear as to whether the Troy businessmen inveigled Foster from the Champlain works, or he induced them into the enterprise located on the north bank of the Saranac River about twenty-one miles from Plattsburg. In any event the Redford Glass Works and the little village of Redford were established and the 3000 acres of Clinton County wilderness acquired by Cook and Corning insured an ample supply of wood. The building of the glasshouse was started in March 1831[43] and in April of the following year the Redford Glass Company was incorporated for twenty-one years by Charles W. and Gurdon Corning, Gershom Cook, and John S. Foster.[44] For some as yet undiscovered cause, Foster departed before the end of 1832 and went across the state to Alexandria, about thirty miles northeast of Watertown in Jefferson County. Selecting a spot about two miles from the village, he built a cylinder glasshouse which he called the Redwood Glass Works.[45] Less than two years after the first glass was blown Foster died. Both houses, though passing through many ownerships, operated with considerable success. The Redford works closed in 1852, the Redwood in 1877.[46]

From the pieces with well-authenticated histories of having been blown at one or the other of these two glasshouses, or at the small furnace which operated for two years from 1841 through 1843 at Harrisburg near Redwood, it is apparent that only when a piece is accompanied by trustworthy history can it be assigned to one of these houses. The brilliant aquamarines appear identical, the forms are similar, and so, too, are the treatments of the applied decorative motifs. Two individual Redford pieces are illustrated on Plate 7. The candlestick, No. 1, is one of the infrequently encountered articles in this type of glass, and the mug, No. 3, while not rare as an article, is extremely so with the applied lily-pad decoration. Another mug, No. 5, Plate 74, also blown at Redford, is unusual because of the threading. The pair of vases, No. 5, Plate 7, and the large deep footed bowl, Plate 16, were blown at Redwood. Other characteristic pieces which are undoubtedly Redwood or Redford, though no one can say which, are illustrated by the three bowls, Plate 22, of which the compote or bowl on standard is most unusual; the sugar bowl and pitcher, Plate 8; the extremely fine footed bowl, Plate 15, and the plate, No. 2, Plate 24—the last, one of only two we have seen with the lily-pad decoration. All of these pieces are ornamented with lily-pad, Type II, except the compote with Type III. The high incidence of these forms of the lily-pad on pieces known to have been made in glasshouses which began production about 1830 or were in operation later has led us to the tentative conclusion that they were evolved after 1830. The Type I, which has a slender, sometimes almost threadlike stem and very small and often beadlike pad, probably was somewhat earlier but still nineteenth-century. As we have said previously, as yet these exact forms have not been found on any foreign glass. Moreover, since their use seems to be confined largely to South Jersey, Keene and Stoddard in New Hampshire, and northern and western New York, it may be that comparatively few blowers practiced the technique.

Four years after the canal connecting the Delaware and Hudson rivers through Rondout Creek was completed in 1828, a group of men from the Willington Glass Works in Connecticut established the Ellenville Glass Works on the canal at Wawarsing, Ulster County, New York. For twenty years, under several ownerships, it was operated for the manufacture of bottles, profitably in good times.[47] A considerable number of individual Ellenville pieces have been recorded which were blown from the usual dark olive-amber, olive-green, and true amber metal used for the commercial products. They have been found principally in the homes near the works and the surrounding countryside, many of them owned by descendants of the blowers or their friends for whom the pieces were made. Some are satisfactory examples of the glass blower's art; some are crude. The dark olive-amber (black) glass pitcher with threaded neck, Plate 37, typical of the more skillfully fashioned vessels, is attributed to Ellenville and probably was blown before 1840.

A late nineteenth-century Ulster County glassworks is said to have operated at New Windsor for the production of window glass. Since as yet we have learned nothing about it beyond local report, it seems little more than a ghostly return of the mid-eighteenth-century venture in that vicinity. The pitcher, No. 1, Plate 39, came to us with the circumstantial history of having been made by a blower named Burgess, as a gift to his landlady, a Mrs. Harriet McCormack, who ran the Clinton Hotel, where the blowers roomed. The pitcher, blown in the 1870s, illustrates a decorative technique almost as old as glassmaking but probably not used in American glasshouses before the second quarter of the nineteenth century.

In the extreme western part of the state there were two rather long-lived bottle houses established in the 1840s.[48] One was built in 1840 at Lockport on the Erie Canal, a few miles northeast of Buffalo; the other, in 1849 at Lancaster, almost in a beeline south of Lockport and just east of Buffalo. By 1860 the New York Central Railroad had reached Buffalo, and Lancaster was one of its stops. The bottle of innumerable types and styles was the commercial product of each factory but each is known to collectors for its historical and pictorial flasks and individual pieces. At Lockport, besides aquamarines, many artificial colors were made, for instance, blues and greens—rich deep greens, yellow-greens, olive-greens, and emerald-greens. Individual pieces in most of these colors have been identified as Lockport, among them the shapely bowl, Plate 4, in a blue shade typical of Lockport. Some of the pieces have the lily-pad decoration, usually Type II. The rare, amateurishly formed little candlestick, No. 2, Plate 89, is another Lockport specimen. Lancaster, too, produced historical and pictorial flasks in a wide range of colors, similar to those of Lockport, but its blue was a lighter shade. The light olive-amber wineglass with sturdy crimped foot, No. 1, Plate 59, is attributed to Lancaster. It is likely that the lily-pad pieces on Plate 6 also were blown there.

The southern counties of New Jersey were exceptionally attractive to glass manu-facturers because of wooded acres, beds of superior sand, nearness to large markets, and transportation facilities, the last exceptional even early in the nineteenth century. As a result South Jersey had a higher concentration of glassworks, principally for window glass, bottles, and other hollow ware, than any other section of the country except the Pittsburgh-Monongahela area.[49] The first American glassworks to achieve any real degree of success, Wistars', was built near Salem in 1739; glass is still being made in South Jersey. One of the main advantages which Jersey glasshouses had over those of inland New England was that, after their wood lots were stripped in the mid-century, the cost of transporting coal was not so great as to be one of the deciding factors in the success or failure of a factory. The same can be said of many New York houses for which the Erie Canal meant cheap transportation, but most of the surviving glasshouses in central New York were bought up and closed up by Pittsburgh interests.

When the nineteenth century opened, one glasshouse is definitely known to have been operating in South Jersey, that started by the Stanger brothers, which was discussed some pages back. Around 1800 Jonathan Haines and William Stanger, one of the seem-ingly inexhaustible family of glass-blowing Stangers, started a glassworks at Clementon in Gloucester County not far from Glassboro. About the same time, or a little earlier, James Lee, of Philadelphia, and his associates built the Eagle Glass Works for the production of window glass and bottles at Port Elizabeth not far from the mouth of the Maurice River in Cumberland County, a section taken from Salem County in 1794. In 1806 Lee with several associates established another works in Millville township, which five years before had been virtually virgin territory, rather flat and very thickly wooded. Some time earlier, in hopes of attracting industry, the navigable Maurice River had been dammed to form Union Pond, as the resulting bulge in the river was named by the owners of the tract. Millville village had been laid out on a sandy knoll below the pond and above the Maurice River bridge linking the turnpike running westward to Bridgeton and southward to Cape May. This road, it was said, was almost unusable except when frozen. The Lee group could have made no better choice of location, not only because of the fuel and shipping, but also because the sand of the riverbanks about five miles below town was soon proved to be so superior in quality for glass that later tons of it were exported to out-of-the-state glassworks. It will be recalled that Thomas Cains's furnace in the South Boston Crown Glass House was one at which this sand was used. The little community of which the Millville glasshouse was the fulcrum was called Glasstown. Through the fat and lean years, in fact until the 1840s, there were several rather rapidly changing ownerships. In 1844 the Whitall brothers purchased the works and ten years later bought the glasshouse in South Millville. This house, established in 1832 by Frederick Schetter, of Baltimore, was located on the river well below the bridge and near Petticoat Branch. Like its neighbor, it had passed through several previous ownerships. In 1857 Whitall, Tatum and Company was formed, a firm still operating in the mid-twentieth century.[50]

PLATE 10

1. Bowl blown from brilliant amber-yellow non-lead glass; circular base and wide-spreading sides with heavy outfolded rim, decidedly lopsided; patterned in a 20-rib mold; double insertion and expanded in design of broken-swirl ribbing.

Height varies from $1\frac{3}{4}''$ to $2\frac{1}{2}''$; top diameter, $7\frac{7}{8}''$; diameter of base, $3\frac{3}{4}''$.

This bowl came from Ohio and is believed to have been made in the early glasshouse located in what is now the village of Kent, Portage County, Ohio. According to the history of Portage County, this glasshouse was built in 1824 by James Edmunds, Henry Park, and Park's brother. It is said that according to some of the early records the spelling of their name was Parke and Edmonds.

2. Blown Three Mold pitcher, pattern GIII-5; lead glass in delicate shade of wisteria; ovoid body, wide cylindrical neck, flaring tooled rim with down-turned pinched lip; applied slender solid semi-ear-shaped handle.

Height, $6\frac{7}{8}''$; top diameter, $4\frac{1}{4}''$; greatest diameter of body, $4\frac{15}{16}''$; diameter of base, $3\frac{3}{8}''$.

This pitcher was patterned in the same mold, or an identical one, used for quart decanters which are common in clear glass. Also we know of one yellowish-green, two blue, and one reddish-amethyst (footed) decanters blown in the same mold. Fragments of Blown Three Mold glass in this pattern were excavated on the glasshouse site at Sandwich, Massachusetts.

3. Blown Three Mold small tumbler or flip glass, in pattern GIII-6; lead glass in same wisteria color as pitcher, No. 2.

Height, $4\frac{1}{4}''$; top diameter, $3\frac{1}{2}''$; diameter of base, $2\frac{7}{16}''$.

Clear flip glasses and a reddish-amethyst tumbler blown in the same mold are known.

4. Blown Three Mold inkwell, pattern GIII-29, in pale aquamarine non-lead glass; very rare in this color and unique because of the three tiny applied swans.

Diameter, $2\frac{1}{4}''$; height, $1\frac{7}{8}''$, to top of swan, $2\frac{5}{8}''$.

Inkwells in this Blown Three Mold pattern in olive-amber, amber, and olive-green were made commercially at the Keene-Marlboro-Street Glass Works, New Hampshire, during the 1815–30 period.

5. Egg cup, one of a pair, blown from brilliant amber-yellow non-lead glass; ovoid bowl flaring abruptly at heavy infolded rim, short double-knop stem drawn from same gather, and applied circular foot; patterned in 16-rib mold and expanded in swirled ribbing. Attributed to Mantua Glass Works, Mantua, Portage County, Ohio. Circa 1822–29.

Height, $3''$; top diameter, $3\frac{9}{16}''$; diameter of foot, $2''$.

Among the many products produced at Millville in its more than one hundred years of existence were window glass and containers of nearly every type, including demijohns for Dr. Thomas B. Welch's grape juice and apothecaries' furniture in opaque white. Presumably the latter were made under the firm of Whitall Brothers; definitely, pressed translucent white apothecaries' jars were made by Whitall, Tatum and Company.[51] We believe there is a possibility that the Victorian hand basin and ewer, to use the advertising term instead of the country "washbowl and pitcher," shown on Plate 26, were blown there. These toilet articles made commercially in cut glass are infrequently encountered among individual blown pieces and the few we have been able to trace were made after 1833. A far cry from common bottles, formed, thanks to piece molds, with little more effort than a puff of breath and flip of wrist, are the intricate paperweights, made by Ralph Barber and his contemporaries at Millville in the early twentieth century. The Millville rose, so closely identified with Barber, has become famous. An example attributed to him is illustrated by No. 2, Plate 98. The rare crocus weight on the same plate is also attributed to Millville.

The name "Coffin" was to become a very familiar one in connection with the New Jersey glass industry for over forty years, as William Coffin, Sr., and his sons built and operated glasshouses and even took over, briefly, a few which were in financial trouble.[52] The first with which one of the family was associated was a bottle house well known to collectors of historical flasks. It was built by William Coffin, Sr., and Jonathan Haines of the Clementon works near a small lake and sawmill on a tract of land owned by Coffin in the township of Galloway, Atlantic County. The glassworks and its little community were called Hammonton, for John Hammonton Coffin, son of William. Coffin was not a trained glassman when he went to South Jersey in 1812, but apparently he became one. In 1836 the firm became Coffin and Hay—Bodine Coffin, another son, and Andrew K. Hay, William Coffin's son-in-law. Late in the 1830s the house was consumed by fire and rebuilt. After the death of William, Sr., in 1844 his sons, John Hammonton and Edwin Winslow, operated the works until about 1851, when it was sold. In the meantime Bodine Coffin and Andrew Hay had taken over the Winslow Glass Works. The Hammonton works did not survive the 1857 depression.[53] The brilliant clear amber bowl, No. 1, Plate 12, came to us with a history of having been blown at the Hammonton Glass Works by William Coffin.

After 1830 southern New Jersey was to outnumber New York in the establishment of bottle and window glasshouses, and the 1830s were the most prolific decade. When the Bridgeton Glass Works, like the Hammonton under Coffin and Hay, well known for its historical flasks, was built by Stratton, Buck and Company in 1836 there were nearly forty houses operating in the southern counties. Bridgeton was a strategic spot for a glassworks, as was Millville. Not only were supplies handy, but the Cohansey Creek, up which the steamboats of the day could travel from Delaware Bay eight miles away, flowed through town. Though started as a window glasshouse the production of bottles was soon added. In 1841 disaster struck. John Buck died and the factory burned to the ground. It was rebuilt by new interests and passed through various hands before becoming the Cohansey Glass Works in 1870, after which it operated until 1917.[54]

The flasks produced at Bridgeton in the early period, that is, prior to 1850, have been recorded in amber, olive-amber, greens including emerald and aquamarine, deep sapphire-blue, and in clear glass. The handsome Victorian pitcher, No. 2, Plate 40, its dense somber amber enlivened by the broad deep loops of opaque white, was attributed by family tradition to the Bridgeton Glass Works. It is one of a pair obtained from a relative of John or Jackie Getzinger, who was said to have been a blower at Bridgeton. The shape—small short globular body and long neck with high arched lip, somewhat similar to that of the ewer on Plate 26—is one which seems to have come in after 1830, as did the frequent use of loopings of one or more colors. Another shape of the period is illustrated by the blue pitcher, No. 1, Plate 40, which has been mentioned in connection with the Glassboro houses under the early Whitney regime.

The Isabella Glass Works, built in 1848 on the Williamstown-Brooklyn Road in Camden County, was another of the small glasshouses which peppered South Jersey, and with which the ubiquitous Stangers were concerned. Local history and tradition disagree as to whether Thomas or Julius Stanger was the founder, but agree that the name Isabella, found on many historical flasks of the later period, was given to the works in honor of Stanger's daughter. In 1857 Stanger died: the house passed into other hands. The record is confused as to whether the glasshouse failed to survive the depression or operated for ten years more.[55] Two offhand individual pieces fashioned in this glasshouse are illustrated, namely, the extremely rare lamp, No. 1, Plate 94, which was acquired from a Miss Stanger in Brooklyn, New Jersey, and the aquamarine mug with opaque white loopings, No. 1, Plate 73.

As it is inevitable that, in over a hundred years of glass blowing in South Jersey's many glassworks, literally hundreds of individual pieces were fashioned, so it is probable that hundreds of surviving pieces can be confidently assigned to the area even though they cannot be attributed to a particular glasshouse. The same can be said of nearly every similar area. The main reason for the first proposition is the persistence of customs; the second, that these individual pieces, American folk art in glass, rarely traveled far from the place of their fabrication. Sometimes, yes; often, no. Consequently such a piece found in South Jersey and having the earmarks of South Jersey type glass is quite likely to have been blown there. However, without some reliable data as to the house, one should stop to recall that there were a great number of houses, interlocking and changing ownerships, and employment of the same blowers in more than one house. The Stangers, for instance, as owners and blowers, were all over like pussley. The same caution should be used when one is tempted to attribute almost any undocumented piece of glass of this type to a maker or house. A few of the typical pieces which fall in the general South Jersey category are the little aquamarine creamer with mulberry loopings, and the miniature with lily-pad decoration, Plate 5; the clear blue salt, No. 9, Plate 58; the aquamarine mug with bold leaf prunts, No. 4, Plate 74, and the creamer with double band of lily-pad, No. 3, Plate 41. The lily-pad illustrates Type I of this decorative device, the type found most frequently on South Jersey pieces.

In the early nineteenth-century Midwestern glasshouses the bottle in its many forms and sizes was one of the principal articles of glass manufacture. As the number of preparations packaged in bottles multiplied steadily, so did the demand for containers, and of its four star roles—medicine, titillator, escape mechanism, and currency—the last was the only one hard liquor relinquished in the course of time. Naturally an article of equal importance was the windowpane. From about 1820, demand and, even more, certain production factors, such as fuel, determined that the westward movement of glasshouses accelerated. Steadily the largest production concentered more and more in the Pittsburgh area, with a much smaller nucleus in Ohio and another in and near Wheeling, (West) Virginia. While the actual number of new houses was greater than either New England's or that of the Middle States it was less than their combined totals.[56] The difference was not great but more of the Midwestern houses survived the assaults of economic blows such as technological improvements in manufacturing and in glass itself, and the depressions which seem to have joined death and taxes as certainties of life. Many survived only to be swallowed by late nineteenth-century and early twentieth-century mergers.

As we have seen, the first nineteenth-century houses established in the Midwest to make flint-glass tablewares soon found it necessary or expedient to add green-glass wares to their output. Our main concern at the moment, however, is not so much with the regular commercial products of any house as with the individual pieces blown in them, whether as gifts or to fill a community need. It is almost certain that in the Midwestern as in the Eastern bottle and window glasshouses before the days of mass production some table and utility household wares were made for local consumption. Moreover, the expensiveness of fine glassware and most Midwesterners' distance in miles and thought from Fashion's orbit undoubtedly prolonged the practice, which would have petered out more rapidly in houses in the neighborhood of the cities when and where the tableware houses began to flourish. There can be no question that such wares and gifts were made in the houses of the immediate Pittsburgh area even after the War of 1812, yet one hears almost wholly of pieces from New Geneva, the Monongahela area, and the Ohio houses of Zanesville, Kent, and Mantua. True, they have been the objects of the most intensive research, but the cause goes deeper. In most instances there is little hope of tracing many specific pieces to any glasshouse located within or near the environs of an urban center, for those areas have been absorbed by the cities, and the families for whom the pieces were made have scattered. The chances, however, are not slight that types made in them were closely similar to contemporaneous pieces identified with the Monongahela area and Ohio.

As in the East the majority of individual pieces were free-blown household utensils, such as jars and pitchers, bowls and dishes, tumblers and "big-bellied bottles" or decanters—pieces of ageless form and without ornamentation which if found in the East would be classified as South Jersey type. Other pieces, the most prized today, were ornamented. And it is still a matter of amazement to many of us that, so far as we know at present, the decorative devices of the South Jersey tradition, that is, glass applied to itself and tooled into any one of many forms, were by-passed in favor of the pattern-mold. This could not have been because the blowers, especially those in the earliest houses, were unfamiliar with the technique. They and those for whom the various articles were fabricated must have preferred the less stolid figures and the play of light and shade of the pattern-molded glass. However, there simply must have been instances when a blower made some ornamental piece on the order of the banks, Plate 96, which would have given him the opportunity to extend his skill to its utmost. John Melish, who, like nearly everyone who visited Pittsburgh, went to Bakewell's, may have recorded such an occurrence. In 1811 he wrote: "I went accompanied by a friend to visit the glassworks which we found in excellent order, and one of the workmen prepared for us some glass ware of curious workmanship." [57] Free-blown plain pieces, cut or engraved pieces would hardly have struck him as "curious" but glass ornamented by itself with quilling or some applied decoration might have.

Once more before we can escape from this 1800–76 well of glassmaking we must slip back, this time to 1815, in Ohio. In that year two houses were planned and erected; one in Cincinnati on the Ohio River and one at Zanesville on the Muskingum River, which flows into the Ohio. Little is known of the Cincinnati works beyond a few rather isolated facts—James O'Hara's old friend and partner, Isaac Craig, was one of the promoters; according to a plan drawn by Elias Pym Fordham on his Western trip, the house was located at the lower end of the city and on the Ohio; it was a "manufactory of green and window glass"; "clean white sand [for the metal] abounded at the mouth of the Scioto," but clay for crucibles was obtained from Delaware; and it probably was the glasshouse which Mr. Fearon found operating "on a tolerably large scale" on his visit between the late summer of 1817 and spring of 1818.[58] But its blowers undoubtedly produced many a pitcher, decanter, and tumbler.

The first Zanesville glasshouse[59] was planned and built by local businessmen who, coming from "homes of culture in New England and Virginia," [60] doubtless appreciated fine glassware, especially crystal, and, aware of Zanesville's strategic commercial location on a main east-west road as well as on a navigable river, anticipated successfully rivaling Bakewell's. It was inevitable that the glasshouse was operated with diminishing returns since not only were most Western markets, including Zanesville, already well supplied by Pittsburgh, or even imports, but in 1815 the shrinkage of war-swollen commerce had started. It seems equally inevitable that in order to operate at all the founders of the White Glass Works, presumably so called because it made clear glass, very quickly extended their production to green glass for bottles and other hollow ware. Bottles and similar hollow ware were the principal products under the Rev. Joseph Shepard, who with two associates took over the plant in 1823 after it had been leased to another group for three years. The historical flask, No. 2, Plate 113, is a relic of the period. Surviving the repeated changes of ownership, the works ran almost continuously for over thirty years.

Quite a body of glass has been attributed to the White Glass Works, largely by analogy[61]— similarity to individual pieces identified by tradition and local history—and by geographical distribution. As a rule the last factor, as we have pointed out, is fairly reliable in the case of this type of glassware, which is non-commercial or of very restricted demand. In any event it has been widely accepted as a reasonable conclusion that a 10-diamond part-size piece mold and a 24-rib dip mold were used at the White Glass Works for both lead and bottle or green-glass wares. The brilliant sapphire-blue lead-glass covered sugar bowl and creamer shown in color on Plate 9 are attributed to Zanesville. Skillfully formed, as are all pieces we have seen which are identified with this house, these two are definitely of the nineteenth century in shape and proportion and the sugar bowl has the galleried rim, a feature not found on eighteenth-century vessels. But each has an eighteenth-century type of foot, the very short-stemmed and slightly flaring type, in this case with the flare tooled to terminate in ten petals. To the best of our knowledge this particular combination of treatments characteristic of two centuries is not encountered on Eastern glass of the period. In addition the bowl has a peculiarly Midwestern double-domed cover with ball finial, all fashioned from one gather, as has the brilliant amber covered sugar bowl, No. 1, Plate 3. This amber bowl was fashioned in a Midwestern variant of a distinctive American shape. The circular drawn foot is an unusual feature even in Midwestern bowls. The essential difference between the Eastern and Midwestern variants, true also of pitchers, lies in the proportions: the Midwestern have a more acutely angled shoulder than the Eastern and the sides flare, whereas on the Eastern shape they spread. All of the Midwestern bowls, of which we now know, having this characteristic shape, with or without the drawn foot *and* with the same type of double domed cover, were either found near Zanesville or had a Zanesville history. This bowl was patterned in a 24-rib mold. So, too, was the light green vase, so very eighteenth-century in feeling, shown on the same plate. Three flasks, the spherical bar bottles, and jugs, all patterned in a 24-rib mold, which are typical of those attributed to Zanesville are shown on Plates 106, 107, and 108.

In 1821, when the depression was well over, David Ladd and Jonathan Tinker, two refugees from postwar conditions in the East, established a glassworks at Mantua, Portage County, Ohio,[62] not far from the Cuyahoga River up which merchandise passed on its way to the Great Lakes region. It was quite fitting that Ladd and his three brothers, Connecticut Yankees, should settle in their state's former Western Reserve. Tinker, from Vernon, New York, was a glass blower and son-in-law of Oliver Lewis, one of the incorporators of the Mount Vernon Glass Works. He superintended the transformation of Daniel Ladd's tannery near Mud Brook into a glasshouse. In January 1822 the first glass was blown. A little less than two years later the house was sold to the Mantua Glass Company formed by Joseph and William Skinner and other local businessmen. Immediately the glasshouse and its output were expanded. Partners came and went. Its last year of operation was in 1828–29 under Oliver Lewis from Vernon, his son, and his son-in-law.

In the meantime Ladd had moved a bit west but not far from Mantua, to a section in which there were two tiny adjoining villages, Carthage and Franklin Mills. Here with one Benjamin F. Hopkins he built another glassworks. By 1826 he had a partnership with Zenas Kent, owner of much land and a good general store. Another glasshouse was started in 1824 by Park, Edmunds and Park. That Kent is the name given to the glass blown in either the works of Ladd or of Park, Edmunds and Park arises from the fact that it is the present name of the community, one given in honor of Marvin Kent, son of Zenas, when the two villages became one in 1863. In the case of individual Kent pieces one cannot be sure of the parent works, except for the Blown Three Mold of which the bowl, No. 1, Plate 14, is an example. All glassmaking seems to have ceased in Kent by 1834. No matter how good or beautiful the glass produced in Portage County was, the paths were beaten to Pittsburgh and possibly Zanesville.

Once more tribute is due the late Harry Hall White for his contributions to our knowledge of early American glass. He made extensive excavations on the sites of the

Mantua and Kent glasshouses and delved into contemporary sources and local history for facts pertaining to their operation. The fragments were sufficient in number so that, besides identifying the Blown Three Mold patterns used at Kent and Mantua, it was possible to determine the variant in each pattern, in other words, the size of the mold, the base design and number and size of the units of each band as they were in the molds. Mr. White established that a three-piece 15-diamond or ogival mold, a 16-rib and a 32-rib dip mold were used at Mantua and a 20-rib dip mold was used at Kent. One distinctive feature of the Mantua 16-rib mold was the terminal ring at the center bottom to which the ribs converged. It is faintly discernible on the Skinner plate, No. 4, Plate 24. This plate, one of a set made at the Mantua Glass Works, was later given as a wedding present to Lois Skinner, niece of Joseph and William Skinner. There is no doubt that the making of table glass as well as bottles and other similar utility vessels was the intent of the owners of the Mantua works, and the Kent as well. In February 1822, about a month after the Mantua furnace was in production, the editor of the *Western Reserve Chronicle* recorded receipt of a gift of a well-shaped decanter and "elegant sweetmeat."

In addition to the Kent and Mantua Blown Three Mold pieces shown on Plates 14, 19, 48, and 86, one Kent pattern-molded and three Mantua pieces are illustrated. The Kent bowl, No. 1, Plate 10, of amber-yellow glass has the great brilliance characteristic of nearly all glass found in Ohio. It was patterned in a 20-rib mold and expanded in the broken-swirl design. As far as we have been able to discover as yet, this ribbed design on a single gather of glass is purely American and Midwestern. It was a variation on the "Pitkin" decorative theme. Instead of following the old half-post method of using two gathers, one was used. The gather was patterned in a ribbed dip mold and, when withdrawn from the mold, the vertical ribs were swirled to right or left; it was then inserted in the mold again, impressing vertical ribs upon the swirled. Finally, by the degree of expansion a wide variety of effects was achieved. At its greatest expansion it appears to be a diapering of lightly drawn diamonds-on-the-diagonal, sometimes called "feathered"; when but slightly expanded, it resembles regimented little popcorn kernels. The shape of this bowl, and also the other Kent bowl on Plate 14, is typically Midwestern and un-Eastern. Rarely do the sides of a bowl rise in an unbroken line, straight or curved. Often after rising vertically for a short distance they will flare quite widely. The lines, while not the most graceful, have the merit of being a distinguishing feature.

The three Mantua pieces are the covered sugar bowl, Plate 31, the egg cup, No. 5, Plate 10, and the wineglass, No. 5, Plate 59, all rare. The light yellow-green sugar bowl was patterned in the 15-diamond piece mold, its cover in the 16-rib mold; the whole piece is decidedly eighteenth-century in form and feeling. The amber-yellow egg cup also was patterned in the 16-rib mold and its ribbing swirled. But as the expansion was slight the ribs are in close ranks and the play of tone and tint in color is less than in widely expanded pieces. The wine, blown from bubbly light but brilliant green glass, has sixteen expanded vertical ribs which tapered to fine threads as the bowl was drawn out. It was in Mr. White's collection and attributed by him to Mantua. The small golden-amber compote or tazza, No. 6, Plate 3, was patterned in a 32-rib mold and quite possibly may be a Mantua piece. So, too, may be the typically Midwestern amethyst salt on the same plate. Amethyst was a color made at Mantua.[63]

Other salts of characteristic Midwestern shape are shown by Nos. 4–6, Plate 58. They illustrate how the eighteenth-century double-ogee form, as shown by Nos. 1 and 2 on the same plate and the salts on Plate 2, was treated in early nineteenth-century Midwestern houses. Occasionally the typical bowl of Stiegel type proportions was fashioned and given a flaring rim as No. 5, Plate 58.

In general we believe that the characteristics of the Ohio pieces, with a few exceptions, are also those of the glasswares blown in the many other Midwestern houses but that the latter are either unrecognized today or gone to cullet or the junk pile. As compared with the Eastern individual pieces in the South Jersey tradition, those of the Midwest, that is, the majority of them, seem rather fragile and more expertly fashioned. Their color range is wider even though those natural to bottle and uncleared window glass predominate, that is, tints and shades of green and amber. The exceptionally beautiful and clear ambers are found in nearly every tone from rich deep brown to golden amber; the greens, from the palest aquamarine to deep olive, and even so-called olive-yellows and citron. As elsewhere, there was sparing use of artificial colors—chiefly cobalt, sapphire, and cornflower blue; more rarely amethyst; very rarely purple; and occasionally clear glass and a cloudy crystal like a polished moonstone.[64]

In the preceding pages we have made a large number of generalizations regarding bottle- and window-glass individual pieces blown from 1800 to 1876. We shall issue now a blanket qualification to insure each generalization and each statement as to regional characteristics, nuances of style and design against being taken as a categorical assertion. That qualification is: These are true in our experience up to the present writing. Many facts, theories, and hypotheses, our own as well as others, seemingly valid when judged by the evidence on which they were based, have been completely exploded from time to time by the unearthing of new information. Therefore to nearly every statement even verging on the categorical should be appended a modifying and cautionary clause. For the collector and student of American glass, as for those in other fields, one generation's truth frequently becomes the next one's myth.

NOTES ON THE MODERN RENAISSANCE OF THE ART OF GLASS

THE American and European eclipse of glass as an art, while never quite total, seems to have lasted over half a century. The passing of its shadow is said to have been started by the French glassmaker, Emile Gallé, and to have been completed in the early twentieth century,[1] almost one hundred years after glassmaking became a firmly rooted industry in the United States. Important as that entire period is, with its marvelous experiments and fascinating developments in the commercial table and ornamental blown glass produced in our factories, it has not been the subject of a single comprehensive comparative study, although some of the facets, such as the late nineteenth-century art glass, have been highlighted in excellent articles. And it is a field which we enter timidly, for, while gathering our research material, like our collection, mainly from other fields, we have merely skirted this vast one. Our survey of available published material has been confined chiefly to a few sources such as articles in *Antiques*, various reports and catalogues of exhibitions of the Franklin Institute of Philadelphia, the American Institute of the City of New York, and several World's Fairs—the London and New York Crystal Palaces, the "Centennial," the World's Columbian Exposition, and the "World of Tomorrow" in 1939. Therefore we wish to emphasize the fact that these notes make no pretense of presenting a deep and complete analysis of the modern renaissance in the art of glass blowing or the decades immediately preceding it.

Even before 1830 the "spirit of commercial exploitation," which, Thorpe points out,[2] led English manufacturers to copy the glass of France and Germany, had motivated the glassmakers in the United States, but it was reined in somewhat by the depression of the late thirties. After that it ran wild. The continuously broadening base of consumption created a demand for and made profitable a tremendous expansion in the variety of glass articles and wares. Between the cut and engraved crystal glass, still and always the luxury ware, and the rapidly expanding varieties of the pressed glass for the majority, there was a widening swath of fancy blown glasswares, many completely imitative of foreign glass and many the results of scientific experiment. It was this glass which struck the keynote for the remainder of the century. And perhaps it was true of our glassware in general that, as New York State's agent to the London Crystal Palace in 1851 reported regarding the American exhibits as a whole, "the character of our articles was such as to show the world that we worked for the great masses, not for the luxurious and privileged few."[3]

Many tendencies evident shortly before 1830 had crystallized even before London's Great Exhibition and our pocket edition of it in 1853, including the Bohemian trend

[132]

toward elaborate decoration of blown glass by enameling, painting, and gilding—and, of course, by engraving. In fact "Bohemian" was a potent sales adjective just as "English," "French," "Irish," and "Dutch" had once been. "Fancy Goods—Vases, Colognes, Card receivers, Allumets [match holders], Decanters and Wine Bottles in China, Terra Cotta, Parian Marble, and Bohemian Ware" and "Beautiful specimens of Bohemian Glassware richly cut and engraved, Toilet Bottles, Fruit Bowls, Flower Baskets, Vases, etc.,"[4] are typical excerpts from advertisements of the mid-century. Unquestionably among the richly cut articles were some of the famous cased or, as it is more frequently called today, overlay glass. If it was not being made by our manufacturers by 1850—we believe it probably was—it certainly was soon afterward. When the 1861 tariff act was passed, Bohemian types, of which cased glass was pre-eminent, were being produced here in such quantities as to warrant provision for specific imposts on the imports.[5] Other types perhaps not quite so important but certainly growing in popularity in the mid-century were "frosted" and "Venetian." [6] Probably some of the glass called Venetian was similar to that blown later by the now famous Nicholas Lutz, who came from St. Louis, France, to the Dorflinger Glass Works and about 1870 entered the employ of the Boston and Sandwich Glass Company. His achievements, which have placed his name among those having a magical charm for many collectors, were in the intricate processes of fashioning the latticinio and similar "striped" Venetian wares.

At London in 1851 two novelties caught the public fancy, both English processes. By one, an invention of William Kidd for "illuminating, embroidering and silvering flat surfaces of glass," designs engraved on the underside of glass seemed to be in high relief on the outer surface; by the other, glass was "silvered." [7] If experiments with the latter process in this country were not conducted concurrently with the English ones, they were made soon afterward, probably by more than one American manufacturer and certainly by the New England Glass Company. Silvered or Mercury glass, also glass probably made by Kidd's process, was exhibited at the New York 1853 Crystal Palace by the New England Glass Company, whose William Leighton in 1855 obtained a patent in connection with knobs of silvered glass.[8] Subsequently Mercury or silvered glass was made by many American houses. The candlestick, No. 1, Plate 90, is an example of this Poor Man's silver, perhaps the first imitation in glass of a more expensive fabric since the development of porcelain glass. While its resemblance to silver is slight, it apparently attained a great popularity in its own right; for its production was carried over into the twentieth century. It was in the natural course of events that silvered glass should be accompanied by a similar "gold" glass, which, however, was not made in the same great quantities.

During the two decades before the first World's Fairs color in glassware had become of paramount importance, and an irresistible attraction for the majority of customers. The old stand-bys—the sapphire and cobalt blues, emerald and other familiar greens, amethysts and rare purple—were now common colors. The most favored colors were light and dark ruby, for the making of which cheaper means than gold had been rediscovered in Bohemia in 1827.[9] Many hues new to transparent and opaque "modern" glass, many shades and tints of old ones had come into use as the result of laboratory experimentation. Among them were canary, "vaseline" and topaz, alabaster and opal, turquoise and pink, chrysoprase and Pomona green. Rich ambers, brown, and "black" were made deliberately and were not "accidents" from impurities in the raw materials. An accompaniment to the expansion of colors and types was elaboration of form.[10] Fancy shapes sometimes almost completely disregarded the function of the vessel if it had one beyond being ornamental. Even a casual glance through illustrated catalogues and articles convinces one that by the mid-century novelty had already become to the Victorian era what the gadget has been to ours.

About 1865 the seed of the glass renaissance had been planted by Gallé and by the time of the Philadelphia International Exhibition of 1876, the "Centennial," had sent out its first shoots. Gallé, who established his own factory at Nancy, France, approached the design of glass with the fixed idea "that commercial glass need not be in bad taste" and approached the execution of design with the ideals of pure craftsmanship. His glass was a far cry from the twentieth-century results of the movements he initiated; he specialized in cased and a primitive kind of cameo glass for which he chose naturalistic subjects as decorative motifs.[11] True cameo glass was the achievement of English glassmen. Shortly after Gallé set his course, John Northwood succeeded in copying the celebrated Portland vase, a copy which broke upon completion. A few years later Joseph Locke, while with Hodgetts and Richardson of Stourbridge, made a replica which, though never quite completed, was exhibited at the Paris Exhibition of 1878.[12] These notable accomplishments in the 1870s quickened the pulse of the classical revival and interest in glass of the ancients. It is said that "without Gallé's experiments and his wide influence, the renaissance in the glass industry would have been long delayed,"[13] which doubtless is true. Still it does seem as though a large measure of credit should be meted out to Northwood and his followers also. And it would not surprise us if someday research reveals unsung contemporary glassmakers whose attitudes and efforts were paralleling those of Gallé's.

Be that as it may, once started, the movement mushroomed far too rapidly for its own sound and healthy growth. Inevitably many of the manufacturers—on the Continent, in the British Isles, and in America—who copied the works of others or contributed colors, metals, or designs did so for purely commercial reasons without either regard for aesthetics or an iota of honest sentiment for the art of glassmaking. The band wagon was overloaded by zealots of the neo. Even by 1876, whetting the appetite for novelty of shape and extravagance of decoration often bordering on the bizarre was common practice—not only in glass, but in everything. By the time of the World's Columbian Exposition in 1893 the peak of extravagance in design and ornamentation and mere virtuosity of execution seems to have been reached. Slightly below it were the results of the rejuvenated passion for classical form. Sometimes odd combinations emerged from the hodgepodge, such as classical shapes with most unclassical overornamentation. Many colors, enameling, gilding, painting, staining, singly and in combination, were used most lavishly.[14] Often the final touch was the application of glass ornament in the form of flowers, leaves, and vines. Under the aegis of the competitive renaissance from the mid-1880s into the early twentieth century many art glasses,[15] technical triumphs in color and metal, were created, and many ancient types were reproduced in "modern" ways. Among the art glasses were Satin or Mother of Pearl glass, Amberina, Pomona, Burmese, Agata, Spangled glass, Crackled glass, and iridescent. Some simulated materials other than glass, as for example the Onyx and the Tortoise-shell glass and the Peach Blow. The last, one of the delicately shaded glasses, imitated the famous Chinese porcelain in the colors of the peach bloom. Ancient glass was reproduced in the Millefiori, Aventurine, and Vasa Murrhina. While in general the pieces made from these metals or in these styles were plain free-blown, occasionally they were pattern-molded, and expanded, usually in vertical ribbing, diamonds, or "inverted thumbprint." A few of the metals were used for pressed wares as well as blown.

On the present evidence it would appear that only a few of the American glass manufacturers were in the vanguard of the experimentation which determined the formulae for most of the art-glass metals and colors. Conspicuous among them were the New England Glass Company at Cambridge, the Mount Washington Glass Works—which had been established in 1837 by Deming Jarves, owned by William L. Libbey in the 1860s and moved by him to New Bedford, where in 1894 it became part of Pairpoint Manufacturing Company—and Hobbs, Brockunier and Company of Wheeling, West Virginia. Just a few years before Edward D. Libbey closed the New England Glass Works the company is said to have originated Agata, Amberina, and Pomona. An Amberina decanter is shown on Plate 99 and a Pomona vase on Plate 101. It also made, some claim originated, the Peach Blow glass. The vase, No. 2, Plate 99, is New England Peach Blow. Burmese, another shaded glass, was originated at the Mount Washington Glass Works in the late 1880s, and Peach Blow may have been, since the firm patented a "Peach Blow" glass. Still another product was a glass shaded like the New England Glass Company's Amberina. The conflict over the use of the terms Peach Blow and Amberina was resolved by an agreement whereby the New England Glass Company retained Amberina and adopted Wild Rose for its Peach Blow, and the Mount Washington Glass Works retained Peach Blow and adopted Rose Amber for its Amberina. Hobbs, Brockunier and Company created several of the art glasses and produced them in far larger quantity and variety of articles than did the Eastern houses. The firm had a fine tradition of glassmaking behind it, for in a very real sense the New England Glass Company was its parent works. In 1845 John L. Hobbs and James B. Barnes from the Cambridge works took over an idle glasshouse in Wheeling and later their sons, John H. Hobbs and James F. Barnes, joined them. The firm of Hobbs, Brockunier and Company formed by the two Hobbs and Charles Brockunier in 1863 was fortunate enough to secure the services of the expert metal and color man, William L. Leighton, also from Cambridge.[16] It was he who worked out the formulae for many of the firm's successful innovations including the Wheeling Peach Blow and Spangled glass. It was he also who years before, in 1864 to be exact, perfected the lime glass which was far cheaper to make than lead metal for fine glassware and was considered the most important contribution to the industry since the pressing machine. Incidentally, we have used the term Peach Blow as two words instead of one because it was so used by both its Wheeling and New Bedford makers.

In 1893, the year of the Columbian Exposition, Louis Tiffany, who had been making ecclesiastical glass since 1878 at his Corona, Long Island, furnaces, had the satisfaction of successfully producing a metal which had the iridescence of long-buried ancient glass. Shortly afterward he started the commercial production of iridescent ornamental wares. Apparently Tiffany, like all true artists and so many glassmen, not all of whom could afford to follow their glassmaking creed, believed he had a responsibility to his medium. A guiding tenet was that only by the age-old techniques of free-blowing and manipulation could justice be rendered to glass as a substance. This attitude as well as the method of production explains the selection of Favrile as the trade name of his wares: it is derived from an old Saxon word meaning hand-wrought.[17] The punch bowl on Plate 102 and the bowl in a Tiffany metal holder, No. 1, Plate 101, are examples of his iridescent glass. From this remarkable innovation Tiffany went on to others. Using another ancient device, that of imbedding in the body of a vessel loops and draggings formed from applied threads of glass, he created some astonishing designs and amazing colorings. The traditional use of this method of decoration is illustrated by the South Jersey pitcher, No. 2, Plate 40, and Pittsburgh vase, No. 2, Plate 51, the Tiffany, by the little Quezal vase, No. 4, Plate 100, and the Emil Larsen vase, No. 5, Plate 103. Inevitably Tiffany's original wares were promptly imitated and similar glass evolved. The Quezal ware is said to have been made by a group of Tiffany workmen who established their own furnace in Brooklyn. Among the glassworks producing similar wares and innovations of their own were the Durand Glass Works, Vineland, New Jersey, and the Union Glass Works, which operated in Somerville, Massachusetts, from 1851 until 1924. The footed bowl, No. 2, Plate 101, is an example of the Kew Blas, an art glass originated by the Union Glass Works.

The Aurene candlestick, No. 3, Plate 100, somewhat reminiscent of Tiffany iridescent ware, represents one of the many types and colorings of glass originated by Frederick Carder, founder of the Steuben Glass Works in the early twentieth century, and one of our noted glass technologists. Mr. Carder, who was associated with John Northwood from 1880 until about 1901 and head designer under him, was one of the leaders in reviving the art of glass.[18] And incidentally, he, like René Lalique earlier in the century, has cast many glass objects by the so-called lost wax process.

Having played the theme of the decadence in the art of glass, we now turn to the other side of the record. For there is another side. We are among those who stubbornly cling to the belief that, deplorable as the vast majority of our commercial blown glasswares from the 1830s throughout the nineteenth and early twentieth centuries were, there were always pieces which, according to the standards of all ages, would be classified as "good." True, most shapes were overfancied or odd, but not all; many were simple, dignified, and graceful, especially in the clear or crystal wares and occasionally in the art glasses after the classical recaptured the eye in the late nineteenth century. These matters of taste always will be the subjects of controversies which can be reported and never settled. But aspects upon which nearly all can agree are those of skillful execution and technical progress. While, especially after the 1840s, the proportion of native blowers decreased steadily because fewer and fewer American boys wished to serve the long apprenticeships, manufacturers still could obtain their expert blowers and decorators from European glasshouses or inveigle them from each other's employ. Mr. Carder told us that when he established his glassworks at Corning he had to "import" its entire staff of master blowers. Thus the skill of the artisan in the United States' table- and ornamental-ware factories and in the glass-decorating shops was of a high degree. The engraver and glass cutter in particular had to be tops in these fields of extrinsic decoration, for more and more demand was made upon his ability to control his grinding equipment as designs for the luxury wares steadily became more intricate and complex. The most expensive of the engraved wares were usually decorated with naturalistic subjects rendered realistically. A three-dimensional effect was expected for the best and was achieved, as a result to which the bottles on Plate 88 bear witness. As on most modern engraved pieces, the decoration of this pair of bottles made about 1890 appears to be in relief rather than intaglio.

Besides a few of the old firms maintaining high standards of quality and workmanship in the fine blown and cut and engraved wares, a few new ones provided other oases of fine glass. One was that of Christian Dorflinger, who made some of the purest crystal metal ever produced in the United States. He was born in Alsace, France, in 1828. Between the ages of nine and eighteen he mastered the fundamentals of glassmaking at St. Louis, in Lorraine, and decided that his personal interest lay in the field of glass decoration, in particular by etching and engraving, enameling and gilding. In 1846, the year after his father died, he brought his mother, brothers, and sisters to the United States, where, having settled his family in Indiana, he became a journeyman blower with a Philadelphia firm manufacturing druggists' ware. In 1852, at the age of twenty-four, he owned his first glasshouse, the Long Island Flint Glass Works, in Brooklyn, New York. By 1860 he had two more glasshouses and was manufacturing fine flint glasswares. Ill-health forced him into retirement in 1863: two years of boredom drove him back to the glassmaking he loved so well. The Dorflinger Glass Works, which he established in 1865 at White Mills, Pennsylvania, achieved fame and honor for its wares. The blowers were European artisans from Brooklyn houses and local farm boys whom Mr. Dorflinger trained himself. From 1867, when the glass-cutting and engraving department was added, all decoration except gilding was done at the glassworks, though the production of blanks for many glass-cutting shops— twenty-two in Wayne County alone—was continued. Sons and grandsons of Christian Dorflinger learned glassmaking at White Mills and eventually carried on the works after his death in 1915. During World War I the impossibility of obtaining raw materials used in the glass posed the problem of changing their formula, which meant an inferior product or closing: they chose to close. After the war the factory operated briefly before changing styles and lack of German potash led to the final drawing of the fires in 1921.[19] The crystal metal made by Dorflinger is superb. We must confess that, given pieces of equal thickness and simple forms, we can detect no tremendous difference between the metal of the Dorflinger pieces and modern crystal, including that of Steuben and Orrefors. A few characteristic examples of the Dorflinger commercial tablewares are shown on Plates 44 and 62. It seems unlikely that many will quarrel with the form or the cutting of the pitcher which was made during the Brooklyn period of operation. The drinking vessels from the White House glass made for Presidents Benjamin Harrison and Theodore Roosevelt show the characteristic deep cutting and the unfortunate, to our way of thinking, late nineteenth-century practice of overdecoration. The other drinking vessels illustrate shapes, engraving, and cutting typical of the best designs of their periods. To many an American eye the Lincoln and Centennial glass may be as pleasing as some of the present-day styles which revert to the late eighteenth and early nineteenth centuries, such as the Steuben examples on Plate 63.

Paperweights, representatives of one of the most fascinating of the arts of glassmaking, have been attributed to the Dorflinger Glass Works and some were made there. However, we have been informed by several members of the family that they were not a commercial product of the house. They, like the lovely rose and other paperweights created by Ralph

Barber and some of his colleagues at Millville, were individual pieces made principally as gifts. At present it would appear that the American manufacturers who produced fine paperweights commercially, such as those shown on Plates 97 and 98, were the New England Glass Company, the Boston and Sandwich Glass Company, the Mount Washington Glass Works before and after it was acquired by the Pairpoint Company, and John L. Gilliland (not Gillerand) and Company of the Brooklyn Flint Glass Works.[20]

The novel in form and decoration which characterized the Victorian era were matters of taste and fashion, the novel in metal—that is, the glass itself—and in color were the results of scientific experimentation. The writer of the preface to the second volume of the American edition of Knapp's *Chemical Technology,* published in 1849, pointed out that there had been "several ingenious American inventions which . . . prove that the intense activity of the American inventive genius has not been dilatory in applying itself to this department [glass] of manufactures." Glass as a substance, the manufacturing equipments from furnace to molds, and the methods of fabrication, all were objects of constant laboratory research and of improvement during this long period. Scientific methods were followed in testing material and composition. The often beautiful metals were the results of careful purification of raw materials and precisely measured batch prepared according to pretested exact formulae followed with exactness. Out of the experiments with materials, effects of heat, and other factors came the art glasses.[21] If one is a glass purist, then few if any of these glasses, such as Peach Blow and Amberina, can be justified, regardless of the beauty of the coloring and regardless of the fine simple shapes in which many of the pieces were fashioned. But even the purist must acknowledge that they represent the triumph of the glassmaker over his materials and equipment and their environment.

It would appear that the first authoritative voice to be heard in disagreement with the trend was that of René Lalique, a French goldsmith turned glassmaker, in the early twentieth century. At least he is credited with probably having "saved the renaissance from becoming hopelessly entangled in préciosité." Lalique performed two extremely important directory feats for the glass renaissance: he revived the interest in clear or crystal metal as an art glass and in "glass *as glass.*" Thereby he "rescued the experimentors from dissipating their abilities in remote technicalities and curiosities."[22] Starting from these points, shortly before World War I, a French painter, Maurice Marinot, introduced the heavy massive forms[23] which, in general, typify Modern glass for most people. From France the movement spread throughout the northern European glassmaking countries and finally across the Atlantic to the United States. The new concepts were adopted here more slowly than had been those of Gallé, Northwood, and their followers, in part perhaps because, whereas the attraction to color and an appreciation of it come naturally, the preference for clear crystal glass is, we suspect, an educated taste. The severely simple and functional forms giving full play to the metal's essential qualities of transparency and fluid brilliance were indeed the fulfillment of the purist's dream of "glass *as glass.*" In general where decoration was not by and through glass itself it was by cutting in broad planes to give form or to bring out the qualities of the metal or by sculptural engraving subordinated to the glass, in perfect balance with the untouched surfaces, or by the contrast emphasizing the characteristics of glass. Such at least appears to have been the ideal, one which has been realized frequently. However, in the case of some Modern engraved pieces it has seemed to us that the glass was merely the mat on which an engraving was mounted.

Several outstanding firms have created commercial table and ornamental glass in the modern manner, in color and combinations of color and crystal as well as pure crystal or clear glass. Among them are the Fostoria Glass Company, Bryce Brothers, Pairpoint, which is no longer operating, Libbey Glass, A. H. Heisey and Company, and Steuben. Examples of the modern in American glass made by the last three producers of blown wares are shown on Plates 23, 53, 54, 63, and 93. Each has an enviable tradition of fine glassmaking behind it. The Libbey Glass of Toledo, Ohio, traces its beginnings back to 1818, to the New England Glass Company in which William L. Libbey became interested in the early 1870s. The closing of that house and the removal to Toledo have been mentioned already in connection with that important early glasshouse. In 1940 Libbey designed a line of new American modern blown table and ornamental glassware. In it the company announced that Libbey craftsmen were writing a "new chapter in the history of fine glassware." The intent and motive as stated in their catalogue was to impart to its design a "character truly American . . . honest, dignified, and one which accentuates the resplendent beauty inherent in the natural forms of a fine material." We regret that photographs of some of their engraved pieces were not available for illustration. The pair of cornucopias and the three bud vases on Plate 53 give only a slight idea of this ware, the production of which ceased during World War II and has not been resumed.

The two interesting vases on Plate 54 were blown at the Newark, Ohio, glassworks of A. H. Heisey and Company, whose satisfyingly attractive tablewares are known to nearly every housewife in the country. George Duncan, whose name is familiar to many collectors of pressed glass, was the grandfather of T. Clarence Heisey, the present head of the company. For a few years from about 1849, though his principal interest lay in iron and lumber, George Duncan was one of the company operating the Pittsburgh City Glass Works for the manufacture of window glass and bottles. Apparently this branch of industry had a fascination for him; in the mid-1860s with Daniel C. Ripley and others he established a glasshouse for the manufacture of cut and engraved flint glasswares, bar goods, and pressed glass. When the works, like so many others, was overtaken by financial difficulties in the panic of 1874, George Duncan assumed the obligations of the company and the firm of George Duncan and Sons was formed. He succeeded in liquidating the indebtedness of the firm but succumbed to the strain of overwork. The business was carried on by his sons and Augustus H. Heisey, his son-in-law, who had been associated with the King Glass Works.[24] Augustus H. Heisey, we are told, was responsible for rescuing "cast glass from the doldrum of mediocrity" and putting it "on a pedestal—thereby making George Duncan & Sons one of the outstanding hand glass plants of its day," as that of A. H. Heisey and Company is today. In response to our queries regarding the vases on Plate 54, Mr. Heisey writes: "the Saturn Optic vase [No. 1] is just one of those things that develop through experimentation . . . something we are constantly doing." The ribs on the vase, No. 2, which remind us of the early Pittsburgh pillar-molded ribbing, we were surprised to learn, were fashioned by manipulation, not in a mold.

The roots of the present Steuben Glass, Incorporated, go back nearly a century, to

1851, when Amory Houghton, Sr., who was considered one of the ablest glass mixers of his time, established the Union Glass Works at Somerville, Massachusetts. Amory, Jr., who was associated with him, was imbued with the scientific approach to the multiplicity of problems inherent in glassmaking and devoted the major portion of his time to laboratory experimentation.[25] The Houghtons' acquisition of the Brooklyn Flint Glass Works in 1864 and the removal to Corning, New York, in 1868 have been mentioned previously. At Corning the policy of systematic research into new glasses, methods, and application of glass is still followed. During World War I, when Corning's facilities were too limited to meet the wartime demand for technical glass, Frederick Carder's neighboring Steuben Glass Works with its staff of highly skilled master blowers was acquired. After the war, as the Steuben Division of the Corning Glass Works, the house resumed production of table and ornamental glass, operating, however, with returns which diminished to the point where its abandonment was seriously considered. It was rescued by Arthur Amory Houghton, Jr., great-grandson of the founder of the Corning Glass Works. The years 1932 and 1933 were momentous not only for Steuben Glass but for the international reputation of American glass. In the first a chemical formula was found for a crystal metal so pure that "laboratory tests have established the glass as second in purity only to fused quartz, or pure rock crystal," and American boys, most of them just graduated from high school, entered apprenticeships in glass blowing. In 1933 Steuben Glass, Incorporated, was formed with Arthur Amory Houghton, Jr., as president, John Monteith Gates as director of design, Sidney Waugh as chief designer, and Robert J. Leavy, who had been at Steuben for some years, as production manager.[26]

After an intensive study of the situation, Houghton, who was concerned deeply with glass as an art medium, had decided that, given Corning's new pure crystal and Steuben's shop of the most expert of craftsmen, only design was lacking to make truly great glass. Therefore he enlisted his friend Gates, a rising young architect, in his project and Gates in turn enlisted Waugh, the sculptor. These two, each with a mind already prepared in the tradition and practice of an art, approached the challenge of glass design by thoroughly familiarizing themselves with the idiosyncrasies of the new medium, its limitations, and its possibilities. Since 1936 Steuben has maintained a design studio in New York City, a practice in American industry to be highly recommended to all who can afford to adopt it. All artists who join the staff of designers have to acquire a complete understanding of glass, as did the three men who started this most exciting adventure in the art of glass in our time. Once a design has survived its critical review, it is taken to Corning by its originator. There, after designer, craftsman, and technician have consulted, a model is fashioned. If, after critical and ruthless appraisal, the Design Department approves the embodied design, it is returned to the Corning technical staff to be judged from the production standpoint. Each design has to pass all these tests before it is presented to the public for approval.[27] The public, in which few dissenting voices are heard, includes many who cannot afford to own the admired glass, for Steuben is a luxury ware as were the fine cut and engraved wares in the old days of the eighteenth century and as are all the fine handmade appurtenances of nice living in this mechanized mass production age.

While the illustrated drinking vessels, candlesticks, and bowls are typical of Steuben glass, they are too few in number to form an adequate picture of its accomplishments in the art of glassmaking. The drinking vessels, excepting the modern highball glass, Plate 63, show the kinship with late eighteenth- and early nineteenth-century shapes characteristic of Steuben stemmed ware, but the tiny exquisitely engraved decorations are Steuben. The candlesticks, Plate 93, are quite eighteenth-century in feeling, which may be one of the many reasons they appeal so strongly to us. The American Ballad Bowls, designed by Sidney Waugh, not only are fine examples of the modern style but, especially for the antiquarian, have the added interest of being engraved with historical subjects. When consideration of some of the modern examples arises there is a slight difference of opinion between the authors of this book but there is utter agreement in the opinion that Steuben glass as a whole is the most beautiful glass made in the United States today, the most beautiful in metal, in form, and in decoration. There are many who believe that Arthur Amory Houghton, John Monteith Gates, and Sidney Waugh are approaching the realization of their "attempt to make the finest glass the world has ever seen." [28] Contemporary recognition of Steuben's achievement in the art of glass has been accorded it by at least eight American museums of art and the Victoria and Albert Museum of London; all of which have included examples in their permanent collections. Time, however, will hand down the final verdict on its inherent merit in relation to the glasswares of the past, present, and future. In the meantime we can be proud today of Steuben glass as the culmination of nearly two hundred years of glass blowing in America.

PLATE 11

1. Small footed bowl blown from deep sapphire-blue lead glass; circular form flaring slightly to plain rim, short stem drawn out from same gather: applied thick circular foot; bowl patterned in same or identical mold as the bottle, No. 3, Plate 1, and expanded in diamond-daisy variant design.

Height, 3–3¼"; top diameter, 4⅝"; diameter of foot, 2⅝".

Two salts patterned in similar diamond-daisy mold are known in deep sapphire-blue and three in yellowish emerald-green. One of the emerald-green salts and a deep amethyst bottle in the same pattern, both in our collection, showed lead content when the spot test was made, as did the blue bowl.

The bottle in similar pattern illustrated on Plate 1 showed non-lead by spot test. All of the bottles in the usual diamond-daisy pattern which we have tested showed non-lead. However, it is possible Stiegel made some of his "perfume" bottles in lead glass, for he advertised flint glass, by which he probably meant glass of lead. Moreover, sugar bowls, like No. 2, Plate 2, creamers and salts, many of which are undoubtedly Stiegel, show a strong lead content.

2. Footed bowl blown from slightly smoky non-lead glass; plain rim; straight-sided foot or base ring formed from a narrow strip drawn out to a width of about five eighths of an inch and applied to base of the bowl. On one side, engraved by copper wheel, a wreath formed by two narrow leaf sprays connected at the bottom by a small daisy-like flower and enclosing initials "M.T." in script, surmounted by a coronet.

Height, 4⅛"; top diameter, 7⅞"; diameter at base, 4¼".

There can be little doubt that this bowl, now in the collection of W. Dan Quattlebaum, was made at the Amelung Glass Works. Not only are the technique and design of the engraving typical but the coronet is almost identical with the one on a large covered flip made at Amelung's glassworks and presented to Charles Ghequiere, of Baltimore, Maryland. This flip, which is in the Henry Francis du Pont Winterthur Museum, is inscribed *"Floriat Commercium," "Charles Ghequiere,"* and *"New Bremen Glassmanufactory the 20th of June, 1788."* This bowl was acquired from Miss Rachel Thomas, of New Market, Maryland, who inherited it from her great-grandmother, Margaret Thomas Brooke, of Montgomery County, Maryland. As Margaret Thomas, who was born in 1769, was married in 1789, the bowl was probably a wedding gift.

PLATE 12

1. Bowl blown from clear amber non-lead glass: wide heavy outfolded rim; applied circular crimped foot.

Height, $5\frac{1}{16}''$; top diameter, $6\frac{3}{8}''$; diameter of foot, $3\frac{7}{8}''$.

    This bowl is attributed to the glassworks of Coffin and Hay, Hammonton, New Jersey, and according to family history was made by William Coffin, Sr., himself. Coffin, in association with Jonathan Haines, built the works about 1817 and continued to operate it until about 1836. Then his son, Bodine Coffin, and son-in-law, Andrew K. Hay, took over.

2. Footed bowl blown from clear blue glass; straight-sided form rounding at base to applied heavy circular foot. Bowl decorated with superimposed gather tooled into lily-pad Type II, applied threading below rim around upper part of bowl. South Jersey. Early nineteenth century.
Courtesy of the Metropolitan Museum of Art, New York City.

Height, about $4\frac{3}{4}''$; top diameter, $4\frac{5}{8}''$; diameter of foot, $3\frac{1}{16}''$.

PLATE 13

1. Large footed bowl blown from clear green non-lead glass; wide outfolded rim; unusual shape: from rim, sides of upper half of body spread slightly and then taper sharply to a large applied petaled foot (seven broad petals). Body patterned in a 24-rib mold and expanded in fairly heavy ribbing swirled to right. Midwestern. Late eighteenth or early nineteenth century.

Height, 5⅝″ to 5¾″; top diameter, 7¾″; diameter of foot, 4⅜″.

This bowl was in a small but very choice collection of American blown glass formed about twenty-five years ago. While we have no data as to its previous history, because of its characteristics we believe it to be Midwestern, possibly Zanesville, Ohio, or some early glasshouse in the Pittsburgh-Monongahela area. Although the glass is non-lead the quality is very fine and the bowl has a resonance equal to that of many of the finest lead- or so-called flint-glass bowls.

2. Large footed bowl of clear green non-lead glass, fairly deep in tone; heavy outfolded rim and applied circular foot. Patterned in a 20-rib mold and expanded into wide-spaced vertical ribbing which, owing to the expansion, takes the form of shallow fluting. New Geneva Glass Works, western Pennsylvania. Circa 1798–1807.

Height, 5″; top diameter, 8¼″; diameter of foot, 4″.

While this bowl was blown from non-lead metal, because of its shape and the excellent quality of the glass it has resonance equal to that of lead glass. It was found about thirty years ago in a private home near New Geneva, Pennsylvania, and with a reliable history of having been blown in the Gallatin Glass Works. On the basis of this history, the bowl's characteristics, and our knowledge of a 20-rib dip mold's having been used at this glasshouse, the piece is attributed to the New Geneva Glass Works—the "Old Works" as the first glasshouse was called in the account sheets among the Gallatin papers in the manuscript collection of the New York Historical Society.

PLATE 14

1. Blown Three Mold bowl with flat base, light green non-lead glass; patterned in mold for making globular decanters or bar bottles in pattern GII-6. Midwestern, probably Kent, Ohio. Circa 1823–30.

Height, about $2\frac{5}{8}''$; top diameter, $8\frac{1}{16}''$; diameter of base, $4\frac{3}{4}''$.

Pattern GII-6 is composed of a wide band of vertical ribbing between bands of diamond diapering and a band of tapered gadrooning which on decanters falls on the shoulder. The gadrooning does not appear on the bowl because it was cut off when the rim was formed. It was established, by excavations made by the late Harry Hall White on the factory site, that a mold for this pattern was used at a glasshouse in or near the present town of Kent, Portage County, Ohio. This was probably the works operated by Park, Edmunds and Park. Bowls in this Blown Three Mold pattern are rare. Those in light green vary in size. Three or four are known in a light olive-green or what might be termed olive-yellow color. They are deeper and, being nearly straight-sided, are narrower at the rim. One footed bowl in green is known. Globular-shaped decanters or bar bottles and pitchers, about quart size, are known in clear lead glass. Two different molds were used. One, that in which most of the pieces were patterned, had forty-five ribs; the other, rarely encountered in our experience, had forty-six ribs. The globular bar bottles were made without stoppers, the taper-shaped decanters with disk stoppers, horizontally ribbed on one side and vertically on the other.

These decanters and bar bottles occur in a considerable color range including pale aquamarine, clear green, deep yellowish green, canary-yellow, pale olive-yellow, deep olive-yellow, brilliant golden amber, all in non-lead glass. The bar bottles occur also in clear lead glass. It is possible that these or identical molds were used in more than one Midwestern glasshouse.

2. Bowl blown from brilliant amber-yellow non-lead glass; wide sides spreading from flat base to heavy outfolded rim; patterned in small 20-rib dip mold, double insertion, and greatly expanded into broken-swirl design. Midwestern, probably Kent, Ohio. Circa 1823–30.

Height varies from $3\frac{5}{8}''$ to $4''$; top diameter, $8\frac{1}{2}''$; diameter of base, $4\frac{7}{8}''$.

Similar bowls also occur in pale olive-yellow. They were patterned in molds customarily used for bottles and flasks and are very rare.

PLATE 15

Large footed bowl blown from brilliant aquamarine non-lead bottle or window glass; very wide-spreading sides with heavy outfolded rim; applied circular crimped foot; bowl with superimposed decoration tooled into lily-pad Type II. Redwood or Redford Glass Works, New York State. Circa 1831–50. Collection of Mr. and Mrs. Mitchell Taradash.

Greatest height, about $4\frac{5}{8}$″; top diameter, $14\frac{1}{4}$″.

So far as we know there is no characteristic distinguishing an individual piece made at the Redwood Glass Works from a similar piece made at the Redford Works. The two glasshouses were in operation during the same period and John S. Foster, the founder of Redwood, had been superintendent at Redford for two years. The individual pieces with superimposed decoration made at these two glasshouses were in the finest South Jersey tradition, in fact, generally speaking, superior in craftsmanship. And the aquamarine glass was more brilliant and frequently with a tone which might be termed turquoise.

PLATE 16

Large footed bowl blown from aquamarine non-lead glass; bowl rounding from a heavy applied circular foot and flaring to a heavy outfolded rim; superimposed gather tooled into lily-pad Type II. Redwood Glass Works, near Watertown, New York. Circa 1833–50.

Height, 7⅝"; top diameter, 12½"; diameter of foot, 5⅜".

The bowl was acquired over twenty-five years ago in a private home in the vicinity of the glass-works. With it came a companion large pitcher of about three-quart capacity and with superimposed lily-pad decoration matching that of the bowl. The pitcher, however, has a flat base instead of an applied foot.

PLATE 17

Deep ovoid bowl on standard, blown from clear deep olive-green non-lead glass; bowl with applied irregular thread just below the slightly flaring rim, and resting on a standard composed of a thick ring surmounting a turned stem and applied circular foot with narrow step. Probably South Jersey. First half of nineteenth century.

Height, about $9\frac{1}{2}''$; diameter of bowl, $7\frac{3}{4}''$ by $5\frac{13}{16}''$; diameter of foot, $4\frac{5}{16}''$.

The shape of the bowl is extremely rare and unique in our experience.

PLATE 18

1. Boat-shaped compote rather crudely fashioned from clear non-lead glass; deep bowl supported by an applied cylindrical stem with large medial ball knop and terminating in a circular step on an octagonal plinth; bowl with a cut design in style somewhat like that encountered on late eighteenth- and early nineteenth-century Irish glass, composed of a broad band of large conventionalized tulips, one placed in middle of each side and at each end, with pointed arches containing strawberry diamonds in the intervening spaces; at the outer edge of the bottom of the bowl, elliptical notches. Found in Pennsylvania and believed possibly to have been made in one of the early nineteenth-century Pittsburgh glasshouses.

Height, about 8″; top diameter, 6¾″ by 9⅜″; foot, 4″ by 4³⁄₁₆″.

The cutting is crude and may have been done by an apprentice.

2. Large compote on standard blown from clear lead glass; circular bowl unusual in shape in that, instead of being flattened across the bottom, it was drawn down at the center into a shallow cone resting on an applied cylindrical stem, with very wide flattened double knop, between double rings, applied wide circular foot; bowl engraved by copper wheel with leaf and "daisy" design characteristic of Pittsburgh glasshouses of the 1815–35 period.

Height, 7¹³⁄₁₆″; top diameter, 8½″; diameter of foot, 6″.

PLATE 19

1. Blown Three Mold footed bowl; clear, fairly deep green non-lead glass; globular body tapering slightly to a heavy outfolded rim and resting on applied heavy circular foot; pattern GII-33, band of diamond diapering between bands of vertical fluting. Mantua Glass Works, Portage County, Ohio. Circa 1822–29.

Height, $5\frac{1}{4}''$; *top diameter,* $6\frac{13}{16}''$; *greatest diameter of body,* $7\frac{1}{8}''$; *diameter of foot,* $4\frac{1}{16}''$.

The mold in which this bowl was patterned is definitely known to have been used in the Mantua Glass Works. It had thirty-nine flutes in the bottom and top bands, separated by a single horizontal rib from the center band of diamond diapering which was two and a half diamonds high and thirty-six diamonds around, and a fluted and ringed base with thirty-three short flutes and double ring at center. As far as we know only five pieces of Mantua Blown Three Mold glass have so far been recorded—this bowl, a quart pitcher, a quart decanter, and a large cover of the flanged set-in type for a bowl, and another quart decanter which turned up in Ohio about 1945. The pitcher, one decanter, and large cover are illustrated on Plate 118, *American Glass.* The pieces are all in a similar clear, fairly deep green glass. We have tested all but one decanter and they are non-lead glass. The decanters were apparently made without glass stoppers. A careful examination of the edge of the rim of the bowl illustrated indicates that at some time it had a cover. If so it would undoubtedly have been like the cover illustrated on Plate 118, *American Glass.* That cover in pattern, color, and quality of the glass matches perfectly the bowl but it is a little too great in diameter to fit.

2. Blown Three Mold bowl on standard; clear lead glass; circular bowl with heavy applied rim of deep sapphire-blue; short applied stem with large globular knop and applied circular foot; pattern GIII-5. Boston and Sandwich Glass Company. Circa 1825–35.

Height, $6\frac{7}{16}''$; *top diameter,* $6\frac{5}{8}''$; *diameter of foot,* $4\frac{1}{4}''$.

PLATE 20

Very large Blown Three Mold footed bowl; clear lead glass; circular bowl with wide heavy out-folded rim and applied Blown Three Mold pedestal foot; bowl, pattern GII-18; foot probably blown in mold for flip glass, shaped into a shallow bowl, and then attached, whether pattern GIII-5 or GIII-6 uncertain as part of the design was lost in forming the folded rim. Sunburst motif same as in bowl, No. 2, Plate 19. Probably Boston and Sandwich Glass Company. Circa 1825–35. *Height, $5\frac{7}{8}''$; top diameter, $9\frac{1}{2}''$; diameter of foot, $6\frac{3}{4}''$.*

PLATE 21

Large compote or bowl on standard; lead glass; circular bowl flaring to outfolded rim and supported by an applied clear stem resting on broad circular foot; bowl made from three gathers of metal—a layer of opaque white on the inside covered by a gather of amethyst decorated with loop-ings of milk-white, and the outside then covered by a casing of clear glass. Pittsburgh. Last half of nineteenth century.

Height, 8⅜"; top diameter, 9⅝"; diameter of foot, 5⅝".

PLATE 22

1. Bowl, straight-sided, flaring to heavy folded rim and blown from aquamarine non-lead glass; superimposed lily-pad decoration Type II. New York State, Redford or Redwood Glass Works. Circa 1831–50. Collection of Dr. George K. Butterfield.

Height, 4⅜"; top diameter, 10"; diameter of base, 5⅝".

2. Small footed bowl blown from deep aquamarine non-lead glass; heavy outfolded rim and applied heavy circular crimped foot; bowl with superimposed lily-pad decoration Type II. New York State, Redford or Redwood Glass Works. Circa 1831–50.

Height, 4"; top diameter, 5⁵⁄₁₆"; diameter of foot, 3¼".

3. Compote, blown from bluish-aquamarine non-lead glass; circular bowl flaring to wide outfolded rim; stem composed of hollow knop (giving the illusion of a large tear in the stem) and circular step drawn out from same gather as bowl; applied circular foot; bowl with broad sweeping superimposed lily-pad Type III. Redwood Glass Works, New York State. Circa 1833–50.

Height, 5"; top diameter, 8⁵⁄₁₆"; diameter of foot, 3⅞".

PLATE 23

STEUBEN AMERICAN BALLAD BOWLS

Set of three bowls of brilliant crystal-clear (lead) glass, exemplifying modern design; each bowl having three structural elements: a deep wide-based bowl with sides spreading slightly to plain rim, heavy ring of solid glass lightened in effect by trapped symmetrical air tears, wide circular foot, which in fact is an inverted shallow dish. Expertly engraved by copper wheel. Larger bowl with four scenes entitled "Exploration," "Colonization," "Independence," and "Expansion"; one of the smaller bowls, engraved with three tableaux below a lettered border, "Commerce & Trade"; the other, with representations of the early locomotive, airplane, and steamboat, below a lettered border, "Transportation." Designed by Sidney Waugh. Steuben Glass Works, Corning, New York, 1946. Courtesy of Steuben Glass, Inc.

Large bowl: height, $7\frac{1}{4}''$; top diameter, $9\frac{1}{8}''$; diameter of foot, $5\frac{7}{8}''$.

"Trade & Commerce" bowl: height, $5\frac{15}{16}''$; top diameter, $7\frac{1}{2}''$; diameter of foot, $5\frac{13}{16}''$.

"Transportation" bowl: height, $5\frac{7}{8}''$; top diameter, $7\frac{1}{2}''$; diameter of foot, $5\frac{7}{8}''$.

PLATE 24

1. Plate, free-blown from clear lead glass; heavy outfolded rim; applied band of narrow trailed circuits or chain decoration—fourteen circuits or links. Probably South Boston, period of Thomas Cains. Circa 1812–23.

Diameter, 7⅜″.

This type of decoration is sometimes called guilloche. Pitchers and sugar bowls with covers are found with similar decoration. It is believed glass of this type was made by Thomas Cains in South Boston, where he operated the first successful flint- or lead-glass furnace in the Atlantic States.

2. Plate, free-blown from aquamarine non-lead bottle or window glass; heavy outfolded rim; band of superimposed decoration tooled into lily-pad Type II. New York State, Redwood or Redford Glass Works. Circa 1831–50.

Diameter, 7½″.

Plates with superimposed lily-pad decoration are extremely rare.

3. Small shallow bowl, blown from brilliant light green non-lead glass; heavy infolded rim and small circular base; patterned in a 10-diamond mold and expanded. Early nineteenth century.

Height, 1⅜″; top diameter, 5⅜″; diameter of foot, 2¼″.

The same or an identical mold was used in making the 10-diamond chestnut-shaped flasks attributed to Zanesville, Ohio. However, this bowl was acquired from an elderly woman who had inherited it with the family history of its having been bought originally by a Mrs. Stevenson in 1818 and of having been made by a man named Duval in Wellsburg, (West) Virginia. On or about 1813, it is said, Isaac Duval, Nathaniel Carr, and John Carr built a glasshouse at Charleston, the present town of Wellsburg, West Virginia. The firm name was Isaac Duval & Company. The glasshouse is said to have operated successfully until the death of Duval in 1828. It is quite possible that the 10-diamond mold or an identical one was used by Duval and also at Zanesville.

4. Free-blown plate of brilliant light olive-yellow non-lead glass; sides flaring from shallow circular base to narrow irregular outfolded rim; patterned in a 16-rib mold and expanded, broken-swirl design. Mantua Glass Works, Mantua, Ohio. Circa 1822–29.

Height, 1″; top diameter, 6⅛″.

This plate was obtained from a Mrs. Evaline Messenger, of Hiram, Ohio, who inherited it from her mother, a daughter of Pleadis Lois Skinner. Lois Skinner was a niece of William and Joseph Skinner, who with others took over the glassworks in Mantua when David Ladd disposed of his interest in 1823. This plate was one of a set of six, with a bowl, said to have been made at Mantua and given by her uncles as a wedding gift to Lois Skinner. The terminal ring around the pontil mark to which the ribs extend on the base of the plate is a distinguishing characteristic of the 16-rib mold used at the Mantua Glass Works.

5. Blown Three Mold plate of clear lead glass; very flat sides flaring almost at a right angle to the circular base, pattern GII-18—a band of diamond diapering between bands of vertical ribbing. Circa 1825–35.

Height, 9/16″; top diameter, 5¾″; diameter of base, 2½″.

6. Blown Three Mold plate of clear lead glass; outfolded rim and small circular base; patterned in a tumbler mold in GIII-21—band of diagonal ribbing to right, one to left, band of alternate sunburst with diamond center and blocks of diamond diapering, band of diagonal ribbing to right, and single horizontal rib between bands. Circa 1825–35.

Height, 1″; top diameter, 6⅛″; diameter of base, 2″.

In the photograph the pattern appears to be pattern GIII-22 with diagonal ribbings running in the opposite directions and the top band of vertical ribbing lost in finishing the rim. This is because one is looking at the inside of the plate. In all Blown Three Mold glass the pattern is described from the outside and from base to top.

PLATE 25

Hand basin and ewer of brilliant aquamarine non-lead glass. Deep bowl, resting on applied circular crimped foot and flaring to heavy outfolded rim. Pitcher, globular body, wide cylindrical neck with slightly flaring plain rim and deep pinched lip; applied unusually broad crimped foot and applied solid semi-ear-shaped handle. Both bowl and pitcher with superimposed lily-pad decoration Type III. Saratoga (Mountain) Glass Works. Circa 1844–60.

Bowl: height, 6–6½"; top diameter, 11"; diameter of foot, 4⅜".
Pitcher: height, 8½"; top diameter, 4¾"; greatest diameter of body, 5⅝"; diameter of foot, 4¾".

This basin and ewer were blown at the first Saratoga glassworks, erected by Oscar Granger in 1844 when he moved his Mount Vernon Glass Works from Vernon, New York, to Mount Pleasant, about eight miles from Saratoga Springs. The new glassworks was known as the Mountain Works.

PLATE 26

Hand basin with ewer, free-blown from a very heavy gather of opaque white non-lead glass. Hemispherical bowl with wide-flaring, slightly downturned rim and resting on an applied broad sloping circular foot. Ewer or pitcher, with short angular globular body sloping to a very long cylindrical neck flaring slightly to plain rim with high broad lip; applied solid handle. Probably mid-nineteenth century.

Bowl: height, $4\frac{3}{8}''$; greatest diameter of rim, $11\frac{1}{2}''$; diameter of foot, $4\frac{5}{8}''$.

Pitcher: height, $11\frac{3}{4}''$; diameter of top, $4\frac{1}{16}''$; greatest diameter of body, $5\frac{7}{8}''$; diameter of foot, $4\frac{5}{8}''$.

The basin and ewer, formerly in the collection of Miss Minnie I. Meacham, one of the early collectors of American glass, were attributed by tradition to the Kensington Glass Works, Philadelphia. We are more inclined to the belief that they were made in South Jersey. Possibly they were blown in the glasshouse of the Whitall brothers, who about 1844 acquired the first glassworks built in Millville, New Jersey, and are supposed to have made apothecary jars in opaque white. Pressed translucent white ones were produced there by Whitall, Tatum and Company, the firm formed about 1857.

The color and texture of the glass in this set are similar to some of the early Bristol opaque white glass.

PLATE 27

1. Sugar bowl and cover blown from clear brilliant amethyst lead glass; deep globular body tapering slightly to a galleried rim and resting on an applied short-stemmed flaring circular foot; hemispherical cover with infolded rim and stemmed flat button finial drawn out of the same gather; bowl and cover patterned in a 12-rib mold and expanded in wide-spaced vertical ribbing. Attributed to Pittsburgh, probably Bakewell's. Early nineteenth century.

Over-all height, $7\frac{1}{2}$"; without cover, $5\frac{5}{16}$"; top diameter, $4\frac{5}{16}$"; greatest diameter of body, $4\frac{11}{16}$"; diameter of foot, $2\frac{13}{16}$".

2. Pitcher blown from deep sapphire-blue lead glass; broad-shouldered body and wide neck with flaring rim and pinched lip; applied solid semi-ear-shaped handle with long crimped end with impressed leaf decoration; body patterned in a 12-rib mold and expanded in wide-spaced vertical ribbing. Attributed to Pittsburgh, probably Bakewell's. Early nineteenth century.

Height, $5\frac{1}{4}$"; top diameter, 3"; greatest diameter of body, $3\frac{1}{2}$"; diameter of base, $2\frac{3}{4}$".

3. Sugar bowl and cover blown from clear deep green non-lead glass; globular body sloping to plain rim and resting on an applied circular foot; small applied solid handle with thumb- and finger-pieces on each side; eighteenth-century type of set-in flanged cover, dome shape with applied double button finial. South Jersey. Found in a private home near Glassboro, New Jersey. Probably last quarter of eighteenth century.

Over-all height, $6\frac{1}{8}$"; top diameter, $3\frac{13}{16}$"; greatest diameter of body, $4\frac{5}{16}$"; diameter of foot, $2\frac{1}{2}$".

4. Pitcher, free-blown from clear deep green non-lead glass; barrel-shaped body, short cylindrical neck with plain rim and tiny pinched lip; applied olive-amber (black) glass broad corrugated strap handle with heavy thumbpiece. Attributed to South Jersey. Probably last quarter of eighteenth century.

Height, $6\frac{3}{16}$"; top diameter, $3\frac{1}{2}$"; greatest diameter of body, $4\frac{1}{2}$"; diameter of base, $3\frac{1}{2}$".

PLATE 28

1. Sugar bowl and cover of dark amethyst non-lead glass, so deep in color that, combined with the thickness of the glass, it appears black in reflected light; the bowl angling at the center and tapering to applied sloping circular foot; high domed cover, straight-sided and fitting over the top of the bowl and resting on a single heavy applied ring—a cover treatment rarely encountered; on each side of the bowl, a small applied looped handle decorated with pinched trailing; on the cover, a stemmed ball finial supporting a crudely formed swan at the center of four leaf-like ornaments; on one side of the bowl, engraved by copper wheel, a characteristic Amelung oval medallion composed of narrow leaf sprays joined at equidistant points by four tiny daisylike flowers; within the medallion, inscription *"To Mis. C. G. In Washington Cty"*; on the front of the cover an engraved floral and leaf spray similar to that found on the covers of Amelung pokals and flips. From the Henry Francis du Pont Winterthur Museum.

Over-all height, $8\frac{1}{4}$"; without cover, $4\frac{1}{2}$"; height of cover to base of finial, $1\frac{3}{4}$"; top diameter of bowl, $3\frac{5}{8}$"; diameter at horizontal rim on bowl which supports cover, $4\frac{1}{4}$"; greatest diameter of body, 5"; diameter of foot, which is irregular, $3\frac{3}{16}$"–$3\frac{1}{4}$"; diameter at lower rim of cover, $4\frac{1}{16}$".

2. Creamer blown from dark amethyst non-lead glass similar in color to sugar bowl, No. 1; ovoid body, broad cylindrical neck with slightly flaring rim with pinched lip, applied circular foot, and applied solid semi-ear-shaped handle; on the front, engraved by copper wheel, a circular medallion similar to that on the sugar bowl, and enclosing a large eight-pointed star. From the Henry Francis du Pont Winterthur Museum.

Height, about $4\frac{13}{16}$"; top diameter, $2\frac{1}{2}$"; greatest diameter of body, $2\frac{15}{16}$"; diameter of foot, $2\frac{1}{8}$".

The sugar bowl with inscription *"To Mis. C. G. In Washington Cty"* was acquired from descendants of a Miss Catherine Geeting who as a child had resided near the Washington-Frederick County line in Maryland, and within a few miles of the New Bremen Glassmanufactory. Presumably the initials *"C.G."* were hers, and the *"Cty"* stood for county. Since Catherine Geeting was married on April 8, 1808, and Amelung had ceased making glass about 1795 it is believed that the bowl was made in honor of an early birthday.

The pitcher was also acquired in the vicinity of Frederick, Maryland. The color and metal are so similar to the sugar bowl that it is quite possible they may have been blown from the same batch of glass.

PLATE 29

1. Free-blown large footed bowl and cover, very heavy, clear non-lead glass with decided smoky tone; circular bowl with a heavy applied ring about one inch below the rim forming a rest for the cover; heavy applied crimped foot; on each side an applied looped handle with thumb and finger rests; bowl decorated with trailed circuits or chains; cover decorated with swagging and a large chicken finial supported by a short cylindrical stem. Attributed to Amelung's New Bremen Glassmanufactory. Circa 1788–94. From the Henry Francis du Pont Winterthur Museum.

Over-all height to top of chicken finial, about 9″; without cover, 4¼″; top diameter, 4 5/16″; greatest diameter of body, 5⅜″; diameter of foot, 3 11/16″.

2. Free-blown footed shallow bowl with high conical dome cover, clear non-lead glass with slightly grayish tone; bowl straight-sided form, very shallow and with heavy applied ring about one inch below the rim forming a rest for the cover; applied short stem and applied circular foot; on two sides, small applied handles with thumb and finger rests, and on the other sides applied irregular bosses; tall dome-shaped cover with applied large bosses toward the top and finial formed of a short cylindrical stem supporting a crude stag with large antlers; bowl and cover each patterned in a 16-rib mold and expanded in vertical ribbing; perhaps intended for holding a sugar loaf. Found in the vicinity of Frederick, Maryland, and attributed to Amelung's New Bremen Glass-

manufactory. From the Henry Francis du Pont Winterthur Museum.

Extreme height to top of finial, 8¼″; without cover, 3¼″; top diameter of bowl, 3 7/16″; diameter of bowl at applied ring which supports cover, 4 9/16″; foot irregular, varying in diameter from 3″ to 3⅜″; diameter at rim of cover, 4¼″.

The cover treatment of these two bowls is similar to the Amelung Geeting bowl, Plate 28. The cover fits over the rim of the bowl and rests on a ring applied about an inch below the bowl rim. This appears to be an Amelung characteristic, in our experience rarely encountered on other glass. In fact, in addition to these two covered bowls and the Geeting bowl, we know of only one other bowl with this cover treatment. That was found in South Jersey near Glassboro and was blown from a heavy gather of aquamarine non-lead glass. The body and cover are decorated with heavy swirled ribbing and the bowl rests on an applied circular crimped foot. The cover has an applied button finial supported by a short cylindrical stem. While attributed to South Jersey because found there, it might well be an Amelung piece made in the first years the works was in operation when, we know, bottle glasswares were being produced. The earliest dated and inscribed pieces in clear glass were made, as far as we know, in 1788, but the glasshouse was in operation prior to that date. This bowl is illustrated (No. 2, Plate 16) in *American Glass*.

PLATE 30

1. Sugar bowl and cover blown from very pale green, probably non-lead glass; deep bowl rounding in lower part and sloping to applied square base; applied bowknot handles; eighteenth-century type of set-in flanged cover with an applied elaborate swan finial supported by a graduated double ring. Attributed to South Jersey, last quarter of eighteenth century. From the Henry Francis du Pont Winterthur Museum.

Over-all height, $6\frac{3}{4}''$; without cover, $3\frac{1}{2}''$; top diameter, $3\frac{1}{4}''$; base, $2\frac{5}{8}''$ by $2\frac{5}{8}''$; width, outside handle to handle, $5\frac{3}{4}''$.

2. Sugar bowl and cover blown from brilliant clear lead glass; deep circular bowl rounding to applied short-stemmed small sloping circular foot; eighteenth-century type of set-in cover with flanged rim drawn out from same gather; applied stemmed ball finial containing seven small tears and a miniature ball on the top; bowl and cover patterned in a piece mold and expanded in large ogival or diamond diaper design, twelve diamonds in lateral chain. Stiegel type. Last quarter of eighteenth century.

Over-all height, $6''$; without cover, $3\frac{1}{4}''$; top diameter, $4\frac{3}{16}''$; diameter of foot, $2\frac{5}{16}''$.

Bowls in clear glass in expanded ogival or diamond design are extremely rare. This specimen may very well have been made in Stiegel's glasshouse at Manheim. It was acquired several years ago in New Jersey, where it had been handed down through the Deacon family. The Deacons were Quakers and had business connections in Philadelphia.

PLATE 31

Sugar bowl with set-in flanged cover (eighteenth-century type), blown from light yellow-green non-lead glass; applied sloping circular foot; cover with button finial drawn out from same gather. Bowl patterned in three-piece 15-diamond mold and expanded in diamond diaper pattern. Cover patterned in a 16-rib mold and expanded into wide-spaced vertical ribbing. Mantua Glass Works, Mantua, Ohio. Circa 1822–29.

Over-all height, $5\frac{3}{4}''$; without cover, $3\frac{5}{16}''$; top diameter, $3\frac{1}{8}''$; diameter of foot, $2\frac{3}{4}''$.

This rare covered sugar bowl is an excellent example of the survival of eighteenth-century forms and details in some of the early nineteenth-century Midwestern glasshouses, especially the small bottle and window glasshouses.

PLATE 32

1. Sugar bowl and cover, free-blown from deep aquamarine non-lead glass; oval in form, with a heavy outfolded rim; at each end, a heavy solid applied handle, crimped at the base, and on each side, an applied short crimped band. Hollow free-blown set-in cover shaped by manipulation from a single gather and closed at the bottom instead of being open, the only cover with this feature of which we have a record; the lower part contracted to fit into the bowl with its sides resting on rim of bowl; hollow finial, formed from the same gather, shaped and finished with a top band of crimping to simulate a flower, and its hollow space giving the effect of a large tear. A crude piece but unique as far as we know. Suncook Glass Works, Suncook, New Hampshire. Circa 1839–50.

Over-all height, $7\frac{3}{4}$"; without cover, $4\frac{1}{2}$"; top, 3" by 5"; diameter of base, 3".

2. Sugar bowl and cover blown from clear lead glass; oblong in form and similar in shape to Staffordshire earthenware bowls of the period. Formed in a full-size piece mold. Probably New England Glass Company. Circa 1818–25.

Over-all height, $5\frac{1}{8}$", without cover, 4"; top, $4\frac{3}{8}$" by $3\frac{3}{8}$"; body, $5\frac{9}{16}$" by $4\frac{1}{16}$"; base, $2\frac{3}{4}$" by $3\frac{1}{8}$".

Round and oval dishes, salts with and without foot or standard, and other articles in various geometric patterns are found in this type of glass. The glass is much thicker than that of the regular Blown Three Mold so that articles normally have a smooth inner surface. A few salts are known in deep blue. The New England Glass Company is believed to have made such glass and so are other glasshouses of the same period. Some pieces of this type, which we call "imitation cut glass," were made in Ireland.

PLATE 33

Blown Three Mold covered dish with plate or stand, blown from clear lead glass; straight-sided bowl with galleried rim; domed cover with flaring folded rim and heavy button finial. Bowl, cover, and stand in pattern GII-18—a band of diamond diapering between bands of vertical ribbing. Probably Boston and Sandwich Glass Company. Circa 1825–35.

Bowl: over-all height, 5″, without cover, $3\frac{5}{16}$″; top diameter, $4\frac{9}{16}$″; diameter at base, 4″.
Stand or plate: height, 1″; diameter, $7\frac{1}{8}$″.

Dishes of this type were probably used for preserves or butter. According to the family tradition handed down with the one illustrated, it was used for honey.

PLATE 34

1. A typical nineteenth-century Pittsburgh-area free-blown sugar bowl and cover of clear lead glass; globular body contracting below a galleried rim and resting on applied knop stem; flaring circular foot; small domed cover with flat button finial. Bowl decorated with copper-wheel engraving of conventionalized flowers and leaf sprays; the cover, with a narrow leaf band; style and character of the engraving typical of Pittsburgh glasshouses of the 1815–35 period.

Over-all height, $7\frac{1}{4}''$, without cover, $5''$; top diameter, $4\frac{1}{8}''$; greatest diameter of body, $4\frac{9}{16}''$; diameter of foot, $3\frac{3}{4}''$; diameter of cover at rim, $3\frac{9}{16}''$.

2. Free-blown sugar bowl and cover, clear non-lead glass; small globular body tapering slightly to plain rim and rounding at bottom to a short drawn stem which terminates in a circular knop resting on an applied wide circular foot; applied solid handles with small thumbpiece. Bowl decorated with shallow copper-wheel engraving of leaf spray on each side. Eighteenth-century set-in cover with wide flanged rim, flat top instead of usual domed or rounded form, and exceptionally well-formed and large swan finial. Believed to have been made in Philadelphia-Baltimore area. Late eighteenth century.

Over-all height, about $7\frac{11}{16}''$, without cover, $4\frac{5}{8}''$; top diameter, $3\frac{1}{4}''$; greatest diameter of body, $3\frac{3}{4}''$; diameter of foot, $3\frac{1}{4}''$.

3. Blown and cut tall sugar bowl with galleried rim and domed cover; bowl clear non-lead glass, cover lead glass; straight-sided bowl rounding at bottom to an applied stem with large hollow globular knop and resting on a broad applied circular foot; decorated with wide band of strawberry diamond and fan cutting above a single band of cut and polished half ovals. Cover with similar cut design and applied ball finial with star cutting on top. Pittsburgh, possibly Bakewell, Page and Bakewell. Circa 1815–35.

Over-all height, $8\frac{7}{8}''$, without cover, $6\frac{3}{4}''$; top diameter, $4\frac{9}{16}''$; diameter of foot, $3\frac{1}{2}''$.

It would be expected that normally bowl and cover would have been blown from same batch. However, since this non-lead cover is evidence that such metal as well as lead glass was used for cut glasswares, and lead and non-lead glass were made at the same period by most of the early glasshouses specializing in tablewares, the mismating is not so surprising.

4. Blown Three Mold sugar bowl and cover in clear lead glass; deep circular bowl with wide galleried rim and applied sloping circular foot; dome cover with stemmed ball finial formed from same gather. Bowl and cover patterned in GI-24, extremely rare in this pattern. New England area. Circa 1820–35.

Over-all height, $5\frac{7}{8}''$, without cover, $3\frac{5}{8}''$; top diameter, $5\frac{1}{8}''$; diameter of foot, $2\frac{3}{4}''$; diameter cover rim, $4\frac{1}{2}''$.

5. Blown Three Mold sugar bowl and cover in clear lead glass; deep bowl with galleried rim; applied slightly domed foot with wide infolded rim and patterned in a small open-top 24-rib mold and expanded in vertical ribbing. Dome cover with infolded rim and flat-topped button finial formed from same gather. Bowl in Sunburst pattern GIII-20; cover in pattern GII-22. Probably New England area. Circa 1820–35.

Over-all height, $6''$; without cover, $4\frac{3}{8}''$; top diameter, $5''$; diameter of foot, $3\frac{9}{16}''$; diameter of cover rim, $4\frac{3}{4}''$.

PLATE 35

Large covered bowl on standard, blown from very heavy gather of non-lead glass, clear with pinkish tone. Deep straight-sided bowl, with flaring tooled galleried rim, supported by an applied short knop stem and heavy circular foot; lower part of bowl decorated by a second gather formed into eleven very heavy tapering and swirled ribs below a heavy rounded horizontal band. High domed cover with tooled rim and similar decoration on dome, but with ten ribs closer together than on the bowl, large flat button finial. General characteristics of the bowl indicate a period about 1820–35. Collection of Mrs. Robert Harvey.

Over-all height, about $10\frac{3}{8}''$; without cover, $6\frac{7}{8}''$; top diameter, $6\frac{1}{8}''$; diameter of foot, $4\frac{7}{8}''$.

PLATE 36

Large jug or pitcher, free-blown from clear olive-green non-lead bottle glass; large globular body, broad cylindrical neck, flaring slightly to plain rim without a pouring lip, heavy solid applied handle. *Height, 8¾″; top diameter, 3⅞″; greatest diameter of body, 7⅝″; diameter of base, 4¼″.*

Wine or spirits bottles in similar size and body shape were a regular product of many bottle houses of the late eighteenth and early nineteenth centuries. The piece illustrated is such a bottle converted by some blower into an individual handled jug or pitcher by expanding the neck and applying a handle. It was formerly in the collection of Miss Minnie I. Meacham, one of the first discriminating collectors of early American blown glass.

PLATE 37

Large pitcher free-blown from heavy olive-amber (black) non-lead bottle glass; globular body, broad cylindrical neck, flaring slightly to plain rim with pinched lip; neck decorated with a few applied threads; heavy applied circular foot. Exceptionally fine individual piece. Attributed to the Ellenville Glass Works, Wawarsing (later Ellenville), Ulster County, New York. Circa 1836–40. *Height, about 8⅜"; top diameter, 4⅜"; greatest diameter of body, 5⅞"; diameter of foot, 4⅛".*

PLATE 38

Large pitcher free-blown from heavy deep reddish-amber non-lead glass, a color sometimes called "blood amber"; symmetrical globular body resting on a heavy applied circular foot and rounding to a wide cylindrical neck, flaring slightly to a plain rim with tiny pinched lip; applied solid semi-ear-shaped handle with heavy crimped end. Neck threaded from base to the rim and body decorated with a superimposed gather tooled into a double lily-pad decoration of Types II and III. Stoddard, New Hampshire. Circa 1842–72.
Height, $7\frac{7}{8}''$; top diameter, $4\frac{9}{16}''$; greatest diameter of body, $5\frac{3}{8}''$; diameter of foot, $4''$.

Only a few pitchers with this double lily-pad decoration are known to us—another in similar blood amber and about the same size as this and two, a little smaller, in olive-amber. Three of these pitchers, including the one illustrated, were in the collection of the late Herbert Delevan Mason, who over a period of several years made a specialized collection of individual pieces made by blowers of the Stoddard and Keene, New Hampshire, glasshouses. He had data indicating that these pitchers were the work of one Matthew Johnson, a skilled blower who was employed at Stoddard for several years during the period of about 1846–70. From about 1842 to 1873 four different glasshouses operated in South Stoddard and Mill Village, settlements about two miles apart in the same township. It is believed Johnson worked in the South Stoddard Glass Company factory of which Weeks and Gilson finally became the sole proprietors, and also in the second glasshouse in Mill Village, which was known as the New Granite Glass Works. Johnson is credited also with having made many of the finest pieces blown at the Redwood and Harrisburg glasshouses near Watertown, New York. There is a very definite similarity between the finest of these New York State pieces decorated with superimposed gather tooled into lily-pad decoration Type III and those made by Johnson at Stoddard.

PLATE 39

1. Pitcher, free-blown from non-lead glass, aquamarine with loopings of milk-white; globular body, resting on heavy applied aquamarine circular foot; broad cylindrical neck with wide-flaring rim and tiny pinched lip; applied semi-ear-shaped aquamarine handle.

Height, $8\frac{3}{8}''$; top diameter, $5\frac{7}{16}''$; greatest diameter of body, $5\frac{5}{16}''$; diameter of foot, $3\frac{1}{2}''$.

This pitcher was a presentation piece made by a workman named Burgess at a glassworks operated around the 1870s at New Windsor, Ulster County, New York. It was presented to a Mrs. Harriet McCormack, who ran the old Clinton Hotel in New Windsor at which some of the blowers were said to have boarded. The pitcher was inherited by her granddaughter, from whom it was acquired some years ago.

The commercial product of this factory was window glass, though possibly bottles were made also. As far as we know, this pitcher, a workman's individual piece, is the only example of tableware so far recorded.

2. Pitcher blown from light aquamarine non-lead window glass; large globular body resting on applied large sloping foot; broad cylindrical neck with flaring rim and broad pinched lip; applied solid handle ending in a long band of crimping. Neck with fine applied threading extending to rim and body decorated with superimposed gather tooled into lily-pad design Type II. Blown by Matt Johnson. Circa 1850–55.

Height, $9\frac{1}{4}''$; top diameter, $5\frac{5}{8}''$; greatest diameter of body, $6\frac{1}{4}''$; diameter of foot, $4\frac{5}{8}''$.

This pitcher was blown in the "North Works" or Keene Window Glass Factory which, prior to about 1825, was the New Hampshire Glass Factory. It was made as a presentation piece by Matthew Johnson (or Matt as his familiars called him) while he was employed at Stoddard but was on one of his periodic visits to Keene, New Hampshire.

PLATE 40

1. Pitcher tree-blown from heavy gather of cobalt-blue non-lead glass; squatty globular body, flattened-out shoulder, long wide cylindrical threaded neck with flaring rim and small pinched lip; applied heavy sloping crimped foot; applied slender semi-ear-shaped handle with single crimp and turned back at end. Whitney Glass Works, Glassboro, New Jersey. Circa 1835–40.

Height, $6\frac{7}{8}''$; greatest diameter of body, $5\frac{1}{4}''$; diameter of foot, $3\frac{7}{8}''$.

According to family history, this pitcher was blown by Joel Duffield, a glass blower at the Whitney Glass Works, Glassboro, New Jersey. This works was a continuation of the Harmony Glass Works which had been started in 1813 by a number of workmen previously employed at the Olive Glass Works, a continuation of the second glasshouse in South Jersey started by the Stangers about 1780-81. Thomas H. Whitney acquired an interest in the Harmony Works about 1835 and a little later his brother, Samuel A. Whitney, became associated with him, the firm name being Whitney Brothers. The plant was known as the Whitney Glass Works. It was finally acquired by the Owens Bottle Company.

2. Pitcher blown from dark amber non-lead glass with loopings of milk-white; fashioned in a form which came into vogue after 1830 and continued in use forty years or so; small globular body with an applied amber glass gather tooled into broad ribbing below a rounded horizontal ring, long wide cylindrical neck terminating in a plain rim with high arched lip and decorated with opaque white loopings; applied short multiple-ring stem and wide circular foot; applied solid semi-ear-shaped handle terminating in a flattened tailpiece with impressed leaf decoration, a detail of handle decoration which came in about 1830 and continued beyond 1870. Bridgeton, New Jersey. Circa 1836–50.

Height, $7\frac{1}{2}''$; top diameter, $3\frac{1}{8}''$; greatest diameter of body, $3\frac{7}{8}''$; diameter of foot, $3\frac{15}{16}''$.

One of a pair of pitchers obtained from a relative of Jackie Getzinger, a glass blower who is said to have made them in the glassworks at Bridgeton, New Jersey.

3. Pitcher blown from brilliant light green non-lead glass; cylindrical body with wide spread at shoulder, short cylindrical neck with plain rim and tiny pinched lip; applied broad flat semi-ear-shaped handle, vertically ribbed; body patterned in a 24-rib mold, double insertion and expanded, broken-swirl decoration; characteristic Midwestern form and decoration. Midwestern. Early nineteenth century.

Height, $7''$; top diameter, $4''$; greatest diameter of body, $5\frac{7}{8}''$; diameter of base, $3\frac{7}{8}''$.

4. Pitcher blown from brilliant light green non-lead glass; straight-sided body spreading at shoulder, cylindrical neck with plain rim and pinched lip; applied semi-ear-shaped broad flattened handle with heavy vertical ribbing and horizontal ribbing on the drawn-out end; body patterned in a 24-rib mold and expanded in ribbing swirled to the right; typical Midwestern shape and decoration. Midwestern. Early nineteenth century.

Height, $7\frac{1}{4}''$; top diameter, $3\frac{15}{16}''$; diameter at shoulder, $5\frac{5}{8}''$; diameter at base, $3\frac{3}{4}''$.

PLATE 41

1. Small pitcher, free-blown from clear lead glass; globular body with wide cylindrical neck with plain rim and pinched lip, and resting on an applied petaled foot (eight petals); applied solid slender semi-ear-shaped handle with crimped end; body decorated with eight applied vertical bands of crimping and rigaree applied before the foot was attached. Probably Midwestern. First half of nineteenth century.

Height, 4⅛"; top diameter, 3"; greatest diameter of body, 2⅝"; diameter of foot, 2 5/16".

2. Miniature Blown Three Mold pitcher, cobalt-blue with clear handle, lead glass; blown in miniature decanter mold in Sunburst pattern GIII-12; neck and wide-flaring rim with down-turned lip formed by manipulation. Boston and Sandwich Glass Company. Circa 1825–35.

Height, 2⅛"; top diameter, 1 7/16"; greatest diameter of body, 1 11/16"; diameter of base, 1 5/16".

3. Small pitcher, free-blown from aquamarine non-lead glass; ovoid body, wide neck with flaring tooled rim and tiny pinched lip; applied irregular crimped foot; applied solid semi-ear-shaped handle; body decorated with superimposed gather tooled into double band of lily-pad Type I. South Jersey. First half of nineteenth century.

Height, about 3½"; top diameter, 2⅛"; greatest diameter of body, 2⅛"; diameter of foot, 1⅞".

4. Small creamer, free-blown from aquamarine non-lead glass; globular body with narrow flattened shoulder and wide cylindrical neck with flaring threaded rim and pinched lip; applied quatrefoil solid foot with slight crimping on underside, an unusual type; applied unusual D-shaped handle with thumbpiece; body patterned in 24-rib mold and expanded in faint vertical ribbing which does not show on the neck because it was flattened out during the tooling to form the neck and rim. Probably South Jersey. First half of nineteenth century.

Height, 4 5/16"; top diameter, 2 3/16"; greatest diameter of body, 2 13/16"; diameter of foot, 3¾" by 3⅞".

5. Pitcher, free-blown from aquamarine non-lead glass; small globular body with wide cylindrical neck threaded to flaring rim with pinched lip, and resting on an applied long hollow cylindrical stem and small circular foot; solid applied semi-ear-shaped handle. Attributed to first Saratoga glass-works located at Mount Pleasant, about eight miles from Saratoga Springs and known as the Mountain Works. Circa 1845–60.

Height, 6⅛"; top diameter, 2¼"; greatest diameter of body, 2⅝"; diameter of foot, 2 11/16".

The stem of this creamer is an unusual feature. We have seen it on very few pieces, two of which were small compotes, also free-blown from similar aquamarine non-lead glass and attributed to Saratoga (Mountain) Glass Works.

6. Pitcher blown from light green non-lead glass; globular body, wide cylindrical neck with plain rim and small pinched lip; body resting on three applied equidistant small feet; applied solid semi-ear-shaped handle; body patterned in a 24-rib mold and expanded in vertical ribbing. Attributed to Zanesville, where it was acquired many years ago. Circa 1816–25.

Height, 6¼"; top diameter, 2 11/16"; greatest diameter of body, 3⅜".

PLATE 42

1. Large blown and cut pitcher; clear lead glass; globular body, wide neck flaring slightly to rim with broad arched lip; applied heavy handle with flat cut thumbpiece. Entire pitcher decorated with cutting in the style followed in the English and Irish glasshouses of the second quarter of the nineteenth century; central design of four large blocks of strawberry diamonds separated by single pillar rib or flute; a horizontal angled rib and band of flat splits above and below the central band; prismatic cutting on neck and lip; long vertical prismatic cutting each side of handle; notched rim; star cutting on base. Acquired in a private home in New York City, possibly originally from the glassworks of John and Richard Fisher, New York City, or John L. Gilliland's Brooklyn Flint Glass Works, or the Jersey Glass Works in Jersey City, in all of which cut and engraved flint glasswares were being made in the second quarter of the nineteenth century.

Height, 8½″; top diameter, 4⅞″; greatest diameter of body, 6 3/16″; diameter of base, 3½″.

2. Blown Three Mold pitcher; clear lead glass; semi-barrel-shaped body, short cylindrical neck with wide-flaring plain rim and deeply pinched lip, applied broad solid handle with wide medial rib; patterned probably in a quart decanter mold in GIII-26, the most elaborate of the Geometric patterns. Boston and Sandwich Glass Company. Circa 1825–35.

Height, 6⅝″; top diameter, 4¼″; greatest diameter of body, 4⅜″; diameter of base, 3¼″.

3. Pitcher free-blown from clear lead glass, typical Midwestern shape, spreading to a narrow shoulder, wide cylindrical neck with plain rim and tiny pinched lip, applied large hollow semi-ear-shaped handle, drawn out at lower end, which is crimped and rolled over; lower part of body patterned in a dip mold and expanded with decoration of twelve contiguous arches with rounded top forming so-called sunken panels; further decoration of a band composed of large daisylike flowers and leaf sprays engraved by copper wheel, and around the neck, engraved leaf sprays. Pittsburgh area. Circa 1815–35.

Height, 5⅝″; top diameter, 3 9/16″; greatest diameter of body, 4⅞″; diameter of base, 3″.

PLATE 43

1. Blown Three Mold creamer, sapphire-blue lead glass; straight-sided body with short rounded shoulder, wide cylindrical neck flaring at rim with pinched lip; tooled horizontal ribbing on rim and upper part of neck; applied solid semi-ear-shaped handle; blown and patterned in a four-piece half-pint decanter mold in Baroque pattern GV-14, sometimes called the Horizontal Palm Leaf, one of the most elaborate of the Baroque patterns—twenty-four short broad vertical ribs; four equidistant dots and four trefoils; four units in the double palm-leaf band; four equidistant dots; sixteen links in guilloche band; four equidistant 5-petal palmettes; rayed base, twenty-four ribs. Boston and Sandwich Glass Works. Circa 1825–35.
Height, 4¾″; top diameter, 3⅛″; diameter of base, 2¾″.

2. Blown Three Mold creamer; light sapphire-blue lead glass; pear-shaped body sloping at shoulder to wide cylindrical neck; flaring tooled rim with pinched lip; flaring circular foot with milled rim; applied solid semi-ear-shaped handle; blown and patterned in half-pint decanter mold in Baroque pattern GV-3, twenty-one long heavy ribs below six equidistant trefoils. Circa 1825–35.
Height, 5⅛″; top diameter, 3½″; greatest diameter of body, 3 7/16″; diameter of foot, 2½″.

As far as we know creamers and half-pint decanters are the only articles found in this pattern. No record is available as to the glasshouse in which this mold may have been used.

3. Blown Three Mold creamer; cobalt-blue lead glass; straight-sided body tapering at shoulders to wide cylindrical neck, with wide-flaring tooled rim with tiny pinched lip; applied wide handle with heavy central rib and crimped end; blown and patterned in a half-pint decanter mold in Baroque pattern GV-8, Shell and Ribbing. Boston and Sandwich Glass Works. Circa 1825–35.
Height, 4½″; top diameter, 3⅛″; diameter at base, 2½″.

Quart, pint, and half-pint decanters, quart and pint pitchers, and creamers are known in this pattern.

4. Blown Three Mold pitcher, brilliant clear lead glass; straight-sided body, sloping shoulder, wide cylindrical neck, and flaring rim with tooled horizontal ribbing and pointed pinched lip; applied broad handle with heavy medial rib terminating in thumb rest at top and impressed leaf on flattened lower end; blown and patterned in quart decanter mold in Arch pattern GIV-6, Gothic arches above heavy short pillar ribs, heavy gadroon ribbing; the ribbing, falling on the neck, much more expanded and swirled than on decanters; plain base. Possibly the New England Glass Company. Circa 1815–30.
Height, 7 3/16″; top diameter, 4¼″; greatest diameter of body, 4½″; diameter of base, 4″.

5. Blown Three Mold pitcher, clear lead glass; straight-sided body rounding at shoulders to wide cylindrical neck with flaring rim and pinched lip; wide tooled horizontal band at base of rim; applied slender hollow semi-ear-shaped handle; blown and patterned in pint decanter mold in Baroque pattern GV-13, heart, guilloche or chain, and heavy short ribbing at bottom; plain base. New England area. Circa 1815–30.
Height, 5¾″; top diameter, 3½″; greatest diameter of body, 3⅛″; diameter of base, 3″.

PLATE 44

Tall free-blown and cut pitcher of exceedingly clear brilliant glass, probably lead; ovoid body, long cylindrical neck flaring at rim with high arched lip; applied solid swan-neck handle arching high above the rim, a treatment characteristic of the period; body and neck decorated with cut facets in honeycomb effect; star cutting on base of foot. Made at the glassworks established by Christian Dorflinger in Brooklyn, New York, in 1852. Owned by Miss Katherine Dorflinger, daughter of Christian Dorflinger.

Height to top of lip, $9\frac{7}{8}''$; to top of handle, $11\frac{1}{2}''$.

PLATE 45

1. Pitcher on standard, free-blown from non-lead aquamarine bottle or window glass; globular body, broad cylindrical neck with wide-flaring tooled rim with small pinched lip; applied short knop stem and comparatively small circular foot; applied solid semi-ear-shaped handle; body decorated with superimposed gather tooled into lily-pad Type I. New London Glass Works, Connecticut. Circa 1856–70.

Height, $7\frac{3}{8}''$; top diameter, $4\frac{5}{8}''$; greatest diameter of body, $4\frac{11}{16}''$; diameter of foot, $3\frac{7}{16}''$.

This pitcher was made at the New London Glass Works, New London, Connecticut, for John Ferguson, who was employed near the factory, for presentation to Delia Craig.

2. Decanter jug, free-blown from aquamarine non-lead glass; globular body, tapering cylindrical neck rounding at top and contracting to a high sloping rim with small pinched lip; applied heavy broad tapering 3-rib strap handle; upper part of body and neck decorated with applied wide-spaced threading. New York State. Probably mid-nineteenth century.

Height, $8\frac{1}{4}''$; greatest diameter of body, $4\frac{3}{8}''$; rim, $2\frac{3}{8}''$ by $3''$; diameter of base, $3''$.

3. Pitcher blown from light sapphire-blue non-lead glass; bulbous body tapering to wide neck and wide-flaring rim with large overhanging lip; applied semi-ear-shaped hollow handle turned over and crimped at bottom; patterned in an 8-rib dip mold with heavy pillar molding, swirled to right on neck and rim. Pittsburgh. Circa 1830–75.

Height, $7\frac{1}{2}''$; top diameter, $4\frac{1}{4}''$; greatest diameter of body, $4\frac{1}{2}''$; diameter of base, $3''$.

PLATE 46

1. Cruet with stopper, blown from purplish-amethyst non-lead glass; ovoid body tapering into cylindrical neck with high arched lip; applied tapering hollow handle with flattened crimped end; body patterned in 25-rib mold and expanded in vertical ribbing; free-blown stopper, with unusually long shank, apparently made from same batch of glass. Pittsburgh area. Circa 1820–50.

Over-all height, 9¼″, without stopper, 8⅛″; greatest diameter of body, 3¾″.

2. Cruet or small decanter jug, free-blown from amber (black) non-lead bottle glass; irregular angled globular body with long tapering neck terminating in two globular knoplike turnings below a high rim with tiny pinched lip; applied flat circular foot; applied solid slender bow-shaped handle. Connecticut glass. Last half of nineteenth century.

Height, 8⅛″; top diameter, 1½″; greatest diameter of body, 3¹⁵⁄₁₆″; diameter of foot, 2¾″.

Whereas the amethyst cruet is typical of early nineteenth-century Pittsburgh commercial glass, this Connecticut cruet is an individual piece, crudely executed but with a certain primitive charm to which all these examples of folk art in glass can lay claim. There is a strange kinship between this cruet and forms encountered in some Persian glass of the seventeenth and eighteenth centuries. It was blown in one of the Connecticut glasshouses operated in the mid-nineteenth century, probably that of the Westford Glass Company.

PLATE 47

"STIEGEL" PANELED VASES

For many years the large paneled vases were called Stiegel. It is now considered doubtful that any were ever made at the Stiegel glassworks. While unquestionably American, they appear to be definitely of the nineteenth century. We attribute them to the New England area and think that perhaps a large percentage of them were made at the works of the Boston and Sandwich Glass Company. The large vases occur in two shades of amethyst, one lighter than the other, cobalt-blue, light sapphire-blue (very rare), emerald-green (also very rare), and in clear glass.

They were all patterned in dip molds and expanded in varying degrees so that the ribs forming the sides of the panels and, in all cases, extending to the pontil mark on the base vary in prominence. The large vases usually have twelve sunken panels, occasionally thirteen; and the small vases, nine. While there is a general similarity in shape there is considerable variation in the curves of the bodies, forming six basic types. In the three illustrated here, the slenderness of the small amethyst vase at the right is the most unusual. Another rare feature is a folded rim; two amethyst specimens with folded rim are known to us, one small and the large one on this plate.

1. Small paneled vase blown from cobalt-blue lead glass; nine so-called sunken panels about two and a half inches in height with rounded tops and very pronounced ribs; only small specimen in blue so far recorded.

Height, 6"; greatest diameter of rim, $3\frac{3}{4}$"; greatest diameter of body, $2\frac{1}{2}$"; diameter of base, $2\frac{1}{2}$".

2. Paneled vase blown from clear brilliant amethyst lead glass; twelve sunken panels, four and three-quarter inches in height with rounded tops and very pronounced ribs; folded rim, only large vase recorded having this feature.

Height, $7\frac{3}{4}$"; greatest diameter of rim, $5\frac{7}{16}$"; greatest diameter of body, $4\frac{5}{8}$"; diameter of base, $3\frac{3}{8}$".

3. Small paneled vase blown from brilliant amethyst lead glass; nine sunken panels about three and five-eighths inches in height with rounded tops and ribs less pronounced than on No. 1 or No. 2; only about seven small amethyst vases recorded as yet.

Height, $6\frac{3}{4}$"; greatest diameter of rim, $3\frac{3}{4}$"; greatest diameter of body, $3\frac{5}{16}$"; diameter of base, $2\frac{1}{8}$".

PLATE 48

1. Handled vase blown from aquamarine non-lead bottle glass; globular body with wide cylindrical neck flaring slightly to rim; applied slightly domed circular foot with wide infolded rim; on each side, an applied solid handle with crimped and turned-over end; unusual superimposed decoration on body, four equidistant lily-pads Type II depend toward base, and on front and back two small lily-pads Type I, on slender stems, joined directly above the lily-pad Type II; neck with wide-spaced spiral ribbing extending to rim. Attributed to Lockport Glass Works, Lockport, New York. Circa 1849–60.

Height, 6¾″; top diameter, 3⅛″; greatest diameter of body, 3⅝″; diameter of foot, 3¾″.

This vase in the South Jersey tradition is extraordinary, not only because of the departure from the norm in lily-pad decoration, but also because of its foot. The type most characteristic of this general category is the solid, often heavy, circular variety, either plain like that of No. 2, or crimped. This blown type, a survival of eighteenth-century treatment and form, is rarely encountered in individual pieces from our bottle and window glasshouses.

2. Small vase blown from bluish-aquamarine non-lead bottle glass; small globular body with superimposed gather tooled into broad, faint, slightly swirled gadrooning topped by heavy rim; wide threaded neck flaring to plain rim; applied knop stem and wide plain circular foot. South Jersey type. First half of nineteenth century.

Height, 4½″; top diameter, 3⅛″; greatest diameter of body, 2⅜″; diameter of foot, 2⅞″.

In general shape this vase, as well as a few others which we have seen, is similar to some of the imported porcelain mantel ornaments, especially French vases of the early nineteenth century.

3. Blown Three Mold vase of light green non-lead glass; cylindrical body with wide-spreading sides contracting sharply at top to form a wide collarlike bulge; short cylindrical neck with wide-flaring rim; blown and patterned in a pint decanter mold in pattern GII-6, and fashioned by manipulation. Probably Kent, Ohio. Circa 1824–30.

Height, 5⅜″; top diameter, 3⅝; greatest diameter of body, 3⅝″; diameter of base, 2⅜″.

PLATE 49

1. Celery glass or vase blown from clear lead glass; deep straight-sided bowl with slightly flaring rim and rounding at bottom to an applied flattened knop stem and circular foot; lower part of bowl decorated with a wide band of gadrooning molded upon a superimposed gather and patterned in a 20-rib mold; upper part of bowl completely encircled by a wide band of copper-wheel-engraved decoration, part of which is of genre character, depicting two farmhouses between which are flowers and leaf sprays and domestic fowls in flight, a scene quite reminiscent of the vignette on the Amelung Repold flip illustrated on Plate 77. Early nineteenth century.

Height, $8\frac{1}{4}''$; top diameter, $4\frac{15}{16}''$; diameter of foot, $4''$.

2. Celery glass or vase blown from clear lead glass, similar in shape to No. 1 but with heavier gadrooning on lower part of body, and a more globular knop in the stem. Elaborate copper-wheel engraving on the upper part of the body: on one side, a heart-shaped cartouche formed by cut and polished ovals, containing the monogram "FN" and enclosed by two large floral and leaf sprays; on the other side, a double-handled urn filled with leaf sprays, and between the two central designs, additional flower and leaf sprays; at the top a band of vintage design. Early nineteenth century.

Height, $8\frac{1}{2}''$; top diameter, $5\frac{3}{8}''$; diameter of foot, $3\frac{3}{4}''$.

A great many vases of this type have been found all through Maryland, Pennsylvania, and adjacent areas. Frequently they have been attributed to Amelung. However, the form is far too late, probably well after 1800. Moreover, all that we have tested, and it is a considerable number, show strong lead content. The engraving may have been done by Amelung workmen employed in later glasshouses. It is likely the vases were made in more than one glassworks and probably in the Baltimore, Philadelphia, and Pittsburgh areas. Some of them have a style of engraving definitely Pittsburgh. While most of them, we believe, were made in the first quarter of the nineteenth century, some of them probably were as late as 1830–35.

3. Celery glass or vase free-blown from clear lead glass with pale améthystine tint; body, with straight sides spreading slightly to rim, and resting on an applied hollow knop and circular foot; in the hollow knop a United States silver half dime dated 1838; on the front just below the rim and in diamond-point engraving "G & J Noble" within crude leaf sprays, and below the inscription in two lines, "Liverpool 1838."

Height, $7\frac{5}{8}''$; top diameter, $5\frac{1}{8}''$; diameter of foot, $3\frac{5}{8}''$.

Our guess is that it was made in the Pittsburgh area as an engagement or wedding gift and that the engraving was done possibly by a local jeweler, for engraving by diamond point was not a technique practiced by glass decorators at that time.

PLATE 50

1. Celery glass or vase blown from clear lead glass; tall cylindrical body flaring at rim, and rounding at bottom to applied circular foot; lower part of body patterned in a dip mold and expanded with decoration of twelve short round-top sunken panels; upper part, decorated with daisy-like flowers, long fern leaves, and conventionalized floral and leaf sprays, engraved by copper wheel in a style typical of the Pittsburgh area. Circa 1820–35.

Height, 7¼″; top diameter, 5⅛″; diameter of foot, 3⅞″.

2. Blown Three Mold celery glass or vase; clear lead glass; bowl with flaring tooled rim, blown and patterned in a flip mold in pattern GII-18; applied low pedestal foot with wide infolded rim, blown and patterned in a tumbler mold in pattern GII-21. Probably New England area. Circa 1820–35.

Height, 6⅜″; top diameter, 4½″; diameter of foot, 3¹³⁄₁₆″.

3. Celery glass or vase, blown from clear lead glass; body with straight sides spreading to a slightly flaring rim and resting on an applied short globular-knop stem and broad circular foot; cut design consisting of a wide central band composed of alternate conventionalized palms on pedestal of fine diamonds and plain Gothic arches, and between a band of flat splits at the bottom and a band of facets at the top; outer edge of rim finely notched. Type which could have been made in any one of the New England, New York, New Jersey, Maryland, Eastern or Western Pennsylvania or (West) Virginia glasshouses which were making blown and cut and engraved tablewares extensively in the 1820–50 period.

Height, 8″; top diameter, 5″; diameter of foot, 4″.

PLATE 51

1. Vase blown from opaque white glass with hard shiny surface; bulbous body tapering to wide cylindrical neck and flaring rim; applied knop stem and wide flat circular foot; patterned in an open-top mold and decorated with eight wide-spaced distinctly marked vertical ribs, type called pillar molding. Pittsburgh area. Second to third quarter of nineteenth century. Collection of Mr. Lowell Innes.

Height, 8½"; top diameter, 4¾"; diameter of foot, 3⅞".

2. Vase, one of a pair, blown from non-lead glass; small globular body, long cylindrical neck flaring at wide scalloped rim; applied clear glass ring at juncture of body and neck; applied clear glass cylindrical stem and wide circular foot; entire vase above stem decorated with loopings of red, white, and blue. Pittsburgh. Circa 1870s.

Height, 9⅝"; top diameter, 4¼"; diameter of body, 3"; diameter of foot, 4¼".

The pair was purchased about fifteen years ago from a woman in Ohio who had inherited them from her mother. One time when the mother was visiting the family of a Pittsburgh glass blower, employed in the Bakewell factory, the blower fashioned the vases and presented them to her.

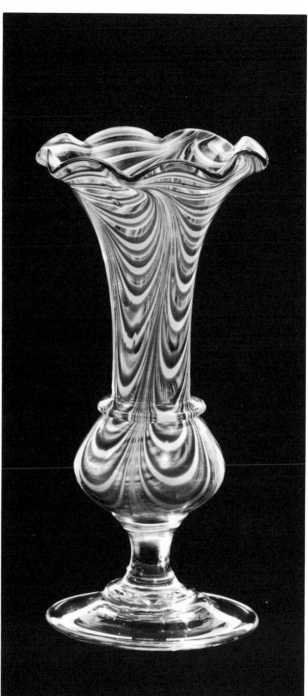

PLATE 52

THE MONITOR AND THE MERRIMAC VASE

Vase free-blown from clear non-lead glass; deep straight-sided bowl with slightly flaring scalloped rim and curving at bottom to an applied short knop stem and bell-shaped foot; body engraved by copper wheel with a vignette depicting the engagement of the *Monitor* and the *Merrimac*, in the war between the North and the South, within an arborlike frame surrounded by vintage decoration; on the foot a circlet of vintage engraving. Circa 1862.

Height, 9⅞"; top diameter, 4⁷⁄₁₆"; diameter of foot, 4⁵⁄₁₆".

This vase is one of the few pieces of American *historical* glass commemorating events in our wars. If any naval engagement was to be depicted on glass, we might expect that it would be this important one which occurred in Hampton Roads, Virginia, on Sunday morning, March 9, 1862. Actually the 40-gun steam frigate *Merrimac,* one of the vessels sunk by the federal government when its Gosport Naval Yard was abandoned in the spring of 1861, had been raised by the Confederates and converted into the first ironclad warship, one having also a cast-iron ram attached to her bow. She was renamed the *Virginia,* and it was as the *Virginia* she raided Newport News on March 8 when she rammed and sank the sailing ship *Cumberland,* then attacked the frigate *Congress.* The latter, forced aground, her commander killed, and with scores of dead and wounded, surrendered. With darkness coming on, the *Virginia* withdrew to await the morning before attacking the *Minnesota, St. Lawrence,* and *Roanoke,* all wooden ships and apparently helpless against the new ironclad.

However, a surprise awaited Buchanan, the commander of the *Virginia.* Having heard of the transformation of the old *Merrimac* at the hands of the Confederates, the Navy Department had accepted John Ericsson's offer to build an ironclad. The *Monitor* resulted. She was laid down at Brooklyn, October 1861, launched the following January, and commissioned in February 1862. Ironworkers at Troy, New York, had provided the armor, the plates, and the rivets. John A. Gris-

wold and John F. Winslow, of Troy, with the aid of President Lincoln, had secured funds to build the *Monitor,* which had the first revolving turret in naval history. Commanded by Lieutenant John L. Worden, she arrived on the scene on the evening of March 8 and about midnight anchored near the *Minnesota.* A pygmy by comparison in size, she attacked the *Merrimac* when the latter arrived on the morning of the ninth to finish her work of destruction. The terrific battle which ensued was not in itself decisive and neither vessel was seriously damaged. However, it saved the Union Navy and was far-reaching in effect, completely revolutionizing naval warfare for many years to come.

The Troy *Daily Budget* on Monday evening, March 10, carried an account of the engagement and repeated the following telegram:

March 9, 1862. To John A. Griswold, Troy, N. Y. The *Monitor* is a noble boat. She saved the *Minnesota* which was aground, also the *St. Lawrence.* Her arrival was indeed fortunate to myself. It saved all the property inside and outside the Fort. She is much superior to the *Merrimac,* the latter had 8 guns and the *Monitor* only 2.

In England the news of the exploits of the *Merrimac* and the subsequent battle between the two ironclads was received with concern bordering on consternation. On March 26, 1862, the London *Times* said, "This startling battle has dumbfounded and dismayed all England. . . . The battle is the one absorbing topic in the Clubs, in Parliament, in Society."

In a subsequent issue of the *Times* it was commented: "What we have been taught by the American example is not the relative efficiency of one type of iron ship over another, but the absolute superiority of iron ships, however imperfectly built, over any wooden ship, however powerful. . . . If a mere makeshift like the *Merrimac,* rudely extemporized on the spur of the moment, can destroy the finest ship, and defy the strongest forts of the Federal Government, what may not be done by a first-rate specimen of the class? . . . If a cheap, half-seaworthy battery like the *Monitor* can bring the *Merrimac* to bay, what may not be done on further trial?"

PLATE 53

Modern decorative wares made by the Libbey Glass Company, Toledo, Ohio, prior to World War II. Courtesy of Libbey Glass Company.

1. Cornucopia, clear lead glass in form of horn of plenty with decoration of brilliant spiral optic drawn into a tightly twisted stem; applied curled foot.
Height, 8".
Group of three graceful bud vases; each intended for a single flower.

2. Cylindrical form spreading at heavy base.
Height, 8".

3. So-called "teardrop" resting on square foot.
Height, 7¼".

4. Long graceful body flaring at circular rim and contracting sharply above a thick rounded base.
Height, 7½".

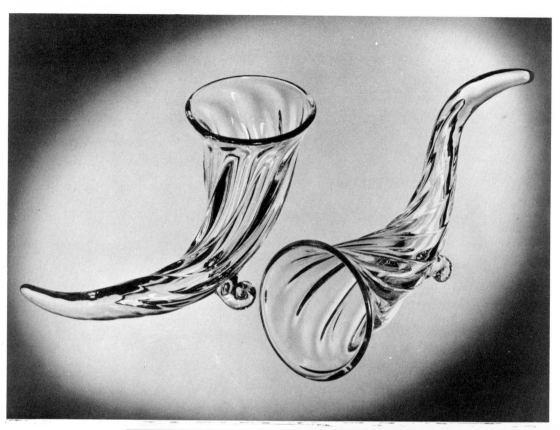

PLATE 54

1. Saturn Optic Vase blown from clear brilliant glass; flip-glass shape, tapering cylindrical form with wide-spaced spiral ribbing; small circular base from same gather. Made by A. H. Heisey and Company, Newark, Ohio. Mid-twentieth century. *Height,* $10\frac{1}{2}''$; *top diameter,* 6''; *diameter of base,* $3\frac{3}{4}''$.

2. Vase, blown from clear glass; long cone-shaped body with flaring, wide scalloped rim; body decorated with very heavy vertical ribs similar in effect to pillar molding but formed by tooling; applied circular foot. Another example of modern decorative wares made by A. H. Heisey and Company. Mid-twentieth century.

Height, $8\frac{1}{2}''$; *top,* $7\frac{1}{4}''$ *by* 8''; *diameter of foot,* $4\frac{5}{8}''$.

These vases illustrated through courtesy of A. H. Heisey and Company.

PLATE 55

Jar free-blown from a very heavy gather of olive-green (black) non-lead bottle glass; body of classical form rounding at shoulder to short wide cylindrical neck with rolled rim or lip.

Height, $9\frac{1}{8}''$; top diameter, $4''$; greatest diameter of body, $6\frac{3}{8}''$; diameter of base, $4''$.

There was no history accompanying this exceptionally well-formed jar. It is of classical form and could have been fashioned in any one of the American glasshouses making bottles in the eighteenth, early nineteenth, or even mid-nineteenth century.

PLATE 56

Large jar or vase free-blown from heavy clear olive-amber bottle glass; ovoid body rounding to broad cylindrical neck tapering to plain rim. From collection of the late Herbert Delevan Mason, and attributed by him to Keene-Marlboro-Street Glass Works, New Hampshire. Circa 1815–40.

Height, 14"; diameter at top, 5⅛"; greatest diameter, 7⅞"; diameter of base, 5½".

The simplicity of design and flowing lines speak for themselves and testify to the creative ability and craftsmanship of the blowers in our early glasshouses.

PLATE 57

A unique small barrel-shaped jar blown from non-lead bottle glass; color, a shade of amber with decided puce tone, one occasionally encountered in historical bottles and flasks which were made in some of the bottle houses operating about the middle of the nineteenth century. Short cylindrical neck finished with a broad crudely applied band just below the rim, entire body elaborately decorated with applied horizontal, vertical, and diagonal quilling or pinched trailing forming a sort of wide-spaced latticework; between the two upper bands of horizontal trailing, three equidistant applied button prunts. On either side an applied small solid handle with thumb- and finger pieces, the upper part attached to the neck and the lower part to the band of trailing on the shoulder. Probably Connecticut, nineteenth century.

Height, 6⅞"; top diameter, 2¼"; greatest diameter of body, 4½"; diameter of foot, 3¼".

The piece was found in a private home between Eastford and Westford, Connecticut, and is believed to have been made either at the West Willington or Westford glassworks. In the family it had always been called a "workman's fancy." The decoration and handles are quite Spanish in style.

PLATE 58

A group of nine salts illustrating various techniques in blowing: plain free-blown, patterned in dip molds or in part-size piece molds and expanded, or blown in full-size piece molds; and dating from the eighteenth through the early nineteenth centuries.

1. Blown from a heavy gather of deep sapphire-blue lead glass; double-ogee bowl with short hollow stem, pattern-molded and expanded with heavy vertical ribbing, slightly swirled on upper part of bowl; applied circular foot.

Height, $2\frac{15}{16}''$; top diameter, $2\frac{5}{16}''$; diameter of foot, $2\frac{1}{8}''$.

2. Blown from light sapphire-blue lead glass; double-ogee bowl with short rim and short bulbous stem; patterned in 12-diamond mold and expanded with diamond pattern pulled into heavy ribbing on the stem; applied circular foot.

Height, $2\frac{11}{16}''$; top diameter, $2\frac{3}{16}''$; diameter of foot, $1\frac{7}{8}''$.

3. Brilliant green, blown from non-lead glass; double-ogee bowl with short stem resting on an applied sloping petaled foot (seven petals). Provenance unknown. Came from New Hampshire. Could have been made in almost any bottle house.

Height, $2\frac{15}{16}''$; top diameter, $2\frac{3}{8}''$; diameter of foot, $2\frac{1}{4}''$.

4. Blown from brilliant amber-yellow non-lead glass; bowl unusual in form, the wide upper part being perfectly straight-sided and small lower part ogee; short stem drawn from same gather; applied slightly sloping foot; bowl patterned in 16-rib mold and expanded, ribbing swirled to left. Midwestern.

Height, $2\frac{3}{4}''$; top diameter, $2\frac{3}{4}''$; diameter of foot, $2\frac{3}{16}''$.

5. Blown from light olive-green non-lead glass, a shade frequently termed citron; double-ogee bowl, with flanged lip and short stem from same gather; patterned in a 24-rib mold and expanded, ribbing swirled slightly to left; applied slightly sloping foot. Midwestern.

Height, $3\frac{1}{8}''$; top diameter, $2\frac{3}{4}''$; greatest diameter of body, $2\frac{7}{8}''$; diameter of foot, $2\frac{5}{16}''$.

6. Blown from pale yellow-green non-lead glass; double-ogee bowl with short stem from same gather, patterned in a 16-rib mold and expanded in broken-swirl decoration, applied slightly sloping foot. Midwestern.

Height, $3''$; top diameter, $2\frac{7}{16}''$; greater diameter of body, $2\frac{15}{16}''$; diameter of foot, $2\frac{1}{16}''$.

7. Blown Three Mold, deep sapphire-blue lead glass; shallow circular bowl with straight sides slanting inward slightly to plain rim, short stem and flaring foot formed from same gather; pattern of vertical ribbing, GI-16, with eight-pointed star in base, very rarely found in salts or in color. Probably Boston and Sandwich Glass Company. Circa 1825–35.

Height, $2''$; top diameter, $2\frac{7}{8}''$; greatest diameter of body, $3\frac{1}{16}''$; diameter of foot, $2\frac{1}{2}''$.

8. Blown Three Mold, sapphire-blue lead glass; double-ogee bowl of unusual type and circular foot from same gather, pattern GIII-13; plain base. New England area. Circa 1820–35.

Height, $2\frac{5}{8}''$; top diameter, $2\frac{11}{16}''$; greatest diameter of body, $3\frac{1}{16}''$; diameter of foot, $2''$.

9. Blown from a heavy gather of clear blue non-lead glass; shallow circular bowl tapering to applied circular crimped foot; bowl tooled into pattern of heavy horizontal ribbing. South Jersey. First half of nineteenth century.

Height, $2\frac{1}{16}''$; top diameter, $2\frac{5}{8}''$; diameter of foot, $2\frac{1}{4}''$.

Nos. 1 and 2 illustrate variations of the typical commercial Stiegel type salt. The Midwestern salts, Nos. 4, 5, and 6, like No. 3, were products of bottle houses and represent the wares made for local trade as well as for the blower's friends or family. The two Blown Three Mold salts, Nos. 7 and 8, were nineteenth-century commercial wares, whereas the South Jersey, No. 9, is an individual piece.

PLATE 59

1. Wineglass free-blown from clear olive-amber non-lead bottle glass; deep bowl with long drawn stem and applied circular crimped foot. History of having been blown at the Lancaster Glass Works, Lancaster, New York, of which the principal commercial products were bottles and flasks. Circa 1850.

Height, $3\frac{5}{8}''$; top diameter, $2\frac{1}{16}''$; diameter of base, $2\frac{1}{2}''$.

2. Tall wineglass free-blown from heavy olive-amber bottle glass; slender deep bowl with drawn slender inverted baluster stem terminating in two graduated knops resting on a small applied circular foot. New York State, possibly the Mount Vernon Glass Works or the Saratoga Mountain Works. Circa 1830–50.

Height, $5\frac{3}{16}''$; top diameter, $1\frac{7}{8}''$; diameter of foot, $2\frac{1}{16}''$.

3. Wineglass free-blown from clear amber bottle glass; bell-shaped bowl with drawn double ball-knop stem resting on an applied broad slightly domed foot. Attributed to New Hampshire, Keene or Stoddard. Second half of nineteenth century.

Height, $4\frac{1}{4}''$; top diameter, $2\frac{5}{8}''$; diameter of foot, $3\frac{3}{8}''$.

4. Wineglass free-blown from brilliant clear deep green lead glass; barrel-shaped bowl with applied angular-knop stem and flaring circular foot. Jersey Glass Company, Jersey City. Circa 1824–40.

Height, $4''$; top diameter, $2\frac{1}{4}''$; diameter of foot, $2\frac{5}{8}''$.

5. Wineglass free-blown from light green non-lead bottle glass; conical bowl with drawn cylindrical stem, patterned in a 16-rib mold and expanded in vertical ribbing; applied sloping circular foot. From the collection of the late Harry Hall White and attributed by him to the Mantua Glass Works, Mantua, Portage County, Ohio. Circa 1822–29.

Height, $4\frac{15}{16}''$; top diameter, $2\frac{1}{4}''$; diameter of foot, $2\frac{1}{4}''$.

With the exception of the wine from the Jersey Glass Works all those shown on this plate are examples of the individual pieces blown in our bottle and window glasshouses in the nineteenth century. Wines are among the less frequently encountered articles in the South Jersey tradition.

PLATE 60

1. Wineglass blown from clear lead glass; conical bowl with drawn stem having a small ball knop at top, and resting on circular foot with wide under-folded rim; bowl and stem pattern-molded and expanded into ribbing forming narrow round-top panels on bowl and slightly twisted ribbing in stem. Possibly Pittsburgh area or New England. First quarter of nineteenth century.

Height, $4\frac{1}{8}$"; top diameter, $2\frac{1}{4}$"; diameter of foot, $2\frac{1}{4}$".

2. Wineglass blown from clear lead glass; delicate cone-shaped bowl, stem composed of slender inverted baluster terminating in a slender true baluster and supported by an applied delicate circular foot with star cutting on the bottom; the stem decorated with cutting and containing a long tear following its contours; the bowl decorated with copper-wheel engraving of a pine tree, leaf sprays, and inscription *"New England Glass Company Boston"* on one side, and on reverse: *"Mass. Cent¹ Head Qʳˢ 1876."*

Height, $4\frac{1}{2}$"; top diameter, $2\frac{1}{8}$"; diameter of foot, 2".

3. Wineglass blown from clear non-lead glass with grayish tone; drawn conical bowl and drawn cylindrical stem; applied flaring circular foot with plain rim; on one side, copper-wheel engraving of a medallion composed of four small conventionalized flowers and four slender leaf sprays enclosing initials *"G.R."* in script. New Bremen Glassmanufactory. Circa 1792.

Height, $4\frac{1}{8}$"; top diameter, $2\frac{1}{16}$"; diameter of foot, $2\frac{5}{16}$".

One of a set made at Amelung's glassworks for George Repold, of Baltimore, two of which were inherited by Miss Margaret Waesche, of Washington, D.C.

4. Blown Three Mold wineglass made from clear lead glass; semi-barrel-shaped bowl in pattern GII-19, applied angular-knop stem and flaring circular foot. Probably New England Area. Circa 1820–35.

Height, $3\frac{15}{16}$"; top diameter, $1\frac{7}{8}$"; diameter of foot, $2\frac{3}{8}$".

5. Firing glass free-blown from clear non-lead glass with grayish tone; deep conical bowl terminating in thick cylindrical stem containing large tear and resting on heavy circular applied stepped foot, formed from one gather; bowl engraved by copper wheel with Masonic emblems within a wreath formed by two floral sprays with a daisy-like flower in each and at top, crudely engraved, "SIELENTIO-DE-FIEDE." Possibly Amelung's glassworks. 1788–92.

Height, $4\frac{3}{8}$"; top diameter, $2\frac{1}{2}$"; diameter of foot, $2\frac{7}{16}$".

6. Firing glass free-blown from clear non-lead glass with grayish tone and with band of deep blue around rim; similar in form to No. 5, large tear in stem, heavy circular foot; crudely engraved on one side with a medallion composed of conventionalized flowers and narrow leaf sprays enclosing initials *"F.C.W."* in script, and on the other side with Masonic emblems. Probably Baltimore-Philadelphia area, or possibly Amelung. Circa 1790–1810.

Height, $4\frac{1}{2}$"; top diameter, $2\frac{3}{8}$"; diameter of foot, $2\frac{3}{4}$".

7. Firing glass of clear non-lead glass with grayish tone, waisted bowl terminating in thick cylindrical stem with tear, and heavy circular foot; on one side, gilded decoration of two long leaf sprays partly enclosing Masonic emblems; rim of bowl gilded. The production of these non-lead glasses, which fall in the category of dram or tavern glasses, was continued in England well into the last quarter of the nineteenth century; on the Continent likewise. And it is probable they were also made at the New Bremen Glassmanufactory, where gilding and enameling as well as engraving were used in decoration of glass.

Height, 4"; top diameter, $2\frac{11}{16}$"; diameter of foot, $3\frac{15}{16}$".

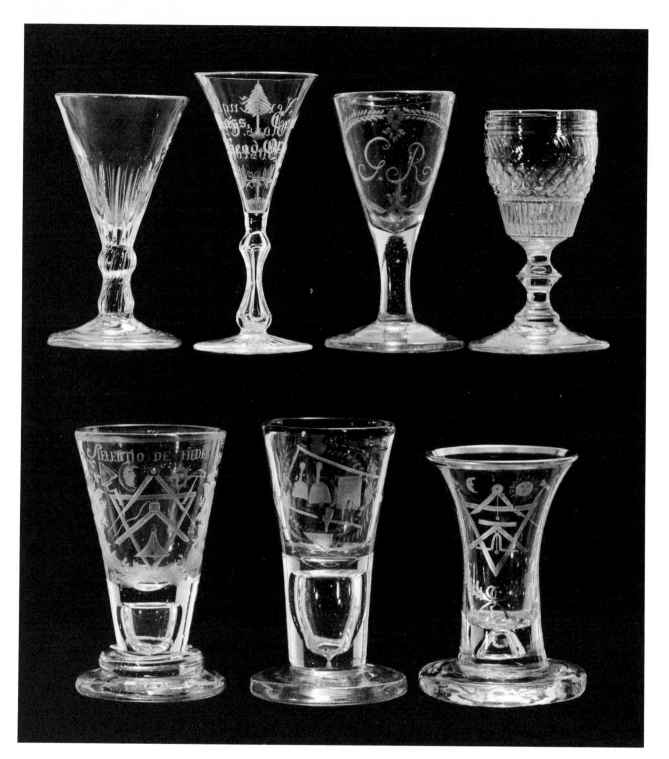

PLATE 61

1. Blown Three Mold cordial glass of clear lead glass; small straight-sided circular bowl with hollow tapering stem and small circular foot drawn from same gather, patterned in GIII-12 in miniature decanter mold. Probably Sandwich. Circa 1825–35.

Height, $2\frac{3}{4}''$; *top diameter*, $1\frac{1}{2}''$; *diameter of foot*, $1\frac{3}{8}''$.

2. Syllabub or jelly glass blown from pale green non-lead glass; deep cylindrical bowl flaring to plain rim and resting on an applied knop supported by circular foot with infolded rim; bowl patterned in a small 18-rib dip mold and expanded with vertical ribbing swirled at top. Late eighteenth or early nineteenth century.

Height, $3\frac{7}{8}''$; *top diameter*, $2\frac{3}{8}''$; *diameter of foot*, $2\frac{3}{16}''$.

3. Blown Three Mold wine, clear lead glass; tapering straight-sided bowl in pattern GI-6, and with applied angular-knop stem and plain circular foot. Circa 1820–35.

Height, $3\frac{3}{4}''$; *top diameter*, $2''$; *diameter of foot*, $2\frac{1}{8}''$.

This pattern is one of those attributed by fragment identification to Sandwich. It may also have been used by the New England Glass Company.

4. Cordial glass blown from light purple lead glass; conical bowl with ball-knop stem from same gather, applied circular foot; bowl and stem patterned in a 12-rib dip mold and expanded in vertical ribbing. Late eighteenth or early nineteenth century.

Height, $2\frac{1}{2}''$; *top diameter*, $1\frac{5}{8}''$; *diameter of foot*, $1\frac{9}{16}''$.

5. Wineglass blown from brilliant light green lead glass; circular bowl with heavy tapering cylindrical stem drawn from same gather, applied broad circular foot with infolded rim. New England area. First quarter of nineteenth century.

Height, $3\frac{13}{16}''$; *top diameter*, $1\frac{15}{16}''$; *diameter of foot*, $2\frac{9}{16}''$.

6. Rare tall free-blown wine in aquamarine non-lead glass; bucket bowl and long cylindrical air-twist stem drawn from same gather, broad circular foot with plain rim. An extremely rare specimen and an individual piece. Late eighteenth or early nineteenth century.

Height, $5\frac{3}{8}''$; *top diameter*, $2''$; *diameter of foot*, $2\frac{5}{8}''$.

7. Wineglass free-blown from pale blue lead glass; circular bowl with heavy tapering cylindrical stem drawn from same gather; applied broad circular foot with infolded rim, very similar in form to No. 5. New England area. First quarter of nineteenth century.

Height, $3\frac{3}{4}''$; *top diameter*, $2\frac{1}{2}''$; *diameter of foot*, $2\frac{1}{2}''$.

PLATE 62

A group of fine drinking vessels made at the glasshouses operated by Christian Dorflinger, first in Brooklyn, New York, and later at White Mills, Pennsylvania. Christian Dorflinger achieved a perfection of crystal-clearness and quality in flint (lead) glass tablewares which up to then had not been excelled, if indeed equaled, by any glassmaker in America. The White House glass tablewares for eight presidents, from Abraham Lincoln to Woodrow Wilson, were made in the Dorflinger Glass Works.

The upper row shows glass from the set made in 1890 for President Benjamin Harrison. The elaborate, deeply cut design is very similar to the Daisy and Button pressed glass which was so popular in the late 1880s and 1890s. The beautifully engraved shield-shaped cartouche with the United States coat of arms is quite overpowered by the all-over cut pattern. The port wine, goblet, and champagne were from the President Harrison set; the highball glass, said to have been the first included in White House table glass, was made for President Theodore Roosevelt.

1. Highball glass: *height*, $5\frac{7}{8}''$; 2. Port wine: *height*, $4\frac{1}{4}''$; 3. Goblet: *height*, $6\frac{1}{4}''$; 4. Champagne: *height*, $4\frac{1}{2}''$.

The lower row shows late mid-nineteenth-, late nineteenth-, and early twentieth-century Dorflinger design and decoration of drinking vessels. At the left, Nos. 1 and 2, are a punch glass and champagne from the set made about 1861 at the Brooklyn factory for President Lincoln. The delicate engraving and cutting of the decoration are exceptionally fine. The expert rendering of the United States coat of arms is less traditional than on the later White House glass. To many, the freer lines seem more pleasing. The cordial glass and tall wine, Nos. 3 and 4, are from a set made for the Centennial Exposition held in Philadelphia in 1876. Again there is a pleasing simplicity of design and ornamentation not found on all glass of the period. In the entire service, no pieces were identical in the detail of the engraved foliated scroll and figure decoration. The cordial has an eagle and a horse; the wine, a horse and a rabbit. The sherry glass, No. 5, with conical bowl flaring slightly at the rim and slender drawn stem, is engraved with the coat of arms of Cuba. It was from a large table service made in 1918, when Mario Menocal was President, for the Cuban Palace in Havana. There were nineteen different types of glasses in the service.

An article by R. Gerald McMurtry, "Lincoln White House Glass and China," in the *Lincoln Herald*, June 1947, stated:

A. P. Zimandy of Washington, D.C., was the dealer who sold Mary Lincoln the glassware. It was manufactured by Christian Dorflinger, in his Green Point Glass Works in Brooklyn, New York. Zimandy's invoice of July 23, 1861 described the goods as "one sett of Glass ware rich cut and Engraved with the U. S. Coat of Arms." The total charge was $1,500.00 and Mrs. Lincoln certified, "This bill is correct" and signed her name on the invoice.

All of these pieces are from the collection of Miss Katherine Dorflinger, daughter of Christian Dorflinger, and are illustrated through her courtesy.

Punch glass: *height*, $3\frac{15}{16}''$; Champagne: *height*, $4\frac{3}{4}''$; Cordial: *height*, $3\frac{3}{8}''$; Tall wine: *height*, $5\frac{1}{2}''$; Sherry glass: *height*, $4\frac{5}{16}''$.

PLATE 63

A group of Steuben Glass mid-twentieth-century drinking vessels: a modern highball glass and stemmed ware in eighteenth-century style. All free-blown from the finest quality of brilliant flint (lead) crystal and fashioned by manipulation; each decorated by a single small motif beautifully engraved. Illustrated through courtesy of Steuben Glass, Inc.

1. Red wine, rounded funnel bowl resting on heavy knop stem with tear and slightly domed foot; bowl engraved with snowflake.

Height, 6"; top diameter, $2\frac{3}{4}$"; diameter of foot, $2\frac{7}{8}$".

2. Highball glass, slender, slightly barrel-shaped, with heavy solid base; engraved with American eagle with olive branch and thunderbolt in talons and encircled by stars.

Height, $6\frac{1}{2}$"; top diameter, $2\frac{15}{16}$"; diameter of base, 2".

3. Cordial, small funnel bowl engraved with squirrel; cylindrical stem with ball knop, circular foot.

Height, $1\frac{3}{4}$"; top diameter, $1\frac{3}{4}$"; diameter of foot, 2".

4. Cordial, bucket bowl, engraved with heraldic horse; cylindrical stem with angular knop, circular foot.

Height, $3\frac{7}{8}$"; top diameter, $1\frac{3}{8}$"; diameter of foot, 2".

5. Red wine, conical bowl with stem drawn from same gather and tooled into large angular knop with tear, resting on small ball knop, circular foot; bowl engraved with a dove holding leaf spray in its bill and perched on a cornucopia filled with produce and resting on a chain of cut and polished ovals.

Height, 6"; top diameter, $2\frac{15}{16}$"; diameter of foot, $2\frac{7}{8}$".

PLATE 64

THE BREMEN POKAL

Clear non-lead glass with slight greenish cast; semi-oviform bowl supported by stem composed of a large globular knop above an inverted baluster resting on a domed foot; characteristic Amelung set-in cover with an applied band tooled into a half round which rests on rim of bowl; engraved by copper wheel: on one side, arms of the city of Bremen and inscription *"Old Bremen Success and the New Progress"*; on the reverse, *"New Bremen Glassmanufactory—1788—North America, State of Maryland"*; on the cover an engraved foliated scroll. Courtesy of the Metropolitan Museum of Art, New York City.

Over-all height, $11\frac{1}{4}$"; diameter of top, $4\frac{7}{8}$".

The stem and foot of the Bremen pokal are very similar to those of the Schley pokal. It was found in Bremen, Germany, where it was said to have been in the possession of a local family for over a hundred years. It is believed to have been one of the first presentation pieces made at the glassworks in New Bremen and sent by Amelung to some of his associates in Bremen who had invested capital in the American glassmaking venture. When the pokal first reappeared in this country about 1928 some were inclined to doubt that it was made at Amelung's glassworks. Consequently the theory was advanced that it had been made and engraved in Germany and sent over here in celebration of the establishment of the New Bremen Glassmanufactory. However, all doubts were soon dispelled by the discovery of other presentation pieces similar in metal, technique, and style of engraving and, moreover, authenticated by family history supported by inscription of names and dates.

All authenticated Amelung pieces which, to our knowledge, have been tested, are non-lead glass.

So far as we know the inverted baluster stem, a characteristic of the Amelung goblets and covered pokals, is not encountered in stemmed drinking vessels made in any other American glasshouse. It is found on early German wines, goblets, and covered pokals but almost disappeared after the third quarter of the eighteenth century, as did the domed foot. Their use by the Amelung workmen might be termed an anachronism. All authenticated Amelung stemmed wares—wines, goblets, and covered pokals—which we have seen have the foot with plain rim. Early German large wines, like those made at the Lauwenstein glasshouse, which in details of the shape of the bowl, type of stem, and domed foot are very similar to Amelung pieces, characteristically have a folded foot.

PLATE 65

Tall goblet or large ceremonial wine blown from clear non-lead glass slightly grayish in tone; deep bowl flaring to plain rim, applied stem composed of a solid globular knop, an inverted baluster with large tear, and a small knop; applied, exceptionally wide-flaring foot with plain rim and rising to slight cone at center.

Height, $10\frac{1}{16}$"; top diameter, $4\frac{1}{2}$"; diameter of foot, $5\frac{5}{16}$".

The former owner acquired this goblet in the New England area many years ago and knew nothing of its history. We believe there is a possibility that it may be Amelung. While the shape of the bowl differs and the foot is not domed as on the inscribed Amelung goblets and covered pokals, it has the typical inverted baluster stem with large tear, plain rim on the foot, and is made from non-lead glass of grayish tone similar to some of Amelung's inscribed pieces. So far as we know this type of stem is not found on drinking vessels made in any other eighteenth-century American glasshouse. All authenticated Amelung stemmed wares—wines, goblets, and covered pokals—which we have seen have the foot with plain rim.

PLATE 66

1. Goblet blown from clear non-lead glass with slight grayish cast, semi-oviform bowl supported by an inverted baluster, with large tear, which rests on a domed foot with plain rim. Bowl engraved by copper wheel with name *"C. Amelung."* in script within a typical Amelung foliated and floral wreath, and on opposite side the inscription *"Metha Repold d. 16. Octo. 1792"*.
Height, 7"; top diameter, 3⅞"; diameter of foot, 4".

The *"C."* is for Carolina, Amelung's wife. Metha Repold was the wife of George Repold, a merchant in Baltimore. This goblet, the large flip shown on Plate 77, and a wine illustrated on Plate 60 (one of a pair) were inherited by Miss Margaret B. Waesche, of Washington, D.C., a descendant of the Repolds, whose name originally was Von Repold. Miss Waesche informed us that George and Metha Repold were intimate friends of the Amelungs.

2. Amelung goblet blown from clear non-lead glass with slight grayish cast, very similar in form to the Repold goblet. The bowl ornamented on one side with an engraved foliated and floral wreath so characteristic of Amelung's work and enclosing the name *"J Amelung"* in script, and on the reverse an inscription. Owned by Mrs. Kennard Weddell.
Height, 6¾"; top diameter, 3¹³⁄₁₆"; foot diameter, 4".

The inscription on the goblet is an odd mixture of Roman (English) and German script which we are told is usual with many of the old German inscriptions written here in America. If the writer did not know the English letter, he substituted a German one. The inscription, according to the family history handed down with the goblet, was the Amelung family motto. Correctly written, it is: *"Suche Tugend und wann due Sie findest so überlasse alles übrige der Vorsehung,"* which, in translation, reads: "Seek Virtue and when you find Her leave everything else to Providence."

The goblet and the tumbler with blue enamel and gilded decoration and initials *"F.C.S.A."* illustrated on Plate 81 were inherited by Mrs. Ethel Amelung McCallum, a great-great-granddaughter of Amelung's oldest daughter, Frederica, through her second marriage to Dr. Philip Somerkamp. According to the family tradition, the goblet was made for Amelung himself. Several years ago Mrs. McCallum gave this goblet to Mrs. Weddell a direct descendant of Amelung through the daughter Frederica. This goblet is slightly shorter than the Amelung-Repold goblet and the dome of the foot not so pronounced.

For the translation of the German inscription, we are indebted to Mrs. Margaret M. Zimmerman, secretary of the Historical Society of Frederick County, Frederick, Maryland.

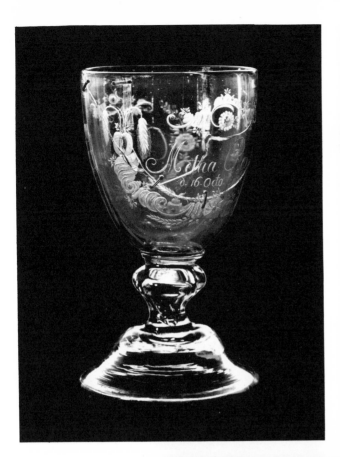

PLATE 67

1. Goblet blown from clear lead glass; globular bowl, double knop at top of stem, heavy circular foot; skillfully engraved by copper wheel with coat of arms of the State of Pennsylvania. Possibly Pittsburgh area. Circa 1810–20. From the Henry Francis du Pont Winterthur Museum.

Height, $4\frac{3}{4}''$; top diameter, $3\frac{1}{2}''$; greatest diameter of body, $3\frac{7}{8}''$; diameter of foot, $3\frac{3}{8}''$.

2. Goblet of clear non-lead glass with faint yellowish cast; semi-oviform bowl separated by cut octagonal merese from cut stem, square foot with cut eight-pointed star on bottom; at bottom of bowl, eight cut panels with rounded top and varying in height; side of bowl decorated by copper-wheel engraving of American eagle with head turned to left, and wings, tail, and legs spread, as on the seal of the United States; large shield on breast; olive branch in right talons, thunderbolt in left; pennant with "E PLURIBUS UNUM" in eagle's beak and surrounded by fifteen small stars; above, clouds and sunrays; just below rim, a narrow engraved band with polished ovals and roped line at each edge. From the Henry Francis du Pont Winterthur Museum.

Height, $5\frac{3}{4}''$; top diameter, $3\frac{5}{16}''$; foot, $2\frac{3}{8}''$ by $2\frac{3}{8}''$.

3. Goblet of clear non-lead glass with grayish cast; semi-oviform bowl separated by cut octagonal merese from cut octagonal stem, square foot; six-pointed cut star on bottom of foot. At bottom of bowl, eight cut panels with pointed top, small sprays of conventionalized flower and leaf design between tops of the panels. Side of bowl decorated by copper-wheel engraving of American eagle,

head turned to left, wings, tail, and legs spread; large shield on breast; olive branch in right talons, thunderbolt in left; pennant with "E PLURIBUS UNUM" in eagle's beak and surrounded by fifteen small stars; above, clouds and sunrays. Just below rim, narrow engraved band with polished ovals from which depend garlands composed of flower and leaf motifs and polished ovals. From the Henry Francis du Pont Winterthur Museum.

Height, $5\frac{1}{8}''$; top diameter, $3\frac{5}{8}''$; foot, $2\frac{1}{2}''$ by $2\frac{1}{2}''$.

The origin of these goblets is largely a matter of speculation. Vermont was admitted to the Union on March 4, 1791, and Kentucky on June 1, 1792, making fifteen states. This seems to date these goblets as having been made between June 1792 and 1796, when the next state was admitted. If American, which we are inclined to think is a possibility, they may have been made at the New Bremen Glassmanufactory, which was in operation in 1792, the date on several inscribed Amelung pieces. However, there is a marked difference in the drawing and rendering of the eagles and other details, indicating that they were either made in different glasshouses or at different times, or engraved by a different workman if in the same glassworks. There must have been two sets. We know of no other glasshouse in America in operation at that time where the work could have been done, but there may have been, probably were, independent engravers and glass cutters in Philadelphia, Baltimore, and other seaboard cities. The feathering of the eagle and so-called olive branch on goblet, No. 3, is very similar to the treatment of the leaf sprays on decanter, No. 4, Plate 85.

PLATE 68

1. Presentation goblet blown from clear lead glass; straight-sided bowl rounding at base to an applied stem composed of a globular knop over a combined inverted and true baluster, each containing large tear; applied circular foot with rayed cutting on bottom. Bowl decorated by copper-wheel engraving of four slender leaf and flower sprays tied with bowknots and enclosing initials "*B. F. McN.*" and date "*Dec. 25th. 1864*"; on the reverse, an upright flower and leaf spray; style of the engraving typical of that found on many presentation pieces made at the works of the New England Glass Company and Boston and Sandwich Glass Works in the 1860s and 1870s.

Height, $7\frac{7}{8}$"; top diameter, $3\frac{11}{16}$"; diameter of foot, $3\frac{13}{16}$".

2. Tall goblet of very heavy clear lead glass; bucket-shaped bowl resting on applied double vermicular collar capping a long cylindrical stem containing red, white, and blue twists; angular knop at base of stem resting on circular foot. Union Glass Works, Somerville, Massachusetts. Circa 1860.

Height, $8\frac{3}{8}$"; top diameter, $3\frac{1}{2}$"; diameter of foot, $3\frac{3}{8}$".

3. Tall goblet or wine blown from heavy non-lead glass with dark greenish cast; semi-oviform bowl, very thick at base, resting on large inverted baluster stem with large tear, supported by high domed foot; in the thick lower portion of the bowl, six small tears circling a slightly larger tear in the center. Handed down in an old Baltimore family and believed to have been made at Amelung's glassworks.

Height, 8"; top diameter, $3\frac{3}{8}$"; diameter of foot, $4\frac{1}{4}$".

4. Goblet of clear non-lead glass; cylindrical bowl flaring at tooled rim; ten oval-top panels encircling lower part of bowl, continued on the ten-sided stem to spread out over the foot; on one side, a large rectangular panel, with border of ruby stain enclosing a vignette of Trenton Falls engraved by copper wheel, and with the inscription "TRENTON FALLS NEW-YORK" cut through the ruby stain at the bottom, somewhat similar to a view of Trenton Falls appearing on Old Blue Staffordshire made for the American market. Second quarter of the nineteenth century.

Height, $6\frac{1}{8}$"; top diameter, $3\frac{1}{2}$"; diameter of foot, $3\frac{1}{8}$".

5. Small Blown Three Mold goblet, clear lead glass; barrel-shaped bowl in pattern GIII-6, flaring slightly at top to plain rim; applied short knopped stem with circular foot; bowl blown in half-pint decanter mold. Boston and Sandwich Glass Company. Circa 1825–35.

Height, $5\frac{3}{16}$"; top diameter, $3\frac{3}{16}$"; diameter of foot, $2\frac{13}{16}$".

6. Goblet blown from clear and milk-white non-lead glass; semi-oviform clear bowl set into a pattern-molded shell or casing of opalescent milk-white glass scalloped at top and patterned in a 30-rib mold; applied milk-white ring-knop stem and circular foot. Said to have been blown at the Ihmsen Glass Works, Pittsburgh, Pennsylvania. Mid-nineteenth century.

Height, $6\frac{5}{16}$"; top diameter, $3\frac{1}{4}$"; diameter of foot, $3\frac{1}{4}$".

PLATE 69

Tall goblet blown from moderately deep green glass, probably non-lead; deep bowl, tapering quite sharply to an applied stem composed of two parts—a solid upper part shaped by manipulation which rests on the lower, a blown hollow ball—the whole supported by a slightly domed circular foot with rim folded under; in the hollow knop a silver medal. Albert Gallatin Company, New Geneva Glass Works, Pennsylvania. Circa 1798–1800. Collection of Mr. Jerome K. Strauss.

Height, $9\frac{1}{8}$–$9\frac{5}{16}$"; top diameter, $5\frac{3}{16}$"; diameter of foot, $5\frac{3}{16}$".

The goblet was found about ten years ago in the little town of Mapleton, Pennsylvania, just two miles from New Geneva. It was in the possession of one of the descendants of Charles Alexandre Mestrezat, a relative of Albert Gallatin and a prominent citizen of Mapleton in the last years of the eighteenth and early years of the nineteenth centuries.

In an interesting story of the goblet published in the magazine *Antiques,* August 1939, Mr. Strauss wrote as follows:

The outstanding feature of this goblet, the silver medallion enshrined in the bulb, has served as a major clue in tracing the origin of the piece. Because the wall of glass that grips it is fairly thick, particularly at the joining of bulb and foot, and because a film covers part of the inner surface of the bulb, the design and lettering on the medallion were difficult to decipher. This film, incidentally, is pale brown where the silver touches the glass, shading to a bluish opalescence, and is presumably silver sulphide resulting from the sulphur content of the fuel used in the glass furnace. However, enough of the medallion was visible to permit a rude sketch to be made of its two faces for the purpose of identification. . . . It appears that such silver medals were awarded as prizes by the Collège de Genève to specially diligent or gifted students, a practice that was carried on from the beginning of the seventeenth century to the early part of the nineteenth. Important for our present purpose is the fact that the dies used up to about 1781–1782 had developed defects and were replaced by a new set of slightly modified design. The medal in this goblet was struck from those in use prior to 1781.

It is, of course, impossible to tell whether medals from the old dies were available for award to students graduating after 1782. However, it is worth noting that Gallatin graduated in 1779. . . .

In conclusion, it seems unquestionable that this goblet was made by Albert Gallatin and Company, or the New Geneva Glass Works. . . . Speculation on the ownership of the medal adds to the interest of the piece. It seems most probable that Charles Alexandre Mestrezat was not the one to whom the medal was awarded, though it might have been won by his father or another of his forbears. But one is easily led to a likely assumption; that the medal represented an achievement in the early life of the great Albert Gallatin himself—that it was at a later date encased in a product of his own factory and given to his relative as a token of esteem and of friendship, to remain forever within the family. . . .

PLATE 70

1. Goblet blown from a heavy gather of pale yellow-green non-lead glass; barrel-shaped bowl resting on an applied stem composed of three graduated rings and short cylindrical shank rising from a broad sloping circular foot; bowl decorated around lower part with a heavy superimposed band of fluting or gadrooning patterned in a 32-rib mold, and around center with a broad applied ring; and just below rim, for space of about one inch, with threading. Found years ago in the vicinity of Greensboro, Pennsylvania, and attributed to New Geneva Glass Works of Albert Gallatin Company. Circa 1798–1810.

Height, $5\frac{3}{4}''$; top diameter, $3\frac{1}{2}''$; diameter of foot, $3\frac{9}{16}''$.

2. Tall goblet or chalice blown from clear deep amber bottle glass; bell-shaped bowl resting on applied heavy stem with medial vermicular collar and applied domed foot with wide under-folded rim. Attributed to Stoddard, New Hampshire. Circa 1842–60.

Height, $8''$; top diameter, $4\frac{5}{8}''$; diameter of foot, $3\frac{13}{16}''$.

An interesting individual piece, this goblet shows reversion to an early form of ornamentation in the vermicular ring which is similar to that on several decanter jugs of the Ravenscroft period, 1675–90. While on spot test the glass shows considerable lead content, this probably is due to lead-glass cullet.

3. Goblet blown from brilliant blue-green non-lead glass; deep cylindrical bowl flaring slightly below plain rim and rounding at bottom to an applied solid stem terminating in a globular knop and resting on an applied circular foot. Attributed to the Rensselaer Glass Factory, Sand Lake, New York. Circa 1830.

Height, $6\frac{7}{8}''$; top diameter, $3\frac{3}{4}''$; diameter of foot, $3''$.

This goblet is said to have been made by John Gabler, a blower at the glassworks about the time it was leased to Stadlers, Rush and Company by the Rensselaer Glass Manufacturing Company, the one incorporated on April 10, 1830. The tenant company supposedly was formed by blowers from South Jersey including the Gabler brothers, of whom John was one. The goblet was acquired in the vicinity of Sand Lake from descendants of John Gabler. The glass is the same in color and weight as fragments from the glasshouse site.

PLATE 71

1. Goblet blown from non-lead glass; clear deep amber bowl, cylindrical form rounding at base; applied solid baluster stem and circular foot of bluish aquamarine. South Jersey. About second quarter of nineteenth century.

Height, 6⅝″; top diameter, 2¹⁵⁄₁₆″; diameter of foot, 3¹⁄₁₆″.

2. Goblet blown from heavy gather of clear deep olive-green non-lead glass; conical bowl with heavy globular-knop stem drawn out from same gather and resting on applied heavy circular foot. Willington Glass Company, West Willington, Connecticut.

Height, 6⅝″; top diameter, 3¾″; diameter of foot, 3⅛″.

The goblet can be dated any time in the early years of this glasshouse—1815–35. After passing through various ownerships the works closed in 1872.

3. Large mug blown from dark olive-green (black) non-lead bottle glass; tapering cylindrical bowl with short hollow stem and small circular foot drawn out from same gather; applied solid semi-ear-shaped handle. Saratoga (Mountain) Glass Works. Circa 1844–65.

Height, 6⅝″; top diameter, 3⅝″; diameter of foot, 2⅝″; diameter at bottom of body, 2¹⁵⁄₁₆″.

The Saratoga (Mountain) Glass Works was located at Mount Pleasant, about eight miles from Saratoga Springs. This was the glasshouse and community which Oscar Granger established in the midst of an abundant supply of wood when lack of that commodity forced him to abandon his Mount Vernon Glass Works at Vernon, New York. In 1865 when he sold the works to the Congress and Empire Spring Company the plant was moved to Saratoga Springs—and re-erected in that part of the village known as Congressville. There it was operated until about 1890, principally to supply the various spring-water companies with their bottles.

PLATE 72

1. Handled mug blown from light green non-lead glass; deep cylindrical body flaring slightly to rim, rounding at bottom, and resting on applied petaled foot (eight petals); applied semi-ear-shaped handle with thumb and finger rests; lower part of body decorated with a heavy band of molded fluting or gadrooning, around the middle section trailed circuits or chain, and just below rim, applied threading. Probably Midwestern. First half of nineteenth century. Collection of Mr. Jerome K. Strauss.

Height, $5\frac{11}{16}''$; top diameter, $3\frac{1}{16}''$; greatest diameter of body, $3\frac{3}{8}''$; diameter of foot, $2\frac{7}{16}''$.

2. Handled mug blown from brilliant clear green glass, probably non-lead; cylindrical form flaring slightly to plain rim; large applied semi-ear-shaped handle with three ribs; body pattern-molded and expanded in swirled ribbing. Midwestern. First half of nineteenth century. Collection of Mr. Jerome K. Strauss.

Height, $4\frac{1}{2}''$; top diameter, $4\frac{1}{8}''$; diameter of base, $3\frac{3}{8}''$.

3. Handled mug blown from clear yellow-green glass; straight-sided form with plain rim; applied corrugated strap handle with large thumbpiece; entire body decorated with applied fine threading. Eighteenth or early nineteenth century. Collection of Mr. Jerome K. Strauss.

Height, $5\frac{1}{8}''$; top diameter, $3\frac{9}{16}''$; diameter of base, $3\frac{3}{16}''$.

PLATE 73

1. Handled mug blown from non-lead aquamarine glass with loopings of milky white; oviform body with wide-flaring rim; applied circular crimped foot; large applied hollow semi-ear-shaped handle of aquamarine glass. Isabella Glass Works, Brooklyn, New Jersey, which tradition says was named after Isabella Stanger, a daughter of one of the Stangers who operated the glasshouse. Circa 1850.

Height, $4\frac{1}{2}''$; *top diameter,* $4\frac{1}{2}''$; *diameter of foot,* $2\frac{5}{8}''$.

2. Handled mug of clear light amber non-lead glass with milky-white loopings; oviform body flaring at rim and resting on applied heavy circular foot of amber glass, solid applied looped amber handle. South Jersey. Circa 1835–50.

Height, $5\frac{1}{8}''$; *top diameter,* $3\frac{3}{4}''$; *diameter of foot,* $3\frac{1}{4}''$.

3. Handled mug of clear amethyst non-lead glass; plain free-blown barrel-shaped body with small applied (4-rib) corrugated strap handle. Circa last half of eighteenth century.

Height, $4\frac{1}{2}''$; *top diameter,* $3\frac{1}{16}''$; *diameter of base,* $2\frac{1}{2}''$.

PLATE 74

1. Miniature handled mug blown from light olive-yellow non-lead glass; straight-sided form with applied solid semi-ear-shaped handle; upper half of body decorated with applied threading. First half of nineteenth century.

Height, 2⅛″; top diameter, 1¹⁵⁄₁₆″; diameter of base, 1½″.

2. Plain free-blown cup and saucer, clear light green non-lead glass. Cup: circular form resting on applied circular foot; applied solid semi-ear-shaped handle. Saucer: fairly deep circular bowl with plain rim, resting on applied very short stem and circular foot. New York State. First half of nineteenth century.

Cup: height, 2¹⁄₁₆″; top diameter, 3⅛″; diameter of foot, 2¼″. Saucer: height, 1½″; top diameter, 5¼″; diameter of foot, 2½″.

3. Miniature handled mug free-blown from non-lead light green glass; straight-sided cylindrical form with applied solid semi-ear-shaped handle. New York State. First half of nineteenth century.

Height, 1¾″; top diameter, 1⅝″; diameter of base, 1⅜″.

4. Handled mug blown from heavy aquamarine non-lead glass; cylindrical form with plain rim; applied solid semi-ear-shaped handle with small thumbpiece; body decorated with six applied leaf prunts in three nearly equidistant groups of two each. South Jersey. Circa 1835–60.

Height, 4⅜″; top diameter, 3³⁄₁₆″; diameter of base, 2⅜″.

5. Handled mug blown from clear brilliant non-lead aquamarine glass with bluish tone; straight-sided cylindrical form with applied solid semi-ear-shaped handle; upper half of body decorated with applied threading. Redford Glass Works, Redford, New York. Circa 1831–50.

Height, 3⅝″; top diameter, 3⅛″; diameter of base, 2½″.

PLATE 75

1. Blown Three Mold punch cup of clear lead glass; globular body and drawn circular foot; applied solid semi-ear-shaped handle; pattern GIII-25, one identified from fragments as Sandwich; a very rare form in Blown Three Mold glass. Boston and Sandwich Glass Works. Circa 1825–35.

Height, $2\frac{1}{2}''$; top diameter, $2\frac{5}{16}''$; greatest diameter of body, $2\frac{1}{2}''$; diameter of foot, $2''$.

2. Punch cup blown from clear lead glass, barrel shape with applied solid semi-ear-shaped handle; wheel-cut decoration composed of band of cut splits with rounded top around the base and strawberry diamond and fan cutting above. Probably Pittsburgh. Circa 1820–35.

Height, $2\frac{3}{4}''$; top diameter, $2\frac{3}{8}''$; greatest diameter of body, $2\frac{1}{2}''$; diameter of base, $1\frac{3}{4}''$.

3. Blown Three Mold handled mug, clear lead glass; straight-sided form, applied solid semi-ear-shaped handle; pattern GIII-13. Circa 1825–35.

Height, $2\frac{7}{8}''$; top diameter, $2\frac{7}{16}''$.

4. Handled mug blown from clear lead glass, straight-sided form with applied semi-ear-shaped handle with heavy medial rib; decoration of wide splits below alternate diamond with fan and printy with blaze cutting; the latter may be the "rising sun" motif mentioned in an advertisement of cut glass in the 1820s. Probably Pittsburgh. Circa 1820–35.

Height, $3\frac{3}{8}''$; top diameter, $2\frac{13}{16}''$.

PLATE 76

THE AMELUNG TOBIAS AND THE ANGEL FLIP GLASS

Tall flip glass and cover blown from a heavy gather of clear non-lead glass, with greenish cast in the very heavy base; straight-sided form, spreading slightly at the top; set-in cover with a large applied baluster finial similar to that on the Schley pokal cover, and with an applied band tooled into a half round to rest on the rim of the flip—a typical Amelung cover. Decoration engraved by copper wheel and composed of a tall arch formed by the inscription, in script, *"Happy is he who is blessed with Virtuous Children. Carolina Lucia Amelung. 1788."* over a handsome medallion formed from conventionalized large leaf scrolls, tiny leaf sprays, and three daisylike flowers enclosing a vignette of Tobias and the Angel; on the front of the cover, a large engraved foliated and floral scroll.

Over-all height, $11\frac{7}{8}''$; *without cover,* $8\frac{1}{2}''$; *top diameter,* $5\frac{5}{8}''$; *diameter of base,* $4\frac{1}{2}''$.

One of the most important pieces of Amelung glass, this covered flip glass bears the same date as the Bremen pokal, Plate 64. Obviously a gift to the glassmaker's wife, it probably was one of the first presentation pieces made at the New Bremen Glassmanufactory when the metal was beginning to approach the desired clearness. Until its discovery Lucia, another given name of Amelung's wife Carolina, was unknown.

From the inscription and the incident depicted from the Book of Tobit, one infers that the Amelungs' family life was a happy one, that John and Carolina likewise had children who observed the fifth commandment. The little scene showing the angel guiding Tobias, son of Tobit, on his journey after catching the fish from which was taken the gall to cure Tobit's blindness, was a favored subject with artists long before Amelung's day. It is likely that a copy or the memory of one of the early paintings served as model for the engraver.

PLATE 77

THE AMELUNG REPOLD FLIP GLASS

Tall flip blown from a heavy gather of non-lead glass, with a very dark amethyst or pinkish cast in the heavy base; straight-sided form, spreading slightly at the top. Decorated by copper-wheel engraving; on obverse, a large medallion formed from elaborate leaf scrolls, floral sprays, enclos-like flowers, and barley and wheat sprays, enclos-ing the initials in script *"G M R"*; on the reverse, a vignette depicting a Maryland farmhouse facing a tall tree flanked by shrubbery, and in the immediate foreground a group of three domestic fowls below two in flight. 1788–92.

Height, $7\frac{7}{8}''$; top diameter, $5\frac{3}{4}''$; diameter of base, $4\frac{1}{4}''$.

From the standpoint of decorative design this flip glass is one of the most interesting pieces, not only of Amelung but also of American glass, known today. It is one of the very few known (and the only Amelung example) that have scenes falling in the category of genre art. The initials are those of George and Metha Repold, of Baltimore, Maryland, who were friends of John and Carolina Amelung. The flip glass was among the heirlooms inherited by Miss Margaret B. Waesche, of Washington, D.C., a descendant of the Repolds. But quite apart from its family history this piece could be attributed on the basis of the execution and style of the engraved decoration.

PLATE 78

1. Flip glass blown from clear non-lead glass with slight greenish tone; straight-sided spreading form; rather crude decoration consisting of a wide ribbon with ends loosely scrolled, outlined in dark green and bearing the name "Mary Russel" upon a gilded background, and between circled tips of the scroll at ends a large eight-pointed star also gilded and outlined in dark green; at the top, a narrow band of gilding above a single dark green line. Last quarter of eighteenth century.

Height, 6"; top diameter, $4\frac{1}{2}$"; diameter at base, $2\frac{7}{8}$".

2. Large covered flip glass blown from clear lead glass with grayish tone in the very thick base; straight, slightly spreading sides; eighteenth-century type flanged set-in cover with applied hollow ball finial on short stem supported by a double ring; shallow crude engraving like that on the eighteenth-century peasant non-lead glass from various continental areas; at the top, a band of ellipses, formed by intersecting pinnated wavy lines, above the name "IOHN REYNOLDS" enclosed in a wreath formed by single long scrolled pinnated leaf sprays tied together by a bowknot beneath the "N" in "REYNOLDS"; on each spray, above the knot, a tiny, crudely formed bird. Presentation piece found in Philadelphia. Last quarter of eighteenth century.

Over-all height, $8\frac{3}{4}$"; without cover, $6\frac{1}{4}$"; top diameter, $4\frac{7}{8}$"; diameter of base, $3\frac{5}{8}$".

3. Large flip glass blown from clear non-lead glass with greenish tone in the thick base; engraved by copper wheel with rather crude floral and leaf spray medallion enclosing the initials *"A.G."* in script.

From the Henry Francis du Pont Winterthur Museum.

Height, $8\frac{3}{16}$"; top diameter, $5\frac{13}{16}$"; diameter of base, $4\frac{1}{4}$".

It is said the initials stand for A. Grosz, who resided in the vicinity of Frederick, Maryland, and that the glass was made at Amelung's glassworks. While the style of the floral and leaf sprays is quite different from any of the dated and inscribed Amelung presentation pieces, the form of the flip, the heavy base, and the greenish cast of the non-lead glass are typical of other flips of proven Amelung origin. The style of the letters is also characteristic of Amelung lettering: for instance, the *"G"* on the Repold flip, Plate 77.

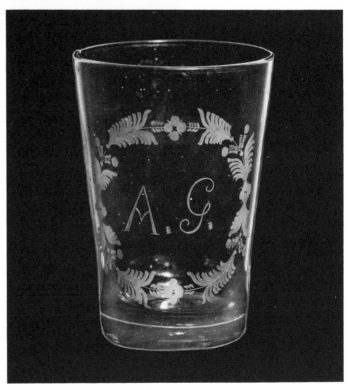

PLATE 79

1. Tumbler blown from clear lead glass with pale bluish tint; straight spreading sides; double-patterned in a 16-rib mold and expanded, broken-swirl design. Midwestern. Circa 1815–35.

Height, $3\frac{3}{4}''$; top diameter, $3\frac{3}{8}''$; diameter at base, $2\frac{1}{4}''$.

2. Small tumbler blown from clear flint glass; straight-sided form; the gather first patterned in a small open-top 22-rib mold and then expanded as it was blown into a full-sized three-piece mold in pattern GIII-8. New England area. Circa 1825–35.

Height, $2\frac{3}{4}''$; top diameter, $2\frac{1}{4}''$; diameter of base, $2''$.

3. Tumbler blown from clear lead glass; straight-sided form with heavy thick base; engraved by copper wheel, view of Washington's tomb with pine trees in background and flanked by two knolls from which rise tall trees in leaf. According to an old label on the base, said to have been made by a skilled engraver, employed in the Philadelphia glassworks of Burgin and Sons, as a gift to Sarah Burgin, daughter of one of the proprietors.

Height, $3\frac{3}{8}''$; top diameter, $3\frac{1}{16}''$; diameter of base, $2\frac{9}{16}''$.

As yet no information has come to light to indicate that Burgin and Sons were engaged in the making of tablewares.

4. Flip glass blown from clear non-lead glass with pale greenish cast; straight spreading sides; decoration in colored enamels; on the obverse, central design of two lovebirds in gray and pale blue perched on a yellow basket containing a spray of leaves in nile-green and resting on nile-green verdure with a brick-red band beneath, flanked by a tall conventionalized flower and leaf spray in many colors—milk-white, gray-blue, nile-green, yellow, brick-red, and black; at the top, encircling the flip, a wavy line of white above a band of yellow, and beneath, a narrow line of white; on the reverse, in white, an inscription in two lines: *"My love you Like me do".*

Found in Pennsylvania, probably American and possibly Stiegel.

Height, $4\frac{5}{8}''$; top diameter, $3\frac{5}{8}''$; diameter of base, $2\frac{1}{2}''$.

5. Tall tumbler blown from heavy clear non-lead glass; cylindrical form; on the obverse, a raised panel framed by narrow bands of fine cross-hatching and engraved by copper wheel, depicting a group of buildings above the inscription "WIDOWS AND ORPHANS ASYLUM *in Philadelphia";* at bottom, a narrow band of fine cut diamonds. On the reverse, at the top, three festoons of very fine cut diamonds above graduated pillar flutes or ribs; on the base, cut rays converging at the center.

Possibly Union Glass Works, Kensington, Philadelphia. Circa 1830–40.

Height, $4\frac{7}{16}''$; top diameter, $3\frac{1}{8}''$; diameter of base, $2\frac{7}{8}''$.

The engraving on the tumbler, we are informed by Mr. Ezra J. Feinberg, is an exact copy of one of the views, engraved by George Strickland, in *Views in Philadelphia from original drawings taken in 1827–1830,* published by C. G. Childs in 1830. The Orphan Asylum, established by the ladies of the Second Presbyterian Church of Philadelphia in 1814, was destroyed by fire on January 24, 1822, and rebuilt. The home built by the Indigent Widows and Single Woman's Society was completed in 1820. The cut decoration is of the 1830 period, the view of topical interest primarily to Philadelphians, the Union Flint Glass Company the most important one in the area making fine cut and engraved glasswares: hence the above attribution.

PLATE 80

1. Blown Three Mold flip glass of clear lead glass; straight, slightly spreading sides; pattern GIII-26 with concentric-ring base, one of the most elaborate of the Blown Three Mold patterns, and one in which quart, pint, and half-pint decanters, quart and pint pitchers, creamers, and small creamers also are recorded. Boston and Sandwich Glass Works. Circa 1825–35.

Height, 5$\frac{13}{16}$″; top diameter, 4$\frac{5}{8}$″; diameter of base, 3″.

2. Flip glass blown from clear non-lead glass; straight, slightly spreading sides; double-patterned in a 16-rib mold and expanded, broken-swirl design. Midwestern. Early nineteenth century.

Height, 5$\frac{5}{8}$″; top diameter, 4$\frac{5}{16}$″; diameter of base. 2$\frac{3}{4}$″.

3. Blown Three Mold flip glass of clear lead glass, straight-sided spreading form, very wide at top; pattern GIII-2 Type II; extremely rare article in this pattern used primarily for decanters. Boston and Sandwich Glass Works. Circa 1825–35.

Height, 5″; top diameter, 4$\frac{3}{8}$″; diameter of base, 3″.

PLATE 81

1. Tumbler of clear glass blown and patterned in a full-size three-piece mold; cylindrical form; wide band of swag ribbing encircling the lower part; above, on one side, the name "LAFAYETTE" and, on the other, "WELCOME." Collection of Mrs. Hugh Williamson Kelly.

Height, about $3\frac{7}{8}''$; *diameter, about* $2\frac{5}{16}''$; *circumference at the top,* 10", *and just above the thick bottom,* 9".

This tumbler, as yet the only known pattern of Blown Three Mold having historical significance, was acquired about twenty years ago from the Strong family in York, Pennsylvania. According to the family tradition, it was one of a set of sixteen which were especially made to be used at a banquet tendered to General Lafayette at McGrath's Hotel in York on Wednesday evening, February 2, 1825.

2. Tumbler, blown from clear glass; cylindrical form, slightly waisted above the thick base; on the front, a scrolled medallion outlined in gold, bearing the gold initials "F.C.S.A." in script, and backed by blue enameling on the inside of the tumbler; around the rim, a narrow gold band.

Height, 4"; *top diameter,* $3\frac{1}{8}''$; *diameter of base,* $2\frac{7}{8}''$.

The initials are those of Frederica Christina Sophia Amelung, the oldest of Amelung's four children, three daughters and one son. This tumbler and two similar tumblers, each with initials of one of the other daughters, were inherited by Mrs. Ethel Amelung McCallum, a great-great-granddaughter of the glassmaker through Frederica's marriage to Dr. Philip Somerkamp. The one illustrated is owned by a niece of Mrs. McCallum, Mrs. Lowell Thomas Murray, who is a great-great-great-grandchild of Amelung. The present whereabouts of the other two is unknown. Years ago Mrs. McCallum gave one to a sister, the other to a brother.

PLATE 82

1. Tumbler, blown from clear lead glass; cylindrical form; decoration of strawberry diamond and fan cutting above a horizontal rib surmounting a wide band of sixteen splits encircling the lower part of the tumbler; in the base, portrait bust of General Lafayette, a white cameo incrustation.

Height, $3\frac{3}{8}''$; top diameter, $2\frac{7}{8}''$.

2. Tumbler similar to No. 1 except that it has an added decoration, engraved by copper wheel, of a delicate rose-vine circlet around the top and on one side a small medallion formed by two rose-vine sprays enclosing the monogram *"F C W"* in script; in the base, a portrait bust of Washington in uniform, a white cameo incrustation · much smaller than that in Nos. 1 and 3.

Height, $3\frac{3}{8}''$; top diameter, $2\frac{7}{8}''$.

3. Tumbler similar to No. 1; bust of Andrew Jackson, also a white cameo incrustation.

Height, $3\frac{3}{8}''$; top diameter, $2\frac{7}{8}''$.

It is our belief that these tumblers with the cameo incrustation, or sulphide, as they are also called, were made in the Pittsburgh Flint Glass Works of Bakewell, Page and Bakewell. The Washington and Jackson tumblers probably were made about 1824, the Lafayette undoubtedly in that year as were so many of the items to commemorate his visit to America. In March 1825 the firm was advertising "LAFAYETTE & MEDALLION tumblers, ornaments" for sale at reduced prices. Apparently their sale had not been up to expectations in 1824.

In the Jerome Strauss collection of glass drinking vessels there is a tumbler similar to No. 2, but with a different monogram and small bust of Benjamin Franklin in the base. In the collection of the New York Historical Society are two other tumblers with different cutting and monogram *"D W C,"* each containing a bust of De Witt Clinton in the base. These tumblers were given to the Society in 1884 by Alfred De Witt, whose father, Peter De Witt, received them from Mrs. De Witt Clinton. They were supposed to have been presented while De Witt Clinton was governor of New York State, 1825–27. Clinton visited Pittsburgh in 1825 and while there was given a public dinner and in the evening a Masonic supper. It is quite possible the tumblers were presented to him on that occasion.

PLATE 83

THE IHMSEN HORNET AND PEACOCK DECANTER

Large decanter, capacity a little in excess of two quarts; blown from a heavy gather of clear lead glass with decided grayish cast; globular body; cylindrical neck with flanged lip and three applied angular collars. Decorated by rather crudely executed copper-wheel engraving portraying the naval engagement between the *Hornet* and the *Peacock* in the War of 1812; the lower part of the decanter engraved to imitate water; the *Hornet* shown standing by the sinking *Peacock* while two boats bring survivors from the British man-of-war to the victorious Yankee ship; on the other side, inscription "THE HORNET AND PEACOK" above two leaf sprays enclosing initials "*J L*". Charles Ihmsen, Birmingham Glass Works, Pittsburgh, Pennsylvania. Circa 1813.

The Hornet and Peacock decanter came to us from Mrs. Leaugeay Phillips Stevenson, to whom it was given by Dr. John Leaugeay Phillips, her father. He was the son of Phoebe Leaugeay Phillips, the daughter of John and Wilhemina Ihmsen Leaugeay and granddaughter of Charles Ihmsen. Charles Ihmsen, who was one of the partners in the first glasshouse in the Birmingham district of Pittsburgh, established in 1810, made the decanter for his son-in-law, John Leaugeay. Whether there was a reason other than patriotic enthusiasm for the selection of this naval engagement off the coast of South America as the subject for the engraving, we do not know. There is no doubt "that splendid naval action" and the events connected with the *Hornet's* captain and crew were in the news for many weeks after the New York *Commercial Advertiser's* scoop, published before the release of Captain James Lawrence's official letter of March 19, 1813, to the Secretary of the Navy. And the *Hornet's* feat in, as Lawrence reported, literally cutting the British *Peacock* to pieces in less than fifteen minutes on that late afternoon of February 24 was a matter of intense national pride. Everyone knew the details, knew also that "the crew of the *Hornet* made a subscription and supplied the prisoners (who had lost almost everything) with two shirts, a blue jacket and trousers each," and that the English tars had published letters of appreciation.

Charles Ihmsen would not have had any difficulty obtaining a model from which to copy his engraving on glass. The battle was recorded on canvas almost immediately. At least one painting was exhibited in various cities and towns. According to the Boston *Columbian Centinel* for September 27, 1813, it was "made from a drawing under the immediate direction of the late, gallant Lawrence." Ihmsen's version is not unlike that which appears in *The Naval Monument*, published in 1816. Even in 1823 J. T. Porter included in his *America Triumphant* the following verse:

> The Lawrence with his Hornet's nest
> If I have not forgot 'em;
> In fifteen minutes sent of John's
> Fine Peacock to the Bottom.

PLATE 84

Quart decanter blown from clear lead glass; semi-barrel-shaped body tapering quite sharply at shoulder to cylindrical neck with flanged lip and three applied double-ring collars; on the obverse, engraved by copper wheel, the American eagle patterned after the United States Seal but with the pennant, inscribed "E PLURIBUS UNUM," extending from under one wing across breast and over the other wing; above, seventeen small stars and arching cloud band; on the reverse, a merchant ship under full sail below the legend "FREE TRADE"; on one side, between the eagle and ship, an anchor, and on the other a circular sunburst medallion containing the monogram "T C M N." Circa 1808–12.

Height without stopper, $8\frac{11}{16}$"; greatest diameter of body, $4\frac{5}{8}$".

While lead-glass decanters engraved with similar American subjects are known to have been made in Irish glasshouses, we are inclined to believe this one is American, perhaps made in the Pittsburgh area. The stopper is not the original, which may have been either of this or the mushroom type.

PLATE 85

1. Quart decanter blown from clear lead glass; straight sides spreading to rounded shoulder and tapering to cylindrical neck with "bar" lip and three applied heavy plain rings or collars; decorated by copper-wheel engraving of the American eagle in flight, thunderbolt and olive branch in its talons and holding in its beak a large shield with "WINE", in place of bars; on either side of shield, a large leaf spray and above eagle seven small six-pointed stars. Probably Pittsburgh area. Circa 1815–35.

Height, 9½″; diameter at shoulder, 4⅝″; diameter of base, 3½″.

2. Half-pint Blown Three Mold decanter of clear lead glass; Blown Three Mold stopper which may or may not be the original; Baroque pattern GV-3, and circular foot with milled rim also formed in the full-size three-piece mold.

Over-all height, 7⅝″, without stopper, 6⅝″; greatest diameter of body, 3¼″; diameter of foot, 2⅝″.

3. Quart Blown Three Mold decanter, clear lead glass; cylindrical form, rounded sloping shoulder, large molded ring at base of the cylindrical neck with flanged lip; Blown Three Mold stopper. Pattern GIV-7, Arch and Fern Leaf, with medallion formed by entwined serpents and containing the word " NIⱭ," upside down and reversed—a rare variant. Boston and Sandwich Glass Works. 1825–35.

Over-all height, 10⅜″; greatest diameter of body, 4¹¹⁄₁₆″.

These decanters are found in quart and pint sizes, usually with a lattice design instead of the name of a liquor in the medallion. The following names are found in the quart decanters: Rum, Gin, Wine, Whiskey, Brandy, and Cherry; in the pint: Gin and Whiskey.

4. Pint, blown, cut, and engraved taper shape decanter, clear non-lead glass; cut flutes on neck, cut flanged lip, and flat cut stopper; on obverse *and* reverse, copper-wheel engraving of two horizontal leaf sprays above a circular sunburst medallion containing the letter *"R"* and resting on a bank of clouds. Collection of Dr. and Mrs. Martin Stohlman.

Over-all height, 11″.

We have a small goblet, one of a pair, blown from clear non-lead glass, with almost identical medallion and leaf-spray decoration, but with the letter *"W"* in the medallion. It was found in York, Pennsylvania, several years ago and was, according to tradition, one of a set made at Amelung's glassworks for George Washington.

5. Tall taper shape decanter of clear non-lead glass; engraved by copper wheel in typical Amelung style, a large medallion formed by four delicate leaf sprays with interspersed daisylike flowers around a frame enclosing the initials *"S G"*, upon the top of which is a bird with raised wings. Plain flat stopper. The style and details of the decoration indicative of workmanship of Amelung engravers. Collection of Dr. and Mrs. Martin Stohlman.

Over-all height, 13″.

PLATE 86

1. Decanter about quart capacity formed and patterned in full-size three-piece mold; clear light green non-lead glass; straight sides spreading to sloping shoulder, tapering neck with wide mouth and flanged lip; probably made without stopper. Geometric pattern GII-33, composed of a band of diamond diapering between bands of vertical fluting; band of vertical fluting on base; one of the two decanters known at present. Mantua Glass Works, Mantua, Ohio. Circa 1822–29.

Height, 8⅜″; diameter of base, 3¼″; diameter of shoulder, 4⅜″.

2. Pint decanter, formed and patterned in full-size three-piece mold; brilliant light green non-lead glass; barrel shape, tapering neck with flanged lip. Pattern GIII-16. Keene-Marlboro-Street Glass Works, Keene, New Hampshire. Circa 1816–35.

Height, 7″; diameter of base, 3″; diameter of shoulder, 3⅝″.

The majority of the decanters in this Keene pattern and blown in the same mold were from olive-green, olive-amber, or amber bottle glass, with plain lip. They never had stoppers. Only a few specimens are known in this light green color. This mold was used also for other hollow wares including pitchers, flip glasses, and sugar bowls. Two sapphire witch balls are known which, so far as we know today, are unique.

3. Half-pint decanter formed from clear lead glass; barrel shape, tapering neck with wide flanged lip; the gather, first patterned in a small open-top 16-rib mold and then blown into a full-size three-piece decanter mold so that the Geometric, Sunburst, pattern GIII-6 was superimposed on the ribbing, a technique used rarely and probably only to make individual pieces. Blown Three Mold stopper, pattern GII-18. Probably Boston and Sandwich Glass Works. Circa 1825–35.

Over-all height, 7⁵⁄₁₆″; diameter, 3¹⁄₁₆″.

4. Miniature decanter, one of a pair, blown from clear lead glass; formed and patterned in full-size three-piece mold; straight spreading sides angling sharply at long shoulder sloping to cylindrical neck with flanged lip; original flat stopper with fine crisscross pattern; pattern GII-19. Circa 1820–35.

Over-all height, 3⅞″; diameter of base, 1⅛″; diameter of shoulder, 1¹³⁄₁₆″.

5. Quarter-pint decanter formed and patterned in full-size three-piece mold; clear lead glass; barrel-shaped body, cylindrical neck with wide flanged lip, and two applied rigaree collars or neck rings; pattern GII-18; diamond indented base; ribbed wheel stopper. Probably Boston and Sandwich Glass Works. 1825–35.

Over-all height, 5⅛″; diameter of base, 1⅝″; diameter of shoulder, 2³⁄₁₆″.

PLATE 87

1. Very heavy Blown Three Mold carafe, capacity a little more than a quart; emerald-green lead glass; semi-barrel shape, shoulder sloping to a wide molded rib at base of very wide cylindrical neck with wide flanged lip; pattern GI-29 (described from base to top): three horizontal ribs, band of eighteen broad vertical ribs, two horizontal ribs, band of twelve fan flutes, and single broad rib; rayed base having thirty-eight triangular rays around the depressed center. Attributed to the Mount Vernon Glass Works, Vernon, New York. Circa 1815–35.

Height, $8\frac{9}{16}''$; diameter of base, $3\frac{5}{8}''$; diameter of shoulder, $4\frac{5}{8}''$; diameter of neck, $2\frac{1}{16}''$; diameter of lip, $3\frac{3}{8}''$.

While the width of the neck indicates this piece was made for a carafe or water bottle, the mold was used customarily for making decanters, which have been found in clear glass, emerald-green, yellow-green, and dark olive-green (black) glass. So far as we know, they were never made with stoppers. Several molds in this pattern have been determined, some of which undoubtedly were used at the Sandwich Glass Works, but the mold in which these carafes and decanters were blown is the one attributed to Mount Vernon.

2. Quart decanter blown from brilliant clear green glass; barrel shape, tapering neck with flanged lip; formed and patterned in a full-size two-piece mold with an elaborate pattern which, beginning at the base, is composed as follows: a wide band containing two panels each with a six-pointed star within a diamond, between blocks of vertical ribs flanked by a plain narrow panel; three horizontal ribs; a band with inscription "MURDOCK AND CASSEL—ZANESVILLE"; a single horizontal rib; a band similar to bottom band, and a single horizontal rib.

Height, $8\frac{3}{4}''$; diameter at base, $3\frac{1}{4}''$; diameter at shoulder, $4\frac{3}{8}''$.

We do not know whether this decanter ever had a stopper. It was made in a glasshouse in Zanesville, Ohio, which was taken over about 1832 by Thomas Murdock and Joseph Cassel and operated by them for several years. Its commercial products were probably window glass and bottles. Two pint flasks made by them are known. One has the same inscription but with the word "OHIO" added after "ZANESVILLE." The other is like No. 2, Plate 113, but with the name "MURDOCK & CASSEL" instead of "J. SHEPARD & CO." As far as we know this decanter, found in Newark, Ohio, in 1928, is the only specimen which has come to light.

3. Quarter-pint Blown Three Mold decanter with original pressed wheel-shaped rayed stopper; dark sapphire-blue lead glass; short straight sides spreading slightly and rounding to sloping shoulder, tapering neck with flanged lip; pattern GIII-26, the most elaborate of the Geometric patterns: a band of herringbone ribbing, single horizontal rib; band of six squares of alternating blocks of diamond diapering and sunburst-in-square, two horizontal ribs; narrow band of sunburst-in-square; wide band of fine vertical ribbing; ringed base. Very rare in this size, and extremely so in blue. Boston and Sandwich Glass Works. Circa 1825–35.

Over-all height, $5\frac{1}{2}''$; diameter of base, $1\frac{7}{8}''$; diameter of shoulder, $2\frac{1}{4}''$.

4. Pint decanter blown from purple-amethyst lead glass; square form with chamfered corners, short cylindrical neck with flanged lip; original matching pressed wheel-shaped rayed stopper; Blown Three Mold pattern GII-28: wide band of forty vertical ribs, two horizontal ribs; wide band of diamond diapering, single horizontal rib; sixteen fan flutes on shoulder. Attributed to Keene-Marlboro-Street Glass Works, Keene, New Hampshire. Circa 1816–30.

Over-all height, $9''$; dimensions of body, about $2\frac{3}{4}''$ by $2\frac{3}{4}''$.

These pint-size square decanters and a quart size also in this pattern were made in clear glass and in a wide range of colors like those of the heavy Keene Masonic flasks which are marked "IP" (Justus Perry), "HS" (Henry Schoolcraft), or "J.K.B." (unknown) like No. 1, Plate 110. The colors include purple, amethyst, blue, and various shades of green from pale to deep emerald. Like the flasks, they are lead glass. The original stoppers were of various styles and include Blown Three Mold, the pressed wheel like the one shown, rayed, mushroom, and ribbed ball. While we believe they were made at Keene because in colors, weight, and type of metal they are like the heavy Keene Masonic flasks, it is probable that some of them at least, in clear glass, were made also by the New England glasshouses in the Boston area.

(Continued on page 296)

PLATE 88

A pair of blown, cut, and elaborately engraved bottles with brilliant faceted ball stoppers; clear lead glass; globular body resting on a heavy circular foot with sunburst cutting on base; eight wide tapering cut flutes on the short shoulder and neck, and flanged lip also cut; elaborate copper-wheel engraving covering entire surface of each bottle and showing a slightly different rendering of similar subject; on the obverse, a group of stable buildings below the initial "R"; on the reverse, a galloping horse and hound; landscape in the intervening spaces. Circa 1890.

Over-all height, 7⅝"; greatest diameter of body, 5"; diameter of foot, 3".

According to the family record which came with these bottles, they were ordered about 1890 from the Corning Glass Company, Corning, New York, by I. W. Wellington, of Corning. He ordered them for a New York banker by the name of Bowden who presented them to his niece, Miss Ellen Rogers. The blanks were probably made at the Corning Glass Works, and the bottles cut and engraved by J. Hoare and Company, a firm occupying premises owned by the glass company. Its fine cut and engraved glass was sold under the name of J. Hoare and Company Cut Glass Manufacturers.

(Plate 87 continued)

5. Quart footed decanter, with original matching stopper; blown from reddish-amethyst lead glass; globular body, tapering to cylindrical neck with flanged lip and resting on hollow flaring circular foot drawn out from same gather; Blown Three Mold pattern GIII-5: a wide band of narrow vertical ribbing, single horizontal rib; wide band of six squares, alternating sunbursts and blocks of diamond diapering; single horizontal rib; narrow band diagonal ribbing to left; single horizontal rib; band of vertical ribbing; rayed base (forty-six rays). Blown Three Mold globular stopper, pattern GII-18.

Decanters with this drawn-out foot are extremely rare—we know of a few in clear glass, only this one in color. The usual barrel shape decanters, blown and patterned in the same or an identical mold, are relatively common in clear glass and occasionally are found in color. We know of two in dark sapphire-blue and one in light green with yellowish tone. The wisteria pitcher shown in color on Plate 10 was blown in the same or an identical mold as the footed decanter. Imitations of pitchers and decanters in this pattern which were produced in clear glass and in colors in 1946 show definite variations in the mold used for them and have other characteristics differentiating them from the originals.

PLATE 89

1. Pair of dark amber (black) non-lead-glass hollow candlesticks, free-blown and shaped by manipulation into an unusual form having a very broad base sloping to a tapering shaft which was tooled into two sausagelike turnings beneath a long nozzle with a plain rim. Westford Glass Works. Circa 1860.

One: height, $7\frac{1}{2}$"; diameter of foot, $4\frac{5}{8}$". The other: height, $7\frac{1}{8}$"; diameter of foot, $4\frac{7}{8}$".

These rare candlesticks are undoubtedly Connecticut glass. They were included in a collection of bottles and flasks purchased in Hartford over twenty-five years ago and were attributed to the Westford Glass Works, a bottle factory. A few years later a similar individual pair was acquired in the vicinity of East Manchester, and likewise with a reliable history of having been blown at the Westford Glass Works. Both pairs are similar in color to the cruet, No. 2, Plate 46, which also has a sausagelike turning.

2. Miniature candlestick, free-blown from aquamarine non-lead glass; fashioned from one gather into socket with a narrow flanged lip and a multiple-knop shaft resting on a small circular foot; the well of the socket, tapering to the top of the bottom knop, is given the appearance of a long graduated tear by the horizontal lines tooled in forming the knops. Acquired in Buffalo, New York, many years ago, and attributed to the nearby Lockport Glass Works. Circa 1840–50.

Height, $3\frac{3}{8}$"; top diameter, also that of the foot, $1\frac{3}{8}$".

3. Small hollow candlestick, free-blown from clear reddish-amber non-lead glass; fashioned from one gather into long socket with narrow rounded flange above a double globular-knop stem and a broad sloping circular foot. Blown in one of the glasshouses in Stoddard, New Hampshire. Circa 1842–60.

Height, 5"; top diameter, $1\frac{1}{2}$"; diameter of foot, $3\frac{1}{2}$".

4. Very rare miniature candlestick, free-blown from one gather of dark olive-green (black) non-lead bottle glass; socket with slightly tooled lip, resting on a solid double globular-knop stem supported by a heavy circular foot. First half of nineteenth century.

Height, $3\frac{1}{2}$"; top diameter, $1\frac{5}{16}$"; diameter of foot, $2\frac{1}{16}$".

This candlestick was discovered in a small village thrift shop in Westchester County, New York, about ten years ago. It is an individual piece which might have been made at the Ellenville Glass Works in Ulster County, New York, or in one of the Connecticut glasshouses such as Coventry, Westford, or West Willington. We have a similar candlestick, a little larger, which is definitely Connecticut.

PLATE 90

1. Mercury glass candlestick, blown from clear glass and silvered; patterned in a full-size three-piece mold, heavy tapered gadrooning on high double-ogee foot and ribbing on stem and lower part of socket. Last half of nineteenth century.

Height, $8\frac{3}{4}''$; top diameter, $1\frac{1}{2}''$; diameter of foot, $4\frac{1}{2}''$.

2. Blown candlestick, one of a pair; ruby glass socket with narrow flange attached by a double ring of clear glass to a clear glass hollow stem shaped like an attenuated hourglass and set into a collar of deep green glass at the top of a heavy sloping circular foot of the same color. Pittsburgh. 1870–80.

Height of each, $9\frac{5}{16}''$; top diameters, $1\frac{3}{4}''$ and $1\frac{13}{16}''$; diameters of bases, $4\frac{1}{4}''$ and $4\frac{3}{16}''$.

The pair was secured in Pittsburgh from the family of a blower who had been employed at the Rochester Tumbler Company in the 1870s. According to family tradition, the sticks were blown as a test of the relative skill of this blower and a visiting blower who had been employed at the Sandwich Glass Works. Each made one stick. The outcome of the contest was a draw; for the result was a pair of almost identical candlesticks.

3. Blown candlestick of clear non-lead glass; heavy circular foot with wide underfold, supporting a composite knop stem including four multiple-ring knops divided by a cylindrical column containing a crude clear and dull red twist; long socket with bulbous base, straight sides, and flanged lip. Found in Philadelphia. Possibly American, eighteenth century.

Height, $10''$; top diameter, $1\frac{5}{8}''$; diameter of foot, $3\frac{3}{4}''$.

PLATE 91

The candlesticks in this group, free-blown and fashioned from heavy gathers of clear lead glass, are typical of the Pittsburgh area. Nos. 1 and 2 probably were made during the first quarter of the nineteenth century; No. 3 in the second.

1. Socket of unusual form having a squatty body with cylindrical neck and flaring upturned rim, and resting on graduated rings at top of a heavy multiple-knop shaft supported by a wide circular foot; in each of two knops, a small bubble or tear. *Height, $7\frac{7}{8}''$; top diameter, $2\frac{5}{16}''$; diameter of foot, $4\frac{1}{8}''$.*

The socket of this candlestick is unusual not only in shape but also in that the body appears to have been formed in a three-piece mold, perhaps a stopper mold, after which the neck and flange were formed by manipulation.

2. Cylindrical socket, with wide flange, set in multiple rings at top of a long shaft composed of a tapering column, with large air twist between two flat rings and knops supported by a broad flat circular foot. *Height, $9\frac{5}{8}''$; top diameter, $2\frac{5}{8}''$; diameter of foot, $4\frac{1}{2}''$.*

3. Clear glass of pale amethyst tint; unusual in form, the cylindrical socket with wide flange and upper part of shaft which is tooled into a "bow tie" on end, formed from one gather; lower part of shaft, somewhat acornlike in shape, patterned in an 8-rib mold and expanded, and supported by a short stem and very wide circular foot. *Height, $10\frac{3}{4}''$; top diameter, $2\frac{1}{2}''$; diameter of bottom of shaft, $3\frac{5}{8}''$; diameter of foot, $5\frac{5}{8}''$.*

PLATE 92

1. Very tall candlestick blown from clear lead glass; socket with flanged lip and solid flattened globular base matching large knop in lower part of shaft; long shaft composed of a tapering column between triple rings at the top and single ring, wide knop, and smaller globular knop at bottom; very broad circular foot; column of shaft with a central air twist within wide spiral bands of light blue. Pittsburgh area. Circa 1815–30.

Height, $11\frac{5}{8}''$; *top diameter,* $2\frac{5}{8}''$; *diameter of foot,* $5\frac{1}{8}''$.

2. Tall candlestick blown from light aquamarine glass, probably non-lead; long cylindrical flanged socket tapering at base to a hollow knop which merges into a very large hollow bulb; applied multiple-knop stem; cone-shaped foot with wide flare to infolded rim. Probably South Jersey. Late eighteenth or early nineteenth century. Courtesy of the Metropolitan Museum of Art, New York City.

Height, $10\frac{1}{4}''$; *top diameter* $1\frac{1}{2}''$; *diameter of foot,* $4\frac{3}{4}''$.

3. Very tall candlestick, one of a pair, blown from clear lead glass; long column of the shaft and deep socket with wide-flaring rim patterned in an 8-rib mold and expanded in decoration of heavy pillar molding; socket and shaft separated by two rings; applied short cylindrical stem and broad circular foot. Pittsburgh area. Circa 1830–40.

Height, $12\frac{3}{8}''$; *top diameter,* $4\frac{1}{4}''$; *diameter of foot,* $5\frac{1}{2}''$.

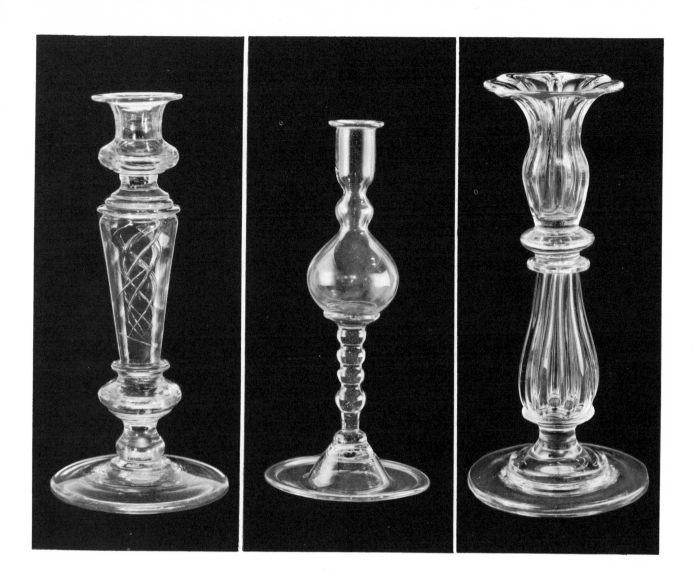

PLATE 93

1. Pair of candlesticks blown and fashioned from light green non-lead glass; broad circular applied foot supporting a long shaft composed of triple graduated rings between two true balusters; upper baluster surmounted by a globular gather tooled into heavy swirled ribbing and supporting the long cylindrical socket with flanged lip. South Jersey. First half of nineteenth century. Courtesy of Metropolitan Museum of Art, New York City.

Heights, 9¼″ and 9⅛″; top diameter, 2⅜″; diameter of foot, 4½″ and 4¼″.

2. Pair of candlesticks blown from clear lead glass; high domed foot with folded rim supporting a multiple-knop and -ring stem upon which rests a long cylindrical socket with rolled-over and turned-down rim; a trapped-air teardrop in the center knop. Steuben Glass Works, Corning, New York. Circa 1945.

Height, 10½″; top diameter, 2⅞″; diameter of foot, 5¾″.

These magnificent candlesticks, as well as most of the Steuben free-blown decanters and stemmed drinking vessels, are very similar in design and execution to the finest of the same types made by the most skillful eighteenth-century craftsmen in English and Irish glasshouses.

PLATE 94

1. Lamp, free-blown from brilliant aquamarine non-lead glass; long cone-shaped font with top sloping to short cylindrical plain lip, and drawn out at base into a graduated multiple-knop stem resting on an applied wide circular foot; applied solid semi-ear-shaped handle; font fitted with tin two-wick whale-oil burner set in cork, probably the original burner. South Jersey. Circa 1848–50. *Height, $7\frac{1}{8}''$; greatest diameter of font, $2\frac{5}{16}''$; diameter of foot, $3\frac{1}{2}''$.*

Lamps are rare among articles in the category of South Jersey type glass. This well-formed individual piece was acquired many years ago by Renwick C. Hurry from a Mrs. Stanger in Brooklyn, New Jersey. It was said to have been blown by Julius Stanger at the Isabella Glass Works, which was so named for Mr. Stanger's daughter.

2. Blown Three Mold lamp fashioned from clear lead glass; globular font similar to peg lamps found in the same pattern, GII-18; applied short button-knop stem supported by cone center of saucer base in pattern GI-20. New England area, quite possibly New England Glass Company. Circa 1820–30. *Height, $5\frac{1}{4}''$; diameter of font, about $3''$; diameter of base, $5\frac{1}{16}$.*

Lighting devices are among the scarce articles in Blown Three Mold. The base of this one was blown in a tumbler mold in pattern GI-20, shaped into a small dish with narrow outfolded rim and center pushed up.

3. Sparking lamp, blown from clear lead glass; semi-spherical font, with short cylindrical neck, drawn out into a short stem with flattened knop; applied circular foot; font fitted with original one-tube tin burner set in cork and having the original wick. Probably New England area. Circa 1812–30. *Height, about $3''$; diameter of font, $2\frac{1}{8}''$; diameter of foot, $2''$.*

"Sparking lamp" is the name given by legend to such as the three shown on this plate. Supposedly when a young man called on his girl her mother limited his sparking time to that during which the lamp burned. "Night lamp" might be a more accurate name.

4. Whale-oil-lamp filler with cover, free-blown from clear lead glass; globular body with applied tapering spout slanting upward diagonally; applied sloping circular foot; small eighteenth-century type set-in cover with flange and small stemmed ball finial, formed from one gather; applied large flattened semi-ear-shaped handle with fine medial rib. New England area. Circa 1812–30. *Over-all height, $4\frac{7}{16}''$; without cover, $3\frac{1}{2}''$; greatest diameter of body, $3\frac{3}{8}''$; diameter of foot, $2\frac{1}{2}''$.*

This and the lamp, No. 3, which is one of a pair, were found years ago in the attic of an old house in New Hampshire. At the time congealed whale oil was still in the filler. Each lamp has the original burner and wick.

5. Blown Three Mold sparking lamp, clear lead glass; flattened globular font; applied solid loop handle; original single-tube tin burner set in cork. Sandwich. 1825–35. *Height, about $1\frac{5}{8}''$; diameter $2\frac{5}{8}''$.*

Sparking lamps like this one were blown for shape and pattern in a mold used for making stoppers for quart decanters. After the gather was taken from the mold the shank was sheared off and a handle applied. The stopper from which they were fashioned was the size and pattern used in quart Arch decanters of pattern GIV-7, like No. 5, Plate 85, and Baroque pattern GV-14.

6. Blown Three Mold sparking lamp of clear lead glass; molded for pattern in cruet bottle or tumbler mold in pattern GIII-23, and fashioned into small ovoid body with short cylindrical neck and with wide heavy circular foot; one-wick burner set in cork. *Height, $2\frac{3}{4}''$; greatest diameter of body, $1\frac{13}{16}''$; diameter of foot, $2''$.*

PLATE 95

1. Bank blown from clear, probably lead glass; relatively small body elaborately decorated with applied strawberry and leaf prunts, pincered and rigaree trailing, and resting on a stem composed of a hollow ball, with applied strawberry prunts, between double rings and supported by a circular foot; extending upward from the top of the body, three graduated groups of four struts, each decorated with applied strawberry prunts and rigaree bands; between the second and third groups, a hollow ball or knop also decorated with similar prunts and rigaree trailings; within the second group of struts, a slender solid column; at top of the third group, a shorter column supporting a double ring in turn supporting a slender twisted column with applied chicken finial.. Boston and Sandwich Glass Works. Circa 1825–50. Collection of Dr. Arthur E. Corby.

Over-all height, 18"; diameter of foot, 4".

So far as we know this is the tallest and most elaborately decorated glass bank in existence. It is said to have been presented by Deming Jarves to one of his blowers as a gift for his infant daughter. For several years it was in the collection of Miss Minnie I. Meacham, one of the first collectors of American glass, and later in the collection of the late Mrs. Frederick F. Fish. It is now owned by Dr. Arthur E. Corby.

2. Clear, possibly lead, glass bank; ovoid body decorated with pincered trailings and resting on an applied triple-knop stem supported by a wide circular foot; curving upward from the top of the body, four struts, with pincered trailing, meeting beneath a double ring supporting a double-knop stem with acorn finial. Attributed to the New England Glass Works. Circa 1818–50. Collection of Dr. Arthur E. Corby.

Height, 13½"; diameter of foot, 4".

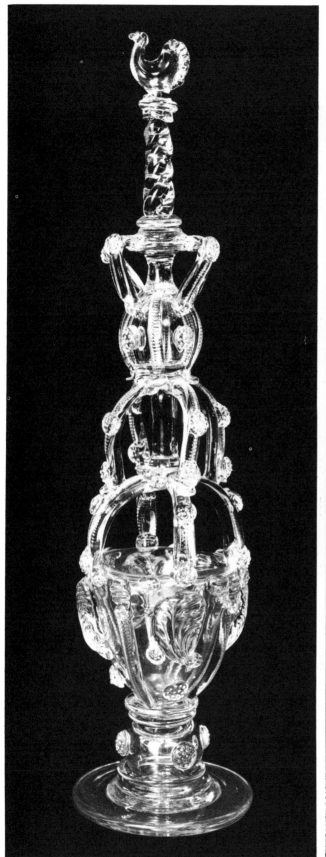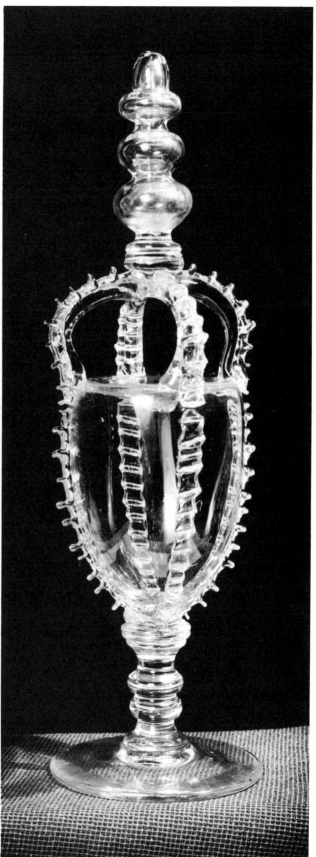

PLATE 96

1. Bank blown from clear glass, probably lead; ovoid body resting on a stem composed of a large hollow ball or knop between double rings and supported by a wide circular foot; body decorated by pincered and rigaree trailing; at the top of the body, four similarly decorated struts converging above the center at a hollow ball, with pincered trailings, supporting a short cylindrical stem with chicken finial; in the hollow ball at the top, a silver half dime dated 1837, and, in that of the stem, one dated 1840. Attributed to Boston and Sandwich Glass Works. Collection of Dr. Arthur E. Corby. *Height, 11¼″; diameter of foot, 4″.*

2. Bank blown from clear glass with milky-white loopings in an ovoid body resting on a stem composed of a large hollow ball or knop between double rings and supported by a wide circular foot; four struts curving from top of the body and converging above center, decorated with pincered and rigaree trailing which extends to bottom of body, further decorated by four equidistant applied strawberry prunts; at meeting of struts, a ring below a hollow ball with ringed stem upon which rests a chicken finial; a gold dollar dated 1851 in the hollow ball at top and, in the ball of the stem, another gold dollar, the date of which cannot be distinguished; said to have been made as a presentation piece by one Joe Miller in 1851 at the Boston and Sandwich Glass Works. Collection of Dr. Arthur E. Corby.

Height, 11½″; diameter of foot, 4″.

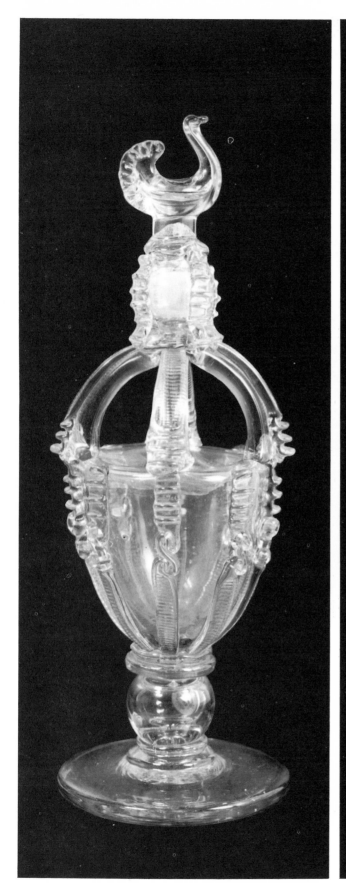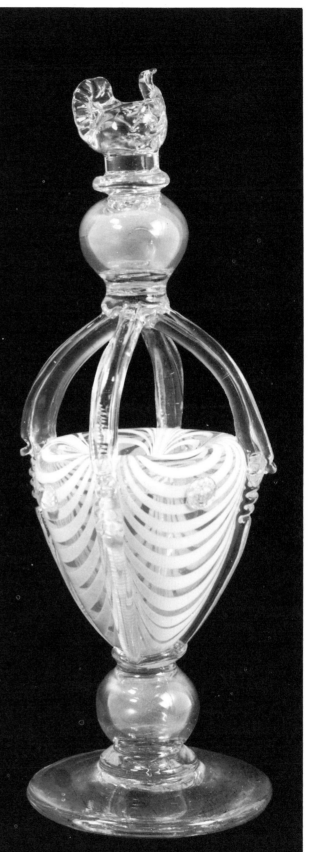

PLATE 97

GROUP OF AMERICAN PAPERWEIGHTS

1. Rare Sandwich upright bouquet with twisted ribbon border: large upright bouquet of white, deep blue, and crimson flowers combined with eleven deeply serrated and pointed dark green leaves, surrounded by a green, red, and white wide twisted ribbon border; a circular concave facet in the top of the weight creating the illusion of a double border.

Height, 1⅛″; diameter, 2⅝″.

The particular use of the twisted ribbon and the flower arrangement make this paperweight a rare Sandwich example.

2. Sandwich pink dahlia on blue and white background: rose-pink dahlia or "pompon," consisting of a yellow millefiori center and numerous delicate double petals, with a short stem bearing five deeply veined leaves of emerald-green and embedded in a jaspideous background of white and dark blue; a rare type of paperweight flower, seldom found on this type of background.

Height, 1¾″; diameter, 2⅞″.

3. Faceted American millefiori on white underlay: twenty-one turquoise, purple, pink, and green millefiori setups of Clichy origin placed in a geometric formation and embedded in an opaque white underlay or background; one concave round facet on the top of the weight and six smaller concave oval facets on the sides.

Height, 1¼″; diameter, 3¾″.

The character of the crystal body and the technical execution of the underlay prove conclusively that the weight was made in America. The rich deep colors and flaring construction of most of the setups and two authentic Clichy roses are also conclusive proof that the millefiori parts were produced at Clichy, France. This unusual and interesting American example bears out the theory that millefiori canes and setups were imported and carried from factory to factory.

4. Sandwich crown: alternating twisted ribbons of crimson combined with deep blue and of chartreuse combined with red, radiating from a center millefiori setup placed high in the weight and depending to the middle of the base.

Height, 1¾″; diameter, 2¾″.

The crown paperweight is one of the few blown, and therefore hollow, paperweights. In the United States it was made only by artisans of the Sandwich factory.

5. Faceted New England Glass Company fruit on latticinio background: five realistic yellow and pink pears and four red cherries clustered within a bed of dark green leaves, resting upon a white latticinio background; an illusion of additional pears and cherries created by clover design faceting on the top of the paperweight; concave oval and triform faceting on the sides.

Height, 1⅞″; diameter, 2⅝″.

The fine craftsmanship of this particular example bears a marked resemblance to that of the French prototype.

6. Faceted Gilliland nosegay with double millefiori border over latticinio basket: a dainty nosegay, composed of deep blue, red, white, and coral millefiori flowers and four deep green leaves and encircled by a double millefiori border of twenty white and black setups containing running rabbit silhouettes and then twenty-eight coral, white, and red setups; a white latticinio basket in the background; brilliance enhanced by elaborate faceting on the top and sides of the weight. John L. Gilliland & Company, Brooklyn Flint Glass Works, Brooklyn, N. Y. Circa 1848–56.

Height, 1⅞″; diameter, 2¾″.

The number of characteristic techniques and colors of the Gilliland factory displayed in this paperweight cause it to be considered an excellent example of Gilliland craftsmanship. Collection of Mr. and Mrs. S. Welden O'Brien. (Notes and description by owners.)

PLATE 98

1. Millville crocus on conical footed base: the crocus composed of ten white petals exhibiting a veined effect accomplished by delicate blending of pink, yellow, blue, green, and red colored glass and flecks of goldstone; among the rarest of the Millville flowers. Collection of Mr. and Mrs. S. Welden O'Brien.

Height, 4¾"; diameter, 3".

Exhaustive research by the owners has revealed no similar type of base.

2. Rare Millville pink rose on footed base: large open pink rose, composed of twelve petals with tips of opalescent appearance, and three large, pointed opaque leaves of light green suspended well above the graceful footed base; the delicate pink, one of the rarest colors found in the coveted Millville rose; because of the perfection of craftsmanship and manner of developing the flower and leaves, attributed to Ralph Barber by the owners. Collection of Mr. and Mrs. S. Welden O'Brien.

Height, 4¼"; diameter of sphere, 3½"; diameter of base, 3".

3. Large open yellow rose composed of fifteen petals within four large pointed brilliant green leaves suspended well above the circular footed base. Made by Emil J. Larson, Vineland, New Jersey. Circa 1934–39.

Height, 3⅞"; diameter, 3⅞"; diameter of foot, 3".

4. Apple, yellow shading to deep red, resting on clear circular base. New England Glass Company. Circa 1840–50.

Height, 2⅝"; diameter, 2⁹⁄₁₆"; diameter of foot, 3".

This paperweight was owned by James F. Barnes, who was at one time associated with his father, James B. Barnes, at the works of the New England Glass Company. It was inherited by his granddaughter, a Mrs. Mallory, from whom it was acquired over ten years ago.

5. Small open blue rose resting within four pointed green leaves with veining in lighter shade of green, suspended above circular footed base. Made by Charles Kaziun. Circa 1946–48.

Height, 2⅝"; diameter, 2½"; diameter of foot, 2⅜".

The early Millville rose weights made by Ralph Barber and other contemporaneous blowers were made principally at the glassworks of Whitall, Tatum and Company from about 1905 through 1918. The rose was made in shades of red ranging from a delicate pink to a deep red, also in yellow and milk-white. The glass was very clear and brilliant.

The Larson rose weights which he perfected about 1934–35 were made in about the same size, beautifully executed, but have four instead of three leaves, and the glass has a slight greenish tone. The Larson roses are in deep red and yellow. Only a limited number were made and they are now quite rare.

The Kaziun weights are smaller, varying in size from small ones about one and a half inches in diameter to those the size of the one illustrated. The glass is almost if not quite as clear as in the older Millville rose weights. The rose was made in shades of red from a delicate pink to a deep red, also in yellow, blue, and milk-white. Small perfume bottles with rose stoppers, and some with rose also in bottom of bottle, were made. In all of the Kaziun weights and perfume bottles which we have seen there is a small letter K in the center of a small millefiori cane placed in the center of the leaves below the rose.

6. Pairpoint spiral and bubbles on footed "crosscut" base: delicate ovoid design of spiraled transparent red and opaque white threads of glass surrounded by a cascade of evenly spaced bubbles; a decorative device peculiar to craftsmen of the Pairpoint factory. Collection of Mr. and Mrs. S. Welden O'Brien.

Height, 3½"; diameter of sphere, 2¾".

7. Sandwich floral bottle stopper; the flower, composed of millefiori center, seven small red petals striped with white and dotted with goldstone, and seven large red petals veined with deep blue, and with a stem bearing six pointed, deeply veined dark green leaves sparkling with dewdrops made of tiny bubbles. Collection of Mr. and Mrs. S. Welden O'Brien.

Length, 3¼"; diameter, 2⅛".

This item of the paperweight family, embodying numerous techniques peculiar to Nicholas Lutz, was acquired directly from his son, William E. Lutz, with an affidavit stating the stopper was made by his father.

The description and notes of Nos. 1, 2, 6, and 7 by the owners.

PLATE 99

On this and the three following plates are shown examples of the art glass, as it is sometimes called, which was developed in the closing years of the Victorian era for table and decorative wares. Elaborate and fancy forms and color effects predominated in these wares which were both free-blown and patterned in molds and expanded. In some cases materials other than glass were simulated. In the main, this glass, made to catch the popular fancy, reflected the late Victorian decadence in the arts and crafts. Nevertheless many of its colors were remarkably beautiful and many of its forms graceful and dignified, in some instances classical. Much of it represents a high degree of technical achievement by American glass manufacturers of the period.

1. Wheeling Peach Blow vase with pressed-glass holder. Vase copied after the famous Morgan Chinese porcelain vase; ovoid in form with cylindrical neck flaring slightly at rim; lead case glass: white lining, casing of yellow shading to deep red, outside coating of clear glass giving glossy finish. Wheeling Peach Blow was also made with a velvety finish from acid bath.
Last quarter of nineteenth century.
Height of vase, $7\frac{7}{8}''$; with holder, $9\frac{7}{8}''$; greatest diameter, $3''$.

2. Peach Blow or Wild Rose vase, homogeneous lead glass (one composition throughout), white shading to delicate rose-pink; on bottom, original paper label with words "Wild Rose" and "N.E.G.W. Patd, March 2, 1886". New England Glass Works. Last quarter of nineteenth century.
Height, $8\frac{1}{4}''$; greatest diameter of body, $3\frac{7}{8}''$; top diameter, $\frac{5}{8}''$.

3. Amberina cordial, non-lead glass; bowl, pale amber shading to cranberry, pattern-molded and expanded in diamond design; foot and stem pale amber. Possibly Mount Washington Glass Works. Last quarter of nineteenth century.

Height, $2\frac{11}{16}''$; top diameter, $1\frac{3}{4}''$; diameter of foot, $1\frac{5}{8}''$.

4. Amberina decanter, pale amber lead glass shading to deep red, pattern-molded in 26-rib mold and expanded in ribbing swirled to right. New England Glass Company. Last quarter of nineteenth century.

Height, $10\frac{7}{8}''$; diameter of base, $3\frac{1}{4}''$.

When the plant of the New England Glass Company at Cambridge, Massachusetts, was closed and Edward D. Libbey moved the business to Toledo, Ohio, in 1888 it was continued under the name of Libbey Glass Company. The manufacture of Amberina glass was continued and pieces marked Libbey are found occasionally. Amberina was made also by the Mount Washington Glass Company, after it moved to New Bedford, and its products are difficult to distinguish from pieces made by the New England Glass Company. We believe that the cordial, No. 3, which is non-lead glass, may be an example of the Mount Washington Amberina. At this glasshouse, Peach Blow wares were made as well as at the New England Glass Works and at Wheeling. As the result of a friendly dispute with the New Bedford company the New England Glass Company adopted the name Wild Rose for its Peach Blow; and the Mount Washington Glass Company, the name Rose Amber for its Amberina.

PLATE 100

1. Burmese candlestick; lead glass; applied, slightly domed foot with folded rim, pale yellow in color; the baluster shaft, applied bobêche and socket, yellow shading to pink; foot, bobêche, and socket patterned in a 12-rib mold and expanded in vertical ribbing; the shaft, pattern-molded in diamond design. Mount Washington Glass Company. Last quarter of nineteenth century.

Height, $7\frac{5}{8}$"; diameter of bobêche, $3\frac{5}{16}$"; diameter of foot, $3\frac{15}{16}$".

2. Vase, probably New England Glass Works Peach Blow; lead glass, white shading to deep rose, glossy finish. Collection of Mr. Raymond D. Allen.

Height, 8"; spread at top, $3\frac{1}{2}$"; diameter of foot, $3\frac{1}{16}$".

3. Candlestick, one of a pair, iridescent pale gold and bluish glass, quite similar in coloring to some of the Tiffany glass. Marked on base, "Steuben Aurene".

   Made at the Steuben Glass Works, Corning, New York, established by Frederick Carder, one of our noted glass technologists, and later operated as the Steuben Division of the Corning Glass Works. Early twentieth century.

Height, $3\frac{7}{8}$"; top diameter, $2\frac{7}{8}$"; diameter of foot, $4\frac{3}{16}$".

4. Small ovoid vase; lead glass, iridescent pearl-white and gold; around shoulder, pale green and gold decoration in style of ancient glass; body patterned in a 16-rib mold and expanded in vertical ribbing; marked on base, "Quezal". Brooklyn, New York. Early twentieth century.

Height, 4"; top diameter, $1\frac{1}{2}$"; greatest diameter of body, $2\frac{3}{8}$"; diameter of base, $1\frac{1}{8}$".

   The iridescent glass known as Quezal was produced by the Quezal Art Glass and Decorating Company of Brooklyn, New York, which, we have been informed, was started about 1917 by blowers who left the employ of Tiffany. The glass, similar to the Tiffany Favrile, was made in a wide variety of forms and coloring. The scarcity of Quezal specimens would seem to indicate that its production was very much less than that of Tiffany. It is said to have always been marked with the name Quezal. It was so named after the quetzal, a bird of the family Trogonidae noted for its brilliant plumage, the members of which inhabit tropical forests in America, Africa, and India. The quetzal is the most beautiful of the species. The upper part of the bird and throat are iridescent greenish, and the underpart crimson. This brilliant bird, native to Central America, was worshiped by both the Aztecs and the Mayas, who associated it with Quetzalcoatl, the God of the Air. Quetzalcoatl, represented as white and bearded, was essentially a god of peace and seldom was honored with human sacrifices. He was associated with many myths; the most famous tells of his having sailed away to Tlapallan, the land of the rising sun, from which he promised to return. The white and bearded Cortez, when he landed in Mexico, was taken for the returning deity, a fact materially aiding his conquest of Mexico. The quetzal has been the national emblem of Guatemala for many years and was depicted on the postage stamps as early as an issue of 1879.

5. Small Mount Washington Peach Blow bowl; non-lead glass, dull finish, white shading to delicate pink; painted and enameled decoration; on the bottom, original label with the inscription, "Patent Peach Blow Mt. W. G. Co.", also Chinese characters. Last quarter of nineteenth century.

Height, $2\frac{1}{4}$"; top diameter, $3\frac{11}{16}$"; greatest diameter of body, $4\frac{1}{8}$".

PLATE 101

1. Circular bowl of iridescent greenish-blue lead glass; patterned in an 8-rib mold and expanded in heavy wide-spaced ribbing; marked, "L C T. Favrile"; original Tiffany metal holder. Tiffany Glass Works, Corona, Long Island. Circa 1892–1920.

Height, 3½"; top diameter, 6½".

2. Footed bowl, mother-of-pearl lead glass; circular form with flaring rim, short stem, and broad circular foot slightly domed; body decorated with three broad leaves outlined in yellow and filled with fine green veins; on the foot, green ribbon decoration; marked "KEW-BLAS" on the bottom; another type similar to Tiffany. Union Glass Company, Somerville, Massachusetts. Late nineteenth or early twentieth century. "KEW-BLAS" is an anagram of the name W. S. Blake, who was general manager of the glassworks at the time the glass was made.

Height, 3⅝"; top diameter, 5⅛"; diameter of foot, 3⅝".

3. Pomona vase, pale amber lead glass with frosted surface covering most of body, and decorated with a single band of pale blue flowers and pale amber leaves; ovoid body with deeply scalloped rim and applied petaled foot. New England Glass Company. Last quarter of nineteenth century.

Height, 6¼"; greatest diameter of body, 4¼"; diameter of foot, 2¾".

PLATE 102

Large punch bowl of iridescent pale gold non-lead glass with bluish tone; leaf decoration in green on bowl and foot; made in two sections, the bowl having a solid cylindrical stem fitting into the hollow pedestal foot with folded rim; on the bottom of the foot, the original paper label with inscription, "Tiffany Favrile Glass Registered Trade Mark." Tiffany Glass Works, Corona, Long Island. Circa 1892–1920.

Height, 11¼"; top diameter, 11⅞"; foot diameter, 8".

PLATE 103

1. Flask blown from light green and clear non-lead glass; slender ovoid body with short neck and plain lip; heavy applied, slightly irregular crimped foot of clear glass; body patterned in an 18-rib mold and expanded in vertical ribbing; each edge decorated with a vertical band of applied heavy quilling or pincered trailing in clear glass and, on each side, two bands of applied fine quilling in pale green, same color as the body.

Height, $8\frac{5}{16}''$; greatest width of body, about $4\frac{1}{4}''$; diameter of foot, about $2\frac{3}{4}''$.

2. Shallow bowl blown from clear lead glass with flashing of ruby; decoration of irregular loopings of opaque white and rim edged with opaque white.

Height, $1\frac{3}{4}''$; top diameter, $7\frac{3}{4}''$.

3. Sherbet glass blown from lead glass; circular bowl, with wide-flaring rim, in pale cranberry color and with decoration of large five-petaled flower formed by milk-white loopings in bottom of bowl; applied slender cylindrical stem and circular foot in golden yellow.

Height, $3\frac{7}{8}''$; top diameter, $4\frac{5}{8}''$; diameter of foot, $2\frac{7}{16}''$.

4. Small tazza of brilliant sapphire-blue and clear lead glass, blown from very heavy gathers; shallow circular bowl with wide-flaring rim; applied angular-knop stem and square plinth in clear glass.

Height, $3\frac{1}{4}''$; top diameter, $4\frac{5}{8}''$; foot, $2\frac{9}{16}''$ by $2\frac{9}{16}''$.

5. Vase blown from non-lead glass; ovoid body, tapering at lower part and flaring to circular base; short cylindrical neck and flaring down-turned sloping rim. Body translucent creamy white with grayish-blue and gold decoration in style of ancient glass; upper surface of rim iridescent apricot color; entire vase with iridescent effect and in style of some Tiffany glass.

Height, $5\frac{7}{8}''$; greatest diameter of body, $3\frac{3}{16}''$; top diameter of rim, $2\frac{7}{16}''$; diameter of base, $2\frac{3}{4}''$.

The pieces illustrated on this plate are all the work of Emil J. Larson, one of the most skillful craftsmen known to the American glass industry in the late nineteenth and early twentieth centuries. He was born in Sweden and in 1887, when ten years of age, came to this country with his father, who was a glass blower. For many years he worked at the Dorflinger factory at White Mills, Pennsylvania, leaving there about 1918. He worked at the Pairpoint factory in New Bedford, Massachusetts, at several other glasshouses, and in Brooklyn, New York, where he made Quezal glass, which is similar to some of the Tiffany glass. About 1925 he went to the Durand Glass Works in Vineland, New Jersey, where he specialized in the iridescent and other so-called art glass, working there until about 1933.

From time to time Mr. Larson acquired metal molds which had been used to pattern glass in glasshouses which had ceased operation. These were small three-piece molds, some of them having a diamond pattern similar to that found on a great deal of the so-called "Satin" glass and other molded glass of the late nineteenth-century period. About fifteen years ago he started a small glasshouse of his own on his premises in Vineland, New Jersey. Here he made a large variety of blown glass, some of it similar to late eighteenth- and early nineteenth-century examples in form and technique. Some of his glass was pattern-molded, some was free-blown with superimposed decoration tooled into lily-pad designs.

Mr. Larson perfected a Jersey rose paperweight which he made in deep red and yellow. His weights were very similar to those made by Ralph Barber and other blowers at Millville, New Jersey. One of his yellow rose weights is illustrated on Plate 89.

PLATE 104

The "Stenger" bottle blown at Amelung's glass-works from a heavy gather of clear non-lead glass of slightly smoky tone appearing greenish when held to the light; about pint size; very thick at base. Engraved by copper wheel; on the obverse, a typical Amelung medallion composed of two leaf sprays interspersed with daisylike flowers and wheat stalks and enclosing the name "*F. Stenger*" in script above the date "*1792*"; on the reverse, a circular medallion formed by two slender leaf sprays joined at top and bottom by a four-petaled flower and enclosing a bottle, a plow, and Masonic trowel and square; the inside of the neck at top ground as though originally fitted with stopper.

Height, $6\frac{5}{8}''$; $3\frac{15}{16}''$ wide by $2\frac{3}{4}''$ through.

This flask was found about 1920 in possession of descendants of Francis Stanger and Elizabeth L. Campbell and with it was their marriage certificate in fractur work dated March 11, 1802. A Francis Stanger was said to have been one of the Stangers who, about 1781, started the first Glassboro works, the second glasshouse in New Jersey. It is a reasonable assumption that the Stenger of this bottle and the marriage certificate is the Francis of the Glassboro Glass Works. The name was a prominent one in American glasshouses of late eighteenth and early and mid-nineteenth centuries and was spelled with both an *e* and an *a*. There can be little question that the bottle was a presentation piece made for Stanger at Amelung's New Bremen Glassmanufactory. The dark cast and texture of the non-lead glass, the style of engraving, and the formation of the letters practically identical with those on other dated and inscribed pieces are conclusive evidence. The emblems may have been intended to indicate Stanger's occupation, place of residence, and fraternity—the bottle for glassmaker; the plow for New Jersey, as one appears in the state's coat of arms; the trowel and square for a Free Mason.

PLATE 105

1. Flask about half-pint size, brilliant light emerald-green non-lead glass; so-called Pitkin type, blown by old German half-post method; flattened ovoid shape, plain lip; double-patterned in a 24-rib mold and expanded, vertical ribbing over swirled to left, producing the so-called broken-swirl design. Midwestern type. Early nineteenth century.
Height, 7⅜"; width, 4⅜".

2. Miniature Pitkin type flask blown from brilliant yellowish-green non-lead glass; flattened circular shape with collared lip (unusual in Pitkin flasks); patterned in a 26-rib mold and expanded, diagonal ribbing to right and vertical ribbing, broken-swirl pattern. Midwestern. Early nineteenth century.
Height, 3½"; width, 2⅞".

3. Pitkin type flask, brilliant deep green non-lead glass; flattened circular shape, plain lip; patterned in 24-rib mold and expanded, ribbing swirled to right and vertical ribbing, broken-swirl pattern. Midwestern. Early nineteenth century.
Height, 6½"; width, 5⅛".

4. Bottle, more likely a snuff jar, blown from dark olive-amber non-lead glass; Pitkin type, ovoid shape, short flaring neck, plain lip; patterned in a 36-rib mold and expanded, ribbing swirled to right and vertical ribbing. Amber glass stopper found in the bottle but not original. Eastern type. Late eighteenth to early nineteenth century.
Height, 5"; diameter at base, 2¾"; diameter of lip, 1⅜"; greatest diameter of body, 3¼".

5. Miniature Pitkin flask blown from olive-green non-lead glass, ovoid shape with flattened sides; plain lip; patterned in a 36-rib mold and expanded in ribbing swirled to right. Eastern type. Late eighteenth to early nineteenth century.
Height, 3½"; width, 2½".

6. Small jar, clear olive-green non-lead glass; cylindrical form flaring at neck to wide mouth, plain rim; patterned in 36-rib mold used for Pitkin type flasks, and expanded, with ribbing swirled to left and vertical ribbing, broken-swirl design. Eastern type. Late eighteenth to early nineteenth century.
Height, 5½"; diameter of base, 2⅝"; greatest diameter of body, 3"; diameter at rim, 2⁷⁄₁₆".

Pitkin type flasks were blown by the old German half-post method in which two gathers of glass were employed. The first gather or post was re-dipped in the metal, thus covering it with a second gather which did not extend the full length of the first and so was called the half post. After securing the second gather it was patterned by insertion in a small dip mold. If the pattern was to be vertical or swirled ribbing there was one insertion; if a double pattern of swirled and vertical ribbing, two insertions and the swirling was obtained by twisting the gather after the first insertion.

The term "Pitkin" was given to American flasks of this type because for many years they were supposed to have been made at the Pitkin Glass Works in East Manchester, not far from Hartford, Connecticut, which operated from about 1788 to about 1830. However, excavations made by the late Harry Hall White proved that "Pitkin" flasks in olive-amber and olive-green bottle glass were made at both the Coventry, Connecticut, and Keene-Marlboro-Street, New Hampshire, glasshouses. Nevertheless, while we have no concrete evidence to prove they were also made at the Pitkin Glass Works, it seems reasonable to assume they were made there even before, as well as at the same time that the Coventry works, not far distant from East Manchester, was a competitor of the Pitkin works. They are definitely eighteenth-century in technique and, long before Mr. White's excavations, had been attributed locally to the Pitkin works.

It was natural that the name "Pitkin" became associated with other flasks blown by the same half-post method and patterned in rib molds, including a large group of flasks made in Ohio, Pennsylvania, and other Midwestern glasshouses. These occur usually in half-pint and pint sizes in brilliant greens, aquamarines, and ambers, of which those illustrated by Nos. 1, 2, and 3 are characteristic examples. Mr. White's excavations definitely proved Pitkin type flasks were made at the Mantua Glass Works, Ohio. They were probably made also at Kent and Zanesville, Ohio; possibly by Isaac Duval at Charlestown, (West) Virginia, later Wellsburg; by Gallatin at New Geneva, Pennsylvania, and at other glasshouses in the Pittsburgh-Monongahela area. It is even within the range of possibilities that Stiegel made flasks of this type at Manheim. The Eastern (Connecticut and New Hampshire) Pitkins which we have recorded were patterned in 32- and 36-rib molds; the Midwestern in 16-, 18-, 20-, 24-, 26-, 28-, 32-, and 44-rib molds. Miniature sizes are very rare, and the quart size extremely so. Only two of the latter have been recorded, to our knowledge; one of these is aquamarine and was patterned in a 32-rib mold and is in a broken-swirl design.

PLATE 106

1. So-called "grandfather" flask, blown from brilliant amber non-lead glass; large chestnut shape, neck with plain rim; patterned in a 24-rib mold and expanded in vertical ribbing.

Height, $8\frac{3}{8}''$; width, $6\frac{7}{8}''$.

These flasks occur in various shades of amber and with the swirled and the broken-swirl ribbing as well as the vertical ribbing. They were probably patterned in the same molds as the globular and straight-sided cylindrical bottles with long neck. While they have been attributed to the early Zanesville glassworks it is probable they were made also in other Midwestern glasshouses. The other flasks illustrated on this plate also are Midwestern.

2. Chestnut-shaped flask blown from very brilliant golden-amber non-lead glass; patterned in 16-rib mold and expanded, broken-swirl design.

Height, $6\frac{3}{4}''$; width, $4\frac{3}{4}''$.

3. Chestnut-shaped flask blown from brilliant yellow-amber non-lead glass; patterned in a 24-rib mold, expanded ribbing swirled to left.

Height, $6\frac{1}{4}''$; width, $4\frac{1}{2}''$.

4. Miniature flask blown from brilliant yellow-amber non-lead glass; flattened circular shape, patterned in a 19-rib mold and expanded in vertical ribbing.

Height, $3''$; width, $2\frac{3}{16}''$.

5. Flask, scant half pint, blown from deep reddish-amber non-lead glass; flattened ovoid shape, sides tapering sharply to cylindrical neck with plain lip; patterned in a 24-rib mold; broken-swirl ribbing with pronounced popcorn-kernel effect.

Height, $5\frac{5}{8}''$; width, $3\frac{1}{16}''$.

6. Flask, half pint, blown from brilliant reddish-amber non-lead glass; flattened chestnut shape, sides tapering sharply to cylindrical neck with plain lip; patterned in a 10-diamond mold and expanded.

Height, $5\frac{7}{16}''$; width, $4\frac{1}{4}''$.

7. Miniature chestnut flask blown from brilliant light amber non-lead glass; patterned in a 16-rib mold and expanded in vertical ribbing.

Height, $3\frac{15}{16}''$; width, $2\frac{1}{2}''$.

Except for the beautiful amethyst diamond-daisy, ogival, and other "perfume" bottles attributed to Stiegel, the pattern-molded pocket flasks and bottles made during the early part of the nineteenth century in various Ohio and other Midwestern glasshouses have never been excelled and seldom equaled in America or elsewhere in brilliancy and beauty of color and delicacy of the molded design. The colors were mainly ambers ranging from golden and topaz tones to deep reddish amber; greens of many shades, from aquamarine to emerald and yellow-greens; olive-greens and olive-yellows and occasionally blues from cornflower to deep sapphire. Those with design of vertical, swirled, or broken-swirl ribbing were patterned in small dip molds and expanded. Where the pattern was that of vertical or swirled ribbing only, there was one insertion of the gather in the mold. For the broken-swirl pattern there were two insertions in a mold, the same mold or one usually with same number of ribs being used for each insertion. At the first insertion, the gather, having been vertically ribbed by contact with the mold, was then withdrawn and given a twist either to right or left to swirl the ribbing. It was then inserted a second time in the mold. Thus on expansion there was a double pattern, expanded vertical ribbing over the swirled ribbing, producing the broken-swirl design. The beautiful patterned hollow wares such as pitchers, bowls, covered sugar bowls, flip glasses, and other articles made in the Ohio and other Midwestern glasshouses were produced by this method.

PLATE 107

A group of early nineteenth-century Ohio and Midwestern pattern-molded globular shape bottles with long neck and collared lip.

1. Blown from brilliant yellow-amber non-lead glass; patterned in a 24-rib mold and expanded in ribbing swirled to left.

Height, 8″; greatest diameter of body, 5½″.

2. Blown from very brilliant yellowish-green non-lead glass; patterned in a 24-rib mold and expanded in ribbing swirled to right.

Height, 7⅞″; greatest diameter of body, 5¼″.

3. Blown from clear olive-green non-lead glass, light tone; patterned in a 24-rib mold and expanded in wide-spaced vertical ribbing, giving a melonlike effect.

Height, 7¼″; greatest diameter of body, 5¹⁄₁₆″.

4. Miniature blown from clear yellowish-green non-lead glass; patterned in a 16-rib mold and expanded in wide-spaced ribbing, giving a melonlike effect.

Height, 3⅞″; greatest diameter of body, 3″.

5. Blown from brilliant clear light amber non-lead glass; patterned twice in 24-rib mold and expanded, broken-swirl design.

Height, 7⅞″; greatest diameter of body, 4¹⁵⁄₁₆″.

While the four larger bottles may have been made at the early Zanesville glassworks which began operating late in 1815, similar bottles undoubtedly were made in other Ohio and Midwestern glasshouses. They range in capacity from about pint size, which is rare, to very large ones holding from four to six quarts. The normal size is from a quart to a quart and a pint. The colors run in about the same range as the chestnut flasks like those illustrated on Plate 106. Straight-sided cylindrical bottles with long neck and collared lip were also made in similar patterns and colors. Many molds differing in the number of ribs were used. The globular bottles in the broken swirl like No. 5 are very rare. The miniatures like No. 4 are extremely rare. A few miniatures are known in swirled as well as the vertical ribbing and also in aquamarine and shades of amber.

PLATE 108

1. Handled jug blown from brilliant light amber non-lead glass; globular shape with short cylindrical neck and collared lip; applied solid handle with crimped end; patterned in a 24-rib mold and expanded in ribbing swirled to left.

Height, $6\frac{5}{16}''$; greatest diameter of body, $5\frac{1}{16}''$; diameter of base, $2\frac{1}{2}''$.

2. Handled jug blown from clear deep amber non-lead glass; ovoid shape with short cylindrical neck and flanged lip; applied wide heavily ribbed handle with heavy crimped end; patterned twice in 24-rib mold and expanded, heavy broken-swirl design.

Height to top of handle, $5\frac{3}{8}''$; greatest diameter of body, $4\frac{3}{16}''$; diameter of base, $2\frac{3}{4}''$.

3. Handled jug blown from very brilliant clear reddish-amber non-lead glass; globular shape with short cylindrical neck and collared lip; applied broad flat handle heavily ribbed, with crimped end; patterned in a 10-diamond mold and expanded.

Height to top of handle, $5''$; diameter of base, $2\frac{1}{2}''$; greatest diameter of body, $4''$.

Only a small number of these handled jugs patterned in the same molds and blown from glass in the same colors as the Ohio and Midwestern bottles have been recorded. We have seen them in brilliant clear green, yellow-green, aquamarine, and olive-yellow. Sometimes they have an ovoid shape slenderer than No. 2. All of these jugs are very rare, in our experience.

PLATE 109

Large jug free-blown from dark reddish-amber non-lead glass; globular body resting on applied circular crimped foot; cylindrical neck with heavy sloping collared lip; applied handle, unduly slender in proportion to size and weight of jug; body decorated with superimposed gather of glass tooled into lily-pad design Type III. Made at Stoddard, New Hampshire, probably by Matthew Johnson at the works of the South Stoddard Glass Company during its operation by Weeks and Gilson. 1853–73. *Height, 10″; greatest diameter of body, $7\frac{5}{16}″$; diameter of foot, $4\frac{3}{8}″$.*

PLATE 110

1. Half-pint flask, clear lead glass with pale amethyst tint. Obverse: small bust of Lafayette in uniform, facing right and partially enclosed by a wreath of laurel branches; above in semicircle, "LA FAYETTE". Reverse: Masonic arch, pillars, and pavement; beneath keystone of arch and between columns, open book with square and compasses, all surrounded by thirteen large six-pointed stars. Fine herringbone ribbing on edges; plain lip; rough pontil. Only specimen so far known to us. Not listed in bottle charts, *American Glass*. Glasshouse not known, but detail of design very similar to Lafayette flasks made at Mount Vernon Glass Works, Vernon, New York. Circa 1824.

2. Half-pint flask, clear light olive-amber non-lead glass. Obverse: Masonic emblems consisting of large five-pointed star between pillars; above star, crescent moon surrounded by seven equally spaced five-pointed stars; below star, hourglass; face clearly depicted in crescent moon. Reverse: same. Edges finely corrugated horizontally; plain lip; pontil mark. No. 246-GIV-29. Attributed to Coventry Glass Works, Connecticut. Circa 1814–24.

During the period of about 1815–28 nearly forty varieties of flasks with Masonic designs were produced, but the anti-Masonic crusade, which developed as a result of the Morgan episode in 1826, seemed to put an end to their popularity. We have no record of flasks with Masonic emblems made after 1830. Several of the Masonic flasks, including the rare one illustrated, had the likeness of General Lafayette on one side. These and other Lafayette flasks were produced in honor of Lafayette at the time of his last visit to this country in 1824. Lafayette was a Mason and was entertained by Masonic Lodges in many of the leading cities of the country.

3. Pint flask, very heavy lead glass, puce color with striations in darker tone. Obverse: Masonic decoration—from a mosaic pavement rise two columns surmounted by archway with keystone in center; beneath keystone, radiant all-seeing eye and between columns, radiant triangle enclosing the letter "G" and above it open book with square and compasses; at left of column, trowel above skull and crossbones; at right of column, "Jacob's Ladder" ascending to "Cloudy Canopy" or "Star Decked Heaven," represented by radiant quarter moon surrounded by seven stars at right of archway; at left of archway, blazing sun; beneath pavement at right, beehive, and at left, crossed level and plumb line; 31 bricks in pavement. Reverse: American eagle, head turned to left; on breast shield with vertical bars, and on upper part twelve tiny dots (three rows) representing stars; wings partly raised and left foreshortened; thunderbolt (three arrows) in eagle's left talons, olive branch in right; above eagle, ribbon with heavy crimping (nine segments or folds in crimping) which resembles heavy beading; beneath eagle, large beaded oval frame containing letters "J.K.B."; significance of these initials unknown. Edges vertically ribbed, plain lip, pontil mark on base. No. 220-GIV-3. Keene-Marlboro-Street Glass Works, Keene, New Hampshire. Circa 1815–24.

The historical flasks illustrated on Plates 110–14 were formed and patterned in two-piece metal molds with intaglio design on the inner surface of the mold. The numbers refer to the bottle charts in the book, *American Glass*.

PLATE 111

1. Pint flask, brilliant olive-yellow non-lead glass. Obverse: early steamboat, with paddle wheel, steaming to right; long narrow flag streaming to left from bow and large American flag, Stars and Stripes, flying from mast back of smokestack; above boat, "THE AMERICAN" in curving line and beneath the water through which the boat is steaming the word "SYSTEM". Reverse: large upright Sheaf of Rye and encircled by inscription "USE ME BUT DO NOT ABUSE ME."; also encircling the sheaf and between it and the inscription, twenty-seven small dots or pearls, possibly intended to represent stars; beneath sheaf, narrow rectangular frame. Herringbone ribbing on edges; plain lip; pontil mark. No. 388-GX-21.

2. Brilliant, very heavy clear green lead glass, about quart capacity; circular shape, with short cylindrical neck and plain lip. Entire flask covered with heavy concentric ribbing except for circular medallion in center with crude American eagle, head turned to right, wings partly raised and left foreshortened, tail curving sharply to the right, and the legs extending downward, apparently grasping a crude olive branch in the talons. Reverse: same. No. 198-GII-76.

It has not been definitely established where this flask, known as the "Concentric Ring-Eagle," and similar flasks, with inscription "NG Co." instead of eagle on reverse, were made. It is believed they may have been made at the Marlboro-Street-Glass Works in Keene, New Hampshire, because in color, weight, and lead content they are similar to the heavy Masonic flasks made at this glasshouse.

The American System flask is one of the most eagerly sought by collectors and one of the rarest of the historical flasks. The phrase was coined by Henry Clay to signify what he staunchly advocated—support of the home industries by protective tariffs and of internal improvements, that is, waterways and turnpikes aided by the federal government. The flask definitely dates in the period from 1818 to 1824 when these matters of national importance and the question of protective tariffs were burning controversial issues in Congress. Pittsburgh was at that time a leading center of the glass industry and of Western trade. Consequently it was vitally and equally interested in transportation and in the fight in Congress over protective tariffs. Henry Baldwin, a young congressman from Pittsburgh, was in the thick of the battle and a strong supporter of Henry Clay. In August 1824 Baldwin was tendered a banquet by leading manufacturers of Pittsburgh in appreciation of his efforts toward securing passage of the Protective Tariff Act. On that occasion he attributed the final victory in Congress largely to the persistent efforts of Henry Clay, and proposed a toast "To Henry Clay and the American System." One specimen of this flask is known with the letters "B.P. & B." (Bakewell, Page and Bakewell) in the oval frame beneath the Sheaf of Rye, and another with the letters "B & M" in the waves just beneath the steamboat, as yet the only specimens of these two varieties which have been recorded. It is not yet known for whom the "B & M" was intended. It is assumed that some moldmaker, possibly Joshua Laird, of Pittsburgh, made the molds for each of the three varieties of this flask, and in each instance for a different glasshouse. A total of perhaps fifteen to twenty specimens of the flask without initials are known.

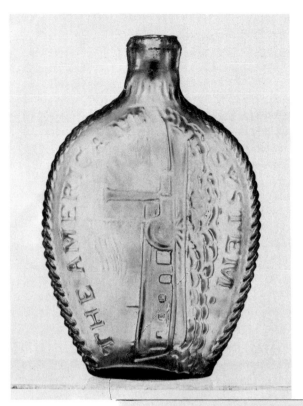

PLATE 112

1. Pint flask, clear lead glass with pale amethyst tint. Obverse: three-quarter bust of George Washington facing left and in uniform; above in semi-circle, "GENERAL WASHINGTON." Reverse: American eagle, head turned to right, shield with seven bars on breast, wings partly raised and right foreshortened, laurel branch in beak, thunderbolt (three arrows) in right talons, olive branch in left; nine six-pointed stars above eagle; eagle stands on oval frame with inner band of sixteen fairly large pearls, and containing initials "I.R."; beneath oval frame, inscription "LAIRD. SC. PITT"; the initials "I." (old-fashioned J) "R.", for John Robinson; "SC." for Sculpsit. Edges beaded with vertical medial rib; plain lip; rough pontil. No. 6-GI-6.

John Robinson was an English glassman who established Pittsburgh's Stourbridge Glass Works, a flint glassworks, in 1823. Joshua Laird, Pittsburgh moldmaker, made the mold for this and a similar flask with bust of Andrew Jackson. Probably molds for many of the earlier flasks of the Pittsburgh-Monongahela district came from his shop.

2. Pint flask, light green non-lead glass. Obverse: three-quarter bust of Franklin facing left; and above, in semicircle, "BENJAMIN FRANKLIN". Reverse: similar bust of Dyott facing right and above, in semicircle, "T.W.Dyott, M.D." On edges two vertical ribs with heavy medial rib, and inscription "WHERE LIBERTY DWELLS THERE IS MY COUNTRY KENSINGTON GLASS WORKS PHILADELPHIA." Plain lip; rough pontil. GI-94. Circa 1820-24.

3. Pint flask, brilliant light green non-lead glass. Obverse: American eagle, head turned to right, wings partly raised and right foreshortened; large shield with six bars on breast, tail feathers showing below shield at right; thunderbolt (three arrows) in right talons, eagle on oval frame with inner band of twenty-eight small pearls; above eagle, nine medium-sized pearls; just below oval frame, diagonal ribbing to right and left. Reverse: large cornucopia coiled to left and filled with produce. Edges beaded and with narrow vertical medial rib; plain lip; rough pontil. No. 128-GII-6. Midwestern, Pittsburgh-Monongahela district. Circa 1820-24.

Thomas W. Dyott, M.D., doctor presumably by his own proclamation, was a colorful figure in the field of glassmaking in America in the first and second quarters of the nineteenth century. He was a poor English boy who arrived in Philadelphia about 1795. According to tradition, his first venture was a small boot-blacking establishment. About 1804 he embarked upon a career as a dispenser of patent medicines, apparently successfully since by 1807 he required a warehouse to hold his stock. Two years later he advertised as the proprietor of Dr. Robertson's Family Medicines, 116 North Second Street. Somehow, by the first of the year 1810, he had become a doctor of medicine, signing himself T.W.Dyott, M.D.; before the end of 1811 he "revealed" that he was a grandson of the celebrated Dr. Robertson, of Edinburgh, whose medicines he sold. In 1815 his claims to an M.D. and the panacean properties of his nostrums were supported by the announcement of his own "long experience and extensive practice in the City of London, the West Indies, and for the last nine years in the City of Philadelphia."

In the meantime, accumulated annoyance at the poor quality of American-made vials and bottles, the high cost of these containers for his medicines, and the war-induced scarcity of them led him to invest in a New Jersey glassworks. This probably was the Olive Glass Works at Glassboro. Its proprietors advertised in 1817, if not earlier, that orders for their products would be received at T. W. Dyott's drugstore on the Northeast Corner of Second and Race streets, Philadelphia. About 1820 he acquired an interest in the Philadelphia and Kensington Glass Works, becoming the sole proprietor within a few years. In 1831 his Dyottville Glass Factories, as they were called henceforth, included four distinct glasshouses; by 1833, five. His works and model community were on three or four hundred acres of land along the Delaware. Having overexpanded, he was caught in the depression of the late 1830s and convicted of fraudulent bankruptcy in 1838, but later re-entered the drug business.

Some of the most interesting early historical flasks were made at the Philadelphia and Kensington Glass Works. So far as we know Dr. Dyott is the only glass manufacturer who had his portrait molded in historical flasks. His likeness appears with that of Benjamin Franklin on three flasks made at the Kensington Glass Works, and on one marked "Wheeling Glass Works", similar to the Kensington flask which is illustrated.

PLATE 113

1. Pint flask, deep cobalt-blue lead glass. Obverse: bust of Columbia wearing liberty cap, facing left; thirteen small six-pointed stars in semicircle surrounding bust; at bottom, ten short graduated vertical ribs. Reverse: large American eagle, head turned to right, shield with ten vertical bars on breast, wings partly raised and right foreshortened, thunderbolt (three arrows with feathered ends) showing in its right talons, olive branch in left; ten short graduated vertical ribs at bottom. Edges with single broad vertical rib; plain lip; rough pontil. GI-119. Circa 1815–30.

Similar flasks occur with inscription "KENSINGTON" in narrow frame beneath bust, and "UNION CO." in similar frame beneath eagle.

2. Pint flask, clear olive-yellow, non-lead glass. Obverse: Masonic arch, pillars, and pavement, twenty-two spaced bricks; within arch, "Farmer's Arms": Sheaf of Rye, pitchfork, shovel, rake, sickle, ax, and scythe; elaborate scroll ornament beneath pavement. Reverse: American eagle, head turned to right, shield with seven vertical bars on breast, wings partly raised, right foreshortened; thunderbolt (five arrows) in its right talons, olive branch in left; eagle standing on oval frame with inner band of twenty-six small pearls and containing word "OHIO"; sunrays surround eagle's head and above rays, in semicircle, "ZANESVILLE," in semicircle beneath oval frame, "J. ƧHEPARD & CO.," the S reversed. Edges vertically ribbed, plain lip; pontil mark. No. 245-GIV-32. Glassworks of J. Shepard & Co., Zanesville, Ohio. Circa 1824–30.

PLATE 114

1. Pint flask, clear light green non-lead glass. Obverse: three-quarter bust of Harrison, facing left, in elaborate uniform showing triple row of laurel branches on breast; above, in semicircle "Wᴹ· H. HARRISON". Reverse: log cabin, tall door with latchstring, window with four panes at right; chimney on roof is capped, and on peak at right United States flag with eight stars, on staff and blowing to left over roof; below cabin, large plow at left, and cider barrel at right. Beaded edges with vertical medial rib; plain lip; pontil mark. GI-63. Pittsburgh-Monongahela District. Glasshouse not known. Circa 1840.

One of the rarest of the historical flasks. Only about five or six specimens known at present.

2. Pint flask, clear green non-lead glass. Obverse: profile bust of Taylor in uniform, facing right; above in semicircle, "ZACHARY TAYLOR" and beneath, "ROUGH & READY". Reverse: tall cornstalk, and above, in semicircle "CORN FOR THE WORLD". Edges vertically ribbed with heavy medial rib; plain lip; pontil mark. GI-74. Attributed to Baltimore Glass Works. Circa 1840–48.

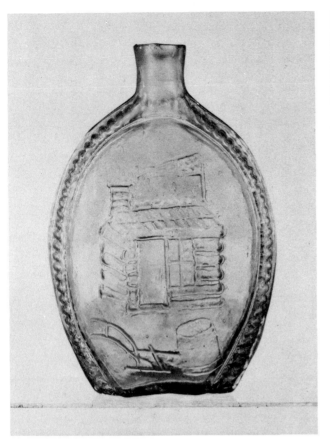

NOTES AND SOURCES

N.B. Where only author's name and page number appear, full reference may be found in the Bibliography.

THE ANCESTRY OF AMERICAN GLASS

1. Eisen, Vol. I, p. 2.
2. Britain, *Specification of Patents,* No. 176.
3. Sources for Chapter I: Eisen, Vols. I and II, in particular, Vol. I, pp. 1–11, 102–17, 128–31, and Vol. II, pp. 749–50; Hartshorn; McKearin, G. S. and H., Chapter I; Thorpe.

GLASSMAKING IN THE COLONIES

1. McKearin, G. S. and H., *American Glass,* Chronological Charts of Glasshouses, pp. 583–613, basis of all glasshouse statistics unless otherwise noted.
2. Knittle; pp. 68–75.
3. Britain, *Specification of Patents,* No. 24.
4. *Captain John Smith's Works,* source of data on the first Jamestown glassworks.
5. *Records of the Virginia Company,* source of data on second Jamestown glassworks (except for material in Note 6, below).
6. New York *Herald Tribune,* "Making of Glass. First Industry in Colonies," January 3, 1949.
7. *Documentary History of New York,* Vol. I, Lord Cornbury's 1705 report to the Lords of Trade, p. 712.
8. Miller, p. 249.
9. McKearin, G. S. and H., pp. 583–613.
10. Hunter, p. 162.
11. Pittsburgh *Mercury,* March 1, 1815.
12. *Documentary History of New York,* Vol. I, pp. 733–35.
13. Hunter, pp. 146–52; Knittle, pp. 107 et seq.
14. New York *Gazette or Weekly Post Boy,* October 7, 1754, quoted by Hunter, p. 149.
15. Hunter, pp. 157–70, data on Wistars and their glassmaking unless otherwise noted.
16. Prime, pp. 153, 154, *Pennsylvania Journal,* October 11, 1780.
17. Maps of the Jerseys, 1777 (one based on 1769 survey). Allowas or Aloes on maps through 1812, later changed to Alloways.

18. Prime, pp. 153, 154, *Pennsylvania Journal,* October 11, 1780.
19. Cushing and Sheppard, p. 332.
20. Bishop, Vol. I, p. 236. Van Rensselaer, p. 124. Maps, see Note 17, above.
21. Prime, p. 152, *Pennsylvania Staatsbote,* September 30, 1765.
22. Ibid., p. 153, *Pennsylvania Chronicle,* July 31, 1769.
23. Johnson, pp. 139 et seq.
24. Prime, pp. 153, 154, *Pennsylvania Journal,* October 11, 1780.
25. Ibid., p. 153, *Pennsylvania Chronicle,* July 31, 1769.
26. For more complete discussion, McKearin, G. S. and H., pp. 27, 28, 37–41.
27. Prime, pp. 153, 154, *Pennsylvania Journal,* October 11, 1780.
28. Ibid.
29. Hunter. Data on Stiegel and his glassmaking unless otherwise noted.
30. Prime, p. 142, quoting *Pennsylvania Archives,* fourth series, Vol. III, p. 333.
31. Ibid., p. 150, *Pennsylvania Gazette,* March 17, 1773.
32. Ibid., p. 145, *Pennsylvania Journal,* July 5, 1770.
33. Wood.
34. *Revolutionary Letters,* p. 219.
35. Prime, p. 150, *Pennsylvania Gazette,* March 17, 1773.
36. For more complete discussion, McKearin, G. S. and H., pp. 57–66.
37. Prime, newspaper ads, pp. 145–50. Hunter, pp. 70, 71, 180–82, 224, 225.
38. For more complete discussion, McKearin, G. S. and H., pp. 48–51, 87–90.
39. 1815 receipted bill, The Bella C. Landauer Collection in The New York Historical Society.
40. For more complete discussion: McKearin, G. S., *Antiques,* August 1939. McKearin, G. S. and H., pp. 90–93.

41. One of twenty-one fragments owned by the Metropolitan Museum of Art, New York City.

42. Dow, pp. 101, 102, Boston *News Letter*, July 11, 1771.

43. Troy *Sentinel*, July 17, 1827 (one of several).

44. Weeks, pp. 80 et seq.

45. Prime, pp. 139, 140, *Pennsylvania Evening Post*, April 15, 1777.

46. Ibid., pp. 137, 150, *Pennsylvania Staatsbote*, August 17, 1773; *Pennsylvania Gazette*, March 17, 1773; and *Pennsylvania Packet*, March 22, 1773.

47. Ibid., p. 137, *Pennsylvania Journal*, December 7, 1774.

48. Ibid., p. 138, *Pennsylvania Packet*, February 27, 1775; and *Pennsylvania Journal*, December 7, 1774, p. 137.

49. *Revolutionary Letters*, p. 225.

50. Prime, pp. 139, 140, *Pennsylvania Evening Post*, April 15, 1777.

51. *Revolutionary Letters*, p. 225.

52. Weeks, pp. 80 et seq.

53. *The American Museum*, Vol. II, pp. 507 et seq.; Vol. III, p. 164; Vol. IV, pp. 57 et seq.

54. Winterbottom (1796 American edition) did not mention glass in his enumeration of manufactures in Pennsylvania. James Butland and Company, one of the operating firms, is listed in the 1800 Philadelphia Directory.

55. McKearin, G. S. and H., pp. 583–613.

GLASSMAKING FROM 1780 TO 1800

1. McKearin, G. S. and H., pp. 583–613.

2. Weeks, p. 89.

3. Jarves (1854 edition), p. 33.

4. Weeks, p. 89.

5. *Revolutionary Letters*, p. 159.

6. Cushing and Sheppard, p. 228. Van Rensselaer, pp. 134, 135.

7. *The American Museum*, Vol. III, p. 593.

8. Cushing and Sheppard, pp. 228 et seq.

9. Bishop, Vol. I, p. 239.

10. McKearin, G. S. and H., pp. 583–613.

11. Dickinson's and the final draft of the "Declaration on Taking Arms," 1775, *Journals of the Continental Congress*, Vol. II, p. 154.

12. *New York Packet. And The American Advertiser*, February 26, 1784, Casca Letter.

13. *The American Museum*, Vol. III, pp. 268, 334 et seq.

14. Ibid., Vol. II, p. 507.

15. Pitkin, p. 30.

16. *New York Packet. And The American Advertiser*, October 25, 1784.

17. McKearin, G. S. and H., pp. 583–613.

18. Burpee, pp. 1261 et seq., 1272 et seq.

19. *The American Museum*, Vol. VI, pp. 48 et seq., "Hints to Manufacturers."

20. Burpee, pp. 1261 et seq., 1272 et seq.

21. Bishop, Vol. I, p. 242.

22. *The American Museum*, Vol. III, p. 490.

23. For more complete discussion, McKearin, G. S. and H., pp. 49, 545, 547, 582.

24. Ibid., pp. 436–38.

25. Davidson, *Antiques*, December 1939.

26. Watson's *Journals*, 1788 and 1821. Spafford (1813), pp. 63, 425; (1824), p. 517.

27. De Neufville Papers. Watson's *Journals*, 1788 and 1821.

28. White, *Antiques*, July 1936; September 1929.

29. *The American Museum*, Vol. II, p. 218.

30. De Neufville Papers.

31. White, *Antiques*, July 1936; September 1929.

32. De Neufville Papers.

33. Ibid.

34. Watson's *Journals*, 1788 and 1821.

35. New York State, Journals of the Assembly, 12th Assembly, pp. 93, 163; and of the Senate, p. 87.

36. Ibid., 13th Assembly, p. 87.

37. Ibid., 14th Assembly, p. 42.

38. De Neufville Papers.

39. Annals of Congress: 2nd, Vol. III, p. 351.

40. Lansingburgh *American Spy*, September 28, 1792. *Vermont Gazette*, September 12, 1792.

41. New York State Laws, 18th Session, Chapter 47.

42. Flick, ms., III: 49–52.

43. New York State Laws, 19th Session, Chapter 54.

44. Albany *Register*, June 20, 1796.

45. Albany *Chronicle or Journal of the Times*, April 16, 1797.

46. New York State Laws, 22nd Session, Vol. III, Chapter 48, and 32nd Session, Chapter 47.

47. Albany *Register*, April 2, 1798.

48. Fessenden, pp. 299, 300. Spafford (1813), p. 199.

49. Bishop, Vol. I, p. 241.

50. La Rochefoucauld-Liancourt, Vol. I, p. 371.

51. Flick, ms., III: 49–52.

52. Boston *Columbian Centinel*, ads in various issues, 1812–14.

53. Fessenden, p. 299.
54. Albany *Register*, May 5, 1794, and May 27, 1796.
55. Flick, ms., III: 49–52.
56. Weeks, p. 81.
57. La Rochefoucauld-Liancourt, Vol. I, pp. 4, 5.
58. Craig, p. 276. Bishop, Vol. II, p. 165. Knittle, *Antiques*, March 1927.
59. Amelung.
60. Ibid.
61. Ghequiere was a steady advertiser in the Baltimore papers for the years we have covered. Repold was listed in the directories as a merchant. Family tradition records the friendship.
62. Amelung.
63. Ibid.
64. Quinn.
65. Amelung.
66. Prime, p. 134, *Maryland Journal and Baltimore Advertiser*, February 11, 1785.
67. Kramer, pp. 5, 6.
68. Amelung.
69. Ibid. June 1790 note added in longhand by Amelung.
70. Amelung.
71. Ibid. June 1790 note added in longhand by Amelung.
72. *Maryland Journal and Baltimore Advertiser*, June 10, 1788.
73. American State Papers, Class IV, Vol. II, p. 62.
74. Annals of Congress, 1st, Vol. II, p. 1620–32.
75. Ibid., 2nd, Vol. III, p. 247.
76. Ibid., 1st, Vol. I, p. 173. U. S. House Doc. 671, Tariff Acts.
77. Annals of Congress, 3rd, Vol. II, pp. 452, 453, 456.
78. About 1791 Thomas Johnson, according to John Ramsay's researches, built one or two glass furnaces near Frederick, one of which was under the management of his nephew, Benjamin, and was offered for sale in 1793 (McKearin, G. S. and H., p. 586). This interest, plus a possible financial interest in the New Bremen Glassmanufactory, may account for the joint memorial. Labes held a mortgage on part of Amelung's land (Quinn). Contemporary ads in the *Maryland Journal and Baltimore Advertiser* also are evidence of his interest in the works.
79. U. S. House Doc. 671, Tariff Acts.
80. *Maryland Journal and Baltimore Advertiser*, May 16, 1789.
81. *Federal Intelligencer and Baltimore Daily Gazette*, March 23, 1795.
82. Quinn.
83. Maryland Laws, 1795, Chapter LXXXIV.
84. Quinn.
85. Annals of Congress, 13th, Coxe's Digest of Manufactures, p. 2628.
86. Knittle, pp. 172–80.
87. Prime, p. 134, *Maryland Journal and Baltimore Advertiser*, February 11, 1785.
88. *Maryland Journal and Baltimore Advertiser*, May 16, 1789.
89. Boston, *The Massachusetts Centinel*, December 17, 1788.
90. *Maryland Journal and Baltimore Advertiser*, March 25, 1788.
91. Ibid., March 1789–June 1790.
92. Amelung. June 1790 note added in longhand by Amelung.
93. Apocrypha, Book of Tobit.
94. Pazaurek, *Antiques*, April 1932.
95. Stohlman.
96. Weeks, pp. 82–83.
97. Innes, *Antiques*, January 1949.
98. Jarves (1854 edition), p. 41.
99. Griffith, p. 111. Weeks, p. 95. Ihmsen family records.
100. Van Rensselaer, p. 195.
101. Quinn.
102. Baltimore directories, research by Richard Wood.
103. Baltimore *Federal Gazette*, August 11, 1802. Van Rensselaer, p. 196.
104. *Baltimore American and Daily Advertiser*, May 15 and June 7, 1803.
105. Quinn.
106. Longhand notations in a 1799 Baltimore directory, New York Historical Society.
107. Innes, *Antiques*, January 1949.
108. Griffith, p. 111. Van Rensselaer, p. 196.
109. Van Rensselaer, p. 196.
110. McKearin, H., *Antiques*, August 1939.
111. Innes, *Antiques*, January 1949.
112. *Standard History of Pittsburg*, p. 74. Gallatin Papers.
113. Weeks, pp. 82, 83. Van Rensselaer, p. 189.
114. Gallatin Papers.
115. Adams, Henry, *The Life of Albert Gallatin* (Philadelphia, 1879), pp. 60, 61, 187.

116. Ibid.
117. Gallatin Papers.
118. Ibid., Articles of Agreement re New Geneva Glass Works.
119. Gallatin Papers.
120. Weeks, p. 82.
121. Gallatin Papers.
122. Knittle, p. 205, quote from May 7, 1803, Pittsburgh *Tree of Liberty.*
123. Gallatin Papers.
124. Weeks, pp. 82, 83. McKearin, G. S. and H., pp. 118, 119, 586.
125. Gallatin Papers.
126. Kramer, p. 22.
127. *The Navigator* (1814), pp. 40, 41.
128. *Writings of Albert Gallatin,* Edited by Henry Adams (Philadelphia, 1879), p. 701.
129. Jones.
130. Weeks, pp. 82, 83. McKearin, G. S. and H., pp. 118, 119, 586.
131. U. S. House Doc. Report on Manufactures (published 1833).
132. Gallatin Papers.
133. Pittsburgh *Gazette,* February 12, 1806.
134. Ibid., March 10, 1807.
135. Gallatin Papers.
136. For more detailed discussion: Gest and Smith; Knittle, pp. 203–7; White, *Antiques,* Vol. XXXVI, pp. 66, 67; McKearin, G. S. and H., pp. 117–24.
137. *The Navigator* (1814), pp. 12–19. The Conewango was only one of several creeks so used.
138. Fordham, p. 59. Annals of Congress, Vol. 15, p. 619.
139. McMaster, Vol. II, p. 189.
140. Ibid.
141. Gallatin Papers.
142. Pittsburgh *Gazette,* April 8, 1797, appearing first or sent to the paper on February 12, 1797.
143. Pittsburgh *Commonwealth,* October 20, 1805.
144. Craig, pp. 276–78, including a June 12, 1797, letter from Major Isaac Craig to Colonel James O'Hara.
145. Weeks, pp. 82, 83. McKearin, G. S. and H., pp. 118, 119, 586.
146. Ihmsen family records.
147. Knittle, p. 211.
148. Pittsburgh *Gazette,* May 20–December 10, 1802.
149. Weeks, p. 84.
150. Ibid., p. 85. O'Hara and Craig advertised in the March 4, 1800, Philadelphia *Aurora.*

General Advertiser that the Pittsburgh Glass Works was operating.
151. Craig, pp. 276–78.
152. Jones.
153. McKearin, G. S. and H., p. 587.
154. Pittsburgh *Gazette,* April 27–June 8, 1804.
155. *Standard History of Pittsburg,* p. 179.
156. Weeks, p. 85, quote from Cramer's *Almanac* for 1804.
157. Innes, *Antiques,* December 1948.
158. Massachusetts Acts and Laws, 1787, Chapter XIII, p. 642.
159. Winterbottom, Vol. II, pp. 168 et seq.
160. Boston, *The Massachusetts Centinel,* December 17, 1788.
161. Boston *Columbian Centinel,* October 3, 1792.
162. Watkins, *Antiques,* June 1940, for detailed discussion.
163. Boston *Columbian Centinel,* October 3, 1792.
164. Fessenden, pp. 295, 296.
165. Massachusetts Historical Society Collection. Series 1, Vol. 3, p. 282.
166. Massachusetts Laws, 1793, Chapter 4, p. 309. Winterbottom, Vol. II, pp. 168 et seq.
167. American State Papers, Class V, Vol. V, p. 492.
168. Watkins, *Antiques,* June 1940, for detailed discussion.
169. *The American Museum,* Vol. VI, pp. 48 et seq., "Hints to Manufacturers."
170. Typical late eighteenth- and early nineteenth-century examples shown by ads of glassworks for sale: Wistars' (Prime, pp. 153, 154), *Pennsylvania Journal,* October 11, 1780. Philadelphia Glass Works (Prime, pp. 139, 140), *Pennsylvania Evening Post,* April 15, 1777. Rensselaer Glass Factory, Boston *Columbian Centinel,* January 3, 1816. Ulster Glass Works, New York *Evening Post,* October 7, 1820.
171. *The American Museum,* Vol. I, pp. 257 et seq.
172. Dyott, and newspaper advertisements.
173. New York State Laws, 50th Session, 2nd meeting, 1827, p. 165, Revised Statutes.

GLASSMAKING IN THE CRITICAL PERIOD FROM 1800 TO 1830

1. Census Reports.
2. McKearin, G. S. and H., pp. 583–613.
3. Annals of Congress, 8th, p. 1471.

4. U. S. House Doc. 671, Tariff Acts.

5. Tabulations of imports based on reports in American State Papers, Class IV, Vol. I.

6. Annals of Congress, 9th, p. 639.

7. Philadelphia *Aurora. General Advertiser,* September 17, 1814.

8. Westropp, *Irish Glass,* export figures, pp. 151 et seq.

9. Annals of Congress, 6th, p. 1291.

10. *Writings of Thomas Jefferson,* Vol. X, p. 238.

11. Annals of Congress, 11th, p. 1929, Gallatin's letter to Congress re report on manufactures.

12. Ibid., 13th, Coxe's Digest of Manufactures, pp. 2370 et seq.

13. Ibid., 11th. Earthen and glass ware section of Gallatin's 1810 report, pp. 2235, 2236.

14. Ibid.

15. Jarves (1854 edition), pp. 44 et seq.

16. Ibid.

17. New York State Laws, 31st Session, Vol. IV, re toll bridges and turnpikes.

18. Davis, Chapter V, "Improvements in the Means of Intercommunication," pp. 191–215.

19. Nuttall, p. 17; pp. 2–18, graphic description of trip over the Alleghenies.

20. Davis, Chapter V, "Improvements in the Means of Intercommunication," pp. 191–215.

21. *Standard History of Pittsburg,* pp. 80 et seq.

22. *The Navigator* (1814), p. 31.

23. Annals of Congress, 11th, pp. 1275 et seq.

24. Auction System Pamphlets. Dyott, pp. 15, 16. Various memorials to 16th Congress. Pitkin, Chapter VIII.

25. McKearin, G. S. and H., pp. 583–613.

26. *Writings of Thomas Jefferson,* pp. 10, 11.

27. Annals of Congress, 2nd, Vol. 3, Appendix, pp. 971 et seq., Hamilton's 1790 report on manufactures and later debates on imports.

28. U. S. House Doc. 671, Tariff Acts.

29. American State Papers, Class IV, Vol. II.

30. *Standard History of Pittsburg,* pp. 209, 210.

31. Ibid., p. 211.

32. Ibid., p. 214.

33. 1820 Census, *Report on Manufactures,* published 1823.

34. U. S. House Doc. 671, Tariff Acts.

35. Troy *Sentinel,* August 28, 1827, report of Harrisburg Convention.

36. Davis, Chapter V, "Improvements in the Means of Intercommunication," pp. 191–215.

37. Ibid.

38. *Nantucket Inquirer,* July 16, 1822.

39. That they were going by some means is evident from advertisements of Western glass in the Boston *Courier* in the 1830s and from claims of the New England Glass Company in its complaint against the Union Glass Company of Kensington, Philadelphia. (Records of U. S. Circuit Court, Philadelphia, 1829.)

40. Davis, Chapter V, "Improvements in the Means of Intercommunication," pp. 191–215.

41. La Rochefoucauld-Liancourt, Vol. I, pp. 366, 399, 469.

42. Boston *Columbian Centinel,* October 3 and 20, November 17, 1819.

43. Washington *National Intelligencer,* March 8, 1825.

44. American Institute of the City of New York, "Report . . . on the subject of Fairs."

45. Troy *Sentinel,* October 17, 1823.

46. Tabulation based on U. S. Treasury Department Reports on Foreign Commerce and Navigation (1821–50).

47. Boston *Columbian Centinel,* January 25, 1823.

48. Tabulation based on U. S. Treasury Department Reports on Foreign Commerce and Navigation (1821–50).

49. Records of the Boston and Sandwich Glass Company quoted by Lee, Ruth Webb, *American Collector,* September 1942.

THE MAKING OF TABLE AND OTHER FINE WARES
IN THE CRITICAL PERIOD

1. McKearin, G. S. and H., pp. 583–613.

2. *The Navigator* (1814), p. 33, Pittsburgh Directory, 1815.

3. Census Reports.

4. *The Navigator* (1814), pp. 66, 67.

5. Sources of data, unless otherwise noted: U. S. House Doc. Report on Manufactures (1833). The Family Book of Bakewell* Page* Campbell, pp. 45 et seq. Jarves (1854 edition), pp. 43 et seq. McKearin, G. S. and H., pp. 138, 589. Pears and Bakewell, Mary, *Antiques,* March 1927 and 1948, respectively.

6. New York City Directories, 1795-1808.

7. Cuming, p. 222.

8. Weeks, p. 86.

9. Jarves (1854 edition), pp. 42, 43.

10. Pittsburgh *Commonwealth,* October 19, 1808.

11. Pittsburgh Directory, 1815.

12. Jarves (1854 edition), pp. 42, 43.

13. Ibid.

14. Pittsburgh *Gazette,* April 12, 1809.

15. St. Louis *Missouri Gazette,* quoted by Van Ravenswaay.
16. Pittsburgh *Commonwealth,* April 5, 1809.
17. Pittsburgh *Gazette,* May 17, 1809, and July 2, 1811, appeared first or sent to the paper on April 12 and June 25, respectively.
18. Pittsburgh *Commonwealth.* Notice of change as of August 31 still appearing December 1, 1813.
19. Pittsburgh Directory, 1815.
20. Pittsburgh *Gazette,* December 23, 1815.
21. Ibid., May 17, 1809.
22. Ibid., April 12 and May 17, 1809; May 12, 1811.
23. Knapp, Vol. II, pp. 15, 31.
24. Pittsburgh *Gazette,* July 12, 1811, appeared first or was handed to the paper on June 25.
25. Harris' and Lyford's 1837 directories.
26. For further discussion: Innes, *Antiques,* December 1948 and January 1949. McKearin, G. S. and H., pp. 138–40. McKearin, H., *Antiques,* October 1947.
27. McKearin, H., *Antiques,* December 1947.
28. Knittle, p. 307.
29. Pears, quoting Alexander Wilson, who visited Pittsburgh in 1810.
30. Pittsburgh *Gazette,* September 14, 1800. *Standard History of Pittsburg,* p. 148.
31. *Standard History of Pittsburg,* p. 202, gives the date as 1808.
32. Pittsburgh *Gazette,* March 10, 1807.
33. Ibid., July 27, 1810.
34. Thorpe, p. 253.
35. Pittsburgh *Mercury,* April 6, 1814.
36. Pittsburgh Directory, 1815. Jones.
37. Fordham, pp. 75, 76.
38. Pears, quoting from Pittsburgh *Mercury,* November 10, 1818.
39. Bakewell, p. 50.
40. Franklin Institute of Philadelphia, Reports . . . on . . . Exhibitions.
41. Troy *Sentinel,* March 4, 1825.
42. Pears.
43. Hartford *Connecticut Courant,* November 9, 1827.
44. Keiron, Marguerite, *Antiques,* September 1943, p. 127.
45. U. S. House Doc. Report on Manufactures (published 1833).
46. Jones.
47. Royall, Vol. II, pp. 110 et seq.
48. New York *Commercial Advertiser,* 1825, various issues, June 8–August 12.
49. U. S. Patent Records.
50. Royall, Vol. II, pp. 110 et seq.
51. *Standard History of Pittsburg,* p. 202, quoting *The Navigator* for 1811. *The Navigator,* 1814, p. 57. Researches of John Ramsay, McKearin, G. S. and H., p. 589.
52. Pittsburgh *Mercury,* November 5, 1812.
53. McKearin, G. S. and H., p. 590.
54. New York *Commercial Advertiser,* November 12, 1814. Boston *Columbian Centinel,* September 27, 1813.
55. Pittsburgh *Commonwealth,* January 1, 1813, appeared first or was sent to the paper on December 23, 1812.
56. Philadelphia *Poulson's American Daily Advertiser,* January 2, 1813.
57. Ibid., May 15, 1815.
58. Pittsburgh *Gazette,* May 11 and July 27, 1816.
59. *Standard History of Pittsburg,* p. 208.
60. Bishop, Vol. II, p. 319. Weeks, p. 78. Knittle, pp. 401, 402.
61. 1820 Census, Report on Manufactures, published 1823. Knittle, personal letters. McKearin, G. S. and H., p. 595.
62. Jones.
63. U. S. Patent Records.
64. McKearin, G. S. and H., p. 596.
65. Lyford's Western Directory. Bakewell, p. 90.
66. U. S. Patent Records.
67. Pittsburgh Directory, 1815. Jones.
68. McKearin, G. S. and H., Chronological Charts: p. 598.
69. Ibid., p. 599.
70. Pittsburgh Directory, 1815. Jones.
71. Jefferson, Josephine, p. 31.
72. Watkins, *Antiques,* June 1940 and September 1945, for detailed discussion.
73. Jarves (1854 edition), p. 36.
74. Weeks, p. 29.
75. Boston *Columbian Centinel,* ads in various issues, 1812–15.
76. Ibid.
77. Boston *Daily Advertiser,* May 28, 1815.
78. Boston *Columbian Centinel,* January 17 and March 26, 1816; June 13, 1818.
79. Ibid., August 6, 1817.
80. New York *Evening Post,* December 4, 1816.
81. Niles' *Weekly Register,* August 14, 1819.
82. Boston *Columbian Centinel,* October 13, 1819.

83. Watkins, *Antiques*, October 1945.

84. Records of the Boston and Sandwich Glass Company quoted by Lee, Ruth Webb, *American Collector*, September 1942.

85. Boston *Courier*, January 4 and April 7, 1831.

86. Jarves (1854 edition), p. 36.

87. Watkins, *Antiques*, September and October 1945.

88. Jarves (1865 edition), p. 116. Pellatt, Apsley, *Curiosities of Glass Making*, p. 94.

89. Westropp, *Irish Glass*, p. 158. Thorpe, Vol. I, p. 340.

90. Ads: Boston *Columbian Centinel*: September 10, 1814; March 26, 1816; July 29, 1820; and (quoted by Watkins, *Antiques*, September 1945) January 17, 1816. Boston *Daily Advertiser*, May 28, 1815. New York *Evening Post*, February 3, 1819. Some running for months.

91. 1815 receipted bill, The Bella C. Landauer Collection in The New York Historical Society.

92. Ibid.

93. Troy *Sentinel*, April 1 and 11, 1828.

94. Watkins, *Antiques*, October 1945.

95. For detailed account of Boston Porcelain and Glass Company and New England Glass Company see Watkins' *Cambridge Glass*.

96. Boston *Columbian Centinel*, November 17, 1819.

97. Jarves (1854 edition), p. 37.

98. Boston *Columbian Centinel*, February 26, 1817.

99. Ibid.

100. Jarves (1865 edition), p. 110.

101. Boston *Columbian Centinel*, October 13, 1819 and March 8, 1820.

102. Catalogues and reports of fairs and exhibitions.

103. Hartford *Connecticut Courant*, November 12, 1827.

104. Ads in Boston *Columbian Centinel* for April 13, July 6–October 20, 1818, October 13 and 20, 1819; March 8, 1820; Hartford *Connecticut Courant*, November 12 and December 31, 1827; Boston *Gazette*, October 4, 1819 and March 27, 1820, pp. 63, 65 in Watkins, *Cambridge Glass*.

105. Knapp, Vol. II, pp. 15, 31.

106. Fish, p. 100.

107. McKearin, H., *Antiques*, September 1947.

108. U. S. Patent Records.

109. McKearin, G. S. and H., pp. 583–613.

110. Ibid., p. 595, information re land purchases from New York City records of conveyances.

111. Hobbs, New York *Sun*, April 1, 1933.

112. New York City Directories, 1833–38, and New York *Commercial Advertiser*, May 8, 1830.

113. American Institute of the City of New York, reports on fairs and catalogues.

114. McKearin, G. S. and H., p. 596.

115. Mechanics *Gazette*, May 24, 1823.

116. Troy *Sentinel*, September 17, 1823.

117. New York *Commercial Advertiser*, November 22, 1824.

118. Philadelphia Franklin Institute reports on exhibitions, 1825, 1826, 1831, 1846. American Institute of the City of New York reports on fairs, 1828–30, 1843, 1845, and address of General James Talmadge at close of 20th Fair, October 23, 1847. London Art Journal Illustrated Catalogue, p. 107, 1851. Rodgers, Charles Y., *American Superiority at the World's Fair* (1851), Philadelphia, 1852, p. 57.

119. Jarves (1854 edition), p. 38; (1865 edition), p. 94.

120. New York City Minutes of the Common Council, January 3 and September 12, 1825; February 3, 1826; May 3, 1828.

121. Knittle, p. 353.

122. Blunt, A. M., *Picture of New York*, 1828.

123. Annals of Congress, 12th, 1st Session, p. 344.

124. New York City directories and ads in New York *Commercial Advertiser, Morning Herald*, and *Evening Post* of years listed in the Bibliography.

125. *Franklin Journal and American Mechanics Magazine*, Vol. II, p. 242.

126. U. S. Patent Records.

127. Ads in various issues of the New York *Commercial Advertiser*, 1824–34; *Morning Herald*, 1831; Philadelphia *Daily Chronicle*, 1831.

128. For detailed account: Jarves, 1854 or 1865 edition. House Doc. Report on Manufactures, 1833. Crane. Lee, *Sandwich Glass*. McKearin, G. S. and H., pp. 144 et seq.; 278 et seq.; 352. Swan.

129. Boston *Columbian Centinel*, ads from May 2, 1812, to April 4, 1814, when the copartnership of Henshaw and Jarves was announced.

130. U. S. House Doc. Report on Manufactures (published 1833).

131. Franklin Institute of Philadelphia, Reports . . . on . . . Exhibitions.

132. U. S. Patent Records.

133. Jarves (1854 edition), p. 39.

134. Mease, *Picture of Philadelphia,* Vol. II, pp. 24, 25.

135. Philadelphia Records of Conveyance, C.W.R. 13, pp. 466 et seq.

136. Records of U. S. Circuit Court, 3rd District, Philadelphia, 1829.

137. McKearin, H., and Rose, J., *Antiques,* November 1943.

138. Mease, *Picture of Philadelphia,* Vol. II, p. 73.

139. Franklin Institute of Philadelphia, Reports . . . on . . . Exhibitions.

140. Records of U. S. Circuit Court, 3rd District, Philadelphia, 1829.

141. Pittsburgh *Mercury,* April 1, 1813.

142. Pittsburgh *Gazette,* May 5, 1826. Name spelled "Jardel"; in Jones, listed as Alexis Jardell.

143. Ibid., April 3, 1829, appeared first or sent to the paper on October 17, 1828.

144. New York *Evening Post,* April 22, 1819, still running January 1820.

145. Annals of Congress, 16th, Vol. II, debates on tariff revision, pp. 1914 et seq.

146. New York *Evening Post,* March 25, 1825.

147. New York *Commercial Advertiser,* steady advertiser from 1819 at least throughout the years listed in Bibliography.

148. Tabulation based on U. S. Treasury Department Reports on Foreign Commerce and Navigation (1821–50).

149. Thorpe, pp. 290 et seq.

150. Ibid. For discussion of cutting see Thorpe, pp. 245 et seq.

151. Ibid., p. 253.

152. Royall, Vol. II, pp. 110, 111.

HISTORICAL AND PICTORIAL FLASKS AND BLOWN THREE MOLD GLASS

1. Pazaurek, *Antiques,* April 1932.

2. Philadelphia Directory, 1807. Pittsburgh *Gazette,* February 16, 1810.

3. Pittsburgh *Gazette,* July 12, 1811, appeared first or was handed to the paper on June 25.

4. For more complete discussion, McKearin, G. S. and H. Material on historical and pictorial flasks based on Chapter XI.

5. Ibid., pp. 514–82, Bottle Charts.

6. McKearin, H., *American Collector,* October 1942.

7. Van Rensselaer, p. 50.

8. Listed by Jones, not by Harris.

9. Stockbridge (Massachusetts) *Star,* April 20, 1801.

10. New York *Man,* March 26, 1834.

11. For more complete discussion, McKearin, G. S., and H., pp. 514–82.

12. Philadelphia *Public Ledger,* February 23, 1848.

13. Ibid., April 8, 1847.

14. Griffith, p. 213.

15. Philadelphia *Public Ledger,* April 13, 1847.

16. Fish, p. 147.

17. New York *Commercial Advertiser,* 1825, accounts of Clinton's trip given in various issues June–August.

18. Ibid.

19. Royall, Vol. II, p. 69.

20. *Standard History of Pittsburg,* pp. 754–59.

21. Annals of Congress, 16th, Vol. II, pp. 1933, 1934.

22. *Standard History of Pittsburg,* pp. 754–59.

23. In spite of the fact that when the glassworks was started, Lancaster, so we are informed by Mr. Ezra Feinberg, had had a railroad (the Buffalo and Attica, now known as the Erie) for five years, it seems likely that the arrival of the New York Central would have been an occasion worthy of commemoration.

24. Philadelphia *Aurora. General Advertiser,* August 22, 1815. Pittsburgh *Commonwealth,* September 9, 1815.

25. Troy *Northern Budget,* January 26, 1822.

26. For more complete discussion, McKearin, G. S. and H. Material on Blown Three Mold based on Chapter VI.

27. Correspondence with M. S. Dudley Westropp, authority on Irish glass, and with E. Barrington Haynes, authority on English glass.

28. McKearin, G. S. and H., pp. 247–63. Blown Three Mold patterns, Plates 84–99; base patterns, Plate 100; sunbursts and diamond motifs, Plate 101.

29. Watkins, *Antiques,* September, 1945.

30. Jarves (1854 edition), p. 36.

31. Boston *Columbian Centinel,* November 29, 1815.

32. Neither Mr. Westropp nor Mr. Haynes has ever seen or heard of one of these labeled decanters in Irish or English glass.

33. McKearin, G. S. and H., p. 263. Sunbursts and diamond motifs, Plate 101.

34. White, *Antiques,* June 1927, September and November 1929, February 1935, February 1941.

35. McKearin, H., *Antiques,* May 1939.

36. Ibid., September 1947.

37. New York *Evening Post,* April 22, 1819, still running January 1820.

38. Boston *Columbian Centinel,* October 13, 1819.

INDIVIDUAL PIECES FROM NINETEENTH-CENTURY BOTTLE AND WINDOW GLASSHOUSES

1. Weeks, p. 85.

2. McKearin, G. S. and H., pp. 583–613.

3. Ibid.

4. Niles' *Weekly Register,* September 1829.

5. For detailed account: Ormsbee, Thomas H., and Craigin, Florence, "Glassmaking at Lake Dunmore," *American Collector,* August and September 1937. McKearin, G. S. and H., pp. 195 et seq., 591, 598.

6. Griffin, pp. 366, 459. Knittle, pp. 242, 243. McKearin, G. S. and H., p. 593. Van Rensselaer, p. 58. U. S. House Doc. Report on Manufacturers (1833).

7. Griffin, pp. 366, 367, 392, 488, 556, 634, 643. McKearin, G. S. and H., pp. 125, 197 et seq., 202, 270, 277, 278. White, *Antiques,* December 1938. Van Rensselaer, pp. 61 et seq. U. S. House Report on Manufactures (1833).

8. Van Rensselaer, pp. 71, 72.

9. U. S. House Doc. Report on Manufactures (1833).

10. For detailed discussion: Watkins, *Antiques,* September 1933. McKearin, G. S. and H., pp. 205 et seq., 604, 605, 607, 611.

11. Watkins, *Antiques,* September 1945.

12. Boston *New England Palladium,* June 20, 1829.

13. Knittle, pp. 369, 370.

14. For detailed discussion: White, *Antiques,* October and November 1940, February and August 1941. McKearin, G. S. and H., pp. 207 et seq., 278, 591, 593.

15. Van Rensselaer, pp. 53, 75.

16. McKearin, G. S. and H., pp. 583–613.

17. Melish, pp. 386 et seq.

18. Troy *Times Record,* January 30, 1937.

19. Troy *Northern Budget,* November 5, 1805.

20. New York State Laws, 28th and 29th Sessions, Vol. IV, pp. 342, 343.

21. "Report of Committee of Commerce & Manufactures," January 12, 1807, Washington, A. & G. Way, Printers, 1807.

22. Albany *Gazette,* October 26, 1812.

23. Ibid., January 21, 1813.

24. Albany *Register,* November 16, 1815. Boston *Columbian Centinel,* January 17, 1816.

25. Troy *Times Record,* January 30, 1937.

26. New York State Laws, 42nd Session, Chapter CLXXXVI.

27. Troy *Times Record,* January 30, 1937.

28. Troy *Northern Budget,* October 26, 1819.

29. Rensselaer County Deeds, Book 15, pp. 156–60.

30. Troy *Sentinel,* 1827–29.

31. New York State Laws, 53rd Session, Chapter 206.

32. New York State Doc. of the Assembly, 56th Session, 1833, Vol. III, No. 204.

33. Rensselaer County Deeds, Books 31 and 41, pp. 462, 146 respectively.

34. Ibid., Books 38, 45, and 52, pp. 265, 306–9, 321 respectively.

35. Troy *Times Record,* January 30, 1937.

36. McKearin, G. S. and H., p. 605.

37. New York State Laws, 11th and 12th Sessions, years 1809–11.

38. White, *Antiques,* July, September, and November 1929, July and September 1930, for detailed accounts of Utica, Oneida, Mount Vernon and Saratoga Mountain glassworks.

39. Boston *Columbian Centinel,* November 12, 1812. Philadelphia *Aurora. General Advertiser,* August 22, 1812. Philadelphia *Poulson's The American Daily Advertiser,* May 3, 1815.

40. Incorporations of the Oneida Glass Factory, 32nd Session, Chapter XXXI, 45th Session, Chapter XLVII, and 59th Session, Chapter 50; of Utica Crown Glass Works, 33rd Session, Chapter XXXVII; of Mount Vernon Glass Company, 33rd Session, Chapter XVI, and 47th Session, Chapter CLXVII.

41. Mrs. Carr, daughter of Oscar Granger. White, *Antiques,* July and September 1930. McKearin, G. S. and H., pp. 185 et seq., 276.

42. McKearin, G. S. and H., p. 598.

43. Gordon, p. 400. French, p. 240. Troy *Sentinel,* March 30, 1832.

44. New York State Laws, 55th Session, Chapter 219.

45. Gordon, p. 487.

46. For more complete discussion, McKearin, G. S. and H., pp. 172 et seq., 192 et seq., 599, 601.

47. French, p. 661. McKearin, G. S. and H., pp. 182, 602.

48. For more complete discussion, McKearin, G. S. and H., pp. 194, 195, 603, 606.

49. Ibid., pp. 583–613.

50. Elmer, pp. 80 et seq. McKearin, G. S. and H., pp. 164, 587, 588.

51. A pressed milk-white jar inscribed "Whitall, Tatum & Co. Phila. & N. Y." on the base is shown on Plate 62, *American Glass,* G. S. and H. McKearin.

52. Ibid., pp. 583–613.

53. Van Rensselaer, pp. 142, 146, 153. McKearin, G. S. and H., pp. 166 et seq., 594, 595, 602, 603, 609.

54. Elmer, p. 56. Stewart, p. 187. Knittle, p. 355. McKearin, G. S. and H., pp. 169, 602.

55. Knittle, pp. 363, 364. McKearin, G. S. and H., pp. 180, 605. Van Rensselaer, p. 144.

56. McKearin, G. S. and H., pp. 583–613.

57. Melish, p. 60.

58. Bishop, Vol. II, p. 217. Fearon, p. 230.

59. Knittle, pp. 372 et seq. for detailed account of Zanesville glasshouses.

60. Ibid.

61. For more complete discussion: McKearin, G. S. and H., pp. 225 et seq. Knittle, pp. 374 et seq.

62. For detailed discussion of Mantua and Kent: White, *Antiques,* December 1934, February, July, and November 1935. McKearin, G. S. and H., pp. 127 et seq., 274, 275, 595, 596.

63. For detailed discussion of Midwestern glass: McKearin, G. S. and H., pp. 51 et seq., 233–37. McKearin, H., *Antiques,* January 1946.

64. Ibid.

NOTES ON THE MODERN RENAISSANCE OF THE ART OF GLASS

1. Chamberlain.

2. Thorpe, p. 291.

3. Johnson, Benjamin P., agent of the state of New York appointed to attend the Exhibition of the Industry of All Nations held in London, 1851. Report. Albany. 1852.

4. Troy *Northern Budget,* November 2 and December 20, 1852.

5. U. S. House Doc. 671, Tariff Acts.

6. McKearin, H., *Antiques,* August 1939.

7. Ibid.

8. U. S. Patent Records.

9. Knapp, Vol. II, pp. 114, 115.

10. McKearin, H., *Antiques,* August 1939.

11. Chamberlain.

12. Keyes. Correspondence with Dr. Alexander Silverman, University of Pittsburgh.

13. Chamberlain.

14. McKearin, H., *Antiques,* August 1939.

15. For detailed discussion of some of these glasses, see *Antiques:* Brothers, August 1934, March and December 1936; Lee, August 1933; Watkins, July 1935; and *The Spinning Wheel,* Kamm, July and August 1949.

16. McKearin, G. S. and H., pp. 601, 602.

17. *Antiques,* December 1926, p. 478. Fox.

18. For more complete discussion, McKearin, G. S. and H., p. 418.

19. Newton; and information from members of the Dorflinger family.

20. Bergstrom, Evangeline H., *Old Glass Paperweights* (Chicago, 1940).

21. Mr. Frederick Carder.

22. Chamberlain.

23. Ibid.

24. McKearin, G. S. and H., pp. 605, 611, 613.

25. Ibid., p. 609, and Corning Glass, which puts the establishment of the Union Glass Works as 1851.

26. Plaut.

27. Ibid.

28. Plaut, p. 5.

BIBLIOGRAPHY

(limited to sources used in preparation of this book)

Amelung, John F. "Remarks on Manufactures, Principally on the New Established Glass-House near Frederick-Town, in the State of Maryland." Printed for the Author, 1787.

American Institute of the City of New York. "Report . . . on the subject of Fairs." 2nd Edition. New York, Printed by J. Seymour, 1829. Annual Reports on Fairs 1829–50.

American Museum, The. Mathew Carey, Editor. Vols. I–VIII. Philadelphia, Carey, Stewart & Co., 1787–92.

American State Papers. March 3, 1789–March 3, 1815. Vols. I and II, Class IV, Commerce and Navigation; Vol. V, Class III, Finance. Washington, Gales & Seaton, 1832.

Auction System Pamphlets. "The Beneficial Tendency of Auctioneering and the Danger of Restraining it." By a Friend to Trade. New York, 1817.
"Facts Important to be known by the Manufactures and Mechanics and all other Classes of the Community. New York. November 1831. Selected from a pamphlet published 1828, under the Direction of the Anti-Auction Committee, entitled 'Remarks upon the Auction System as Practiced in New York. . . .' "

Bakewell, B. G. (compiler). *The Family Book of Bakewell*Page*Campbell.* Pittsburgh, 1896.

Baltimore City Directories. 1799, 1807.

Bishop, J. Leander. *A History of American Manufactures,* 1608-1860. 3 Vols. 3rd Edition. Philadelphia, Edward Young & Co., 1868.

Brothers, J. Stanley, Jr. "American Ornamental Glass," 3 Parts, *Antiques,* Vols. XXVI, XXIX, XXX, August 1934, March and December 1936.

Buckley, Wilfred. *The Art of Glass.* London, George Allen, 1939.

Burpee, Charles Winslow. *History of Hartford County. Connecticut,* 1633–1928. Vol. II. Chicago, S. J. Clark Publishing Co., 1928.

Captain John Smith's Works: A Map of Virginia. The Proceedings of the English Colonie in Virginia. The General Historie of Virginia, New England and the Summer Isles, The Fourth Book. The History of Virginia. The English Scholar's Library. Edited by Edward Arber. Montague Road, Birmingham, 1884.

Chamberlain, Dorothy. "Contemporary Glass for the Collector Ahead," *Antiques,* Vol. XXXII, August 1937.

Craig, Neville B. *The History of Pittsburg.* Pittsburgh, 1851.

Crane, Priscilla C. "The Boston and Sandwich Glass Company," *Antiques,* Vol. VII, April 1925.

Cuming, F (ortescue). *Sketches of a Tour to the Western Country.* Pittsburgh, 1810.

Cushing, Thomas, M.D., and Sheppard, Charles E. *History of the Counties of Gloucester, Salem and Cumberland, New Jersey.* Philadelphia, Everts and Peck, 1883.

Davis, Emerson, D.D. *The Half Century.* Boston, Tappan and Whittemore, 1851.

Davison, Mary E. "The Glass Industry of Cleveland, New York," *Antiques,* Vol. XXXI, April 1937.
———"The Glass of Peterboro, New York," *Antiques,* Vol. XXXVI, December 1939.

De Neufville Papers. Manuscript Collection, New York Historical Society. Letters from James Gray, John Heefke, and Ferdinand Walfahrt in New York City to Leonard de Neufville at Albany and Dowesborough. Petition by Leonard de Neufville for assistance, to New York State Assembly, dated Albany, Jan. 1789.

Documentary History of New York. Vol. I. Albany, Weed, Parsons & Co., Public Printers, 1849.

Dow, George Francis. *The Arts & Crafts in New England. Gleanings from Boston Newspapers.* Topfield, Mass., The Wayside Press, 1927.

Dwight, Timothy. *Travels in New-England and New-York.* Vol. I. 1821.

Dyott, T. W., M.D. *An Exposition of the System of Moral and Mental Labor established at the Glass Factory of Dyottville in the County of Philadelphia.* Philadelphia, 1833.

Eisen, Gustavus A. *Glass.* Vols. I and II. New York, William Edwin Rudge, 1927.

Elmer, Lucius O. C. *History of the Early Settlement and Progress of Cumberland County, New Jersey.* Bridgeton, N. J., Nixon, 1869.

Fearon, Henry Bradshaw. *Sketches of America.* 2nd Edition. London, 1818.

Fessenden, Thomas Green. *The Register of Arts, or A compendious view of some of the most useful discoveries and inventions.* Philadelphia, 1808.

Fish, Carl Russell. *The Rise of the Common Man, 1830–1850.* (Vol. VI, *A History of American Life.*) New York, The Macmillan Company, 1946.

Flick, Hugh M. Extract from *Elkanah Watson: Gentleman Promotor.* III: 49–52. Ms. copy of Ph.D. dissertation.

Fordham, Elias Pym. *Personal Narrative of travels in Virginia, Maryland, Pennsylvania, Ohio, Indiana, Kentucky: and a residence in the Illinois Territory. 1817–1818.* Reprint. Cleveland, 1906.

Fox, Dorothy M. "The Glass of Tiffany," *Antiques,* Vol. XLIV, November and December 1943.

Franklin Institute of Philadelphia. Reports by Committee on Premiums & Exhibitions 1824–1848.

French, J. H., LL.D. *Gazetteer of the State of New York.* 8th Edition. 1860.

Gallatin Papers including Articles of Agreement in re establishing the glassworks at New Geneva. Manuscript Collection of The New York Historical Society.

Gest, Neil C., and Smith, Parke G. "The Glassmaking Kramers," *Antiques,* Vol. XXXV, March 1939.

Gordon, Thomas F. *Gazetteer of the State of New York.* Philadelphia, 1836.

Greene, Evarts Boutell. *The Revolutionary Generation. 1763–1790.* (Vol. IV, *A History of American Life.*) New York, The Macmillan Company, 1946.

Griffin, S. G. *A History of the Town of Keene.* Keene, N. H., Sentinel Printing Co., 1904.

Griffith, Thomas W. *Annals of Baltimore.* Baltimore, Printed by William Wooddy, 1824.

Harris' Pittsburgh Business Directory. 1837.

Hartshorn, Albert. *Old English Glasses.* London and New York, Edward Arnold, 1897.

Hunter, Frederick. *Stiegel Glass.* Cambridge, Houghton Mifflin Company, 1914.

Innes, Lowell. "Pittsburgh Glass," Parts I and II, *Antiques,* Vols. LIV and LV, December 1948, January 1949.

Jarves, Deming. *Reminiscences of Glass-Making.* 1st Edition. Boston, Eastburn's Press, 1854, Revised Edition. New York, Hurd and Houlton, 1865.

Jefferson, Josephine. *Wheeling Glass.* Mount Vernon, Ohio, The Guide Publishing Co., 1947.

Jefferson, Thomas, The Writings of. Collected and edited by Paul Leicester Ford. Vols. IX, X. New York and London, G. P. Putnam's Sons, 1898.

Johnson, R. G. *An Historical Account of the First Settlement of Salem in West Jersey by John Fenwick, Esq. Chief Proprietor of the same.* Published by Orrin Rogers, 1839.

Jones, S (amuel). *Pittsburgh in the Year 1826.* Pittsburgh, Printed by Johnston & Stockton, 1826.

Kamm, Minnie Watson. "Iridescent Glass," *The Spinning Wheel,* July and August, 1949.

Keyes, Homer Eaton. "Cameo Glass," *Antiques,* Vol. XXX, September 1936.

Knapp, Dr. F. *Chemical Technology or Chemistry applied to the Arts and to Manufactures.* Vol. II. Philadelphia, Lea and Blanchard, 1849.

Knittle, Rhea Mansfield. *Early American Glass.* New York, The Century Company, 1927.

Kramer, LeRoy. *Johann Baltasar Kramer.* Printed and bound for the Author by American Printers and Stationers, Chicago.

Krout, John Allen, and Fox, Dixon Ryan. *The Completion of Independence, 1790–1830.* (Vol. V. *A History of American Life.*) New York, The Macmillan Company, 1944.

La Rochefoucauld-Liancourt, Duc de. *Travels Through the United States of North America, the Country of the Iroquois and Upper Canada in the years 1795, 1796 and 1797.* 2 Vols. London, printed for R. Phillips, 1799.

Lee, Ruth Webb. *Sandwich Glass.* New York, 1939. "Peachblow Glass," *Antiques,* Vol. XXIV, August 1933.

Lyford's Western Directory. 1837.

McKearin, George S. "Wistarberg and South Jersey Glass," *Antiques,* Vol. X, October 1926.

——"A Study of Paneled Vases," *Antiques,* Vol. XXXVI, August 1939.

——"Jenny Lind in Glass," *American Collector,* March 1935.

——"Rare Flasks from Early Houses in Pittsburgh and Monongahela Districts," *American Collector,* October 1937.

McKearin, George S. and Helen. *American Glass.* New York, Crown, 1941.

McKearin, Helen. "Early Nineteenth Century Glassmaking in Ohio," *Antiques,* Vol. XLIX, January 1946.

——"Glass at Worlds' Fairs," Parts I and II, *Antiques,* Vol. XXXVI, August and September 1939.

——"Blown Three Mold Fragments Excavated at Sandwich," *Antiques,* Vol. XXXV, May 1939.

——"French Glass and China. A Public Sale Dec. 20, 1816," *Antiques,* Vol. LIV, October 1948.

——"Historical Flasks. American Primitive Portraits," *American Collector,* October 1942.

——"New England Glass Company Invoices," Parts I, II, and III, *Antiques,* Vols. LII and LIII, September, October, and December 1947.

McKearin, Helen, and Rose, James. "Cup Plates of the Philadelphia Area," *Antiques,* Vol. XLIV, November 1943.

McLaughlin, Warner. "Glass Making in the Champlain Valley and Northern New York," *Vermont Quarterly,* New Series, Vol. XIV, No. 1, January 1946.

McMaster, John Bach. *A History of the People of the United States.* Vols. I-VIII. New York.

Maryland, Laws of. 1795. Chapter LXXXIV.

Massachusetts. Acts and Laws Passed by the General Court of Massachusetts. 1787-1794.

Mease, James, M.D. *The Picture of Philadelphia.* Philadelphia, 1811.

——(continued by Thomas Porter). *Picture of Philadelphia.* Vols. I and II. Philadelphia, 1831.

Melish, John. *Travels in the United States of America in the years 1806 and 1807, and 1809, 1810 and 1811.* 2 vols. Philadelphia, 1812.

Memorial History of Hartford County, Connecticut. Edited by J. Hammond Trumbull. Vol. II. Boston, Edward L. Osgood, Publisher, 1886.

Miller, John C. *Origins of the American Revolution.* Boston, Little, Brown & Company, 1943.

Navigator, The. 8th Edition. Pittsburgh, published and sold by Cramer, Spear and Eichbaum, 1814.

NEWSPAPERS

Albany.

Albany *Chronicle.* February 27, 1797–October 2, 1797.

Albany *Gazette.* (Incomplete Files.) 1812-15.

Albany *Register.* (Incomplete Files.) 1798-1815.

Baltimore.

Baltimore *American & Commercial Daily Advertiser.* 1803.

Baltimore *Daily Intelligencer.* 1793, 1794.

Federal Intelligencer, and Baltimore Daily Gazette. 1795.

Maryland Journal. 1788-90.

Maryland Journal and Baltimore Advertiser. 1788-90.

Boston.

Boston *Courier.* Issues in 1828, 1830, 1831.

Boston *Daily Advertiser.* Issues of 1813-15.

Columbian Centinel. 1790-1793, 1812-20.

The Independent Chronicle. Issues of 1814.

The Massachusetts Centinel. 1788, 1789.

New-England Palladium. 1820-30.

Hartford.

Connecticut Courant. Scattered issues. 1797-1804, 1827-29.

American Mercury. Scattered issues, 1798.

Lansingburgh, New York.

American Spy. 1795-96.

Lansingburgh Gazette. 1827-29.

The Northern Budget. June 20, 1797–May 5, 1798.

Nantucket.

Nantucket *Inquirer.* June 23, 1821-22, 1824, 1828-30.

New York City.

Man. 1834.

Mechanics' Gazette. 1823.

New York *Commercial Advertiser.* February 24, 1813-15, 1820-34; issues of 1835-38.

New York *Daily Advertiser.* 1824.

New-York *Evening Post.* 1816–20, 1825.

New York *Morning Herald.* Issues of 1829–31.

New York *Packet. And the American Advertiser.* 1784.

Troy.

Northern *Budget.* May 5, 1798–1808, 1817–29.

Troy *Budget.* 1833.

Troy *Post.* September 1814–September 1817, 1820–22.

Troy *Sentinel.* 1823–32.

Philadelphia.

Aurora. General Advertiser. November 4, 1799–1801, 1812–15.

Claypoole's American Daily Advertiser. 1796.

Daily Chronicle. 1831.

Poulson's American Daily Advertiser. 1800–9, 1812–16.

United States' Gazette for the Country. 1816.

Pittsburgh.

(Newspapers in libraries of the New England Antiquarian Society and New York Historical Society.)

The Commonwealth. Issues of 1805–07, 1810, 1812–14, 1817, 1827.

The Mercury. Issues of 1811–17, 1820.

Pittsburgh *Gazette.* Issues of 1786, 1789, 1793–99, 1802, 1804, 1809–11, 1814–16, 1819, 1826, 1827, 1829, 1835.

The Tree of Liberty. Issues of 1800, 1801, 1803, 1805, 1808.

Newton, Janet Foster. "Dorflinger Glass," *Antiques,* Vol. XLV, January 1944.

New York City Directories. 1794–1865.

New York State. Journals of the Senate and the Assembly of the State of New York, 1788–92. Laws of, 1789–1834.

Niles' (Baltimore) *Weekly Register.* 1811–37. (Baltimore) *National Register.* September 1847–March 1848.

Nuttall, Thomas Green, F.L.S. *Journals of Travels into the Arkansas Territory. During the year 1819.* [From Philadelphia through visit in Pittsburgh.] Philadelphia, Thomas H. Palmer, 1821.

Pazaurek, Gustav E. "A German View of Early American Glass," Parts I and II, *Antiques,* Vol. XXI, April and May 1932.

Pears, Thomas C., Jr. "The First Successful Flint Glass Factory in America," *Antiques,* Vol. XI, March 1927.

Pitkin, Timothy. *A Statistical View of the Commerce of the United States of America.* 2nd Edition. New York, James Eastburn & Co., 1817.

Pittsburgh Directories. 1815, 1826, 1837, 1850.

Plaut, James S. *Steuben Glass.* New York, H. Bittner & Company, 1948.

Prime, Alfred Coxe. *The Arts and Crafts in Philadelphia, Maryland and South Carolina. 1721–1785. Gleanings from Newspapers.* The Walpole Society, 1929.

Quinn, Dorothy Mackay. "Johann Friedrick Amelung at New Bremen," *Maryland Historical Magazine,* September 1948. The Maryland Historical Society, Baltimore, Md.

Records of the Virginia Company of London, The. Vols. I and II. *The Court Book;* Vols. III and IV. *Documents.* Edited by Susan Myra Kingsbury. Washington, Government Printing Office, Vols. I and II, 1906; Vol. III, 1932; Vol. IV, 1935.

Rensselaer County Deeds. Books 15, 31, 38, 41, 45, 52.

Revolutionary Letters. Translated by William L. Stone. Albany. Munsell's Sons, 1891.

Royall, Mrs. Anne. *Mrs. Royall's Pennsylvania or Travels Continued in the United States.* 2 vols. Washington, printed for the Author, 1829.

Spafford, Horatio Gates. *A Gazetteer of the State of New York.* Albany, H. C. Southwood, 1813, 1824.

Standard History of Pittsburg, Pennsylvania. Edited by Erasmus Wilson. H. R. Cornell & Company, 1898.

Stewart, D. J. *Combination Atlas Map of Cumberland County New Jersey.* Philadelphia, 1876.

Stohlman, Martin and Elizabeth. "Excavating and Collecting Amelung Glass," *Antiques,* Vol. LIV, October 1948.

Swan, Mabel M. "Deming Jarves and his Glass-Factory Village," *Antiques,* Vol. XXXIII, January 1938.

Taussig, F. W. *The Tariff History of the United States.* 7th Edition. New York and London, G. P. Putnam's Sons, 1923.

Thorpe, W. A. *A History of English and Irish Glass.* Vols. I and II. Boston, Hale, Cushman & Flint, 1929.

UNITED STATES GOVERNMENT PUBLICATIONS

Annals of Congress. (The Debates and Proceedings in the Congress of the United States. 1789–1824.) Washington, Gales & Seaton, 1834.

Treasury Department. Foreign Commerce and Navigation of the United States. 1821–1850.

House of Representatives Executive Documents. Document Relative to the Manufactures in the United States. 22nd Congress, Doc. Nos. 3 and 14. Published 1833. Tariff Acts passed by the Congress of the United States, 1789–1909. Doc. 671 Patent Records.

1820 Census. *Digest of Accounts of Manufacturing Establishments in the United States and of the Manufactures made in pursuance of a Resolution of Congress of 30th March 1822.* Published 1823.

Van Ravenswaay, Charles. "Glass in Old St. Louis," *Antiques,* Vol. XLIV, August 1943.

Van Rensselaer, Stephen. *Early American Bottles and Flasks.* Revised edition. 1926.

Watkins, Lura Woodside. *Cambridge Glass.* Boston, 1930.

——————"The Boston Crown Glass Company," *Antiques,* Vol. XXXVII, June 1940.

——————"Glass Making in South Boston," Parts I and II, *Antiques,* Vol. XLVIII. September and October, 1945.

——————"Shaded Glass of the Massachusetts Glasshouses," *Antiques,* Vol. XXVIII, July 1935.

——————"Stoddard Glass," *Antiques,* Vol. XXIV, August 1933.

——————"The Union Glass Company," *Antiques,* Vol. XXX, November 1936.

——————"American Silvered Glass," *Antiques,* Vol. XLII, October 1942.

Watson, Elkanah. *Men and Times of the Revolution or Memoirs of Elkanah Watson.* Edited by his son, Winslow C. Watson. 2nd Edition. New York, Dana & Co., 1856. *Journals.* 1788,

1821. Manuscript Collection of the New York State Library.

Weeks, Joseph D. *Report on the Manufacture of Glass, including a History of Glassmaking.* (At the 10th Census, 1880.) Washington, 1883.

Wertenbaker, Thomas Jefferson. *The American People.* New York, Charles Scribner's Sons, 1926.

Westropp, M. S. Dudley. *Irish Glass.* Philadelphia, J. B. Lippincott Company, 1921. "Molded Glass," *Antiques,* Vol. XIV, December 1928.

White, Harry Hall. "The Albany Glass Works," *Antiques,* Vol. XXX, July 1936.

——————"Henry Rowe Schoolcraft, Glassmaker," Parts I, II, III, *Antiques,* Vol. XXXIV, XXXV, December 1938, February and April 1939.

——————"Keene, New Hampshire," *Antiques,* Vol. X, November 1926.

——————"The Lancaster (New York) Glass Works," *Antiques,* Vol. XII, October 1927.

——————"More Light on Coventry and Its Products," Parts I, II, and III, *Antiques,* Vols. XXXVIII and XXXIX, October and November 1940, February 1941.

——————"New York State Glasshouses," Part I (The Oneida Glass & Iron Co., The Utica Glass Co.); Parts II and III (The Mt. Vernon Glass Co.), *Antiques,* Vol. XVI, July, September, November, 1929.

——————"New York State Glasshouses," (Mount Pleasant), *Antiques,* Vol. XVIII, July and September 1930.

——————"The Story of the Mantua Glass Works," Parts I, II, III, and IV, *Antiques,* Vols. XXVI, XXVII, XXVIII, December 1934, February, July, November 1935.

——————"The Wilmington Glass Company," *Antiques,* Vol. XL, August 1941.

Winterbottom, W(illiam). *An Historical, Geographical, Commercial and Philosophical View of the United States of America.* The First American Edition with additions and corrections, in four volumes. Vols. I, II, and III. New York, Printed by Tiebout and O'Brien for John Reid, Bookseller and Stationer, 1796.

Wood, Kenneth T. "A Gratuity for Baron Stiegel," *Antiques,* Vol. VII, January 1925.

The Art Journal Illustrated Catalogue. Industry of All Nations. London, 1851.

Final Report of Executive Committee of Award's Columbian Commission. 1893.

Gems of the Centennial Exhibition at the Philadelphia International Exhibition of 1876. New York, 1877.

Great Exhibition of the Works of Industry of All Nations, 1851. Official Descriptive and Illustrated Catalogue. Vols. II and III. London, 1851.

Illustrated Catalogue of the Centennial Exhibition Philadelphia 1876. New York, Harris H. Hayden.

The Illustrated History of the Centennial Exhibition Philadelphia 1876. Bentley, Thomas. New York, Harris H. Hayden.

International Exhibition, 1876. Official Catalogue. Philadelphia, 1876.

List of Awards made by the United States Centennial Commission to the American International Exhibition, 1876, at Philadelphia. From the official lists. Philadelphia, 1876.

The Masterpieces of the Centennial International Exhibition 1876. Vol. II.

Official Catalogue of the New York Exhibition of the Industry of all Nations. 1853. First Revised Edition. New York, 1853

The Official Directory of the World's Columbian Exposition. A Reference book by Mose P. Handy. Chicago, 1893.

The World of Science, Art and Industry. Illustrated from examples in the New York Exhibition, 1853–1854. Edited by Professor B. Silliman, Jr., and C. R. Goodrich. New York, 1854.

INDEX